Please remember that this is a library book,
and that it belongs only temporarily to each
person who uses it. Be considerate. Do
not write in this, or any, library book.

Neurosis and Treatment:

A Holistic Theory

John Wiley & Sons, Inc., New York · London · Sydney

Neurosis

and Treatment:

A Holistic Theory

BY THE LATE Andras Angyal

Edited by E. Hanfmann

and R. M. Jones

Brandeis University

Library of Congress Catalog Card Number: 65-12721
Printed in the United States of America

Foreword

This jewel of a book undoubtedly will be hailed as a classic in the field, one to be read and enjoyed by all psychologists and psychiatrists. Perhaps even higher praise, I can also recommend this book to the nonprofessional reader who wishes to learn more about human nature. Its lucidity and clarity, its X-ray like penetration to the simpler structures beneath the surface, and its freedom from professional jargon permit it to be directly understood. It is clear that the author "has been there," that he speaks as a deeply concerned participant in the encounter and not merely as a spectator. His knowledge of the neurotic entanglements and of their solutions is obviously deeply felt, and thus communicates itself by helping the reader *feel* what the words are trying to say. As he becomes immersed in Angyal's description of the basic neurotic patterns, the reader will realize that we all share to a greater or lesser degree in "vicarious living" and "noncommitment." Nor are any of us exempted from the tasks of managing love and anger, and from the basic task of countering fear with courage. Thus we can all see ourselves in this book; it is a book about common human nature, and it furthers self-understanding.

For professionals, the main theoretical importance of this book is that it is one of the very few thoroughgoing efforts to integrate psychodynamics with holistic theory. That this effort has been successful there is no doubt, for the book is full of demonstrations of how these two emphases are synergetic, how each makes the other more powerful. To put it in an oversimplified way, Freud was too atomistic, too inclined to split, to dichotomize and to reduce; on the other hand, the Gestalt psychologists were generally too "cool," not "deep" or dynamic enough. Goldstein demonstrated that the two approaches could be merged and that such a merger could be fruitful. And so did Angyal in his first book. Now he has done it again, and in my opinion, more convincingly, more dramatically, more fruitfully, because in his new book he has made use of rich pathological and therapeutic material. Certainly the holistic-dynamic approach to psychology and psychiatry must be taken seriously henceforth.

v

Perhaps some other readers will be fascinated, as I have been, to dis-cover how much Angyal's treatment of the problems of neurosis is con-sistent with the "existential-psychological" approach. Even though he hasn't spelled it out, it is easy enough to discern his dissatisfaction with the medical model of psychological illness and therapy. His conception of neurosis as a total *Weltanschauung*, a life-philosophy, or a personal unconscious mythology, has many consequences for our conceptions of "symptoms" and of "illness," of the "therapist's" role in "treatment," of the meaning of "cure." Each and all of these words are now moot, transitional, obsolescent. For my part, I dislike them all—as representing a condescending authoritarian attitude of an over-proud person to an over-humble person—and I suspect Angyal did too. Certainly he did not consider himself exempted from the troubles he writes about, and I think this helped him to assume what Adler called the "brotherly" attitude rather than that of an omnipotent god, an attitude that was also quite compatible with his character outside his professional role. He speaks of his patients with compassion, with respect and with fellow feeling.

What is it that makes us reject as inadequate the division of all people into the healthy and the sick, into "normal people" and "patients"? It is not an absence of differences between these two groups but the pres-ence of major similarities. All human beings share the human condition and the common human fate of growth, joy, pain, grief, death. In this respect we are all alike, therapists *and* patients. Our common strivings and our common fate form the ground against which therapist-patient differences are figured. The realization of these commonalities lessens the distance between the two and emphasizes their essential human equality. Angyal's thesis that the human strivings, the basic moti-vational trends, are identical in neurosis and in health provides this feeling of fellowship with a sound theoretical basis. Yet anyone who would conclude from this that Angyal tends to minimize the dif-ference between neurosis and health would be mistaken. He never tired of pointing out the magnitude of the handicap neurosis creates and the monstrous waste of human life in which it results; his therapeutic fer-vor, his persistent search for more effective methods of combatting neurosis, came from these insights. While the "sick" ones are human, they are also diminished, inhibited, self-defeating in their pursuit of the common human goals. Angyal views these limitations and distortions as arising from an unrealistic philosophy of life; if this philosophy were in fact correct, the neurotics' behavior would be reasonable and sensi-ble. In a sense then, neurosis is as much a cognitive disorder as an emotional one, and "recovery" is equivalent to an acquisition of a new orientation toward life.

The theory of health and neurosis advanced by Angyal explains effectively how these two orientations, in most respects polar opposites, can coexist in the same person; both their differences and their similarities are clarified. This function of "encompassing" and "clarifying" is typical of the holistic propositions and concepts used by Angyal. Through the use of these concepts many of the contradictory opinions, e.g., concerning the factors that are effective in therapy, are resolved and the conditions stated for each factor's effectiveness. Examples of such controversial issues that seem to me to be successfully clarified or resolved by Angyal are the issues of the role of thinking and of feeling in therapy, of "insight" and "experience," of neurotic guilt and real guilt, to name only a few. Above all, Angyal's concepts shed welcome light on the interrelationship of "analysis" and "synthesis," of demolition and reconstruction in therapy, and on the contrasting and complementary roles of "transference" and the "real relationship." Angyal leaves no doubt about what factors he considers to be of the greatest importance in therapy, but his conceptual framework permits a consideration of a wide range of factors and their interrelationships.

It is regrettable that Angyal did not leave sufficient material pertaining to psychodynamics of religion for inclusion in this book. This was one of his major interests in his last years. I recall a bus trip a few years ago during which we spent several hours attempting to express various religious concepts in psychodynamic terms, and then turned to expressing psychodynamic concepts in religious terms. He told me of his intention to do just such a job in a systematic fashion, but apparently he never wrote it up fully.

This book could not have been prepared without the cooperation of Angyal's family and friends. We owe a debt of gratitude to Dr. Alice Angyal for preserving and sorting the manuscripts and notes and to Dr. Istvan S. Angyal for collaborating with us in making the publication plans. I also wish to express my personal gratitude—and I am sure the gratitude of many others—to my colleagues Dr. Eugenia Hanfmann and Dr. Richard M. Jones for undertaking the huge task of organizing this book out of many components and fragments.

ABRAHAM H. MASLOW

Editors' Preface

When Andras Angyal's heirs turned over to his colleagues at Brandeis University the manuscripts and notes pertinent to the book he was working on at the time of his death, we were confronted with extremely heterogeneous material, not yet organized for presentation. Some topics had been fully worked out, mostly in connection with occasional lectures given by Angyal at meetings and symposia; the rest consisted of notes of varied length obviously stemming from different periods of clinical work. Both editors were conversant with Angyal's thinking on neurosis and therapy. We were members of the seminars he conducted in the Department of Social Relations at Harvard in 1951 and 1952, when his theories had already crystallized; he had supervised our therapeutic work both privately and in his capacity of Psychiatric Consultant to the Psychological Counseling Center of Brandeis University. Nevertheless, we would hardly have been able to organize the material in a manner consistent with Angyal's own plans were it not for two additional sources that were available to us: the tape recordings of a major part of a seminar Angyal gave at the Brandeis Summer Institute in 1957, and recordings of a similar series of talks delivered in 1958 at the Greater Framingham Mental Health Center, where he also served as a psychiatric consultant. These two series contained several additional topics which had been worked out in obvious anticipation of their use as chapters of the book. They also provided us with the sequence which Angyal had chosen, at least for the purposes of a condensed presentation. The written materials included notes for a preface and several outlines for the book; we selected the outline that was most complete as our guideline. The topics outlined fell into three parts: basic concepts, neurosis, and therapy. This still left us with several decisions to make regarding the organization of the three parts of the book.

Angyal's outline indicated that Part 1 was to be a revision of the chapters of his earlier book * most pertinent to his theory of neurosis.

* A. Angyal, *Foundations for a Science of Personality*. The Commonwealth Fund, New York, 1941.

He had begun to implement this plan by reworking the chapter on homonomy and had marked some of his notes for inclusion in the chapters on autonomy and on psychological functions. We followed these directions, using the original chapters in a condensed version. We also decided to include, in an abbreviated form, the other three pertinent chapters: Integration of Personality, Disturbances of Integration, and The Course of Life as a Gestalt; the first two were merged into one chapter.

In Part 2, dealing with the theory of neurosis, the sequence and organization of topics was clear from Angyal's seminar presentations and outlines. We subdivided the material on neurosis in general into four chapters (Chapters 6–9), and combined into one chapter (Chapter 12) the sections dealing with the comparison of the hysterical and the obsessive-compulsive patterns, including the therapeutic problems presented by each.

For Part 3, dealing with therapy, Angyal left no detailed outline, but the material was plentiful. The Brandeis and Framingham lecture series contained a vivid presentation of the total course of therapy, and a detailed description of the holistic approach to interpretation was available in manuscript form; the rest of the material consisted of a mass of unorganized notes on various aspects of therapy. The material already organized by Angyal forms the content of the first four chapters of Part 3 (Chapters 13–16); we subdivided the description of the course of therapy into three parts and supplemented the text with pertinent material from the notes. The remainder of the notes was organized into four additional chapters under the headings of Insight, Resistance, Reviving the Pattern of Health, and The Patient and the Therapist (Chapters 17–20). To make the presentation more systematic, we also reiterated in these chapters some points already made in the description of the course of therapy as a whole. Part 3 required a greater amount of organization than Parts 1 and 2; in it we also had to fill more gaps by providing a discussion of some points merely mentioned in the outlines and notes. Many of these gaps were in the area of therapeutic techniques, and we were usually able to fill them from our pooled memories of the suggestions made in supervisory sessions.

Since Angyal's lectures and notes did not contain enough examples to illustrate all his points, we supplemented the text with examples from our own treatment cases giving preference to those which he had supervised. As in the case of filling the gaps in the text, we were confident of having used these additional illustrations in a manner consistent with Angyal's intentions, and did not feel it necessary to differentiate the additions from the rest of the text.

We kept the few references to other authors that we found in Angyal's notes, but made no attempt to increase their number or to trace, on our own, the relation of his theories to those of others, as Angyal himself had done for the topic of anxiety. In his basic theoretical orientation Angyal must have been influenced by other holistic thinkers such as W. Stern and K. Goldstein; in the field of clinical theories he acknowledged having learned much from psychoanalysis and from H. S. Sullivan; his approach to therapy was congenial with that of the theorists whom Maslow has designated as the "third force" in psychology and, in some points, with that of existentialists. He was, however, no one's disciple. A highly independent thinker, Angyal learned much more from experience than he did from books or formal training. In the field of psychotherapy he was practically self-taught. Angyal's high valuation of personal discovery is reflected in his remarks to a group of beginning therapists who were preoccupied with the relationship of his formulations to what they had previously learned, criticizing alternately the deviations and the agreement.

> Suppose that all of this has actually been said, in different terms, by psychoanalysis. It would still be of value for you to see the therapeutic issues from a viewpoint different from the familiar. All formulations are worn out and killed by repetition. In therapy, an insight repeated over and over in the same words in a foreseen context becomes dull and ineffective. To have impact the same thing must be said to the patient in many different ways. To learn to do this the therapist must cultivate his ability to perceive what happens in therapy in fresh ways, from a variety of angles, and not merely as a confirmation of familiar knowledge.

Angyal himself possessed this ability in a high measure, and the impact of his formulations is due, among other things, to their having arisen from a "fresh look." Doubtless he would have provided his book with many more references than we found in his notes but would still have followed the policy of his first book, where, to ". . . facilitate the flow of the argument digressions to point out differences from and similarities to other theories have been largely omitted." *

Since we had to work with both written and spoken material, style was an issue. Knowing that Angyal had wanted his book to be accessible to laymen, we tried, in editing, to preserve the vivid nontechnical language of his oral presentation in the seminars and to simplify the more formal style of the written chapters; we tried to keep at a minimum discussions and terms that presuppose technical knowledge. We were unable to achieve a uniformity of style, but we hope to have

* *Ibid.*, p. xii.

achieved our main objective, clarity. We wish to express our gratitude to Gertrude Vakar who assisted in the editing of Part 3.

Grateful acknowledgment is made to the National Institutes of Health for the grant that made this book possible * and to all those who, in various ways, assisted us in obtaining this grant: Dr. G. Bibring, Dr. A. Maslow, Dr. C. Rogers, Dr. P. Sapir, Dr. D. Shakow, Dr. A. Stanton, and Dr. R. W. White. Brandeis University provided some secretarial help and some funds for transcribing the tapes. We wish to thank Dr. N. Cohen and Dr. M. Schlank for making available to us the recordings of the seminars Angyal conducted at the Greater Framingham Mental Health Center, and to thank the Commonwealth Fund and the Harvard University Press for permission to reprint, in condensed form, several chapters from *Foundations for a Science of Personality*.

This completes the "Editors' Preface," but as therapists who have learned much from association with Angyal, we wish to say a few words about our motives in undertaking a task that we knew would be arduous. Angyal was a rare instance of a therapist whose theoretical interests and therapeutic concerns functioned in complete harmony and to mutual benefit. His absorbing interest in the theoretical relevance of his clinical observations did not detract from his singularly tenacious way of holding on to the goal of bringing about significant lasting change in his patients. The patient was to get what he came for—whether or not he had bargained for it—before accounts opened by the therapeutic encounter could be closed. This attitude—reflected in Angyal's clinical style of a gently compassionate taskmaster—was responsible for his theoretical innovations at least as much as was his allegiance to the holistic approach. He tells us that his theory of neurosis, the theory of "universal ambiguity," arose out of his search for ". . . a conceptualization of personality adequate for the practical tasks of education and therapy." † And indeed his formulations provide a sound basis for combining therapeutic optimism with a sober appraisal of obstacles to radical change in cases of entrenched neurosis. They also provide, in Angyal's handling, a basis for developing methods that can do more than increase self-knowledge. Angyal was signally successful with the type of neurosis that is highly resistant to change, the obsessive-compulsive character neurosis. Therapists of all orientations will find suggestions in the chapters on treatment that may stimulate their own thinking and experimenting. There are still too many tragic failures in therapeutic work and too many people who have not been

* The work was supported by a PHS research grant No. M-5737 from the National Institute of Mental Health, Public Health Service.
† This book, p. 99.

helped substantially by years of intensive work to permit Angyal's death to rob us of the new thoughts he had hoped to pass on to his fellow therapists.

The book forms a coherent whole and is most profitably read in sequence. However, both laymen and those whose interest is primarily clinical may find portions of Part 1 too abstract; they might prefer to start with Part 2 and turn to Part 1 if they should become intrigued with the theoretical foundations of Angyal's clinical conceptions.

EUGENIA HANFMANN
RICHARD M. JONES

Waltham, Massachusetts
November, 1964

Author's Preface

This book is an outgrowth of the holistic theory of personality, which I put forward many years ago, and of my subsequent therapeutic work with neuroses. In my earlier book,* starting from the premise that personality is a dynamic whole, I dealt with it in terms of concepts that are "psychophysically neutral" and adapted to the description of "biospheric" processes resulting from an interplay of organismic and environmental forces. The usefulness of my theory in formulating specific problems and interpreting data remained to be tested by empirical methods of inquiry. A few years after the appearance of *Foundations* I went into private practice, and my next fifteen years were devoted to therapeutic work with neurotic problems. In following my patients through the mazes of neurotic entanglements and trying, together with them, to make sense of seemingly inconsistent patterns, I found the general concepts I had developed earlier to be useful guides. They gave me fresh insights into the origins of neurotic phenomena, into the complex structure of the fully developed neurosis, and into the reasons for its stubborn retention by the patient; these concepts also supplied a rationale for the factors and sequences that did facilitate change.

From the multitude of individual patterns observed and traced, certain general features eventually emerged, which provided the basis for the theory of neuroses and their treatment, which is the topic of this book. In some of its aspects this theory is not novel and could not possibly be: the study of neuroses has been an increasingly active field since Freud's ground-breaking work. My formulations take previous achievements into account; on some points they largely agree with those of other theorists, on others they differ. What I believe is distinctive about my work is my having consistently placed the findings, old and new, within the holistic framework. It was through the application of my ideas about the nature and action of systems to the problem of neurosis that I was led to formulate the theory of "universal ambiguity," which is the central theoretical part of my contribution.

* A. Angyal, *Foundations for a Science of Personality*. The Commonwealth Fund, New York, 1941.

The basic tenet of the holistic approach is that personality is an organized whole and not a mere aggregate of discrete parts. Its functioning does not derive from the functioning of its parts; rather the parts must be viewed in the light of the organizational principles governing the whole. In my reading this implies that concepts referring to broad trends, under which many manifestations of human life can be subsumed, are preferable to concepts based on specific partial functions. One can, of course, make valid generalizations about human nature at any point of the specificity-generality continuum, and references to the most specific functions may have the appeal of obviousness: all human beings undoubtedly have to breathe, eat, and so forth. However, any attempt to view the total human life as deriving from these fixed physiological features is bound to lead to a good many forced constructions. The approach "from above," from general patterns and trends, enables us to keep the perspective on the whole and offers a comprehensive framework for the understanding of the specific. The generality of this framework permits us to remain unbiased and alert to the many individual patterns the general trends can form; a theory of this kind is not likely to violate concrete reality.

In terms of this conception the early personal manifestations, important as they may be in shaping the person's future, are no more real or basic than the later ones. Both express the same human trends—through the medium of functions that are available or prominent at a given developmental level; this accounts for the similarity of their patterning. Normal development can be viewed as a process of successive approximation of the state of complete realization of the basic human trends. The meaning of the early primitive expressions of a trend is clarified by our knowledge of its later mature expression: to understand an embryo we must know the structure of the mature organism.

To illustrate my point of view, let us take the concept of castration anxiety, a concept centered on a specific psychic content but commonly applied to anxiety about any vital injury or loss. If this use of the term implies that the actual fear of losing the penis is the origin and nucleus of all other homologous fears, which are merely its derivatives or disguises, I cannot agree with this usage. I should consider the issue involved to be a broad one, that of response to a severe threat to one's safety and integrity. Fear of the loss of penis is a very common reaction to such a threat, because this extremely plastic and concrete image is a good vehicle for emotional ideas formed at an early level of development. Since at that stage the child's experience is not differentiated and not organized conceptually, these images are equated with that which they represent. Thus the idea of castration becomes a central symbolic concretization of the general threat of which it is a striking expression, but not the only expression; in the case of a girl, it can become an explanation of the already experienced rejection resulting in a feeling of worthlessness.

All this may sound like undue insistence on mere terminological precision or like metaphysical speculation about the nature of ultimate reality. It seems obvious to me, however, that the type of concepts we choose has definite implications for the outcome of our efforts to form an adequate conception of personality. If we work downward from the broad pattern to the specific, we minimize the risk of being left with a collection of fragments difficult, if not impossible, to combine into a unified whole.

In presenting my approach to neuroses and their treatment, I wish to share with others who are professionally or personally interested in this field the ways of viewing the problem that have proved clarifying to me and to my patients. I hope that I may have helped to demonstrate the fruitfulness of the holistic approach by having applied it to a sector of life that, far from being small and isolated, reflects in its very distortions the crucial issues of human existence.

ANDRAS ANGYAL

Contents

PART THREE: TREATMENT

Part One

Foundations

1. The Trend toward Autonomy

The existential form of the organism is dynamic; life is a process and must be studied as a dynamic whole. Every whole is organized according to some leading principle. Consequently, we must begin by defining the leading principle in the organization of the process of life. *What is the general pattern of the organismic process?* An adequate definition of this pattern has far-reaching consequences for the actual study of the organism. Every organismic part process is a manifestation of the dynamism of the total organism. The part processes gain their meaning from the general pattern of functional organization and can be correctly understood only in the context of this organization. In Chapter 1, I shall discuss one aspect of this general pattern.

Life as a Process of Self-Expansion

Most of the existing definitions of life have one element in common—a theoretical nucleus which could be called the "immanence theory of life." This can be roughly stated in the following way: The organism consists of a number of parts, or organs, which have specific functions. These functions lead beyond the organ itself. The heart irrigates with blood not only its own tissues but all the tissues of the body. The function of each organ is to maintain both itself and other organs in working condition; this organized self-maintenance defines the pattern of the total organismic process, making it a closed circle, comparable to a wheel turning on its own axis without progressing. The function of each organ is defined by what it accomplishes for the rest of the organism, but the meaning of the whole cannot be derived from these part functions. From this point of view, a functional definition of the total life process seems impossible, and life as a whole

3

appears as functionally meaningless. The part processes function to maintain life, and life is the sum of these part processes. Although this formulation may look like a caricature, the hypothesis of immanence, the "closed-circle" conception of life, is implicit in all theories postulating the maintenance of equilibrium, or self-preservation and survival, as the main trend of life.

This hypothesis neglects some highly significant facts. A little reflection will show that life in all its forms is not a purely circular process. The circle is open at two points, there is *assimilation* (intake) on one side, and *production* on the other.

The most primitive form of assimilation, common to every organism, is a material one. A stream of material (food substances, oxygen, carbon dioxide) flows from the environment into the organism; this stream is maintained and directed by the activity of the organism itself. The organism reaches out into the surrounding world, draws material from it, and transforms this material into "living matter," i.e., functioning parts of the organismic system. On the psychological level a similar process takes place. Experience is acquired, assimilated and preserved in memory. Assimilation can be defined as the process by which any factor originally external becomes a functional part of the organism.

The second break in the circle of organismic processes is production. Each living being creates something that transcends its own limits, be it a new organism or far-reaching changes in the external environment produced through muscular and mental activities. Theories that define life as a two-dimensional process of anabolism and catabolism, or storing and dispersing matter and energy, make the mistake of equating catabolism with dispersion. The biological function of catabolism is not energy dispersion but energy mobilization. When anabolism is completed, the next step is the productive utilization of the energy mobilized by catabolism. The dispersion of matter and energy, their escape from the organismic system, is only an unavoidable by-product of living. The stored energy is not wasted, and not all of it is turned back to support further assimilation of raw material. It is used, at least in part, for productive activity; there is a "net profit." Unless one takes into account the inwardly and outwardly directed streams of assimilation and production, the self-transcending character of the functional pattern of living does not become obvious.

Assimilation and production can be viewed as expressing a single organismic trend. By incessantly drawing in foreign material from the outside world and transforming it into its own functional parts, the organism grows and expands at the expense of its surroundings. It also expands through its creativeness. Instruments and other devices invented by man extend the capabilities of the organism—its sensory, mental, motor activities—far beyond their original limits. Such man-made products, by carrying out important functions in the biological process, become integrated in the total activity of the organism; some of these products are almost like organs added to those we originally possess. By converting a large range of external objects into devices such as shelters or tools, the organism extends itself into the external world. Thus, as a first approximation, we may define life as a *process of self-expansion*. The dynamism of life does not result in a closed circle but in a process which through its two phases evolves in a definite direction. This process does not take place within the organism but between the organism and the environment. The organism cannot expand within itself; it can expand only in a medium originally external to it. The life process embraces both organism and environment; they are the two indispensable poles of a single process, life.

Autonomy and Heteronomy

To define the trend toward self-expansion in a more precise way, we must consider the distinctive feature of living organisms, their *autonomy*. The organism is not—as mechanistic philosophy assumes—an inactive point in which various causal chains intersect. Life is, to a large extent, a *self-governing* process. The biological process is not a resultant of external forces but is governed by specifically biological endogenous factors. To a large extent, the organism itself is the cause of its functions; it is endowed with spontaneity.

The organism lives in a world in which things happen according to laws which are heteronomous, i.e., foreign to the organism as such. It is subjected to the laws of the physical world but it can oppose self-determination to external determination. An animal dropped from a height falls according to the law of gravitation like any other body, simply as a mass and not as an organism. Its fall, however, can be modified by influences originating within the organism—a cat, by means of its righting reflexes, manages to land on its feet whatever its position was at the start of the fall. Clear examples of autonomous self-regulation are the functions that serve to maintain homeostasis; thus heat regulation in the warm-blooded animals enables them to maintain a fairly constant body temperature despite considerable changes in the temperature of the environment. Phenomena of adaptation—such as the eyes' accommodating for distance and adapting to light and dark-ness—demonstrate the organism's ability to modify the function of its sense organs according to the demands of the situation. Selection, choice, self-regulation, adaptation, regeneration are phenomena which imply an autonomy of the organism. In fact, not a single life process could be understood without this assumption. In every stimulus-response sequence the external influence does not cause, but merely prompts, the response. The organism responds in its own specific way, i.e., in an essentially autonomous fashion.

Because the organism lives in a world independent of itself, its autonomy is only partial and must be asserted against the heteronomous surroundings. (Thus every single organismic process, and also the life process as a whole, is always a resultant of two components, autonomy and heteronomy—self-government and government from outside.) Every organismic process can be characterized by the ratio $a : h$, where a stands for autonomy, h for heteronomy. The values of both a and h must be greater than zero, but they vary for different processes. The ratio varies also from individual to individual and from species to species. If the environment of a plant becomes poor in food substances, the plant has few possibilities of struggling against this condition; an animal in a similar situation is more autonomous since it can move to other regions to seek food, or in some cases can store it. Similarly, in many kinds of plants the process of fecundation is dependent on external conditions, such as the action of insects and the wind. The fate of the seed, its survival and growth, also depends on external circumstances. In animals, who can deposit the fertilized egg in a protected place, make a deposit of food near it, and care for their young after birth, the reproductive process is less dependent on environmental conditions, although this does not necessarily mean higher efficiency.

The organismic process shows a definite trend toward an increase of the relative value of a in the $a : h$ ratio, i.e., *a trend toward an increase of autonomy*. This trend has no fixed objective but only a general direction. At each stage of the biological process the tendency is toward a situation marked by a greater degree of autonomy than the preceding situation, even if this tendency cannot always be carried through. This trend is equally apparent in the functions concerned with assimilation and with production. Environmental factors, such as food substances, undergo stages of successive modification which bring them more and more under the control of the organism until they are completely integrated with it. The processes of production—raising crops, building shelters, making tools—result in increased mastery of heteronomous happenings by the organism, which permit it to put them at the service of life. In both cases there is a shift of the $a : h$ ratio toward a higher relative value of a.

In apparent contradiction to this trend, we observe a large group of regressive episodes; in these sequences the successive stages of the organismic total process are marked by a reduction rather than an increase of autonomy.

The phenomena of regression fall into two groups: passive setback and strategic retreat. A passive setback is analogous to the situation of a man swimming against the current. His activity aims at progression in a given direction but it is impeded by the force of the stream. The resulting movement depends on the relative strength of the two components, but even if the man is carried backward we still can say that his tendency is to move upstream. The tendency of the organism is toward increased autonomy, even if strong heteronomous influences result in a decrease of autonomy. Similarly, in the case of strategic retreat the goal itself remains "progressive." Regression may occur when a situation becomes untenable at a complex level, and the person retreats to a more primitive and familiar one to gather his forces for a new advance. Hypotheses postulating a large-scale regressive trend in the organism itself, such as the hypothesis of the death instinct, are not very convincing. The facts which are attributed to the death instinct, such as extreme cases of neurotic self-sabotage, can be explained more plausibly on a different basis.

Organism and Environment

In the preceding formulations the organism is considered not as a static structure but as a dynamic organization, a process which takes place not within the confines of the body but between the "organism" and the "environment." This conception, which alone does justice to the nature of the biological process, should replace all attempts to define organism and environment in structural terms. Their morphological separation is impossible; if attempted it would lead to endless hairsplitting dialectics. If belongingness to the organism were to be determined merely by an item's spatial position "within the skin," then not only food substances in the oral cavity and air in the lungs would have to be parts of the organism, but even any foreign object, or any substance injected into it. It would seem more logical to regard, e.g., the contents of the gastrointestinal tract not as a part of the organism but as an insinuation of the environment into the body. But if one starts making such distinctions endless questions arise. Do nutritive substances, after being absorbed and passed from the intestines into the current of lymph and blood, become part of the organism, or would it not be justifiable to call the noncellular components of the blood "environment"? One could carry the argument even further and ask whether the metabolically inactive intercellular substances are as much a part of the organism as the metabolically active cells.

The conception of organism and environment as entities separable in space is inadequate for the description of biological phenomena. They become fundamental biological concepts only if we define them as dynamic factors, as opposing direction in the biological total process. In these terms organism is self-government, and environment is heteronomous influence. The two presuppose each other, the external world becomes "environment" only when and insofar as it is in interaction with the organism. Every process which results from this interaction is part of the life process, irrespective of whether it occurs within the body or outside it.

Such a definition of organism may seem to contradict common sense since we do experience ourselves as distinct units, with firm boundaries. Although the boundaries, in fact, are far from being firm and set, the formulation given in the preceding paragraph should be qualified by the statement that not all variations of the $a : b$ ratio are gradual and continuous. There are sharp gradients between the ratios typical of different groups of functions. The high degree of control we have over the movements of our body tends to create a sharp separation between this unit and the objects and events over which our control is less immediate and certain. Thus the "organism" and "environment" of common sense are the "structural precipitates" of autonomy and heteronomy. The factors which are prevalently under autonomous government constitute the person, or the subject, while those prevalently under heteronomous government form the objects of the environment. This is the basic organization of the "biosphere," of the realm in which life takes place, and it is reflected in the basic differentiation of our conscious experience of the world into "I" and "non-I." Yet within the unit to which we commonly refer as "a person" different groups of processes also have varying degrees of autonomous determination, as demonstrated by the difference between a voluntary act and a knee jerk. Under pathological conditions the $a : b$ ratio of certain functions may change; what has been previously experienced by us as our own activity may appear as not coming from ourselves. The line we draw between the person and the environment is not stable; where we draw it is determined by many factors.

Some Expressions of the Autonomous Trend

In arguing that the life process tends toward an increase of autonomy, rather than to a mere preservation of the status quo, I do not mean to postulate an entity, a force hidden behind the scene. I am merely attempting to give a generalized description of the observable pattern, of the way in which the life process unfolds. Insofar as this pattern implies only a certain direction in which life processes tend to move, and not any specific goal or end state at which they aim, my point of view is not strictly teleological but merely *directional*. A general tendency, of course, cannot appear except in specific manifestations, and some of these manifestations will take the form of pursuit of special fixed goals. But it is the intrinsic pattern of direction that determines (or codetermines) what objects or states can become the organism's goals. Objects which are, so to say, scattered along this direction may become goals for organismic activity.

The life pattern in man has such a great variety of expressions, differing from person to person, that it would be futile to attempt a complete inventory of all the channels through which the trend toward increased autonomy can be expressed. This is clearly demonstrated by the attempts of different authors to compile lists of human drives, instincts, or wishes; the estimated number has varied from a few to a thousand, depending on the level of specificity at which the survey was made. An additional difficulty in exemplifying the autonomous tendency with instances of actual behavior is that a single act may have, and usually has, more than one meaning. Since the trend to increased autonomy is not the only human trend, we can only show, in a given instance of behavior, that *some* of its features manifest the autonomous tendency. The following brief discussions merely point to some types of specifically human activity which serve as outlets for autonomous strivings for large groups of people.

I shall omit those processes and activities that are determined directly by the structural features of the human body, such as metabolic processes and reflexes, or standard reactions to standard physiological needs—although complex structures of subsidiary activities and meanings developed around some of these needs can subserve the autonomous human strivings in other than purely physiological ways.

Perhaps the clearest and most direct expression of the organism's tendency to impress its determination on a wide range of events is the drive to act, to make things happen for the mere joy of action and for the sake of experiencing oneself as the cause of changes. Such activities may be observed even in the infant. When the child's physiological needs are satisfied and no distress is present, he will move his limbs, produce noises, and later manipulate and explore objects. When he begins to acquire language and to exercise his imagination, the child will use them in a similarly playful fashion. When he learns that with words he can make the adults do what he wants, he exercises this "word magic" untiringly. As development proceeds, the child will no longer be content with doing things for the sake of mere action. To be satisfying the activity must lead to some tangible result, have a definite purpose. In adults, relatively few forms of behavior express a mere drive for action; but although such a drive seldom occurs in "pure culture," it is a component in many activities, including work. Apart from its practical purpose, one enjoys the achievement aspect of work, the overcoming of obstacles, and the increase in efficiency. One may even deliberately seek difficulties as a challenge for mastery.

Curiosity, the eagerness to explore and to know the world, is another manifestation of the trend toward increased autonomy. That which one knows is to some degree conquered. Knowing the properties of objects and the laws of various processes facilitates prediction and management. While knowledge may serve practical purposes, it may also be pursued for the sake of knowing, as an expression of the self-expansive tendency. Another common expression of the trend toward increased autonomy is the drive to acquire and accumulate property. Possessing goods, of course, is important for the satisfaction of physiological and other needs, present and future, but it can also express the trend toward mastery more directly. One's property differs from other objects in that one can do with it, to a large extent, whatever one wants. To own something may mean conquest, a greater possibility of dominance. The defense of one's inviolacy and integrity against interference from outside is also an aspect of autonomous strivings. A person seeking an expression for his self-expansive tendencies through any form of behavior will resent and resist any intrusion into his activities; he will oppose domination by others, assert his right to his property, protect his privacy, and in general resist any encroachment of his sphere of freedom and mastery.

When the drive for expansion and mastery is directed not toward impersonal environment but toward one's fellow man, it appears as a tendency to dominate, to compete with, or to gain superiority over others. These tendencies seldom occur in pure form, although they are a common aspect of interpersonal behavior. If they manifest themselves in an excessive degree, at the expense of other kinds of relationships, they must be viewed as distortions of the trend toward increased autonomy; such distortions may be based on very complex dynamics.

It is not by chance that the purest and strongest manifestations of the autonomous trend appear during the period of development, particularly in early childhood. The child's speedy growth is paralleled by his intense drive to utilize and master his developing functions and to expand into the world. The infant's exercise of autonomy is limited to his organic functions and to the expressive behavior which serves as a signal for the adult to try and guess its needs; the satisfaction of these needs is the function of others. The child's needs for food, warmth, etc., may be adequately met; yet before long he will want to "do it myself," even when he is not ready for it, and will protest against being helped. If not discouraged by those around him, he will enjoy a variety of spontaneous activities, not limited to the gratification of physiological needs, and will practice his new functions in a persistent deliberate fashion. Starting life in a state of dependency, he steadily grows toward independence and self-government and thus achieves greater fulfillment in one crucial aspect of living. A person whose autonomous strivings have been abundant and successful in a variety of areas becomes resourceful and competent. These qualities have an instrumental value in relation to his specific goals, but they are also values in themselves; as expressions of fullness of life they are unquestioned and unquestionable. Developing competence and self-reliance is a part of the normal growth of personality and an important aspect of our ideal of maturity.

Disturbances of Autonomy

Neurotic living has for its constant concomitant an impairment of autonomy in some form and degree, though the specific dynamics that bring it about are different in different cases. This aspect of neurosis has been pointed out by various authors. Impairment of autonomy is one aspect of the "weak ego" concept of psychoanalysis. It is central in Adler's conception of the inferiority complex, and it plays a part in the formulations of those authors who, like Fromm, emphasize the reduction of personal freedom in neurosis.

Phenomenologically, the manifestations of impairment or of distortion of the autonomous trend may appear as either a *lack* or an *excess* of autonomous striving, although the roots of the two groups of conditions may be similar. When the lack of autonomy is a generalized one, the person's course seems to be determined by external happenings; he becomes a straw in the wind, a piece of driftwood carried by currents, a creature of circumstances. This state of affairs is created by the person himself. A self-image strongly colored by feelings of impotence, whatever its origins, will affect the person's behavior and way of living and may eventually bring about an actual reduction of self-determination.

Other people, and the social and cultural situations created by them, are the most vital aspects of the human environment. Consequently, the impairment of autonomy has conspicuous and far-reaching results when it manifests itself in interaction with others. Lack of self-government in interpersonal relations can take many shapes: excessive conformism, an inability to disagree with anybody, or dependence on the help of others far in excess of the objective necessity are examples familiar to everyone. In most cases the genesis of these forms of behavior cannot be understood without taking into account the role played by tendencies other than the autonomous. Thus the equation a child may have made between being loved and having things done for him may be at the root of his persistent clinging to dependence; it explains the often observed recurrence of helplessness after the arrival of a sibling. Perhaps one of the most paradoxical manifestations of impaired autonomy is the behavior of a person who not only fails to assert himself but effectively invites exploitation. By giving another the power to use him, this person exchanges his status of living organism for that of a mere tool.

The distortions which take the form of excessive autonomy are often compensations for real or felt lacks, reactions to threat. Extreme resentment and rejection of any influence exercised by others is typical of the developmental phases marked by struggles for emancipation; in some neurotic forms rebelliousness and intolerance of any interference remain fixed patterns in adulthood. The counterpart of clinging to dependence is the wish to be completely independent of others and to accept no help; this is sometimes a reaction against being babied, a protection against being destroyed as a self-determining individual. Another variant of behavior which appears as an overstrong drive for autonomy is the repetitive testing or "proving" of oneself by acts reasserting one's competence and mastery.

Disturbances of autonomous strivings form an important aspect of work inhibition, an ubiquitous condition in neuroses. This impairment may reflect a fear of failure based on feelings of incompetence and helplessness—a reluctance to try in earnest, lest the outcome of a valid test should confirm one's worst fears—or it may express opposition to requirements felt to be imposed from outside. In both cases the presence of autonomous strivings in a distorted form is quite obvious, and these are only two examples of many possible kinds of distortion.

Perhaps the most general structural feature of work inhibition is the disruption of integration in the dimension of *progression*, i.e., segregation of one part from the whole in the means-end sequence of behavior. (See Chapter 4.) For a healthy person the activity itself (though promoting some practical purposes, some other manifestations of autonomous coping with the world) retains its self-expressive value. The activity is enjoyed for its own sake, not merely as a means to an end. In fact, in cases of good integration the "end" is the totality of the work process of which the means are as much a part as the outcome. In doing the parts one is doing the whole. One does not merely want to "get there" but enjoys the total process of getting there, both the stretches of smooth functioning and the challenges presented by problems and obstacles. Disturbances and inhibitions arise when, for whatever reason, the end result becomes dissociated from the activity as such.

> The following is a patient's testimony: "I love fixing engines, and I love driving the go-cart in the race, but the thought of hooking the engine onto the go-cart and getting the cart to the track drives me crazy; at the thought of it I can't lift a screw driver." This patient enjoyed his sessions but missed many hours because he could not bear the thought of driving to them. It was the same each morning; he liked the thought of being up but could not bear to go through the process of getting up.

Such situations often develop if the outcome of an activity—seen, e.g., in terms of earnings or prestige—becomes all important. The "means" activities then are no longer a source of pleasure but merely an annoying obstacle, or at best a peripheral devitalized process. Thus work deteriorates into a chore. Since in our culture work forms the bulk of adult activities, this transformation does not merely diminish one's effectiveness, it also greatly reduces the joy of living potentially available to the person.

The integrated functioning of any general trend presupposes a harmonious balance between the trend itself and its specific content, the processes which embody the trend and give it concrete existence. Some of the expressions of the trend toward increased autonomy—such as those insuring the intake of food—are prescribed by physiological necessity; some are made inaccessible for the person by his state of physical or mental development, by cultural prohibitions, or by the external circumstances. Yet normally the person still has a wide range of autonomy-increasing activities available to him from among which he can choose, and shift, according to his preferences. Thus communication between "surface" and "depth" is maintained. The underlying trend, the dynamic Gestalt, retains its transposability, and a variety of specific activities can acquire vital meaning as embodiments of the trend. Each activity is valued as an expression of the basic trend and is also enjoyed in its specificity, in the particular patterning it contributes.

If for some reason this coherence between the pattern and its potential material gets disrupted, the general pattern becomes schematic and empty, and the concrete activities become either meaningless or too important in their specifics. In some cases autonomous strivings can be expressed only in very special limited ways—a situation analogous to that of a person who must limit his diet to one kind of food. Should this food not be easily available, most of his efforts must be spent on obtaining it. Or a person may focus all his strivings on one particular goal only to find that when reached it fails to bring satisfaction. The overvalued goal has become segregated from its roots and lost its function of expressing the basic trend. A different case of disturbed balance between the trend and its expressions is that of a person who finds no concrete ways to embody his autonomous strivings, which are consequently fated to remain shadowy and unreal; witness the feeling of some patients and of many normal adolescents that they cannot focus on anything because they are attracted by everything, or wish to actualize *all* their potentialities. A striking expression of an "empty" unembodied autonomous drive is the passionate assertion made by an adolescent who feels that he is fighting for his freedom and integrity, but cannot define his goals in any positive terms: "I want to do what I *myself* want to do, but I don't know what it is." To anticipate the topic of the next chapter, we find a similar disturbance in the functioning of the other major trend in those adolescents who are "in love with love," the concrete objects of this love being highly changeable or remaining elusive. All disturbances of this type may be viewed as instances of disruption of integration in the *vertical* or depth dimension, i.e., of segregation of an underlying trend from its concrete expressions. This disruption may also result in disturbances of the *transverse* structure of behavior, i.e., in a lack of coordination between various personal pursuits. (See Chapter 4.)

2. The Trend toward Homonomy[*]

Human behavior cannot be understood solely as a manifestation of the trend toward increased autonomy. Seen from another angle, human life reveals a basic pattern very different from self-assertiveness, from striving for freedom and mastery. The person behaves as if he were seeking a place for himself in a larger unit of which he strives to become a part. In the first orientation he is struggling for centrality in his world, trying to mold and organize objects and events, to bring them under his own control. In the second orientation he seems rather to strive to surrender himself and to become an organic part of something that he conceives as greater than himself. Processes concerned with procreation are evidence that even at the physiological-biological level the individual is integrated into superindividual units. At the cultural level, the person's conception of the larger unit to which he belongs, or to which he strives to belong, varies according to his cultural background and personal orientation. The superordinate whole may be represented for him by a social unit—family, clan, nation—by an ideology, or by a meaningfully ordered universe. The objective existence of such superindividual wholes is a metaphysical question with which the empirical scientist need not be concerned. For the student of personality, the important fact is that the trend toward *homonomy*, the wish to be in harmony with a unit one regards as extending beyond his individual self, is a powerful motivating source of behavior.

Many theories of personality have explicitly or implicitly recognized the existence of this trend. The double orientation of human life has

[*] Angyal reworked the chapter on homonomy completely, feeling that his earlier formulations had failed to convey the full meaning of his concept. To preserve the informal fluent style of Angyal's seminar presentation, we decided against punctuating the text with subheadings.

found reflection in various attempts to formulate the broadest system principle of the person, such as self-preservation and preservation of the species, or the will to power and *Gemeinschaftsgefuehl*. I think the existence of both trends is obvious to the majority of people. Still the tendency persists among theorists to view the second trend as less basic, as perhaps derived from the first in some circuitous way, or as being of lesser importance. I have been asked by people who have discussed my concepts with me whether I would not agree that autonomy was more important than homonomy. I am certain that the second trend is quite as basic as the first. I do not consider it a superstructure, a luxury which comes only after all other needs have been fulfilled. It is just as much a part of human existence as the autonomous needs, at least in a fully functioning human being. To ask which is more important makes no more sense than asking whether hands or feet are more important. From the psychiatric point of view, the second trend is, if anything, more crucial, because if things go wrong in our lives we have more trouble in that area than in any other.

One difficulty in making the manifestations of the homonomous trend vivid and obvious to the reader is that actual samples of behavior can never be ascribed exclusively to one or the other orientation. The behavioral items, particularly in a well-integrated person, always manifest both orientations, although in varying degrees. While the autonomous trend is the predominant moving force in such areas as technology, relatively pure manifestations of homonomy can be found in certain forms of artistic, religious, and social behavior. We shall touch on the artistic or aesthetic experience later. In the context of the topic of this book, the expression of the homonomous trend in the so-called higher aspects of human life, such as art, is less important than its expression in the relationship of one person to another, of husband and wife, child and parent, among friends. These relationships may have all kinds of patterns and qualities, but they always extend beyond the individuality of the participants. They clearly show that in the human being life is not contained within his individual self; it extends into the world and particularly into other human beings. What we call love is a manifestation of the homonomous trend in the relationships among people, and in a more general sense the whole concept of homonomy could be equated with love.

Clarification of the meaning of love is of paramount importance for psychiatry, for more than one reason. Neurotic difficulties are universally attributed to not having received love, or certain qualities of love, in childhood. In some approaches to therapy it is felt essential that this deficiency, among others, be made up in the process of treatment.

Clarifying what is meant by love thus becomes a crucial problem both in matters of prevention and in matters of therapy. Perhaps no other word suffers from such a confusion of meanings. It is used for dependence and possessiveness, for sexual attraction, for maudlin sentimentality, even for hate and exploitation. Love should be defined in a way that would make comprehensible the crucial import that everybody believes it to have in people's lives. We cannot begin to understand the trend toward homonomy until we can say with some precision what we mean by love. This can hardly be achieved by definitions. Before listing what I consider to be the essential characteristics of love, I shall try to elucidate the trend I am talking about by approaching it from a number of different angles.

In one of the preceding paragraphs, I said that homonomous strivings were an inherent part of human existence. Let us stop here to consider the meaning of the term *human existence*. Let us take, for example, such a trite statement as "Life is a struggle for existence." All right, it is. But what do we mean by that? We find that this depends on the sector of life or the level of existence we have in mind.

Physically, we exist in a very tangible way as anatomical structures in which a cycle of rather well-standardized functions takes place. On this level the struggle for existence simply means maintaining this structure in a properly functioning condition—maintaining an already manifestly existing entity. We must fulfill the needs inherent in our biological design—take in food, protect ourselves from excessive heat and cold or other damaging conditions—and we struggle to make these necessities available to ourselves. Such needs call to us in a rather unequivocal manner. When we need food we feel hungry; when we need fluids we feel thirsty. At this level, everything is quite well defined and clear.

There are, however, other sectors or levels of existence, levels on which the specifically human struggle for existence unfolds. Let us take, for example, a person in his late adolescence, who must decide what kind of occupation he will pursue. He must take into account the prevailing economic conditions and opportunities; but a wise decision must also contain a personal element. The occupation must correspond to his inner potentialities, to his abilities and inclinations. But how does he know what his inner potentialities are? To find this out is quite a job and may require a great deal of experimenting and self-observation: What do I really want to do if I disregard what the Joneses do? We have a great urge to fill out our lives rightly, with the right goals, the right activities, but the signposts to guide us toward the choices that are right for us are few and unclear. Before we reach the stage of choosing our life activity, we go through a standardized educational process without having much choice in the matter—nor would we be likely to make early constructive decisions if we had freedom of choice. So personal existence on this level is not an actuality, not anything clearly known; it is there only potentially and has to be found laboriously. In looking for it one makes mistakes of many kinds which, in fortunate circumstances, one may be able to correct by reversing earlier decisions. The struggle for existence on this level is a struggle to become and to be what one really is, to discover ways of living in accordance with one's potentialities.

There is a third level, the most specifically human of all. This is where a person's true aspirations, joys and sorrows, apprehensions and hopes, failures and fulfillments reside. These are the human problems that face us as therapists.

The struggle for existence at this level is for meaning and significance of our person. To be, to exist on this level, *is to mean something to someone else*. On the physical level we have only to maintain what we already clearly are. On the second level we have to actualize the direction of our pursuits out of an initial state that is given to us merely in the form of vaguely perceived multiple potentialities. On the third level we do not start even with potentialities. We start with nothing. We are nothing within ourselves, nonexistent. To be is to mean something to someone else. This existence we cannot directly create for ourselves; it can only be given to us by another.

The true human problem is this: in a sense that matters to us above everything else, we are nothing in ourselves. All we have is a profound urge to exist and the dreadful experience of nonexistence. A poem written in a language that no one can read does not exist as a poem. Neither do we exist in a human sense until someone decodes us. A man in the most crucial way is a symbol, a message that comes to life only by being understood, acknowledged by someone. Otherwise, his existence has no more meaning or reality than an inscription on a rock on an uninhabited planet. William James said that there could be no worse punishment for a human being than to be unnoticed by everyone. Starting with the small child who urgently wants to be noticed, we all want to have a life in the thoughts and feelings of others, to have them reflect our individual existence, and reflect it in an understanding affectionate way.

As so often happens, this general trend can be seen in a particularly striking, exaggerated form when it has to assert itself in unfavorable conditions, against frustrations and difficulties. Why *do* people want to leave a mark behind them? Why are they so gratified if a person who has only met them briefly remembers them? Why do some cut their names in the bark of trees? Certain neurotic states show, in an especially clear fashion, the conditions under which the wish to be understood and accepted can be frustrated, the ways in which the person can be tormented by such frustration, and the means he uses to combat this intolerable state. I said that the person would be nobody if he were alone on the earth, that life would not be worth living; we are restless and not at peace until someone comes and decodes us. This immediately brings to mind a neurotic condition, the picture of a morbidly dependent personality. Such a person cannot stand solitude even for a short time. He suffers terrible feelings of loneliness and wishes that his wife or his friends were there to comfort him. Sometimes, in describing their feelings, patients say: "When I am alone I feel as if I weren't alive." They themselves associate the feeling with nonexistence. If the patient (who is often a woman) feels that she needs love and must have it at any price, she may say, in talking about the man whose love she wants, that with him she could do anything, be everything, but without him she is nothing. Some of these neurotic counterparts of the healthy trend look so similar to the real thing that when one describes them almost any person can say: "That's me!" Actually there are essential differences, as a more detailed description of the total neurotic picture would readily show. But these examples serve to emphasize that existing in the thought and affection of another really is a very concrete level of existence, and that it is essentially on this level that the problems arise with which we have to deal in therapy.

The unquenchable longing to come into existence in this sense is not a prerogative of reflective or sensitive natures. Only the conscious formulation of this need requires a degree of sophistication. The need itself is an all-embracing need of everyone, whether he be clever or stupid, sophisticated or ignorant, sensitive or callous. The need does not depend on the degree of maturity. Only the manifestations of the need are determined by that. It is the crux of our existence from the cradle to the grave. When we are babies this need expresses itself in things that concern us as babies, and when we are adults in things that concern us as adults, but it is the same superordinate trend of our life at all stages. We exercise our capacities in reference to this broad trend, and our physiological functions, whatever their degree of autonomy and standardization, work within this frame of reference.

I want to emphasize this aspect of human life because my view of it has been misunderstood many times, and I do not want to be misunderstood again. This is not poetry. This is earthy reality. And you cannot begin to understand human beings if you do not see the importance of this realm, not just in the general way in which I am presenting it here, but in its very specific manifestations.

Let us approach the same trend from a different angle. In explaining human behavior we usually talk in terms of needs as sources of motivation, and one thinks of a need as being a lack of something that is necessary for the functioning of the individual as such, as a self-centered unit. It is of course true that a person's own needs and wants are a powerful driving force. But there is something else. We ourselves want to be needed. We not only have needs, we are also strongly motivated by *neededness*. To be of no use to anything or anybody would make life intolerable. What is the main problem of old people? Some of them are well provided for and do not suffer from the insecurity that arises out of losing one's earning power and thus the satisfaction of one's "needs." But they are not happy. They suffer from the diminution of their usefulness, from the feeling that they cannot be of help to anybody any more. This would not make any sense if the human being were merely an egocentric organization complete within itself. We are restless when we are not needed, because we feel "unfinished," "incomplete," and we can only get completed in and through these relationships.

We are motivated to search not only for what we lack and need but also for that for which we are needed, what is wanted from us. We struggle to find out what is demanded from us, and we are restless until we find and fulfill these demands. No one would deny, because it is factual, that men do assume duties and seek to live up to what is expected of them. The question is only whether this characteristic of man's motivational structure is basic and primary or is derived, is a tool in the service of his needs in the narrower sense of the word. In most psychological theories, the second alternative seems to be implied. Assuming obligations, responding to the needs of others, is regarded as payment for obtaining satisfaction for one's own needs. This may be true in many cases but by no means in all. Consider, for example, our relationship to children. People can have children for many reasons; they may acquire them simply as a result of satisfying their sexual needs. But why do some people adopt children, deliberately assuming burdens and responsibilities? Among all the possible motives the wish to take care of the needs of someone else must figure high. The fact that the "neededness" motivation is seldom present in its pure form, that other motives are also detectable, should not be taken to mean that they are all that is there. One could say that the feeling of being needed increases one's feeling of personal importance, one's self-respect and value. This is true, but it does not place the motivation back within the realm of individual needs. It remains significant that self-respect is heightened by the person's being of value to *another*.

Whatever other meanings and functions may attach to the tendency to serve the needs of others, fundamentally it does express one's homonomous integration. The need to belong, to participate in larger wholes, is an abstraction, a general pattern; it does not exist in this abstract way but must always be manifested in some concrete relatedness. One of the concrete expressions of this need to belong is to be of some use or service to another person, group, or cause. This is one of the important ways for an individual to avoid or overcome his separateness and isolation. The dread of isolation does not originate merely in the fear that without others one would be incapable of providing for one's own needs, although this, too, may be involved. Essentially the dread of isolation asserts that, for man, individual survival is meaningless as such, that human life is lived not in oneself alone but also in others. The threat of isolation arouses not only anxiety but also anger that one's existence should have to be limited to the boundaries of one's individual self.

Like any other trend, the tendency to serve others may deteriorate and suffer a variety of distortions. One of the most notable of these distortions is the tendency to assume responsibilities which, because of their extent or their nature, are more than the person can or actually wishes to carry. This overcommitment inevitably leads to resentment. The unhealthy superstructure can be built around the healthy nucleus in various ways. The needs and expectations of others may be misperceived or unrealistically exaggerated. The person may not dare to reject demands made on him even if they originate in misconceptions of his possibilities or in the neurotic needs of others, either because he wants to be liked or because he fears to disappoint or to hurt the other. The fear of hurting may be very strong, and it is often a crucial feature in the assumption of hated responsibilities. If the person seeks love and obtains it but feels unworthy of it, he may, in order to really deserve it by being of service, pile obligations on himself to the limit or beyond the limit of his capacities. The fact that through his attitude he greatly tempts the exploiting tendencies of others makes matters worse. Concentration on service may also result from an inhibition and impoverishment of the total expressive gamut of the person. If few other ways of expressing affection are open, overservice may be the consequence.

In some situations the necessity to respond to neededness, even in the absence of a loving relationship, imposes itself so forcefully that the person cannot escape it without guilt. This seems to be the case, e.g., when a person accepts responsibility for an invalid relative even if it nearly wrecks his own life. It is very difficult to disentangle the healthy, the basically human, from the neurotic in some of these cases. But even the worst cases of neurotic overcommitment have some of their roots in the tendency that is common to all of us. Even the compulsive need to make promises, to feel compulsively obligated by them and compulsively unable to free oneself from these obligations when they become hated burdens can be better understood, and the strength of the compulsion more fully appreciated, when one sees it as a distorted complex formed around the nucleus of a basic human trend.

I shall try to elucidate this basic trend further by still another approach to its meaning. Let us start with the analysis of an everyday concept, the concept expressed in the word *possession*. When we possess something we say, "It is mine." But we can mean very different things by these words. We may mean them in the sense of the autonomous orientation: I can do with it what I want; it is under my control; if I want to I can use it; if I don't like it I can throw it away; I can break it or destroy it—it is mine. This is one meaning of possession, but there is another. Consider your relationship to your child or to your wife. It would be strange if you thought you could do with her or him whatever you please. Yet we say "mine," and we say it meaningfully. What do we mean by that? We mean that we identify with the person so that we feel our life extending beyond ourselves and involving these other people. If we say, for example, we the Smiths, or we the Cohens, do things in such and such a way, we define a unit with whose every part we identify, to which we feel we belong.

Now it is interesting that we designate such different attitudes by the same term, "mine." This is not just a verbal matter; it reflects the fact that the homonomous tendency can become neurotically distorted. One of the most frequent distortions is that identification becomes possessiveness. Another person becomes one's possession in the first sense of the word. A similar double meaning can be shown to attach to the phrase "give and take," the first meaning deriving from the trend toward autonomy and the second from the trend toward homonomy. Give and take in one sense means "I will give you this, but shall take from you something to make up for it." This implies the idea that I deprive myself of what I give you: "Now *you* have it, not I; you possess it in the sense of having mastery over it. It is either you or I." But possession in terms of the second trend is an entirely different matter. In this case it would be much truer to say that one is possessed by, not that one possesses. Anything to which you "give yourself," be it an activity, a person, or a goal is yours not through somebody else's being deprived of it. You "possess" it by giving yourself to it, not by taking from it, and in giving yourself to it you can still remain whole; nothing of you gets lost. This is a very different meaning. Obviously, what I am speaking about now is love in the true sense of the word. It may be love of one's work, but it applies particularly to love between people.

The idea of giving and taking in a material sense, where you cannot take without depriving another and cannot give without depriving yourself, frequently becomes neurotically involved in matters of affection. Affection then is treated as if it were merchandise and as if the only possible fun were in getting it. Usually one has little doubt about whether one gives enough affection; one always feels that one gives plenty. Some people have doubts about that, too, but it is much more common to feel: "I don't *get* affection; I don't get enough." If you look at this feeling closely, it implies an interpretation of affection as a material object. A new complication arises from this dealing in affection as though it were merchandise. The exchange of merchandise becomes a substitute for affection. I once had a wealthy patient who went on an excursion with his best friend. The friend was not well to do but could afford this pleasure trip. Everything started happily, but before they left the hotel they settled accounts, and my patient felt he had been shortchanged. It was a matter of a few dollars, a sum that meant nothing to him. (Most of us would like to possess a fraction of his taxes.) But a quarrel developed, and he broke with his best friend because the friend had taken advantage of him, taken something away from him. It is, of course, fantastic to act in such a manner—he could have thrown a hundred times that amount out the window and never noticed it. But to him it meant that his friend had shortchanged him in affection. Some people's troubles with the giving and taking of affection take a more complex form. For example, some cannot accept a present; it makes them feel very uncomfortable. Others feel they must make presents all the time. In whatever form, if the exchange on this material level becomes troublesome and psychiatrically significant, it is almost always a symbolic matter; the actual trouble is with affection. The observed disturbance is an indication that the person interprets affection primarily as a deal, a giving and taking accompanied by counting: "How much am I getting?" "Am I getting the right compensation for what I give?" All of which is based on a superficial analogy with material exchanges between people.

I have discussed three important areas to indicate what kind of human tendency I am speaking about. The first discussion showed that in a very real sense we do not exist on the specifically human level unless we are discovered, noticed, loved, and loved right, by someone else. Another indication of the same basic tendency is that we do not only have needs but are also strongly motivated by "neededness." I mentioned that this is most clearly seen in old people. Some of them have material security, their needs are satisfied, they can sit in the sun, but they feel useless, superfluous. If human beings were living merely within themselves, why on earth should they care, as long as they were comfortable? But we are not comfortable when we are not needed. The third example was in the area of give and take, of possession. There I tried to show the difference between the possession of material things, after which distorted human relations may be patterned, and calling something "mine" in the sense of participation and devotion, in the sense of being "possessed by." None of the experiences I described are exceptional. All people have them in one form or another. All people want to be loved and to love, and their lives are enlarged through both aspects of a loving relationship. One who is loved lives not only within his own skin but also in the love and affection and thought of the other person. To be received in this way into the life of another seems to be one of the most important issues for human beings. The one who loves extends his life by participating in the life of another with all its joys, hopes, and disappointments. Through the community and the communication established in an affectionate relationship the person becomes a part of a unit extending beyond himself.

There is a possible pitfall here which I want to mention. It hinges on the use of the word love, which is open to so many distortions. People very easily assume that if one loves, if one participates in the life of another, this necessarily results in great pleasure for oneself—a lot of fun and very pleasant, cheering moments. Such a romantic conception of love makes us forget that participation in another's life implies also shared suffering, which is not a gain. Loving means that one's life is larger but not that it is necessarily easier or more pleasant. A mother whose child has gone wrong—has done something criminal, let us say —does not reproach the child but suffers for him, and she suffers under something that can only be described as guilt. This does not necessarily mean that she blames herself in a neurotic fashion. Whether or not she has any real reasons to blame herself for the child's trouble, and apart from any specific self-reproaches, she still participates in her child's guilt. Identification means something very positive—the enlargement of one's life, psychologically, far beyond one's own confines. But it does not always mean pleasure, and sometimes it means great pain. It does not have to, but sometimes it does. Usually it means some of this and some of that, both joy and suffering. You do not choose one and discard the other. If you sit up at night with a sick child, let us say, you would not want to give up this experience: you do not want anyone to relieve you so that you can go out and have a good time; you are not in a mood to dance and sing. You want the child to be well, but if he is sick, you want to be there. You accept this enlarged experience. This is also true in relations other than the mother-child relationship, which comes closest perhaps to what a loving relationship can be at its fullest. Of course I am talking about the relatively normal situation, not the kind of parent-child relations we hear so much about from our patients. I think we have to keep the healthy ways in mind as well, if we are really to understand what went wrong with the patients.

I shall now try to round out what I have been saying by listing what I consider to be the three main characteristics of the loving relationship: the experience of a certain fundamental belongingness and unity between lover and loved, the recognition and acceptance of the difference, of the "otherness" of the loved person, and the understanding of the other, an understanding of a special kind.

The first of these characteristics has already been discussed as an identification with the person whom one loves. My use of the term "identification" might be misleading for some. I do not use it in the specific sense that it has in the psychoanalytic theory but simply to indicate the experience of a certain sameness, or communality, which permits those who share the relationship to share also in each other's lives. It is not brought about actively. In loving someone the person recognizes that this identity exists. The term "we-feeling" may have been coined to indicate the kind of "identification" I have in mind—an inclusion into the same unit, a sense of oneness that exists, emotionally, in spite of the recognition of separateness. The second characteristic, the acceptance of difference, is no less important than the first. In an ideal case the person who loves, in spite of his identification with the other, allows the other to live his or her life and does not want to take over. He realizes the other is different from himself, a person in his own right, and in a very real way the person who loves stands off, enjoying whatever direction the other is taking, even if it is not what he had expected or what he would have preferred the other to do. The recognition and acceptance of the otherness of the person also implies an understanding of him, and this is a very essential condition. One cannot love unintelligently and love well.

In saying this I do not mean that one should be able to formulate one's understanding of the other person clearly. If this were so, simple people who are poor at verbalization would not be able to love, but they do love: they do have understanding, though they may not be able to say any clever or poetic things about it. The understanding of the person you love is primarily on an intuitive level, although if you are trained to crystallize your feelings into thought, you may find formulations for it. Essentially, however, it is an intuitive understanding involving deep insight. It is said that love is blind, but I believe that real love is not blind. I think real love is visionary; it sees further than other people do. Sometimes we wonder about a woman who loves a man. That drunk, we think, that person who has done such terrible things. . . . How can she? But she sees something different in him, not because she is blind but because she sees further than we do. She sees the essential core of the person, which means she can love. You can see that I use the word understanding in a special sense. This kind of understanding is different from the one that is limited to the surface. Some shrewd people, including some psychiatrists, have an excellent knowledge of people's weaknesses; they are in a certain sense knowers of men. Such knowledge has practical value. It often enables us to predict the other's reactions, but it is certainly not conducive to love. Real understanding of a person means seeing the real self behind and within his weaknesses and his neurotic distortions.

Such understanding is not the same as idealization, which is a distortion of the truth. Suppose a patient tells me that I am a wonderful person, ascribes to me all kinds of characteristics that I do not have. In the therapeutic setting this will eventually be worked out; it may even be favorable for therapy that he feels that way now. But it is not true. It does not matter in this case. It will be worked out and will not cause any trouble in the long run. But what about a person who sees his father or mother in someone he loves and resents the other whenever he or she does not live up to that image? He does not really love, because he does not love that particular person but a phantom behind that person. To love someone you must understand him in the sense of knowing him as he is. In reality, of course, this understanding will often be imperfect. There are biases and distortions in love, but they may be indications that it is a relationship in which one has some personal axe to grind.

The issue of understanding has some bearing on the attempts to influence the attitude of parents toward children. The public is becoming increasingly aware of the importance of the parental attitudes for personality development, and some people try to bring up children according to books. It is to be feared that very little good can be derived from greater enlightenment. One can suggest methods of educational procedure to parents, and, by providing pertinent information about children's emotional and mental development, one may hope to increase the parents' understanding of them. However, the kind of understanding children need for emotional growth depends less on information than on the parents' attitudes, which are not so easily influenced and changed. Even the question of whether or not the parents use physical punishment—important though it is—is less important than the question of whether they love the child in the right way. If they do, this love will be conveyed unintentionally. If something essential is missing from their love it cannot be compensated for by knowing the "right method." It all depends on how far the parents are loving, and how far they can be loving depends on how free they are from emotional disturbances and difficulties.

With some qualifications this holds also for the relationship of a therapist to his patients. Unless the therapist deliberately remains aloof there will be a natural development of feeling as in any other situation of prolonged acquaintance. As he learns to know and understand his patient he also learns to like him, and the more this feeling approximates devotion, the more help he will be able to give. If the attitudes that the therapist develops are right, and are not strongly colored by his personal problems, he can be confident they will transpire and be convincing to the patient. A therapist who holds these beliefs and follows this course is involved in the therapeutic process more personally and deeply than one whose ideal it is to remain a mere screen for the patient's projections.

Manifestations of the homonomous trend are not limited to the field of interpersonal relations. We cannot pursue here in detail its expressions in the various fields of cultural endeavor, but we shall say a few words about one instance—aesthetic experience—which throws some additional light on the dynamics of homonomous processes. The conceptual categories of stimulus and response, even if holistically interpreted, do not fit the aesthetic experience. An aesthetic impression is not perceived as a biospheric opportunity or contravention. We resonate to it but it does not stimulate us to do something about the situation. Correspondingly, an artistic expression does not aim at molding or conquering the environment. Both impression and expression may be likened to communication; we can view impression as receiving a message and expression as sending forth a message. When the two meet communication takes place.

What does such a conception, or such a simile, imply about the nature of aesthetic experience? The "message" is not an intellectual or factual one, and in the case of a true artistic expression it can hardly be improved by rational formulation. Similarly, the general nature of aesthetic experience, its common denominator, cannot be conveyed through simple description. We can only try to hint at it indirectly, either by a concrete metaphor or an equally inadequate "intelligent" statement.

Every object and every creature in the world is somehow expressive of the kind of world in which such creatures and such objects can exist. They are not isolated existences unto themselves. Each is a sample, an expression, an indicator of the kind of world we live in. When an object is perceived in its expressive function one has an aesthetic experience. An aesthetic or beautiful object does not end with its confines, but points beyond itself; an aesthetic experience opens onto wide infinite vistas. Though an expressive valence attaches to every object, it varies in richness and degree. It is the artist's task to enhance the expressive quality of his production so as to maximize its power of pointing to some general feature of existence. Media and styles may vary, but the aesthetic value of a work of art depends on whether it points beyond the specific object or pattern that forms its content and leads the mind of the beholder toward the perception of expressiveness. The perception of opening horizons, of widening meanings, makes the aesthetic experience a striking expression of the homonomous orientation. The person's separation from the world is overcome together with the separateness of objects, and wider patterns emerge. I believe that experiences of this kind, marked by intensity, clarity, and harmony are the nuclei of the "peak experiences" described by Maslow. A similar effortless emergence of new patterns of relations and meanings also characterizes some phases of creative work, both in art and science.

The nature of the aesthetic experience points up some essential features of the homonomous person-world interaction. Both in the homonomous and autonomous trends the person aims at overcoming his separation from the "object," but the object is not the same in the two kinds of reunion, even when it is "physically" identical. The object of mastery is *nothing but* an object. It is foreign and dissimilar to the person—meaningful only insofar as it can be made to serve him and thus be assimilated into his sphere. The object of homonomous strivings is conceived of as having a "selfhood," a meaningful existence of its own—either that of another human being or of some other intrinsically valuable entity with which it is possible to form a community. The interaction here is not that of discreta having an impact on each other but the interaction of parts in a whole. The message of the nature and state of one entity is received by the other, and through this communication a community, a unit, is formed. Impression and expression are vehicles of communication, modes of holistic interaction through which all homonomous exchanges are carried out.

The directions of the autonomous and homonomous trends are different, and they appear to be opposites, but in a well-integrated person the two orientations are complementary rather than conflicting. In fact they logically presuppose each other. As one strives to master and govern the environment, one discovers that one cannot do this effectively by direct application of force, by sheer violence. One must understand and respect the laws of the environment, go along with them, so to say, which means assuming a homonomous attitude. On the other hand, bringing one's best to a loving relationship requires not only a capacity for self-surrender but also a degree of proficient mastery of one's world, of resourcefulness and self-reliance. Without these qualities one does not have much to offer the other, and the relationship may deteriorate into dependency and exploitation. It is true that in some pathological formations mastery and love are played one against the other and may clash right and left. The problem of how best to combine them, how to be for oneself *and* for others, do what one wants to do and be loved for it, looms large for most people at some points or periods of their lives. Yet a wide range of possible forms of integration is available to a person if neither of the two basic satisfactions are essentially threatened or reduced to fixed channels. It is astonishing to see how quickly and fully the previously baffling conflicts are solved once these inner threats have been removed. Within a healthy organization mastery and love can mesh in and work together in an almost endless variety of ways which up to now have not been systematically explored. This is a challenging topic for future studies.

Far from being irreconcilable opposites, the autonomous and the homonomous trends can be viewed as part aspects of one trend or perhaps as one trend functioning in two directions—downward and upward. To put it abstractly, the human being behaves as if he were a whole of an intermediate order, comparable to the cardiovascular system or the central nervous system, each of which is a whole, an organization of many parts, but at the same time a part of the total physical organism. The human being is both a unifier, an organizer of his immediate personal world, and a participant in what he conceives to be the superordinate whole to which he belongs. His striving for mastery is embedded in his longing for participation.

3. The Psychological Functions

The Symbolizing Function

It is the symbolic nature of psychological processes that distinguishes them from all other phenomena in the world. Symbolism is a triadic constellation whose terms are: the object A, the symbol B, and a third member—the subject—for whom the symbol *means* or *represents* the object. The crucial factor is this third member who has to be endowed with the capacity of meaning function, that is, of "mentation." The connection between symbol and referent is set up by him, and if we eliminate this third member, the symbolism is destroyed. Thus the symbolic relationship is unique to the psychological realm and actually defines it. We may rightly say that the symbolic relationship is just as general and fundamental for the humanistic sciences as the causal relationship has been for classical physics. Psychological activity may be called the symbolizing function of the organism. This implies that not only some but *all* psychological functions can be understood as processes of symbolization. To demonstrate this we shall briefly review the principal groups of psychological functions, following for the moment their conventional classification into percepts, images, concepts, emotional and conative phenomena. First, however, a few words should be said about the general issue raised by the existence of conscious states as such.

Mental phenomena and their relation to physiological processes are frequently looked upon as a sort of miracle. That conscious phenomena, such as the "raw feel" of sensation, do exist is no more miraculous than the existence of physical phenomena or of anything else in the world. Conscious states are demonstrable data and beyond the domain of reasoning. Difficult problems arise only when we consider the possibility and mode of interaction between mental and physical phenomena. The holistic view bridges this fundamentally artificial gap between mind and body by recognizing the psychophysically neutral total organism. The person is neither physiological nor psychological but is a holistic unit, which implies the capacity of both physiolgical and psychological functioning. If we do not identify the personality with the body alone, it is no more miraculous that the person can produce ideas than that he can produce bile—although, in a sense, both are miraculous enough. We do not have to answer the question of how two such different "substances" as mind and body can act on each other, since we do not assume that such an interaction occurs. The total organism is active, in all its manifestations, but in some of these activities psychological features are prevalent and in others, physiological features. Thus, for practical purposes, the two fields can be distinguished. Neural processes cannot produce ideas, and thoughts cannot make the muscles contract, but the total organism, the person, can do both.

Symbolization in Cognition

Turning now to the phenomena of *perception*, we may say that the organism elaborates perceptual mental images on the basis of *tangential* engagements with the environment in the physiological sensory processes. We call these contacts tangential to distinguish them from direct and obvious forms of interaction such as taking nourishment or avoiding danger. After the perceptual data have been produced and actively elaborated by the organism, they are used as symbols for objects of the environment. Each of these environmental objects is far richer in traits than the perceptual datum that indicates the object for the observer. When one sees a white bird, what is visually given is only a white spot of a certain form, but one perceives through it the object "bird." When we state that the bird is an animal, that it lives, flies, eats, etc., we are obviously referring to something different from the visual datum, the white spot. The visual datum will vary if one sees the bird from the front or the side, when it is at rest or is flying, but the bird will remain the same bird. The object is incomparably richer in content than its visual appearance. The visual datum is the symbol for the whole object. It refers to the object and indicates it for the observer. In the terminology of F. Brentano, the perceptual datum is characterized by "intentionality" toward an object. The data given in perception are much simpler than the object itself; hence the great economic value of perception for the organism.

Images are still more simplified symbols, and the organism is able to operate with them with still greater ease and freedom. The advantage of images as compared with perception does not lie in their greater simplicity alone. They allow the organism to deal also with objects that are not included in the situation of the moment. Images broaden the perspective and sphere of the organism over spatially distant parts of the environment—as well as over the past (memory) and the future (foresight). Symbolization is still more effective in *thought processes* because of the use of very remote, but extremely condensed and simplified, symbols. A single concept stands for a whole series of objects and relationships. The symbols involved in thought processes are representative of relations and system connections between objects. With the aid of these symbols a wide range of intellectual operations of high economic value for the organism is possible.

Symbolization in Emotion and Striving

Perceptions and images are symbols which refer primarily to the environment. There also exists a wide range of psychological phenomena that indicate the states of the *organism*. The sensations of pain, hunger, thirst, and other internal sensations belong to this group. The main forms of expression of the state of the organism are, however, the *emotions*. The feeling tone of emotions, their pleasantness-unpleasantness component, is the *experience of the state and of the situation of the person under the aspect of value*. The biological situations are constantly evaluated by the organism from the point of view of their significance for the life process. The emotional tone is the experience of such significances, an experience not embodied in detached thoughts and judgments but given in a very intimate and immediate manner as joy and sorrow, depression and elation, pleasure and pain. Because of the immediacy and "ego-closeness" of emotional experiences, their symbolic nature is not as obvious as, for instance, that of perceptions, in which the symbol and the referent are more clearly distinguishable. It may be useful, therefore, to clarify what is the symbol and what is the *primary fact* to which the emotional experience refers.

The primary fact is a situation having a positive or negative value for the person. Success, failure, threat to one's personal security, disappointment in one's expectations, the loss of a close friend, or, on the other hand, the opening up of new opportunities, an attained goal, a lucky constellation of events creating a fortunate turn in one's personal affairs are examples of situations that have a distinct positive or negative value for the person. Such ego-relevant situations are in themselves not experiences but actually existing biospheric constellations. They are the primary facts which function as referents in the formation of a symbolic relation. The value aspect of these situations is *experienced* in the form of emotion. In other words, emotional experiences are symbols of value-laden, person-relevant facts. Emotion is an evaluative experience, the most immediate form of personal evaluation. Explicit value judgments may precede, accompany, or follow emotional experiences, but they are by no means indispensable to them. A person may feel sad, anxious, or happy without any reason known to him.

Conative processes are no less symbolic in character than any other class of psychological phenomena. The organismic total process is characterized by a directional trend leading from states of lesser autonomy to states of greater autonomy and by the homonomous trend toward participation in larger wholes. Both trends branch out into a number of specific manifestations such as drives and urges, which in themselves are not psychological but organismic, psychophysically neutral. These basic organismic urgencies and their specific ramifications are elaborated symbolically and experienced by the organism as conscious conative processes: wishing, craving, willing. The referents both for emotional tone and conation are not physiological but totalistic organismic states and processes, in which environment is always a participant. In conation these processes are translated not only into psychological processes but frequently also into gross bodily action. As concretizations of the organism's basic trends, drives and urges are neither direct causes nor effects of emotions, but there is a connection between the two. When the vital relevance of a situation is not only acknowledged in thinking but also experienced in the form of emotion, this evaluation is much more likely to result in action. Whether or not the action will be adaptive depends, to a large extent, on the integrational state of the organism. Given a state of chronic conflict, emotions may reflect contradictory evaluations and have disorganizing rather than energizing effects.

If emotions are evaluative experiences, we cannot view any of them as energies stored within the organism, which must periodically have an outlet if the person is to remain healthy. Anxiety and hostility are not present in anyone in fixed quantities; they are emergency reactions to circumstances that interfere drastically with the realization of the basic human strivings. In the neurotic, these emotions always lurk in the background and erupt on frequent occasions because neurotic life is a threatened life. A healthy person rarely experiences disorganizing anxiety or rage; in his case fear and anger, which symbolize more moderate and circumscribed threats, often have an organizing effect on behavior. These two emotions reflect two ways of dealing with threat. Which is "chosen" depends on the magnitude of the threat and the person's confidence in his capacity to deal with it. When the confidence level is high, one can deal with an obstacle either by effectively molding it or by alertly avoiding it, and either activity can be pleasurable. When the threat is stronger, or confidence weaker, anger that can lead to courageous fighting is aroused, but with still greater threats anger is replaced by fear and anxiety. Still, the alternate emotion is never far off. Our anger is aroused only by what we fear, that is, by dangers with which we may not be able to cope, and we are apt to be enraged at whatever drives us into anxiety; this rage can also be turned against oneself—for being weak, inadequate, cowardly. It makes good sense in some contexts to consider anger and fear as two forms of the same emotion, but anger, when it remains outward-directed, is the more constructive of the two because it implies greater self-confidence and self-respect.

Defects of Symbolization

Because human life is carried out partly on a symbolic level, psychological functioning provides the organism with a new means of expressing its inherent tendencies. Symbolic activities greatly widen the field that can be brought under the autonomous government of the organism or used for homonomous integrations.

The symbolic representations of the environment and of the individual are not perfect. The psychological phenomena are not always entirely reliable indices of the primary objects to which they refer. Illusions of perception and falsifications of memory are examples of distortion. In the field of emotion and conation we also find distorted pictures somewhat comparable to illusions. We may experience as pleasurable a state of our organism which is harmful for its welfare, at least in the long run, and we often wish and strive for things that we do not need. Conscious intention frequently misses the real target of one's deeper urgency, a fact of which psychoanalysis has made us keenly aware. The "mind," the ability to have a symbolic grasp of things, is the greatest power given by nature to some of its creatures, but it is also the deepest source of error and suffering. One of the important tasks of an organismic consciousness-transcendent psychology should be to shed light on the processes of distortion brought about by the "mirror of the mind," and to indicate the means for correcting the imperfect pictures.

The Self-Image

Of particular interest to us are the limitations and distortions of symbolization which concern the self-image. We have defined the subject, or the self, as those factors or processes in the biosphere that stand under prevalently autonomous government; this is the person, or the biological self in the broad sense of the word. When this self is psychologically elaborated it appears as self-awareness, or consciousness of self; this is what psychologically we experience as ourselves. Since self-awareness is the conscious image of the biological subject, the features which can be observed in this conscious phenomenon are good indicators of what is going on in the biological subject. Nevertheless, these indicators are often unreliable and insufficient.

With the conscious elaboration of the biological subject-object relationship, a peculiar split appears in the subject organization. It is a remarkable fact that we exclude from self-awareness certain factors which are very important components of the subject. I do not refer here to pathological exclusions like compulsive phenomena, loss of ego reference, and the like but to a fact which is characteristic of the human personality organization in general. When we act under the influence of strong affects, we feel that we do not have entire control over our actions but seem to be carried away by the affect or "passion" as by a foreign force. The word passion has a definite reference to passivity. When we later account for such actions we may use expressions like "I was not myself" or "I was beside myself." A similar example is that state of inspiration in which ideas seem to come from the outside while one experiences oneself as a passive receiver. Such states have often been ascribed to supernatural forces ("divine inspiration," "intuition").

It is beyond doubt that affect, inspiration, and similar experiences originate in our personality, that they are activities of our organisms. Why then does one not experience them as part of one's self? The important fact is that such processes—although determined by the autonomy of the organism—are not governed by our *will*. The conscious self which is only a part, namely the conscious or symbolized part of the biological subject, tends to establish its own autonomous government. What we call "will" represents autonomous determination, the self-government of this narrow conscious or symbolic self. The symbolic self becomes a state within a state. Thus a split is created within the subject organization.

This split is greatly aggravated by the fact that the symbolic self tends toward hegemony, tends to take over the government of the total personality, a task for which it is not equipped. Symbolic processes have a high economic value. Many problems of living are solved not by direct interaction between concrete individual and concrete environment but between symbols indicating the state or characteristics of each. Because of the high economizing value of the symbolic function, the organism tends to utilize it to excess—hence the trend of symbolic functioning toward a hegemony over the total personality. But the psychological self is not equipped to govern the total organism. Only a small part of the biological subject reaches the level of symbolization; and that which is symbolized may be distorted in the process. Some parts of the total biological process may appear only in hazy images, or not at all, as is the case for many of the functions of our internal organs. Thus the symbolic information we obtain about ourselves, and about the environment, is not an entirely true picture of reality and is never complete. When the psychological self attempts to govern the biological total process on the basis of this unreliable and insufficient information, it may become a destructive factor and bring about great damage to the organism.

The discrepancy between the biological total process and what is symbolized is partly due to an inhibition of symbolization of certain personality factors. This inhibition may be a part of a useful selection between relevant and irrelevant factors; it may accompany the automatization of a previously conscious activity, or may be due, as in repression, to the incompatibility of a personality factor with the psychological self. Lack of symbolization, however, is not caused merely by inhibition. Such a lack represents a more fundamental incongruity between the total organism and the psychological self. Only part of the biological total process is symbolized by man in his present state of evolution.

The split between the conscious self and the total organism becomes even more marked because certain factors elaborated on the symbolic level remain segregated on that level and do not penetrate into the depths of personality. This phenomenon of resistance of the total personality against accepting certain symbolic facts may be viewed as the counterpart of repression, or of the inhibition of symbolization. Although we may know quite clearly that something is not good for us, or that it is unreasonable, we still sometimes cannot help doing it. This is an extremely important and difficult problem in the therapy of personality disorders. We see again and again that the patient has perfect insight, but that this insight does not penetrate sufficiently into the personality to change his behavior. The relative segregation of the symbolic self within the organism is perhaps the most vulnerable point of the human personality organization.

I have deliberately avoided using the term *unconscious* in the foregoing discussion of organismic versus conscious processes. Psychoanalysis, which has popularized this term, is in fact a study of the manifestations of the integrated organism, of the biological total process; it has contributed more to our knowledge of the total personality than any other single system. However, the mentalistic terminology in which psychoanalysis describes all personality processes can be confusing and at times misleading. Rather than speak, e.g., of "unconscious wishes," I prefer whenever possible to use different terms for those dynamic trends that are not elaborated symbolically, although they may be revealed by the person's behavior. Attitudes, or sets, which refer to the organism's readiness to behave and perceive in certain ways when certain situations arise are good examples of such holistic, psychophysically neutral concepts. Attitudes can be active without being conscious; although they may become conscious through an additional symbolic elaboration. I shall not be pedantic about terminology, however, and shall occasionally use mentalistic terms, designating, e.g., as unconscious or implicit fantasies those patterns of cognitive sets or attitudes which, if symbolized, would fall in the category of fantasy.

Effects of Symbolization

The description of symbolic processes given so far makes them appear as passive states, as mere reflections of external or internal reality. It does justice neither to the activity involved in the elaboration of symbols by the organism, even in the case of simple perception, nor to the far-reaching effects that symbolization in turn has on reality, on the total course of biospheric events. When, in a symbolic act, we give meaning to an event or an item, defining or identifying it as useful or harmful, loving or unloving, difficult or easy, we do not merely grasp or mirror these features of the biosphere but also potentiate them. This holds true both for the environmental situation and for the person himself. It is not the presence or absence of hostile, loving, fearful, envious, generous, etc., tendencies that distinguish one person from another, or distinguish between the neurotic and the healthy state of the same person. All these potentialities are part qualities of the person at both times, but they are organized in different ways. This organization is not only reflected in the symbolization of the self but is also influenced by it. What the person will be and how he will conduct his life depends primarily on the patterns with which, or in terms of which, he identifies himself.

Self-identification, or self-definition, e.g., as loving, or hateful, or inadequate, is a process which is only partially symbolized; yet its conscious aspect is not a mere epiphenomenon but can have dynamic effects. In therapy this aspect provides means for the preparation of deep-reaching changes, and sometimes it can provide leverage for crucial shifts. A great many therapeutic insights can be described as "renaming," reidentifying one's impulses, strivings, purposes, attitudes. One of the significant results of these redefinitions is the recognition by the patient of his constructive tendencies and possibilities, of alternative ways of conducting his life. These changed significances may prepare the way for a decisive shift in self-definition, for "throwing in one's lot" with the newly recognized constructive alternatives. In all stages of this process, significant events can be at least partly steered, and sometimes triggered, by conscious deliberation.

The attribution of definite meanings to external events has similar far-reaching effects; situations tend to become what we name them. "Fortune" and "misfortune" may seem to pursue a person throughout life, or at least through long periods until the trend changes in some "miraculous" way. On close inspection it may be observed that one person sees opportunities in a variety of events (both good and bad) while another sees in the same events only contraventions, obstacles, threats of misfortune. The second type of person, out of fear, misses opportunities which the first recognizes and grasps. These selective expectations have an extraordinary power in interhuman relations. Everyone consistently calls forth, or invites, only a certain selection from the many attitudes and action potentialities of other people. In analyzing this process of inviting certain reactions to ourselves, we usually find a priori expectations which imply a view of the other person as hostile or helpful, understanding, stupid, belittling, or exploiting. These expectations produce results. There are few people who are so inveterate in one of their modes of behavior that they can be impervious to the other person's conception of them, if this conception is vividly expressed in the mode of interaction he tends to establish. The selective invitation of reaction to oneself is a striking demonstration of the interactional nature of the biosphere and of the extent to which the person creates his environment.

Imagination

The act of defining or identifying is essentially a function of imagination; correspondingly, the shifts in definition and self-definition with which therapists are concerned reflect an imaginative process. We shall therefore consider the workings of imagination in some detail, taking the term in the wide sense which includes thinking and evaluating processes along with the production of concrete images.

The term "imagination" evokes contradictory connotations. When the layman talks about "mere imagination" or says, "It is all in his mind," the implication is not only that the imagined things are not true, but that fantasy as such is a negligible event, not deserving attention, because it produces no tangible results. Another aspect of the popular conception is that imagination has no concern whatsoever for truth, that everything is possible in fantasy, and that in general the production of images is a purely arbitrary affair, a matter of whim which has nothing of substance behind it.

We know, of course, that none of these assumptions are true in this extreme form. Images are not produced out of nothing. There is behind them the energy of a drive which determines their quality; without a need or a wish no image will arise. Nor is it quite true that, given a definite wish, we are free to pursue it in imagination just as we please, without any concern about the realistic possibilities of its fulfillment. There are limitations to this freedom and they exist not only in the case of realistic or semirealistic planning in which imagination is subjected to strong controls. It is difficult, and under certain conditions impossible, to visualize clearly and vividly something that is contrary to reality. In one of my studies of space orientation the subjects were asked to imagine the room in an inverted position.* This seemingly simple task proved impossible to accomplish for most people. Though their eyes were closed, the subjects' knowledge of their factual position in relation to the room interfered with the visualization of the "wrong" position. In studying daydreams we find that the dreamer often expends considerable effort in attempting to surmount obstacles that would realistically present themselves, to resolve difficulties in a quasirealistic fashion. Arbitrary turns, *deus ex machina*, do occur, but a daydream is not satisfying if too many incongruities are left; one tries to resolve them and to make the whole story as plausible and

* A. Angyal, "Die Lagebeharrung der optisch vorgestellten raeumlichen Umgebung." *Neue Psychol. Stud.*, 6:293–309, 1931.

consistent as one can. Concern for reality is not completely abandoned in fantasy.

The assumption that fantasy is ineffective appears to be totally wrong. Imagination has numerous effects. It can produce or affect other mental states—e.g., arouse or allay emotions or stimulate decisions; it can lead to somatic changes of various kinds, well substantiated in psychosomatic medicine; imagination can also produce vital changes in the person's environment, especially the social one. Neurosis provides perhaps the most obvious and striking example of the potency of imagination, particularly of the implicit assumptions not symbolized in consciousness. Yet the conception of imagination as ineffective, as a mere nothing, also has a basis in fact; we have only to think of the futility of most daydreams. This contradiction points up that images may vary from zero effectiveness to extraordinary potency. What are the conditions which make of imagination either an insubstantial reverie which adds little of essence to one's life or a powerful agent which can both help to maintain the status quo and induce transformations in the direction of sickness or health?

Effective Imagination

For an image to be vivid, strong, and effective, two conditions have to be fulfilled; they are interrelated, both referring to the integrational state of the processes connected with the production of the image. Let us assume that behind the image is a need, or a wish, i.e., an incomplete Gestalt which, in accordance with the principle of system action, tends to completion. The stronger the need, the more vivid will be the image, and the more it will prove effective as a step toward the fulfillment of the wish. The strength of the need in turn depends on its position within the personality system and its subsystems. The more directly the need is connected with the central invariable trends of the person, the stronger it will be. If, because of some disturbance of integration, a specific wish is not connected with the deeper more general trend, to which it could serve as an adequate expression, this wish may lack substance and energy, be almost farcical. It might be entertained, e.g., because its object is held desirable by others. Someone may dream of becoming a writer, not because he has the need to write, but because of the prestige of this vocation, of the fame he would like to achieve. The need for fame (which may be a particular formulation of the need to be loved) is present, but the need for writing is not; the surface wish does not correspond to any real need.

The real need for writing arises when the person has something to say. When this is behind the wish, the activity of putting one's thoughts on paper is supported by a powerful structure which this activity serves to complete. But shadowy wishes, not supported by any directly connected need structure, may be satisfied by such shadowy things as daydreams. In the neurotic life there is a great deal of apparent need, desire, ambition, and too little activity to lead toward real fulfillment.

The second condition required for the production of dynamically effective images is wholeheartedness, or absence of conflict and doubt. This is where the imagination's concern with truth serves as a pointer to the central feature of its dynamism. For the image to be effectual its content must be pictured as true, with the conviction that it can be and will be. One could say that only those things that are possible are fully imaginable, i.e., can be imagined with belief. The presence or absence of belief determines whether or not the image will be effective. What we have strong implicit faith in we expect to happen, and this expectation facilitates its own realization. But if we doubt the reality value of the image, it has no dynamic leverage.

If conviction of truth were based only on factuality, convincing images would be mere translations of known facts, and "imagination" would be a meaningless and superfluous term, a duplication of perception and memory. But the "reality," or convincingness, of a given item is based predominantly on an integrational constellation, namely on the consistency of this partial item with the system principle of the whole. The lack of consistency, the conflict between a given experience and the principles governing reality as we know it, leads to doubt and disbelief. For an image to become strong and potentially creative this inconsistency, this contradiction or opposition arising out of our established system of beliefs, must be somehow eliminated or reduced.

Achieving Consistency: Restriction and Extension

Reduction or elimination of inconsistency is possible because reality, the range of what is believed to be factual, is not fixed but variable. A doubtful item, contradicted by reality, can become consistent with it if the field of factuality is changed in one of two ways. Its range can be restricted, so that what is contradictory to the image is obliterated; or it can be extended to include, as lawful possibilities, factors that had formerly been excluded and that would support the given image.

Strong vivid images can be produced through a narrowing of the total field, such as occurs in dreams, in hypnosis, or in experiments involving sensory deprivation. In dreams not only the criteria and controls provided by perception fall away, but the known lawfulness of the world recedes into the background, is "forgotten," so that imagination can take over unopposed. In hypnosis the realm of the "factual" is essentially restricted to the suggestions of the hypnotist, conflict and doubt are eliminated, and strong effective images are produced accordingly. In sensory deprivation the environment is artificially impoverished to such an extent that imaginative processes can take on hallucinatory proportions. Sensory deprivation is only a specific example of a much more general phenomenon, that of the narrowing of the field by dissociation from familiar reality toward which one has a habitual vital orientation. This can happen not only through impoverishment but also through a drastic change from the accustomed environment to one which is quite alien and therefore initially devoid of any cues to its possible biospheric relevances.

Those daydreams that carry some "conviction" which is expressed in excitement and gratification also achieve this effect through a dissociation from one's actual life, particularly from one's own conduct. Thus a man may dream of becoming a great scientist though he cannot bring himself to sit down with a book for ten minutes. If his present state were ever so distant from the dreamed-of goal, but included some activities leading toward it, his fantasies might approach constructive imagination and planning. But daydreams as such can give gratification only insofar as one can forget everything else. In fact, the more the person feels deficient and despairs of success in the particular area he chooses to daydream about, the more vivid and satisfying the dream. In delusions, the strength of the pathological conviction arises from its consistency with the underlying need, but to maintain the delusion one must exclude all contradictory evidence.

The increased vividness and potency of images produced within a narrowed field can be utilized to bring about specific changes, e.g., in the case of hypnotic suggestion. Since, however, the restriction is temporary and the contradictory aspects of the accustomed reality eventually reappear, these changes are often impermanent. Even if a specific image remains effective, this effectiveness is limited; it cannot spread, because to remain undoubted it must also remain isolated from its possible roots and connections. If someone has been "cured" of his fear of cats by having accepted, under hypnosis, the image of cats as lovable animals, little has been achieved. It was not cats as such that he was afraid of, and whatever it was has not been discovered and changed.

An elimination of inconsistencies and doubts that leads to a revitalization of imagination can be achieved in a more real and enduring fashion by a process which is the opposite of restriction or dissociation. An extension of reality, of the range of lawful possibilities, may lead to the realization of the spuriousness of previously perceived contradictions and to a changed patterning of experience. Within the new pattern the previously doubtful image or thought may become system-consistent and consequently convincing and effective. The extended vision of what is real or possible concerns both the image of the external world and the person's image of himself, usually in an interrelated fashion.

The extension of the range of lawful possibilities differs from the opposite process, the narrowing of reality, in that it must needs be a prolonged gradual process. Reality as we know it is not a conglomeration of unrelated items to which new ones can be easily added but a system governed by definite principles which exclude contradictory evidence. Thus we find ourselves faced with a seemingly unsolvable circular situation. For an image, a new thought, to become credible and effective, the existing system of belief has to be loosened, extended, modified; this, however, cannot happen if any new contradictory evidence is automatically excluded. The history of science shows how often even repeatedly observed facts are neglected because they contradict established theories. Revolutionary changes and new hypotheses may be required to extend the field and scope of science. Similarly, if someone's individual world is so structured that to be loved unselfishly is impossible in it, is excluded by the "laws" of the world, contradictory observations may remain ineffective, permanently or temporarily. On the other hand, if through a variety of loosening and modifying processes the person reaches a state in which he can have at least a tentative glimpse of this sector of reality, this first vision can open new horizons and gradually lead to a reliable extension of the range of what is believable and imaginable.

The various stages of the process of extension and reorganization of the assumed "lawful possibilities," and the means that can be used to facilitate these consecutive steps, will be discussed in detail in the chapters on therapy. To make the patient receptive to the new contents, the therapist attempts to reduce or relax those personal states that express and maintain the rigid established definitions by which the patient delimits both his world and his self. In relation to the self these efforts are directed against the autonomous position of the conscious self, against its segregation from the total self. As this segregation is partially overcome, and the previously definite outlines of the self-image are blurred, those contents and processes that have remained outside the self-image become symbolizable and emerge into consciousness in various forms: as dreams, fantasies, memories, unfamiliar impulses, novel self-observations, and eventually realizations of connections and patterns not previously seen. Some of these experiences are akin to intuitional states and to certain stages of the creative process in that they may appear to the subject to come from somewhere outside, while he himself is merely a passive recipient of the message. As new, fresh symbolizations, these experiences may possess to a higher than usual degree the feature of all symbols—that of pointing beyond itself, an openness to the referent which is absent from our limited everyday "truncated" symbolizations. Convictions that are gained through such processes of extension are not logical or labored, they are founded on an experience which is self-transcendent as such.

The therapist cannot produce new symbolizations in or for the patient but he can assist their development, can help "translate" nonconscious personality processes into consciousness by such means as noting and emphasizing new experiences, interpreting dreams, or bringing together material that might lead to the discovery of a personal pattern. The extension and reorganization of consciousness, of the "I-connected" highly differentiated realm of existence, will in turn exercise an influence on the total organismic process out of which it arose. In cases of successful therapy or of a similar spontaneously developing process, the reorganization that has been achieved on the symbolic level through redefinitions, re-evaluations, insights, does not remain just a new view, a changed perception of oneself. It may actually recede into the background of consciousness, but the evidence of personal changes (such as changes of mood and of somatic state) going far beyond what can be deliberately achieved indicates that through some kind of "back absorption" the conscious processes have contributed to the enrichment and reorganization of the biological total process.

4. Integration
and Its Disturbances

The Structure of Wholes

For a holistic study of personality we need logical tools adequate for dealing with the structure of wholes. We need, in fact, a new type of logic, a logic of holistic systems, which would be the counterpart of the conventional logic of relations. This is a large order and a task for the future. As a first step in this direction I shall try to clarify some of the logical properties of systems and to apply the insight gained to the problem of personality integration. In the following discussion the term *system* denotes holistic organization, while the term *whole* refers to the concrete organized object.

In order to demonstrate some of the logical characteristics of systems I shall compare them with relationships, using as an example of a system a static, geometrical one: a straight line *A–B* containing points *a, b, c, d*. The essential differences between relationships and systems may be summarized in the following four points.

1. A relation requires two and only two members (*relata*) between which the relation is established. *A system may involve any number of members and is not analyzable into pairs of relata;* it is not a complex relation. In our example it is impossible to say what the relation between the points *a* and *b*, *b* and *c*, *c* and *d* should be in order to make them form a linear system. If a formulation involving a multitude of members—e.g., a causal chain *e-f-g-i*—can easily be resolved into two-term relations: *e-f, f-g, g-i*, we are dealing with a compound relation and not with a system.

2. In a relationship, the connection of the relata is direct, going without any mediation from *a* to *b* and vice versa. Between the members of a system, the connection is of a more complex type. The points

a, b, c, d of a straight line are connected only in that they form a linear whole. *The members of a system as such are not significantly connected with each other except with reference to the whole.* Their relationships to each other are secondary; they are determined by a superordinate factor.

3. A relation requires an aspect out of which the relationship is formed. For instance, the relations of identity, difference, or similarity between two objects may be based on their color, size, or weight, i.e., on some immanent attribute. This does not hold for systems. *Items become constituents of the system* by means of their distribution or arrangement, *by their positional value in the system and not by their immanent qualities.* In a linear system it is immaterial whether points, crosses, or circles are its members as long as the positional values in the arrangement remain the same. We may transpose a melody a few octaves higher or lower and it still remains essentially the same melody, although the two variations may not have a single individual tone in common. That the whole is, to a large extent, independent of individual parts has been frequently pointed out.

This statement, however, needs some qualifications. The parts have to have certain attributes to enable them to fill the positions required by the system. In a triangle the parts have to be lines, although their other properties (for instance, their absolute lengths) are irrelevant. Thus certain properties of the constituents are relevant, that is, they are necessary to permit the occupancy of a given position, while other properties are irrelevant. The more highly the whole is organized, the more the inherent properties of parts are utilized as codeterminants of positional values. The human organism, for example, is highly economical in this respect. It carries a minimal load of irrelevant properties of parts; most of its properties are "utilized," that is, they codetermine the positional value of the part.

4. Any relationship between items and any arrangement of items presupposes their separation. Multiplicity of objects is possible only in some kind of dimensional domain, of which space and time are the clearest examples. Although the dimensional domain is a necessary condition for both relationships and systems, its function differs in the two cases. In a relationship, the role of the dimensional domain is merely disjunction of the relata; to be compared, two objects have to be separate, e.g., in space or time. *In systems, the dimensional domain not only serves to separate the parts but also participates in the formation of the system.* The system itself is dimensional. A system is a distribution of the members in a dimensional domain.

The increasing awareness of the problem of wholes on the part of biologists and psychologists has led, in the last decades, to the discovery of certain general principles, which are best formulated by the Gestalt psychologists: Wertheimer, Koehler, Koffka. It will be useful to examine briefly some of these principles and definitions in the light of the formulations given above.

Wholes have been characterized as *unitas multiplex*. Let us consider the second word first. Since a system is a way of arranging parts, the role of multiplicity is obvious; a single factor cannot be arranged. The first word of the expression refers to the fact that every system has one and only one construction principle—the *system principle* of the whole. For example, the system principle of the cycle is equidistance of all points from the center. In a given whole, the system principle may be realized either perfectly or only approximately. There are wholes in which all the significant positions of the system are occupied in perfect accordance with the system principle; and there are wholes in which only a limited number of positions are occupied in this way, while other members are out of position. The terms "good" and "bad" Gestalt refer to this difference; the degree of *Praegnanz* a Gestalt may have depends on the extent to which the positions of the parts conform with the system principle of the whole. In some cases enough positions are occupied to indicate the system principle, while the other positions are not filled. These are the "open" *Gestalts*, to be distinguished from "closed" ones, in which all the significant positions are occupied.

Dynamic Wholes

So far I have discussed systems in general, but at this point a distinction has to be made. This distinction applies to relations as well as to systems. Certain relations, as, for instance, comparative ones (*a* is larger than *b*), could be called static, whereas others could be called dynamic. The prototype of dynamic relations is the causal relationship. In the same way one can distinguish between static and dynamic systems. In application to the latter, the formulations of the general laws of systems must be specified so as to take into account their dynamic functional properties. Thus, applied to dynamic wholes, the statement that the parts are determined by their position in the system means that a given part would *function* differently depending on the whole to which it belongs. We would also expect the whole to have its own characteristic dynamics, different from that of causal connections. Certain principles of holistic dynamics have been formulated by the Gestalt psychologists, as, for instance, the "tendency to closure" and the "tendency to *Praegnanz*." These tendencies could be regarded as subvarieties of a more inclusive tendency—the *tendency toward a complete realization of the system principle*. This is accomplished in the case of closure by filling in the unoccupied positions; the tendency toward *Praegnanz* aims at a rearrangement of parts that would move the outlying items into positions required by the system principle. System dynamics—or at least *one* basic principle of system dynamics —would then consist in a movement toward a greater approximation of the system principle.

The possibility of the dynamic action of a system would probably be rejected a priori by many students. In the last analysis causality is just as inexplicable as system action and might even be an extremely simplified form of system action; yet a formulation of the dynamics of a given happening in terms of causality is generally felt to have greater scientific validity than its formulation in terms of system action. Causal thinking has been used in science for such a long time, and in certain fields with such success, that it is almost generally considered to be *the* scientific thinking, although it may well be only a subvariety. It is, in any case, a firmly rooted habit, not easily changed to a basically different approach. Dealing with relations and dealing with systems involves quite different psychological processes. In causal thinking and research the task is to single out, from a multitude of data, pairs of facts between which there is a necessary connection. In system thinking the task is not to find direct relations between items but to find the superordinate system in which they are connected or to define their positional value within such a system. It might well be that the distinction Jaspers makes between two processes of knowing, *Erklaeren* and *Verstehen* (explanation and understanding), refers precisely to the difference between relational thinking and system thinking.*

Personality as an Organized Whole

The preceding analysis of the structure and functioning of wholes has definite bearings on the problem of personality integration. To establish a framework within which some of these implications can be developed, we must first see how the main concepts used in our general analysis apply to personality. This involves stating the nature of the *material* that is organized in the personality structure, the nature

* K. Jaspers, *General Psychopathology*. The University of Chicago Press, 1963.

of the *dimensional domain* within which the part processes are arranged, and the *system principle* which defines this holistic organization.

To start with the last, according to our theory the system principle of the total process of living is the double dynamic pattern formed by the two major human trends: the trend toward increased autonomy and the trend toward homonomy. These trends divide and subdivide, branching out from the very general into more and more specific attitudes toward specific objects and values and ultimately result in concrete needs and drives. These drives seek expression in actual behavior which always involves an interaction of personal trends with the opportunities and contraventions presented by the environment. Thus, although the subject, the pattern of organismic trends, is the organizing factor of the life process, the material that is being organized also includes various aspects of the environment. The position within the personality system of any factor, subjective or environmental, is characterized by its function; it is determined by whether the given factor promotes or handicaps the realization of the basic dynamic pattern and by the specific ways in which it does so.

The domain in which life processes are distributed and arranged has at least three dimensions. The first is the *vertical dimension* leading from *depth to surface*, from potentiality to actuality. The depth of the personality is formed by the basic human trends in their increasingly individualized elaboration, and the surface is formed by the manifest behavior which alone is accessible to direct observation. The arrangement within the vertical structure is such that a factor closer to the surface is a concretization, a partial manifestation of the nearest deeper-lying factor; in this dimension the relationship between part and whole is the relationship between the expression and the expressed.

When a general trend reaches the surface in the form of a specific drive, need, or wish, it usually leads to some action aiming at the satisfaction of this drive. As a rule the goal cannot be achieved at once but only through a series of successive phases. The dimension along which these successive phases are arranged could be called the *dimension of progression*. Organization along this dimension is a teleological or a *means-end* organization, each phase being the end for the preceding and the means for the following phase. In studying such sequences one has a certain choice as to the size of the parts, or phases, one wishes to consider, but the division cannot be purely arbitrary. It must follow the internal articulation of the process, which in turn is determined by the nature of the goal one has chosen for study.

The "vertical" and the "progressive" dimensions do not exhaust the ways in which part processes may coexist within personality. If they are not differentiated from each other as means and ends, or as surface and depth, the part processes may be assumed to exist side by side, in a *transverse dimension,* the dimension of *breadth.* This would hold for those expressions of a basic trend which have the same position on the vertical dimension, none lying deeper than the rest. Similarly, in a complex movement involving several muscles, their simultaneous contractions do not stand in a means-end relationship to each other but exist side by side, i.e., in a transversal arrangement. The organization along this dimension is one of coordination or synergy. Each item of behavior can be described in terms of its position on these three scales, although they do not exhaust all imaginable *principia individuationis,* i.e., all the significant ways in which part processes in personality can be differentiated from one another.

Personality may be viewed as a highly organized whole, a *hierarchy of systems.* The significant positions in its overall organization are occupied by parts which themselves are systems; the constituents of these secondary systems may also be systems and so on. Since in systems the dimensional domain in which the parts are distributed participates in their patterning, the dimensions enumerated also provide the general bases for the formation of these hierarchies of systems. A hierarchy may be organized along the "vertical" dimension. Thus some personal "axiom of behavior," an implicit assumption of wide bearing which consistently affects action, may be viewed as a subsystem of the person's implicit "philosophy of life" and may itself have subsystems corresponding, e.g., to various areas or methods through which this axiom is implemented. A long-range personal goal may organize a multitude of activities into a hierarchy of subordinate goals or into a coordination of multiple efforts, i.e., along the "progressive" or the "transverse" dimensions.

About the actual content of the various subsystems of personality little can be said that would be of general validity. Within the realm of physiological functions, certain systems—the alimentary, the respiratory, etc.,—are clearly distinguishable, but this uniformity does not hold for the personal functions whose organization is influenced by the individual's characteristics and fate. In mapping out the significant areas of personality functioning one can start with those organized by the cultural and social situations, e.g., the person's attitudes and actions in his family, at work, in his profession, etc. One will soon find, however, that the personal structuring of experiences cuts across the culturally defined roles and follows different paths in different people. An essential gap in our research skills is the lack of well formulated and tested methods by which we could ascertain, in an individual case, which processes belong to one and the same system or subsystem.

An important characteristic of systems or wholes is the degree of their *differentiation* into parts; this concept has been best formulated theoretically by W. Stern.* A part may stand out or it may be embedded in the whole. When a person crosses a brook by stepping on the stones that are above the water surface, every step has to be individually planned and stands out as a separate act. In ordinary walking the single steps have little individuality and are more embedded in the total activity. In a diffuse homogeneous system, the total function is more or less evenly distributed over the entire whole. When, however, more complex functions are required from a given system, a kind of division of labor takes place and more specific functions are assigned to different parts. Transient changes of differentiation take place continuously both in the subjective and in the object-related aspect of the organism's functioning. In every state or situation one can distinguish a more differentiated component which, at a given moment, stands in the foreground ("figure") and the rather diffuse remainder which forms the background. What forms the figure can change from moment to moment, but there are also more lasting changes. Many maturational sequences and many types of learning can be best viewed as processes of successive differentiation. Even experimental conditioning, traditionally viewed as a concatenation of isolated reflexes, is probably more adequately described as a formation of a new figure-background differentiation. Successive differentiation is one way in which subsystems of personality are formed.

System Action in Personality

In studying the hierarchy of systems from the dynamic point of view, it is useful to distinguish the dynamics within a given subsystem and between systems of different orders. How do changes within a system take place? A change in the "irrelevant" properties of a part will not change its positional value and consequently will have no effects on the system, for example, walking from one place to another may remain the same system even if the internal structure of the single steps varies considerably. On the other hand, any change in a part that involves a change of its positional value will affect the structure of the whole. Such change calls for some kind of rearrangement,

* W. Stern, *Studien zur Personwissenschaft, I: Personalistik als Wissenschaft.* Barth, Leipzig, 1930.

and this is effected by certain positional value changes of one or more parts of the whole. Thus *changes within the system do not spread directly from one part to another, but always follow the course from a part to the whole or from the whole to a part.* The stimulus-response connection, from my point of view, is not a part-to-part relationship but an instance of system action, proceeding from the part to the whole and from the whole to the part. Only that factor can become a stimulus which, through its biological relevance, causes a change of constellation in a system—by creating either an "open Gestalt" of a need or a wish, or a "bad Gestalt" of a disturbance of functioning, or an opportunity to express in a particular way the trend that governs the system. The "response" in every case is a rearrangement aiming at a more complete realization of the system principle. Those perceptual data that are indicative of neither environmental opportunities nor contraventions do not become active stimuli. The greater part of these data are simply registered and kept "in reserve" as being of potential significance to the organism.

In considering the patterns of interaction between different systems, one must take into account the difference in the degree of *plasticity* that the systems may have. Plastic systems are those in which parts have variable functions, the variation depending on the constellation of the whole. In rigid systems, parts have fairly fixed positions, i.e., they carry out highly standardized, uniform functions. The sensory-neuro-muscular functions which have a broad range of variation, corresponding to the high variability of conditions in the external environment, are an example of a plastic system; no fixed functions would be adequate to manage such a range of changes. The visceral functions, on the other hand, form a more rigid system which deals adequately with a more standardized, highly homeostatic environment. Because of the "fixation," of the low variability of functions, processes that go on in rigid systems are rather localized happenings; processes in plastic systems spread upward and downward, to superordinated and subordinated systems.

Before we consider the manner in which a change in a given system spreads to other systems, we must clarify the concept of part from a new angle. Unlike fragments, which are results of arbitrary divisions, parts are articulated out of a whole by its own inherent organization. The parts of the process of walking are steps, whereas, e.g., the last fourth of the first step, together with the first half of the second step, is a unit resulting from an arbitrary fragmentation of the total process. The implicit criterion we use in singling out natural parts is the extent of their contribution to the whole. The function of walking is the change of place. The body is not yet displaced when the leg is only lifted; progression is made only when the foot reaches the ground again, i.e., when the step is completed. Thus the part must be relatively complete in itself and contribute *directly* to the function of the whole.

This implies that the concept of parts should be reserved for immediate parts. The restriction is necessary if the concept is to have any meaning or value. It would not mean much, e.g., to state that the word "man" is part of a textbook of sociology in which it occurs, or that the sound "o" is a part of a paragraph dealing with social issues. A sound cannot be a part of a sentence without being a part of a word, and the word cannot be a part of a treatise unless it is a part of a sentence; meaningful analyses of part-whole relationships can be made only in terms of immediate parts. In other words, part and whole refer to connections between neighboring regions or systems.

This situation has important implications for the dynamics of wholes. Since system action consists of a change progressing from part to whole, or vice versa, and since the part-whole relation is always that of neighboring regions, it follows that the *spread of change from any section of the whole is continuous*. In application to the hierarchy of systems this means that a change in one system cannot *directly* affect a distant region in the hierarchy. To affect such a region the change must spread downward or upward across the intermediary systems. For this reason, attempts to establish direct relationships between processes belonging to distant sectors of the organism's functioning are of limited value, even if they result in sizeable correlations. Most of the studies of personality functioning which follow this model without attempting to trace the chain of system action connecting these distant segments prove very unenlightening. The continuous spread of change in a composite system may be regarded as one of the basic laws of system dynamics.

Multiple Utilization of Parts

What has been said so far might seem to imply that the subsystems of personality are at all times clearly separated from one another, the parts being permanent "possessions" of a given system and of no other. Such a conception would be misleading. We must correct it by describing a situation which is of paramount importance for the understanding of disturbances of integration.

If a given function has been identified as part of a given subsystem, this connection is usually not permanent. In a plastic system an individual function *a* may at one time be a part of the subsystem A, at another time a part of the subsystem B or C. New functions can arise not only through differentiation from the old ones but also through a *rearrangement of the same part functions to form different total functions*. Thus an individual muscle contraction may on different occasions be a part of widely different motor patterns.

The organism works in a very economical way, carrying out a great many functions with the aid of a relatively small number of individual items. This is possible only if several functions are assigned simultaneously or successively to a given part. Such a situation might be described as functional overcrowding; occasionally it manifests itself also as morphological overcrowding. A good example is the anatomical combination of the urinary and sexual organs; the urethra in the male, for instance, is just as much a part of the urinary as of the genital system. Another example is the close association of the nutritive, speech, respiratory, and some additional minor functions which are carried out by means of the morphological structures of the "oral zone." The functional overcrowding of the organism is greatly increased by the fact that secondary meanings may be superimposed on primary biological functions. Multiple functioning applies also to environmental conditions. A given environmental factor may present opportunities for the formation of several systems. Multiple motivation of a single act is not an exception but the rule in personality dynamics.

Since the part functions of the organism serve various purposes, an orderly way of functioning is possible only by means of precisely working mechanisms which prevent interference between systems having equal claim to the same group of part functions. These mechanisms are the *setting* and the *shifting of set*, comparable to setting the typewriter to write small or capital letters. *Setting can be defined as the construction of a system.* The parts have multiple functional possibilities, but after being arranged in a given system, they function in one definite way, namely, in accordance with the system principle. The other functional possibilities of the parts are excluded; they become activated only when the parts are rearranged in other systems and work in accordance with the new system principle, i.e., after a shift of set. Setting and shifting may thus be regarded as the key mechanisms of organized activity.

Competition of Systems

The multiple utilization of part functions is a most economical arrangement, but it represents at the same time a serious vulnerability of the organism. In spite of the high efficiency of the setting and shifting mechanisms, *the mutual interference of systems* is inevitable in an organization as complex as the biological total process. Competition between two or more systems is the basis of certain pathological conditions as well as of many everyday phenomena. By competition of two systems is meant a configuration of two tendencies aiming to utilize the same part functions in two different systems. Frequently the configuration is such that one of the system-forming tendencies has a greater potency and becomes the leading system, A; the system of smaller potency may be called the interfering system, B. If A and B have one part function, *a*, in common, *a* comes under the influence of two forces, each tending to make it function according to a different system principle. This may have various effects, depending on the balance of the two forces.

An interfering system which lacks the strength to displace the leading system may become manifest merely by inhibiting the leading function. The leading function in this case has to assert itself against the pressure of the interfering system. The ensuing phenomena, which may be called *symptoms of pressure*, often take the form of fatigue and tenseness. Fatigue is characterized by the slowing down of the leading activity or by an increasing difficulty in carrying it out. This may happen not only because there is insufficient energy available for the function, but also because the function has to proceed against the pressure of interfering systems. So-called "mental fatigue" seems to be prevalently of the second type. Sometimes the balance of forces between the two systems may oscillate. The interfering system may come close to breaking through, be repelled, then again come close to breaking through and so forth. We may say metaphorically that in such instances the interfering system does not exert a uniform pressure on the leading function but pounds at it. Such a constellation of forces manifests itself in the syndrome commonly called "nervousness," i.e., restlessness, irritability, and jerkiness of behavior. The pathological condition that used to be called neurasthenia is characterized mainly by pressure symptoms: fatigue, difficulty in concentrating, and tenseness. Similarly the so-called "experimental neurosis," which can be produced in animals by the artificial setting of conflicting functional systems, manifests itself in restlessness or in fatigue-like phenomena occasionally leading to sleep.

Symptoms of pressure appear when the balance of forces between the competing systems is markedly in favor of the leading system. When the interfering system is somewhat stronger but still not strong enough to displace the leading system, it may intrude into it at various points. The phenomena which thus arise may be called *symptoms of intrusion.* The seemingly unmotivated appearance of compulsive and obsessive phenomena, which intrude on the course of the leading activities, are good examples of this group of symptoms. The interfering system may modify or twist the leading activity. Good examples of such twisting are the *Fehlhandlungen*—slips and other "paraphenomena" which have been extensively studied by psychoanalysts. The expressions of the interfering system not only twist the functioning of the dominant one but get twisted themselves in the process. One of the common ways in which an inhibited tendency can seek and find expression is by reaching closure through a short cut, that is, leaving out essential intermediary steps, thus forming a closed but incomplete Gestalt. When inhibited tendencies find an outlet in fantasy (skipping action), this may be considered an example of a short cut.

An even more severe form of system interference than that of intrusion is present when neither of the conflicting systems predominates over the others. This may give rise to such phenomena as retardation, indecision, ambivalence. In severe cases it leads to a *mutual invasion* of the competing systems. This invasion manifests itself in a chaotic constellation in which no function is leading, and fragments of systems are intermingled in a disorderly way, none of the incipient activities reaching completion. Such a picture can be observed in the various kinds of confusional states, e.g., in the mutual invasion of thought systems resulting in fragmentation of thinking. Systems of psychomotor activity may also mutually invade each other and result in a chaotic confusional picture. This situation can be observed in a mild form even in states of embarrassment; it is quite marked in the "catastrophic reactions" described by Goldstein.* Extreme disintegration of activity is occasionally found in schizophrenic patients. Mutual invasion of systems may take various forms, depending on the systems involved. I have described certain forms of spatial disorientation, for instance, as states of confusion resulting from the mutual invasion of contradictory orientation schemata.† The mutual invasion may be a relatively local affair, or it may involve the whole personality.

The interfering system may gain in potency with the passage of time and push the leading system into the background. Then the roles are changed; the interfering system becomes the leading one and vice versa.

The successive appearance of the various types of symptoms arising from competition of systems can be observed in many cases of schizo-

* K. Goldstein, *The Organism.* Beacon Press, Boston, 1963.
† A. Angyal, "Ueber die Raumlage Vorgestellter Oerter." *Arch. ges. Psychol.,* **78:**47–94, 1930.

phrenia during the onset of the illness. The early signs may be only symptoms of pressure: fatigue, inability to work, difficulty in concentrating. Restlessness may follow. The threat of intruding tendencies is frequently anticipated by the patient who has a sense of undefined impending danger. Isolated intrusions of interfering tendencies may then appear, frequently followed by a period of confusion, panic, or other form of mutual invasion of systems until finally the interfering tendencies break through and assume the lead in the guise of frankly psychotic behavior.

Interference of systems is a very common phenomenon and is not pathological in itself. Inhibited functions may be ventilated during sleep, find an outlet in fantasy, or be disposed of in some other way; sometimes they fade away or weaken with time. System interference becomes pathological only when the interfering system is persistent and when the personality strongly resists its expression; this constellation represents a serious menace to the existing personality organization.

Segregation of Systems

Competition of systems is not the only source of disturbances of integration. They can also arise from a lack of coherence and of regular communication between systems, resulting in *segregation of systems*. Capacity for extensive differentiation is the normal feature of personality organization which facilitates the disjunction or segregation between systems. The greater the differentiation of a system, the more the parts are individualized and independent of the whole. Differentiation always involves the danger of too great an independence of the part functions, that is, a danger of disintegration. A whole may differentiate into so many specialized parts that their unification and control may present a serious problem. Although normally, through a process of synthesis, the differentiated parts are again closely integrated into the whole, under certain conditions which interfere with this process the organism may fail in this task.

The segregation of systems shows various pictures according to the systems involved. When there is a break in the continuity of the "vertical" dimension, depth and surface become disjointed. Since the surface is the specific expression and concretization of the depth, incongruity between the expression and that which is expressed may result. Personal tendencies remain unexpressed; surface manifestations, no longer expressing deeper tendencies, become superficial and shallow.

When the break is in the dimension of progression, that is, when the means-end organization is disrupted, the activity may be aborted before it can reach completion and "closure" is prevented. A real segregation of systems occurs when subordinate goals become independent and lose contact with the main goal of activity, which may result in a fragmentation and disintegration of the total function. Segregation in the transverse structure may be called dissociation. This type of segregation consists in a lack of coordination between the parts of a whole and manifests itself in a kind of dysplastic behavior, in a lack of coordination between the various tendencies and attitudes of the person.

Segregation in one dimension is usually followed by segregation in other dimensions. In cases of good integration the connections of a given act or a given experience extend over a wide range of systems, but in the case of segregation the occurrence becomes a more or less localized affair. We refer to this difference in daily life when we say that one person is doing something "half heartedly" and that another is involved "body and soul." Activities severed from other parts of the personality are less forceful and energetic than those that are well integrated with the rest of the personality and consequently are supported and reinforced by many subsystems. The amount of energy which propels activity depends to a great extent upon the integrational status of the person.

Bionegativity and Its Origins

The discussion of the disturbances of integration has led us into the field of pathological behavior. However, since we are discussing not only severe but also mild and transitory conditions, we shall substitute the term *bionegative* for the term *pathological*. Bionegative behavior can best be defined in terms of integration. In an ideally healthy organism the various part processes are integrated in such a way that they subserve and promote the total function of the organism—its twofold dynamic pattern. *Abnormality, or bionegativity, may be defined as a personality constellation in which one or more part processes disturb the total function of the organism.*

This definition has various implications. Bionegativity is an integrational status, a specific relation between part and whole. Neither the personality as such nor any of its part processes in themselves can be called bionegative or abnormal; these terms refer to their relationship. Even in the most sweeping personality disorders, the total personality tends to behave according to its inherent tendencies, although their expressions are distorted in consequence of severe bionegative constellations. A given factor may be bionegative in one personality organization and biopositive in another. (Some conditions, however, would be bionegative in any personality organization, e.g., a damage or lack of some part function which is essential for the total function, as is often the case in brain injuries.) A condition that is statistically abnormal may in some instances be an indication of bionegativity; such a condition also tends to become bionegative because of society's intolerance of too much deviation from the average. However, the correlation between the bionegative and the statistically deviating is not high enough to make a distinction superfluous.

For a thorough understanding of various bionegative conditions it is essential to keep in mind that a disturbance of integration rarely remains localized and isolated; very often it induces further disturbances, and the picture becomes increasingly involved. In attempting to follow such a complex picture in all of its articulations, one must be aware that the various observed symptoms may represent different orders of phenomena, in terms of their nature and origins.

The original source of disturbance may be a trauma, i.e., the interference of some outside agent with the functions of the organism. The traumatic origin—one traceable to a gross physical or chemical agent, or to pathogenic micro-organisms—can be demonstrated for organic diseases of known etiology. For the congenital diseases, traumatic origin can be reasonably assumed to be some kind of damage to the germ cell. In personality disorders, although the endogenous origin of some cannot be excluded, a traumatic origin is very likely; a healthy organism would hardly begin to malfunction without the interference of some noxious agent. The organism is continuously exposed to traumata. Life itself, by its very nature, can be considered a traumatic process. While the organism is governed by its inherent dynamic tendencies, the environment follows its own laws without regard for the needs of the organism. Therefore contact with the environment always involves some traumatic aspects, either in the form of active interferences with the functions of the organism or of inadequacies of the environment with regard to the organism's needs—the traumata of scarcity.

Some symptoms can be viewed as direct effects of the traumatic agent. When a sharp object is thrust into the body the resulting discontinuity of tissues and the flow of blood are determined only by the properties of the object and by the physical and chemical properties of the organism. At this stage its organismic qualities are not as yet drawn into activity. Next, however, the organism reacts to the discontinuity of tissues in its own way, a proliferation of connective tissues and blood vessels starts from the walls of the wound and slowly seals up the gap, forming a scar. This may be the end of the process, but very often it is not. The reaction of the organism to the traumatic damage is an unusual condition, and as such it may act as a further trauma. The scar, after retraction of the connective tissues, may cause a second trauma. The scar on a tubular organ might cause stenosis, in the brain it might cause mechanical irritation. Here we deal with a symptom that is a causal derivative of an organismic reaction. The new damage calls for new adjustive measures on the part of the organism. If the second reaction does not put the organism in equilibrium, further malfunctioning may ensue followed by further adjustive reactions. Thus we may have, besides the first trauma, causal derivatives of the first, second, etc., order and, correspondingly, organismic reactions to the original trauma and to the causal derivatives of the various orders. This is a chain of events in which instances of causation alternate with organismic system action. In this way a very complex state of disturbed integration may gradually come into being which, in the case of personality disorders, can be analyzed and understood only if one knows enough of the patient's past history and has an adequate conceptual framework to guide the analysis.

To analyze the disturbance correctly is important also from the practical point of view, in order to choose the correct therapeutic approach. Some schools of psychopathology deal with every symptom entirely in terms of causation, i.e., from the mechanistic point of view; others tend to view most disturbances almost entirely in terms of purposeful organismic reactions. If a patient hallucinates, the mechanist would want to know what *caused* the hallucination and would explain it, for example, by the toxic irritation of a certain cortical area. A purposivist would concentrate on the question of how the symptom serves the patient, of what he is *driving at* by hallucinating. The inadequacy of a strictly mechanistic point of view is obvious, but the exaggeration of the purposivistic approach must also be warned against. The planfulness of the organism does not exclude mechanistic happenings, whether they are effects of trauma or causal derivatives of a purposeful action, and the phenomenology of the symptom does not always reveal its origin.

Let me use a fanciful analogy. According to a popular belief, the rabbit, before he leaves his warren in wintertime, makes a number of long jumps around the warren, covering a large area with irregularly distributed footprints "in order to make it difficult for his enemies to find his trail." Should this be the case it would be an example of a purposeful organismic action. But when the rabbit, in seeking food or in escaping an enemy, runs through a snow-covered field, it makes no sense to ask what he means by putting his footprints in the snow; the making of footprints is merely a causal derivative of a purposeful action.

In personality disturbances, a symptom of traumatic origin may be subsequently utilized for personal purposes; this does not justify the assumption that the symptom itself expresses the organism's purpose or that the suffering it entails results from the patient's masochism. In bionegative constellations both causal effects and organismic reactions are responsible for symptom formation. To separate the two factors is the task of symptom analysis.

5. Personality
as a Time Gestalt

The dynamic nature of life makes it necessary to view personality as evolving through time. In modern personality research, increasing emphasis is laid on studying the biography of the person. The biographical approach brings up a number of important theoretical questions. The time aspect of personality, the relationship between past, present, and future, the articulation of the life history into phases, the problem of self-determination and chance, are some of the issues that need clarification.

Nobody questions the fact that personality is significantly determined by its past. The study of life histories enables us not only to fill the gaps in our knowledge of the present status of the person but also to gain a deeper understanding which no other method can give. Only historical analysis which reconstructs the succession of events can reveal how one biospheric constellation led to another, that is, how the person has become what he is.

One can subscribe to all this and still maintain that the concept of personality should be limited to the constellation of present factors, and that the past belongs to the person only insofar as it is preserved and carried over into the present. Within a holistic framework such a view cannot be held valid. Instead of considering personality as a constellation of simultaneous factors, we must view it as a *time Gestalt*, i.e., a temporally extended whole. In such configurations the parts are distributed along the dimension of time. A sentence and a melody are examples of this. Similarly, life as a series of occurrences forms a time Gestalt.

As in any whole, each part in a time Gestalt is significantly determined by the rest of the whole. The last word in a sentence or the final part of a melody gain their meaning from what went before, although the last part carries no traces of its antecedents. To see personality as a time Gestalt means to assume that it exists not only at a given moment, that the person is not only what he is here and now, but that he is an organized process extending through time, comparable to the tracing of a crayon moving along on the designer's sheet. The line drawn at any particular moment forms a meaningful structure in conjunction with the lines drawn previously and those to be drawn later. To consider personality a time Gestalt means to assume that the past *qua past* has an influence from a temporal distance upon the present. This implies the unification and dynamic togetherness of factors distant from each other in time.

One objection to this conception is based on the view that the past is fixed, irreversible, and that the future is incalculable, "a closed book," so that neither can be a part of a dynamically vital whole. A *dynamic* whole a large part of which is unchangeable is in fact a contradiction in terms. But is the past of the person really unchangeable? In a sense it is; what has happened cannot be undone. However, in personality, as in all wholes, single events have significance only in relation to the whole of which they are a part; they participate in a whole not by means of their intrinsic qualities but by means of the position they occupy in the whole. As life goes on and the time Gestalt of life history shapes itself into new forms—although immutable if viewed as so many isolated items—past occurrences gain new "positional values," new significance in the changing personality. Since new experiences to some extent change the meaning of the life history, and the single items of the life course gain in turn a different significance within the new whole, we may rightly say that the past of the person is in continuous change. To give some simple examples: years of effort spent in trying to reach a certain goal will have very different meanings in cases of success and failure; missing a train or a plane can be changed from a calamity to supreme luck by later events, be it a crash or a change in the personal plans to which the journey was relevant. Nor is it true that the future is entirely incalculable and separate from the present and past. The future is that region of personality which is not crystallized, is still in the making; yet, as the experiences of wishing, hoping, and planning imply, the future is active in the present as potentiality and disposition.

When one lets the life course of a person pass before one's eyes, one sees him toiling to reach first one and then another goal, attempting to achieve this or that individualized expression of the tendency toward increased autonomy or toward participation in some meaningful whole. But beyond the specific goals to be achieved the person has the broader motivation of shaping his life itself into a coherent meaningful whole. The course of life is comparable to a work of art which one creates, shapes, and perfects by living it; if one is fortunate enough, one may even put the finishing touches to it. The person may be only vaguely conscious of this concern, but it is definitely there, and a feeling of responsibility goes with it. Life is regarded as a unique opportunity, and shaping the life course into something worthwhile is felt to be one's personal task. If one fails in it, the realization of having wasted one's life is experienced with remorse. Death itself may be feared less as the end of life than as an arbitrary stop put to an unfinished work. After a well-completed life course, death is not too disturbing a thought; only the broken, uncompleted life is tragic.

The desire for self-realization, a tendency to shape one's life course into a meaningful whole, gives coherence and unity to the life history. The personal development thus becomes a process of Gestalt formation. In the dimension of *progression* a structure of means-end relations is built. This is the most tangible aspect of the life course, the history of the person's achievement along the lines of mastery, domination, production. This history does not lead directly to a main goal but is usually marked by hesitancy and changes. As a rule, the main goal to be achieved takes shape very gradually in the person's mind and many people never find it. A clear and fully accepted purpose increases the efficiency and productivity of the person. In the dimension of *depth* the person grows from a median position toward both the depth and the surface: he grows toward an increased anchoring of the self in a system of values giving meaning to his life and toward greater facility and perfection in expressing these values in actual behavior. This aspect of development is a struggle for self-expression; sometimes the struggle is so prominent that it becomes the *leitmotif* of the life history. Simultaneously the person may grow in the dimension of *breadth*, opening up more channels for the expression of his basic tendencies. Defective development in this direction results in narrowness, and frequently goes with a rigidity of the personality. Growth in the dimension of breadth also implies a good coordination of the various channels of expression. When the person broadens out while the various channels of expression are but loosely coordinated, one has the picture of dissipation of energy, the person is "spreading himself thin." The fullness of life depends upon the harmonious growth of the personality structure in all three dimensions.

The course of life is essentially the development of a Gestalt from diffuse beginnings to greater differentiation. This process is governed by the same laws as any other Gestalt formation: the tendency toward closure and the tendency toward *Praegnanz*, or, as I would put it, a tendency toward the perfect realization of the system principle. This tendency covers a variety of phenomena. It is a common characteristic of the personality organization to build strong and intricate reaction systems around defects and minor handicaps; this phenomenon is the central theme of the Adlerian psychology. At first sight it may seem rather peculiar that a single deficiency should become the main concern of the person, more important than all the excellent qualities and opportunities he may possess. This becomes understandable if one considers personality development as a Gestalt formation. The concentration upon every incongruous element in the personality organization is an effect of the law of *Praegnanz*. The various "mechanisms," the knowledge of which we owe to psychoanalysis, may also be regarded as attempts—successful or unsuccessful—to bring incompatible, incongruous elements into harmony with the rest of the personality and thus to approach a perfect Gestalt.

Single occurrences which exert a persistent and intensive influence upon subsequent behavior have one characteristic in common; they have not been sufficiently assimilated by the person and have remained unsettled. To understand this, we must recall that the evolution of any whole takes place in successive stages of differentiation and of re-embedding of the differentiated parts into the whole. Differentiation always involves a kind of disequilibrium, because it leads beyond the present status of the whole. The connection between part and whole becomes looser, and the part stands out distinctly and gains an individualistic character. In the process of re-embedding, the part loses this character and again becomes integrated into the whole which may itself be enriched and changed in the process.

The embedding capacity of the person is not unlimited, however. Some occurrences are so sharply incompatible with the personality organization that no assimilation is possible. Then a constellation arises in which certain partial factors are not integrated into the personality in any orderly fashion; these unassimilated elements have persistent and often destructive effects upon later behavior. Thus we see that the past exerts an influence either in an orderly or an unorderly manner. In the first case, a past biospheric occurrence becomes a well-organized but indistinct part of the temporally extended person, while in the second case no such assimilation takes place.

Like all wholes, life history shows an intrinsic articulation; it is more or less distinctly divided into a number of phases which form its subwholes. In each phase the person is confronted with some particular vital problems which form the central theme of the given phase. The life of a newborn child, for instance, is centered around food and sleep; the source of food is the all-important factor, and an undifferentiated union with the mother is the central part of existence. The rest of the environment seems to be experienced by the infant as a disturbance to which it reacts by avoidance. Gradually the child discovers the opportunities presented by the environment and by its own body for exercising its self-assertive tendencies. At first it does not recognize the heteronomy of the environment and attempts to deal with it in an arbitrary fashion. The gradual realization that changes are brought about not by wishing and imagining but by acting in accordance with the properties of the objects ushers in a new phase. This phase is characterized by an insatiable curiosity and the drive to explore the properties of the surroundings. Puberty, through the profound changes which take place at that time, stands out distinctly as a separate phase of the life course with its specific problems and meanings. For the period of adulthood, also, the empirical data clearly indicate the phasic character of the life course.*

In general the phasic course of life histories shows a certain degree of uniformity created by the regular sequence of organic changes in conjunction with certain cultural factors; the life course of people living in the same culture area tends to be uniform. The study of typical life phases may serve as a valuable aid, but not as a substitute, for the analysis of phases in individual cases. Significant occurrences in the personal life may superimpose an individualized phasic differentiation upon the generalized pattern of the life course. Certain forms of maladjustment may have their source in an abnormality of phasic development.

The relationship between individual and environment is an interplay of organismic and heteronomous forces. When this relationship is viewed longitudinally, the autonomous determination appears as an organismic or holistic evolution, and heteronomous determination appears as chance. In the discussion of the problem of determinism in the course of life, these two factors have to be considered separately.

Organismic evolution is the aspect of change determined by factors inherent in the person, i.e., by biological laws in the broadest sense of the word. When we speak of changes which occur *by chance* we mean those processes in the environment which—though relevant to the person's life—originate and proceed independently of the organism. What we call chance are not random happenings. They are only beyond the control and foresight of the individual. Chance occurrences, although they are strictly lawful processes, are practically incalculable factors in a life history; it is impossible to know which external factors

* Ch. Buehler, *Der Menschliche Lebenslauf als psychologisches Problem*. Hirzel, Leipzig, 1933.

may become relevant for the person's life. If predictions about the course of life are at all possible, they can be based only on the intrinsic laws of personality development and can be only approximate.

There is good reason to believe that the reliability of prediction in the biological sciences will always lag behind the reliability of prediction in the physical sciences. Strict determinism, in the sense of classical physics, implies that a given constellation of antecedent factors can result in only one effect. In biological processes, too, the effect is lawfully determined, but it cannot be narrowed down to a single possibility; it comprises a range of possibilities. Only the general kind of biological response is predictable from its antecedents. This statement is a logical deduction from the structural characteristics of holistic processes. Part processes are determined by the whole in the sense that they take place according to its system principle. A part, however, is not defined by the whole in all its individual details, but only insofar as its position in the system is concerned. This allows a certain degree of individual variation in filling the positions determined by the system principle; it allows a range of possibilities. Which of the possibilities shall be realized is probably a matter of chance, i.e., of the constellation of factors that are independent of the subject.

Holistic evolution and chance are intimately interwoven in the person's life course and are practically inseparable. What at first glance seems to be a matter of chance may be largely determined by the personality structure of the individual and vice versa. The incalculability of chance makes life to some degree a matter of gambling. One never can be entirely certain of the later effects of any steps one takes in life. To take reasonable risks is absolutely necessary, otherwise one would be doomed to inactivity.

As the life course proceeds, it becomes more and more deterministic. At the early stages the person is a rather diffuse whole with many vague possibilities, but this whole becomes more and more crystallized and the range of possibilities contracts. The person becomes increasingly differentiated, and the personality structure becomes more and more rigidly patterned. Every decision or choice narrows down the possibilities of the future; not only such important steps as the choice of an occupation or of a mate but even minor steps may have this effect. What a person does at any time commits him to a future course to be taken, sometimes far beyond any realistic necessity. Social mores and a kind of inner obligation to be self-consistent prompt the person to follow the course to which he has implicitly committed himself by his previous actions.

The increase of determinism with the progression of one's life course is based on a general law of Gestalt dynamics, the "law of closure." Every incomplete whole tends to a continuation which is in accordance with the system principle of that whole. In an early phase of the life course only a few initial lines of the life Gestalt are given, and the system-adequate continuation may take many different forms. The more the Gestalt approaches completion, the fewer are the possible variations of a system-adequate continuation.

Part Two

Neurosis

6. The Nature of Neurosis

The general formulations offered in Part 1 provide reference points from which we can now proceed to describe and analyze the neurotic personality. I know that it is considered adequate in some quarters to conceive of a neurosis as a focal emotional disturbance in an otherwise healthy organism, like a bad spot in an otherwise good apple. From such a conception it would follow that some procedure comparable to surgery could eliminate the trouble; something has to be taken out, but the rest is all right. To my mind, however, the term "emotional disturbance" in application to neurosis is at best a euphemism.

Neurosis is not a partial disturbance limited to just one province of personality. Neurosis is a sweeping condition. It is, in fact, a way of life—self-destructive to be sure, but nonetheless a way of life. If it were not so, if neurosis were only a twist here and there on a basically healthy psychological organization, the great difficulty in overcoming it and the strong reluctance on the part of the sufferer to relinquish it would be incomprehensible. One would, on the contrary, expect the healthy functional organization to eliminate or correct any incongruity spontaneously or with minimal help. But a neurosis is not merely a conglomeration of incongruities. It is itself an organization with its own goals, attitudes, and motivations, its own pains and pleasures: anticipated dangers that are feared with unusual intensity, animosities that are pursued relentlessly, promises of pleasure that are most tempting and compelling. The neurotic way of life tends to appropriate all the primary faculties and functions of the person and to use them in accordance with its own system principle. It tends to transform the person's thinking, to create illusory feelings and wishes, and it may even fashion the bodily functions so as to express and serve the aims of the neurotic organization. The strength of a neurosis is due precisely to the fact that it is not a mere collection of separate items but an *organization* with its own vitality, which is sustained and perpetuated by the principles of system action and cannot be obliterated or dislodged by any segmental partial changes. In this chapter I shall give a general outline of the genesis and nature of this deviant organization.

Anxiety and the State of Isolation

Let us start with discussing anxiety which, as practically all theories agree, is the crucial issue, the basic phenomenon in psychopathology. It is anxiety that creates, or marks, the parting of the ways between health and neurosis. Phenomenally anxiety, even when it is intense, is usually vague; its object is not clearly defined, as it is in normal fears. When the object appears to be clearly defined, as in the case of phobias (e.g., fear of narrow spaces or wide open spaces), this definition is a secondary development. The vague, general fear is concretized by being focused on some object or other which is not its original object. In speculating on the true object of anxiety, theorists generally agree that what is felt to be threatened is something that is basic to the human being, something so essential that the person's whole life is felt to hinge on it. That which precipitates anxiety may be a seemingly trivial matter, but it is felt to imply or presage a threat to the very core of the person. This fear of total destruction is felt in the absence of any realistic danger that could have effects of such magnitude.

I have spoken so far of acute conscious anxiety. Conscious anxiety occurs in some neurotic conditions, e.g., in homosexual panic or in anxiety hysteria. In these conditions the person knows only too well that he is anxious and is going through hell; acute anxiety is a most tormenting emotional state. Yet overt anxiety occurs in only a small fraction of neurotic conditions. In a chronic obsessive-compulsive neurosis, e.g., it is very hard to detect any conscious anxiety. There are states, however, behind which anxiety seems to be lurking without being experienced as such: a hurrying, rushed, driven feeling; a general inner restlessness; a continuous state of strain evidenced by strong muscle tension; or a state of lassitude when everything appears as a colossal task, and one feels reluctant to tackle even minimal action. These states are much more constant concomitants of neurosis than are acute anxiety outbreaks.

One way to deal with this range of phenomena is to make a distinction between conscious and unconscious anxiety and to subsume the states just described under unconcious anxiety. However, for reasons that have been explained in Chapter 3 (The Psychological Functions), I prefer to reserve the term "anxiety" for the conscious experience, for the actual feeling of anxiety. Like all emotional experiences anxiety is an expression, a symbolization, of a particular state of the person which may or may not be reflected in consciousness. It is customary to describe this state as unconscious anxiety, but I consider it more adequate to define it not by reference to a feeling but in the more general terms of a life situation; and since the life process always plays between the subject and the object poles of the "biosphere," the definition, too, must reflect this double reference. I propose to define the life situation of which anxiety is the most dramatic and revealing manifestation as a *state of isolation*. The term covers both the state of being isolated from one's world and the conscious experience of this state. This realization can take different forms, including that of a relatively detached judgment. If, however, the state of isolation is reflected in an emotional experience—which always represents an implicit evaluation of a personal situation—the experience is that of anxiety. The state of isolation of which anxiety is an expression is to be found at the bottom of every neurosis. To explain and justify this statement, we must start by outlining the origins and development of the state of isolation in the child.

The Genesis of Isolation

When we speak of the situation of the newborn or the infant as it might be reflected in the child's mental states, we obviously have recourse to inference. When we say, for simplicity's sake, that in a certain situation a young child must have felt, thought, or concluded such and such, we speak of the unknown early equivalents of mental processes which we know in their advanced articulated form in adults. But, although much of what we assume about the early mental states is either speculation or inference, at least one of these inferences has been so strongly supported by the accumulated evidence of systematic observation of children that it may be considered a fact. The characteristic which I have in mind disappears only slowly and gradually, so that our observations can be validated by the verbal reports of older children. This characteristic of early mental states, which is very difficult for an adult to imagine, is the absence of differentiation, of a clear distinction between the "I" and the world, the subject and the object; to the young child, they are one. This unitary perception reflects the complete embeddedness of the child in its environment, particularly during the prenatal stage. The original unity if the organism and its environment is disrupted in the process of birth, and probably very soon after that the child begins to develop an awareness of his separateness, a growing differentiation between the "I" and the "non-I."

This gradual differentiation, though it depends in part on physiological maturation, seems to be brought about mainly by two kinds of experiences. First, pain, cold, and other disagreeable sensations which disrupt the child's organic equilibrium and stand out from the basically comfortable unified state, begin to be moved out of this unity and located somewhere outside. The second source of differentiation is "the disobedience of the object." If I want to move my hand, for instance, it moves; if I want the moon to move closer to me, it doesn't. Thus the world gradually separates into two parts: the "close" part, about which I have a say-so, and the rest of the world, the outside objects which do not obey my wishes. The main characteristics of the world which has been constructed in this way are its "alienness" and its tremendous size and power as compared with the smallness of the child's own sphere of autonomy.

The shock of realization of his separateness, of the alienness of the world, comes to every child. Although the experience of isolation brought about by the dissolution of the original unity is the primary source of anxiety, it cannot be considered pathogenic in itself. In fact, this isolation represents an opportunity to become human; it requires the child to re-relate himself to the world by exercising the two basic human trends, mastery and love. These basic trends have an opportunity to arise only after the original unity has been dissolved to some degree. If there is nothing outside of me, there is nothing to master; everything is under my jurisdiction from the start. But if things have an independent existence, I must struggle to relate to the world in the way of mastery, to bring them under my government. Similarly, a loving relationship is possible only with another who is separate from me. The experience of one's self as a separate, limited entity leads to a sense of incompleteness which creates an urge to become a part of a larger life, to share in the lives of others. So the child combats isolation by insistently seeking to re-relate himself to the world in many single ways, all of which fall under these two broad categories, increased autonomy and homonomy. He finds his place within the world by learning to master his environment, and, in a stabler way, by establishing communication and community with others through loving relationships.

It should be clear from what I have said that I do not share Rank's view of the trauma of birth as the primary basis of neurosis. Birth certainly can be called a trauma in the sense of being a tremendous environmental change and a change in the modes of physiological functioning. When the umbilical cord is cut and the oxygen supply shut off, the child begins to breathe laboriously with the unskilled lungs which until that point were just sponges pressed together against its back. The transition to the new mode of functioning is painful, and it plays its part in undermining the security of the organism's original unity with its environment. This transition, however, is also a step toward a situation that represents a challenge and an opportunity for the child to relate himself to the world as a distinctly human being, to manifest his essential nature. "Birth trauma," which is suffered by all, can hardly be considered the basic cause of neurosis, except insofar as it is a step in individuation which is a precondition of both health and neurosis.

What, then, are the conditions determining which direction the child's development will take during the early stage of his coping with the new separateness? The essential condition of health is that while the differentiation of the self from the world is taking place, there should be ample opportunities for the child to begin to exercise his two basic trends: opportunities to explore, to learn how to handle his surroundings, and opportunities for emotional relatedness, for feelings of closeness with others. Actually the awareness of isolation and the efforts to re-relate to the world through mastery and love do not represent successive developmental stages, as our schematic description might seem to imply. The processes of differentiating and of re-relating oneself go hand in hand, so that when the independent existence of the outside world is firmly established, the child is not completely helpless and isolated in relation to this heteronomous world. He has been learning all along how he himself can affect it, and his life has been anchored in affectional relations with the care-taking adults. In such favorable conditions isolation and anxiety are present only in minimal amounts, as unavoidable correlates of individuated existence. For all practical purposes we can regard as healthy all those in whom isolation and anxiety are minimal.

The picture is very different when circumstances make it difficult for the child to re-relate himself to his surroundings, when situational factors prevent the development of loving relations and an effective exercise of mastery. I shall not attempt here to enumerate all the situations that may have this effect; they are well known to clinicians and their range is quite large. If opportunities for mastery and for experiencing love are too meager, or the obstacles to a successful exercise of these functions are too strong, the world remains alien and the child's state of isolation persists. This persisting heightened isolation is the basis of neurosis. An alien world that can be neither mastered nor communicated with is potentially threatening, comparable to the world of a strange planet where events are governed by unknown laws and whose inhabitants speak an unknown untranslatable language. In this situation, marked as it is by a peculiarly urgent sense of heightened isolation, a turn in the development occurs which leads to the formation of a nuclear neurosis. Instead of making direct and vigorous attempts at relating himself to the world, the child now diverts a large part of his efforts toward protecting himself from the world. In so doing he himself becomes the agent through whom his isolation is maintained and increased; he initiates the vicious circle which typifies neurotic development.

Figuratively speaking, the person surrounds himself with a wall in order to obtain protection, a safe retreat from the dangers which he feels are inherent in any interaction with the world. This attempt at problem solving, however, is doomed to failure; within the self-constructed wall he feels even more isolated and looks out from the enclosure even more fearfully. The real world of varying possibilities for love and mastery thus becomes more forbidding than it was originally, and as the person erects ever stronger defenses against the world, he alienates it still more. Thus when a person, who by acting shy and retiring makes it difficult for others to approach him, is eventually left alone he gets further convincing proof that no one really wants him. The same result may be achieved in other ways. A person who feels very insecure in another's affection may swamp the partner with so much attention and "giving" that the other can only regain freedom by leaving. New protections have to be erected against the possibility of repeated rejection, making it even more difficult to relate to people. The process goes on in a snowballing fashion until neurosis reaches the point of crystallization, i.e., until a structure is worked out which is relatively stable and within the confines of which the person can function after a fashion.

The basic situation in neurosis is that of life lived in isolation; it is a state of being "narrowed in," working one's course within narrow confines, not daring to move out into the wider areas that could be encompassed by personal life. The relationship of this state to anxiety is suggested even by language. The word "anxiety" comes originally from the word "narrow." In German, for instance, the expression *sich aengstigen*, to feel anxious, means literally becoming narrow, being narrowed in. Anxiety is the emotional expression of the state of being narrowed in, but the presence of this state can be objectively determined, even in the absence of anxiety, through the observation of the person's behavior and the general pattern of his life. You can see, e.g., how he sits on the edge of the chair, or hides in a corner, how he shrinks when you try to talk to him; you know that although he feels miserable in his job he has kept it for thirty years; or that he always stays home even though he professes to love company. The self-limitation need not always be as obvious as this; it can take a variety of forms and be subtly disguised. However, by closely examining the person's total mode of living one can determine whether he treads a narrow path or is genuinely expansive. This possibility of objective verification is one of the advantages of defining the central phenomenon of neurosis in terms of a life situation rather than in terms of its emotional reflection, the feeling of anxiety as such.

The Basic Neurotic Assumptions

As the state of isolation is established, maintained, and increased, it results in certain fantasies about one's self and the world. These implicit assumptions, even though not clearly formulated, shape and determine everything the person thinks, feels, and does. The self is felt to be small, weak, and inadequate; correspondingly the world, that immense alien realm, appears unmanageable and overwhelming. Its alienness makes it inapproachable. One would like to communicate and to establish bonds with people, but this is hardly possible if everything and everyone is so separate and different from oneself; one cannot feel close to something that is utterly alien. So the world appears cold, and one finds oneself unloved. Yet being weak and unloved is not the worst part of it. In time the child begins to feel not only unloved but unlovable, secretly concluding that he is unworthy of love. This conclusion undermines even the hope that anyone could ever love him and marks a crucial step in the development of the neurosis. The total resulting image is that of a weak, inadequate, unlovable person facing an indifferent, cold, essentially hostile world which can easily crush him.

This set of assumptions is elaborated in many individual ways, determined perhaps in part by the person's constitutional features, but mainly and traceably by the kind of damaging situations to which he has been exposed in childhood. The assumption, e.g., that people are hostile, may be expressed through the anticipation of physical assault, criticism and ridicule, or exploitation. Similarly, the assumption that one is unlovable can be concretized in various ways, focusing on personal characteristics that range from major to trivial. An example is the case of the adolescent girl who wants to have an operation performed on her perfectly well-shaped nose, feeling that some small defect of this feature makes her generally unattractive and unlovable. At the other extreme, hopelessness about oneself may be expressed in a sweeping fashion. One of my patients felt that only a "reincarnation machine" could help him; another, a girl, expressed her view of herself by telling of an iron her mother had broken years ago which proved "beyond repair."

My observations convince me that the fateful change from feeling merely unloved to feeling unlovable comes about through the urgent need of the child to have good loving parents. He tries to maintain this image at any cost, and if his experiences endanger it, he concludes that if his wonderful parents do not treat him well, there must be something fundamentally wrong with him, that he must be unlovable, some kind of monster. To quote the young woman who felt damaged beyond repair: "I can't ever do enough to make up for something that was incredibly wrong about me in their (her parents') eyes." Another patient, a son of very destructive parents, discovered in therapy that he "never gave up wanting to love them, never gave up trying to love them, but I never made it." Opportunities for loving are so desperately needed, and therefore the belief that one has good parents is so compelling that the self is sacrificed to it. This attitude remains operative even when later attitudes of rejection and hostility toward the parents have been superimposed upon it. Regardless of all individual variations on the themes of one's worthlessness and weakness and the latent hostility of the world, these assumptions can always be uncovered in the therapy of neurotics; they form the basis of all further elaborations of the "mythology of the neurosis."

Dire Expectations and Hope

What do these basic assumptions mean in relation to the person's general expectation from life? Essentially they mean that it is really impossible to live humanly. If these assumptions were true, the person would have to resign himself to a merely vegetative existence and renounce the pursuit of the strivings which express the basic human trends. But here human nature allows no compromises. The specific manifestations of these trends can be given up or changed but not the trends themselves; this exceeds the human potentiality. And so the neurotic does a seemingly paradoxical thing. He decides, as it were, to live and exercise his basic funtions in some roundabout way in a world in which it is impossible to exercise them. This generalization about what the neurotic is trying to do can always be arrived at in therapy when the implications of the patient's individual attitudes have been made obvious. This discovery affects the patient strongly. He is shaken when he finds that what he is trying to do is to live and be happy in a world in which, according to his own assumptions, it is impossible to be effective and to be loving and loved.

Light can be thrown on this paradoxical undertaking of the neurotic by further phenomenological analysis of the feeling of anxiety. In the neurotic anxiety there is always a vague ominous sense of approaching doom, of threatening death. We can now formulate clearly the nature of the vital personal core that is felt to be threatened; it is the person's twofold relatedness to the world which alone makes life worthwhile and which cannot be achieved in isolation. A total destruction of this relatedness may well be likened to death. The point that I want to make, however, is that the expectation of doom in neurotic anxiety is not held with absolute certainty. This becomes particularly clear when anxiety is compared with depression. In severe depression the patient feels, without qualification, that he is no good, is guilty, that no one loves him, that he harms the whole world. The neurotic also harbors a similar black picture, but he is not entirely convinced of its truth. Doubt is an essential element of phenomenal anxiety, and correspondingly it contains also a modicum of hope. If the element of doubt were missing we would have depression instead of anxiety. In reactive depressions this transition is actually manifested. When some external event, e.g., a loss, confirms the person's anxious expectations, hope disappears and the black picture is all that remains. In neurosis as such, however, there is always a flicker of hope that it may be possible to relate, possible to govern, even though this must be done in tortuous indirect ways.

These roundabout ways represent the complex dynamics of the fully developed neurosis. Their function is to enable one to exercise the basic human trends despite the fact that one's world and one's self appear to exclude this possibility. The person still feels that there might be a small chance, and so he keeps trying, even if he tries with very poor methods which are likely to complicate his life even more. An elaborate structure, the neurotic edifice, is built around this slim chance with a view to circumventing the obstacles and succeeding in some oblique way.

Neurosis thus reveals itself as the complex consequence of an attitude which the child acquires in the course of his early attempts to relate himself to the world, attempts prompted by a dawning awareness of his isolation. We may ask whether difficulties in re-relating oneself to the environment must occur before a certain age for a neurosis to be the ultimate outcome. Without attempting a guess at the exact age, I should say that the critical period lasts up to the point when a clear-cut differentiation is established between the self and the world. If no seeds of neurosis have been sown during the period when both differentiation and re-relating proceed at a high speed, it seems plausible that the danger of a neurotic development has passed; in a differentiated world, if one has some firm anchoring, threats are likely to be specific and partial, not absolute. This statement, however, should not be construed as a basis for optimism. Experiences which could form a basis for later neurotic developments are never entirely missing during this stage and, consequently, there are no people who do not carry within them any potentialities for neurosis. They may not be doomed to neurosis, but later events can tip the balance in that direction.

Fortunately, the reverse is also true. There are no neurotics whose early childhood did not contain some constructive elements, some substantial gratifications, some sources of affection. If all these were lacking, the patients would have been damaged more severely. They would not be just neurotic and would not continue to be oriented toward the outside world, even if fearfully. The withdrawal would be much more radical, as it is in schizoid development. In therapy it can be observed fairly regularly that toward the end of treatment the patient begins to talk about his childhood, and particularly about his parents, in a more positive vein than before. A great deal of hostility toward them may have been uncovered earlier in therapy, but now memories of happy episodes are revived, of instances in which the child was treated with kindness. The elements of childhood that emerge now are those which were supportive of health and which, had they been stronger, might have prevented neurosis. Factors promoting health and factors promoting neurosis are to be found in the past of neurotic and normal people alike, even if in unequal proportions, and so neurosis, as a potentiality, is an ever-present part of the human condition.

The General Characteristics of Neurosis

Let us now turn from a description of the genesis of neurosis to a consideration of its outcome, of the world view and the life style typical of the developed neurosis. Despite the specificity of elaboration, all neuroses are characterized by certain features which are directly related to the structure of the basic neurotic situation. The person feels and functions as if he were not really a part of the world; he does not feel that the world is his home. As a result of his isolation, both his capacity to exercise mastery, to determine his own fate, and his capacity to love are impaired; one cannot reach out to others and share in their lives without coming out of one's shell. Beyond these basic impairments it is possible to delineate certain features common to all neuroses.

In the following paragraphs I shall enumerate some of the more outstanding features, omitting those which are elaborated differently in different types of neuroses as, e.g., the style of interpersonal relations. The enumeration does not aim at completeness or at a systematic ordering of the traits described. They could just as well be grouped under different headings. In spite of their generality, these formulations have an important function in therapy, because they serve to point out to the patient the all-pervasiveness of the neurotic trends in his life. For instance, it may be a revolutionary insight for a person to realize that his life is fear-motivated, even though this is true of neurotic life in general.

Most of the characteristics to be mentioned can be grouped under two main headings: the prevalence of *fear*, the predominance of the negative over the positive motivation, and the determining role of *fantasy*, the predominance of the substitutive over the direct experience.

A fundamental characteristic of the neurotic person is an *overemphasis on security*. Safety first is the motto. Of course, in the face of real threats everyone tries to defend himself, but for the healthy person this does not become the main issue in life. It is a rather sad commentary on our culture that a very high concern for security can pass for a healthy need. For the neurotic, almost his entire life is devoted to the pursuit of safety, to protecting himself against danger. When he is making decisions his considerations are overwhelmingly centered on the dangers to be avoided rather than on the objectives to be achieved. This balance is regularly in evidence when the patient speaks about the goals he wishes to achieve through therapy; he is very articulate and clear about what he wants to get rid of but vague and inarticulate about positive goals. The kind of safety which the neurotic achieves is like that of the warrior in medieval times who was clad from head to toe in impenetrable protective armor; when he was pushed from his horse he could not get up because of the weight of his own weapons and needed servants to help him to his feet again. Similarly, the excessive defenses of the neurotic make him impotent. The methods of defense can vary from the extreme of putting on a fierce mask to frighten the enemy to the other extreme of advertising oneself as a weak, harmless creature who could not hurt a fly, in order to avert the anger of the presumed enemy. Behind the angers and hates of the neurotic person fear is always lurking. Anger is also a prominent emotion, but its expression is timid and more often than not covert and indirect. This indirectness is well illustrated by the fantasy of one excessive gift giver in which he, from high up, was gently throwing pretty pebbles to a friend below; no single one could hurt but in their accumulation they buried the receiver.

The neurotic's sense of danger finds expression in another general feature of his wishes and actions, which is often referred to as *compulsivity*. Although I cannot offer a more descriptive term, I prefer to reserve the term "compulsive" for the more specific symptoms which we meet in the obsessive-compulsive neurosis. Let us try to approach this general quality concretely. How does a therapist become aware of its presence? Suppose a person wants to do something or to avoid something. When does his wish begin to look neurotic, quite apart from its specific content?

The intensity of the wish is not the criterion; it is the desperate quality of this intensity that gradually impresses us as specifically neurotic. It is not "I would like to do this or that," but "I must do it *or else*." "I have to avoid it *or else*." This is not specific to any particular wish or situation but pervades the person's whole stock of motives. There is a conspicuous absence of the sense of choice; the neurotic feels that he *has* to do it, or *has* to omit it. If he is prevented from carrying out the wish, he feels threatened. The feeling that appears at this point seems to be a direct expression of basic anxiety. The person feels that his world is going to pieces. It is as if the specific goal he is pursuing were the only possible way to obtain essential satisfaction. If there are indications that something may go wrong with his plan, this possibility is not measured and evaluated in terms of the importance of the plan or of the degree to which it can go wrong. The person feels that this is the beginning of the end, that everything is collapsing.

Although the neurotic suffers anxiety when his plans miscarry, his gratification in case of success is marred by an *absence of real fulfillment*. For a healthy person, consummation is the important aspect of experience. When he wants to do something and plans for it, he wants to carry out the plan and to get some enjoyment and satisfaction from it. The neurotic does not even know this category of experience very clearly; he does things not for the sake of enjoyment but in order to prove or disprove something. Consider, for instance, the person whose sexual life does not come up to what it could be. It may not matter to him whether he gets pleasure or not. He may merely need to prove again and again that he is a man; this may be much more important than whether or not he receives pleasure, enjoys closeness, or has any of the other gratifying experiences that are normally derived from the sex act. Most human pleasures are sacrificed as life ceases to be lived and is increasingly conducted as though it were a legal case being tried in a court that never adjourns. The tragic thing is that none of these proofs ever prove anything; new proofs are required again and again. There is no end to this process.

One of the results of the neurotic's lack of positive satisfaction is his peculiar relationship to time. His life is *not lived in the present*. The present is not happy; if anything good is possible at all it must lie in the future. Thus the neurotic lives in a constant state of expectancy, in a continuous inner flight from the dangers and displeasures of today to the hoped-for satisfactions of tomorrow. This tense expectancy often finds expression in a generalized impatience which makes any waiting a trial. When the person goes somewhere by train, for instance, he is impatient to arrive; he cannot relax and sit back or look at the landscape; he must tense his muscles as if he had to push the train to make it go faster. Paradoxically, this impatience causes him to waste time. He cannot utilize time while waiting tensely for some specific event. Because of his general attitude of expectancy, he often does things just to kill time and this lack of real absorption results in ineffectual performance.

Man's distinctive capacity to symbolize his experience and thus to enhance his commerce with the world has its reverse side in his ability to affirm a state of affairs that does not exist—the ability to lie and to live his lies. For the neurotic, the outer world as well as his inner realities are overlaid, obscured, and substituted for by appearances. He begins at an early stage to develop fantastic assumptions to account for his state of isolation, and he continues to live partly in *a world of fantasy*, a world of invented situations populated with nonexisting figures, ghosts of an ill-perceived past.

I am not referring here to the explicit formulations of fantasy, such as are found in daydreams; excessive daydreaming, if present, is only a minor manifestation of the prevalence of fantasy in the neurotic's life. More important is the fact that the patient has fantastic images of people, of himself, of relationships, which, without being clearly formulated, influence his perceptions and actions. He may not entertain these fantasies consciously, but he behaves as if he believed certain imaginary things to be true. These implicit fantasies are not discrete separate items; they are interrelated and well connected. If these connections are followed through, we arrive at a system of basic assumptions, the underlying *mythology of neurosis* which provides a basis and a justification for the fear and anger that dominate the neurotic's life.

The "enemy" in this mythology is a dark, irrational force with whom no communication, no understanding is possible: his main attribute is utter and absolute alienness. This mythical conception usually attaches to certain selected people—e.g., to all those in authority, or to all women—and becomes the basis for irrational attitudes toward them. Much of the neurotic's implicit philosophy, which provides guidelines for his conduct, consists of similarly fantastic images and assumptions. If in therapy this underlying philosophy is articulated for the patient in an abstract, generalized fashion, it will not mean much to him. But if he is confronted with a sufficient number of cases in which he has behaved *as if* he believed certain false things to be true, these "as ifs" gradually add up, and the patient reaches a point where he himself can discover the general pattern of his fantastic beliefs.

One of the best and most reliable indications that implicit fantasies are at work is the marked *inadequacy* of the person's responses to the situation. The emotional response may be excessive. If the patient is afraid to go out or has some other phobia, one knows that he is responding to a fantasy, that there must be a bogeyman behind the real situation. Usually, however, the fantasy must be detected from slighter indications than phobias. Instead of being excessive, the feeling may be inappropriate to the occasion, or it may be absent where it would be expected. One patient, in talking about the goals of his analysis, asked the therapist: "Well, what do you think? What will the finished product be like?" The impersonal terms in which this self-reference is couched may well make the therapist wonder out loud exactly what kind of product the patient thinks he is, and a product of what. Fantasy about oneself may be also deduced from intense emotion being aroused by an inanimate object; this was true in the case of the patient who spoke of his old car as "unique," "with many rough edges but mixed with elegance" but also as "a padded cell," and so full of faults that it would require "an impossible effort" to correct them.

The *repetitiveness* of certain interpretations or responses is another indication that the person's perception is determined by fantasy. Normally a person's response to different people will vary, depending on their characteristics and their behavior toward him. If someone acts as if every person he meets were out to humiliate him, this repetitiveness indicates a fixation on some mythological conception about himself, about people, and about life in general. Normally a person may say to himself: "Because this person behaves in such and such a way, I must be careful." The neurotic does not even have to take a second look. Even before he has met the person he has already decided how he will react. These fantastic assumptions may be constructed from memory, i.e., from a real situation in the remote past, or they may have other roots, but in any case they are meaningful personal constructions which have a brand of logic of their own. The repetitive, uniform, indiscriminate character of perception and response indicates the presence of fantasies.

Early fantastic assumptions and later substitutive maneuvers transform not only the world around the person but also his own self, so that he lives as a counterfeit image of himself. Some authors call this state *alienation from the self*. This transformation is the result of profound despair. The early traumas have already convinced the person that he is weak, unworthy of love, and cannot under any circumstances truly matter to anyone. Inevitably he is further estranged from himself by the imagined causes of his unlovableness. All he can do is cover his assumed worthlessness with practiced pretenses. If he cannot be, he can at least appear to be and thus glean a semblance of gratification for his basic needs. If one cannot be loved, at least one can have fame, prestige, a reputation, titles, and other external trappings; the person himself becomes an appendage of his badges. In other cases, genuine wishes and wants are replaced by obligations, and life becomes a set of hated demands one halfheartedly tries to fulfill.

There are many ways of selling out, of exchanging being for appearing; the wish to get *at least* something is a typical attitude of the neurotic and an ever-present motive in the formation of substitute goals. Yet this compromise is unacceptable to the person since he keeps wanting "the real thing." Despairing of finding real worth in himself, he may substitute instead the ideal of absolute perfection—if he were perfect, and only then, he could not doubt his worth. His initial self-derogation is then augmented by scorn of himself for not having lived up to this "idealized image," * for not being all-powerful, beautiful, all-loving, supremely intelligent. This is one of the vicious circles in which neurosis abounds; the internal maneuvers meant to improve the situation increase the neurotic predicament. Building up pretenses results in new conflicts and makes the person's situation more and more painful and precarious.

In the process of formation of substitute goals, the basic urges may undergo such profound transformations that they eventually lose any resemblance to their original roots. The person does not know what he really thinks, really feels, and really desires. When his true needs which originate in his basic self reach him as conscious wishes, they are so changed and distorted that he cannot recognize them for what they are. For example, when he needs love, he may feel a ravenous appetite or a compulsive urge to go on a shopping spree.

* K. Horney, *Our Inner Conflicts*. Norton, New York, 1945.

When one asks people what they want, one of the most common responses is "lots of money." This sounds reasonable since money can be exchanged for a variety of things. If, however, one asks a neurotic how he would spend the money, after mentioning a few necessary or frivolous things, he becomes strangely vague about it. By implication he often conveys the feeling, "I really don't know what I want, but should I ever know it I want to have the possibility of getting it." It is this long, and tortuous road from one's basic needs to one's conscious wishes that makes the neurotic way of life so frustrating and exhausting. Structurally, a wish is an open Gestalt. In an integrated organism the appearance of a wish, the formation of a Gestalt open at a given point, is a function of the total organization; so also is the fulfillment, the closure of the Gestalt, which is powerfully supported by the entire organized system. Activity in pursuit of the wish is relatively effortless in this case. In a disunited structure, everything becomes an almost insuperable effort.

The last general characteristic I must mention is the *limitation of performance* common to all neuroses. The neurotic simply cannot give his best. This may be true of most people, but in neurosis the discrepancy between what one can do and what one actually does is particularly great. The specific ways in which the impairment comes about vary widely, but one extremely common phenomenon is *hesitancy*, a correlate of uncertainty and anxiety. The brief phases of hesitancy with which a neurotic's activity may be interspersed appear to be a trivial matter. Yet these dead points can insidiously corrode life: the moments of trivial hesitancy form lacunae in the lived time which, even in one day, add up to a waste of impressive magnitude. When this becomes an issue for the person, it is usually referred to as chronic procrastination. A look at concrete instances of these vacuous moments shows they occur with great frequency when the person is about to initiate something, e.g., to turn to the next activity or the next phase of an activity. The interruption, which can last for hours, is typically introduced in this way: "Before I start let's take a little break, smoke a cigarette, sit down or stretch out for a moment; it is time for a little snack." Or one notices that one is thirsty or has to go to the toilet; one remembers an errand one should do first or wants to look over the work already accomplished. Some need is being conjured up, or some subliminal need pushed into the foreground, as a more or less transparent excuse for avoiding continuing or initiating an activity. These maneuvers have the earmarks of anxiety, as if one were doubtful of the outcome or were striving to postpone "the evil hour."

In therapy the discrepancy between the neurotic's performance and ability must be kept in mind, because when the patient attempts to draw the therapist into an argument about his potentialities, he will use the evidence of his poor performances, his inadequacies, incorrigibilities, etc., in very convincing ways. The facts, of course, are true and you cannot disregard them, but the patient's conclusions are not necessarily true. Suppose a man runs a certain distance in five minutes. The next time he makes it in thirty minutes, another time in twenty; he made it in five minutes only once. What is his true level? One cannot run faster than his true level. The five minutes are more representative of his true level than all the other counts, when he must have been running under a handicap. Similarly the best sample of a neurotic's behavior is likely to be his characteristic level of achievement once his handicap has been removed.

If one considers the person's total course and conduct of life, what is it ultimately that makes neurotic living different from healthy living? The basic human tendencies are the same in normal people and in neurotics, and all the potentialities are the same. There are as many gifted, finely organized people among neurotics as among healthy people, if not more. I think it would be very difficult to defend the thesis that neurotics are basically inferior because of constitutional factors; such theories exist, but they do not have much empirical support. Neurosis is nothing but an attitude acquired by the child in the process of re-relating himself to the world after his original separation from it. On the basis of the experiences he has had at the time, one or another kind of attitude may develop. In either case the person pursues the same general goals, but in a different spirit, with different kinds of expectations about the outcome of his efforts.

No one can have complete certainty about how things will turn out. In weighing the chances we all extrapolate from what we know, from what has happened in the past. The factor of nonrational expectation may enter this process and tip the balance toward an optimistic or pessimistic outlook. A person's attitude can be a confident one: "I am all right. I can do things, and I have enough to offer so that I am likely to be accepted by someone." In relation to the world the non-neurotic person may feel: "True, there is plenty of misery in the world; still things can be worked out one way or another. It is possible to love and to be loved, to manage in the world as it is, and it is possible on occasion to change the world a bit for the better." The difference between a healthy and a neurotic picture of one's chances is essentially a product of imagination, of symbolic generalization and elaboration.

The appalling fact is that fantasy eventually becomes reality. One cannot be afraid of anything for very long without having it become partially real. If, when I meet people I expect rejection and act accordingly, I shall sooner or later be rejected. It is particularly illuminating to observe the numerous ways in which such expectations are fulfilled, although at first glance the ruling factor may seem to be pure chance. Pure chance does not exist in such matters. We say it just happened that someone had an accident, and then we find that he has had twenty accidents in the last few years! It has been proved reliably that accident proneness is a personal characteristic. There is also proneness to marrying and to not marrying, proneness to success and to failure, and to many other states and events. Even in reference to positive events, to strokes of "good luck," there exist various kinds of proneness which are not a matter of pure chance. We shall have more to say in later chapters about how these tendencies perpetuate themselves as dominant influences in a person's life, but their effects are unmistakable. Whereas healthy behavior contains the seeds of success, neurotic behavior is *inherently* doomed to failure.

Other Conceptions of Anxiety

In concluding this discussion of the general nature of neurosis let me return briefly to the basic issue of anxiety in order to compare my formulation of it with the conceptions of other theorists.

I feel that formulating the core issue of neurosis in terms of a total life situation rather than in terms of the feeling of anxiety, besides being in line with the holistic approach, has two distinct advantages. First, a life situation is something that exists apart from the person's feelings and can therefore be determined objectively; to do so we need not resort to the concept of an unconscious feeling, of an anxiety that does not feel like anxiety. We have the basic situation of isolation which at times, under certain conditions, reflects itself in consciousness as anxiety. At other times it does not—overt anxiety is a major problem in only a small fraction of neuroses—but the condition itself exists nonetheless and can be observed.

The other advantage of this formulation is that it puts the concept of anxiety into the framework of a general theory on a definite basis. As noted before, almost everyone who has worked seriously on the problem of anxiety assumes that it is a threat to the very core of the personality; not a partial threat to which we usually respond with more crystallized and localized fears, but a threat to one's very existence. In introducing the life situation of isolation as the basic concept, we can say more specifically what it is that is being threatened. It is the person's relatedness to the world through mastery and through love which alone makes life worthwhile and which cannot be achieved in isolation. In defining anxiety in these terms, we relate the theory of anxiety to our theory of human nature as such. This holistic definition is not inconsistent with the formulations offered by other authors, as a cursory examination of their views will show.

According to some views, anxiety is directed at a rather specific object; we should come to terms with these views. Freud * assumed that the threats involved in the anxiety reaction are the separation from the mother, primarily in the processes of birth and weaning, and the imagined threat of castration in the Oedipal crisis. In some of Freud's formulations the separation from the mother is equated with castration, since the child is assumed to experience the world and its most important part, the mother, as part of his own body. Because there is no clear subject-object differentiation, her loss is like the loss of a highly valued part of his body.

Freud's point of view is not basically different from the point of view presented here, provided that we allow for the difference of theoretical orientation, namely Freud's preference for formulations which emphasize the specific while implying the general. Separation from the mother implies the basic neurotic constellation as it has been described in this chapter, i.e., the situation of isolation. After some subject-object differentiation has taken place, the mother *is* the rest of the world as far as communication is concerned. She is the first community in which loving relations can be formed; she is also an object for the autonomous strivings of the child who tries to make her fit in with his wishes. After the experience of isolation, the mother—who is practically equated with the world—becomes the first embodiment of the mythical enemy with whom no communication is possible and who is potentially dangerous to the child's mastery and freedom. This is reflected in the psychoanalytic descriptions of the pre-oedipal mother as cold, unloving, devouring, dangerous, etc. Similarly, castration may be conceived as typifying a deprivation which prevents the person from initiating a loving or a masterful relationship because of a *defect in him*. Here we have the other effect of the state of isolation, the subjective sense of being unworthy of love and inadequate to cope with an overwhelming and dangerous world. The difference, then, between the Freudian position on anxiety and the one advanced here is a difference of conceptual preference rather than of empirical substance.

* S. Freud, *The Problem of Anxiety*. Norton, New York, 1936.

The theories of other authors, including the neo-Freudians, also fit in with the view presented here, as can be seen from the following examples. Rank * distinguishes two kinds of fears in anxiety: fear of life and fear of death. Fear of life is due to separation, fear of death is a fear of losing one's individuality, of being swallowed up by the world. When Rank defines neurosis as a lack of synthesis between these two anxieties I think the wording is poor, but the intent of relating anxiety to a threat to the two basic human trends is clear nevertheless.

For Sullivan † anxiety is the reaction of the child to a threat to his security by the disapprobation of the significant adult. As I see it, what Sullivan calls "security drives" coincides closely with the homonomous trend, and "security" refers primarily to security in the love of others. "Disapprobation" then means something much more radical than the word would suggest; it means both rejection, resulting in the child's emotional isolation, and derogation, which stamps the child as inadequate and unworthy of love. Once again the two sides of the neurotic world-person relationship appear essentially as we have described them. A reference to being "narrowed in" is also present since, according to Sullivan's thesis, that which has been disapproved of is excluded from the self; this exclusion limits and narrows one's life.

Fromm ‡ views anxiety as arising from the isolation which results from the severance of early ties inherent in the process of growth toward independence. If the ensuing loneliness impels the person to establish a premature integration with others via submission, "escape from freedom" is the result. The importance of both basic trends is implicitly acknowledged in this description, even though the evaluative emphasis is on autonomy.

Horney § considers anxiety a reaction to the danger that one's hostile feelings will erupt against those on whom one depends; anxiety arises out of the conflict between dependent and hostile impulses. At first this view seems quite different from mine, but this difference disappears when the nature of the child's dependence is spelled out. The child is normally dependent on adults both for a safe exercise of his autonomous functions and for loving and being loved. The breaking through of hostility in response to vexatious situations may well be expected to trigger anxiety if it threatens, or is felt to threaten, these basic conditions of living. The role of conflict in anxiety is stressed or

* O. Rank, *Will Therapy*. Knopf, New York, 1945.
† H. S. Sullivan, "The Meaning of Anxiety in Psychiatry and in Life." *Psychiatry*, 11, 1948.
‡ E. Fromm, *Escape from Freedom*. Farrar and Rinehart, New York, 1941.
§ K. Horney, *The Neurotic Personality of Our Time*. Norton, New York, 1937.

implied also by some of the other theorists (although they differ in their conceptions of what the conflicting tendencies are). My own view of the "basic conflict" will be presented in Chapter 8 (The Theory of Universal Ambiguity).

This brief review indicates that although different theorists focus on different sources and aspects of the basic neurotic constellation, their views, on being translated into a holistic framework, prove not divergent but convergent and congruent.

7. The In-Group
and the Stranger

In describing the genesis of the neurotic world view I have stressed *alienness* as the main characteristic of the mythical "enemy," the central figure of the neurotic mythology. He is the utter "stranger." This image results from the persisting state of isolation of the child whose attempts at relating himself to the world have largely failed, so that no communication and no real community has been established. The early failure of communication between the child and the care-taking adult can result from a range of circumstances not limited to drastic neglect or mistreatment; in the early childhood of many neurotics there were no obvious losses, no great disruptions and no conspicuous traumatizing events. But even when the image of the stranger, of an unresponsive and incomprehensible agent, was formed under circumstances entailing no acute suffering for the child, his complete separateness joined with his overwhelming power invariably turns into malevolence in the child's mind or at least into a cold hostile indifference.

This assocation of alienness and assumed hostility is readily observable in adults in a variety of situations. Many a patient discovers that when thinking of people who are outside his familiar circle he feels himself in an atmosphere of ill will; "they" are always vaguely malevolent. The less we know the person, the easier it is to ascribe to him our own feelings, or qualities that would justify our fears. A man who is afraid of drunks is not afraid when his friend gets drunk; a man who is afraid of policemen would not be afraid of a particular one if he knew well this policeman's private life and circumstances.

Correspondingly, it is only too easy to be aggressive and exploitative toward a stranger. The fact that people often behave irresponsibly when traveling in foreign places is multiply determined, but the alienness of the inhabitants of these places is one of the prominent factors.

Many of the soldiers who steal and rape in a foreign country would never think of doing it to the people they know. In the war one shoots at "enemies," not people; in the communist state one can be ruthless toward the "class-alien element." It is easy to treat others inhumanly when their differences from oneself are perceived as making them strangers—differences of race, custom, language, social class. One of the marked characteristics of people who enjoy vigorous psychological health, and from whose world the mythical enemy is absent, is that they do not see any people as strangers. Neurotics, on the contrary, maintain their fixed attitudes of fear and hostility by refusing to learn to know as people those with whom they have some limited contact.

The idea of stranger, originating in the early state of isolation, is revived in the later developmental stages as the child's world expands and becomes structured. The differential response of the young child to the approach of an unfamiliar person is a precursor of the later realization that his world, the family circle, is surrounded by a larger one, the outside world inhabited by strangers. But long before these outsiders acquire a pronounced significance for the child in a positive or a negative sense, he experiences most intensely the in- and out-group formation within the family itself. While normally his first community, the prototypal all-encompassing "group," is the mother, this first community becomes an in-group as soon as other family members begin to emerge on the periphery of his life. As time goes on relationships with these others are formed, but the inclusion of new members in the original group is not a smooth process.

The specifically sexual aspect of the Oedipus situation is only one component of a larger problem facing the child, i.e., that of adding a third member to the original dyad. Under the best of circumstances this second step in the series of homonomous integrations is not easy to take. The constant centering on each other, or of one person on another, is possible only in a dyad, not in a larger group, so that what the child gains in enlarging the community to include the second parent is achieved at the cost of some pain. Coming to terms with siblings presents similar problems, their elaboration being determined by the family constellation. But whatever specific forms it takes, the process of in- and out-group formation, of inclusion and exclusion, is unavoidably accompanied by jealousy and rivalries; it abounds in experiences which, in unfavorable circumstances, can have a traumatizing effect on the child. A successful resolution of these conflicts by the child combines participation in various subgroups, in relationships with individual family members, with the secure sense of being a part of the larger group, the family as a whole. This solution takes the child a long way on the path toward widening and deepening homonomous integration.

What I want to emphasize in this context is that, in this process of group formation, the new member—the father, the new sibling—is at first experienced as an intruding stranger. Children's fantasies often give expression to this idea and to the fear aroused by it. As the child achieves integration within the larger family group, the others cease being strangers and become parts of his home. But even if there is no harmony and no real closeness in the family, the mere familiarity achieved by contact mitigates the terror aroused by the unknown and enables the child to make at least some superficial adaptations to the ways of his family.

Whatever the internal structure of the family, this closely or loosely organized group functions as an in-group more or less sharply demarcated from the outside world as an out-group. The significance of this in-group decreases with time and the out-group increasingly gains in importance. The child's future lies in the outside world, and the attitudes he gradually forms toward this out-group will contribute to shaping this future. These attitudes may not be important while the child's life is still encompassed by the family, but they will be of vital significance when relationships to people outside the family become major issues. How he solves these issues will depend not only on the nature of his integration within the family but also on what attitudes toward the outside world the family fosters.

The family community is suited to the developmental state of the child only as long as it provides adequate opportunity for the satisfaction of his needs for belongingness and mastery. As his interests expand, this community becomes too narrow for him, and the old forms of participation become confining. Every family community has some degree of exclusiveness and is potentially limiting. When the discrepancy between growth tendencies and the possibilities inherent in the nature and structure of the family reaches a certain point, a conflict arises between moving ahead and remaining a part of the community which has had the child's undivided loyalty.

The conflict can be solved only if the others, primarily the parents, are willing to give up the current form of family integration without resentment, if not without pain, for the sake of the child's growth. In renouncing exclusiveness in their relationship to their child, the parents are giving up a community that may be all important to them, a form of life into which they may have put everything; it is a real sacrifice that is demanded of them. But once achieved the renunciation involved in giving freedom of growth to the child brings great rewards. Through this act of creative love the personality of the giver is deepened and enlarged in a way that lends dignity and grandeur to human existence, and, paradoxically, he or she is enabled to regain the community that had to be given up. A new relationship is created with the child whose sphere of life is enlarged, and, through the continued mutual affection, the parent now participates in this enlarged life. Since this new form of integration transcends the child's initial conflict between growth and belongingness, he is freed from anxiety and from any guilt of disloyalty.

A precondition of such an outcome is that the parents be capable of accepting and meeting the child's needs at every stage of his growth and capable also of paving his way into the world outside the family. This second aspect of their competence depends on the degree of the family's integration with the outside community and on their attitudes toward this out-group. These attitudes make it easy or difficult for the parents to "cede" the child to the world and, to a great extent, determine also the child's expectations of it. Families' attitudes toward the "outside" world vary widely. In the ideal case, the parents' own manifold integrations with people and issues bring the "outside" to the child in a gradual and positive way and facilitate his future transition beyond the confines of the family.

At the opposite extreme, certain marriages which to a casual observer may appear to be ideal seem, on closer observation, to be based on the motto, "We two against the world." In such a union a limited community is formed, but it is based, mutually or unilaterally, on complete exclusion of the rest of mankind which is viewed as alien. Mutual love and harmony may be valued highly, but any manifestation by the partner of the homonomous trend outside this unit, no matter how minor and harmless, is felt to be a betrayal, a threat to the marriage or the friendship. Usually no attempt is made to inhibit the partner's self-assertiveness and mastery outside the closed unit. He or she may be encouraged to achieve, expand, stand up for himself; in fact it may even be demanded that the partner pick a fight at the drop of a hat. But no positive expression is felt to have value unless it is intimate. An entertaining story, a joke told by the partner cannot be enjoyed if the pleasure of hearing it is simultaneously bestowed on others. Jealousy is a constitutive element of such a relationship; it need not be in the open but it is a constant overtone. A young woman may express real puzzlement as to why her secure harmonious relationship with her boy friend suddenly yields to an insecure tense mood in the presence of others—*any* others. She feels she must strenuously hold her own in competing with everyone for her friend's attention. In fact he now appears to be an entirely different person, one on whom she no longer can rely, although he acts as his usual self and she does not doubt his affection.

A community of this kind is a particular reconstruction of the basic neurotic situation of isolation; it has something wrong with its inner structure, and not only with its relation to the outside world. The partner is still suspected of being the mythical enemy; in some circumstances he might desert the other or turn against him. Fear of being compared with others implies also self-derogation, a suspicion of being unlovable. But, in comparison to the state of complete isolation, this feeling of one's own weakness and worthlessness is mitigated by some degree of confidence in the strength and support of the unit. In some marriages of this kind, if the need for exclusiveness is bilateral, adjustments are worked out which protect and stabilize the relationship. The intense mutual absorption of the partners may even cause these unions to appear exceptionally close and satisfying.

A marriage of this kind may remain childless by the partners' choice, or the child may remain a secondary concern of the parents, a marginal member of the family. In the more frequent cases of less extreme exclusiveness, the in-group is extended to include the children and may function as a closely knit family, the degree of harmony within it varying from low to fairly high. Yet, regardless of the nature of its cohesion, this larger group may still maintain a position toward the outside community strikingly similar to that of the individual person toward the world in the basic neurotic situation. The unity of the family, affection and mutual support among its members, may be stressed strongly, but people outside the family are (overtly or covertly) viewed as dangerous, ruthless, exploitative, not to be trusted. Being feared and disliked, they are often devalued as inferior. These attitudes are conveyed to the children in many unmistakable ways. Combined with family loyalty they result in developing one moral code of behavior in relation to the family members, a different one for behavior toward outsiders. Thus the child gets an education in fear and hostility toward the stranger, the whole outside world.

The contrast between the family and the out-group, when elaborated in this way, is fraught with conflict. A series of neurotic difficulties arises when, in the course of development, the child is propelled by both cultural and internal pressures to form ties with people who have been strongly suspected of evil. In exploring the origins of their interpersonal difficulties, patients often date them back to their first encounter with groups of their age equals, in school or in the neighborhood. They may have been extremely timid with these strangers: "My mother always had to take me by the hand and ask the children in the street to let me play with them"; or they may have behaved awk-wardly or aggressively, although all they remember is having been victimized and rejected by others. Patients frequently explain these early troubles as being due to the lack of previous opportunity for contact with children, usually ascribed to residential conditions or to chance, though rejection of available playmates by parents may also be mentioned. Whatever the contributing circumstances, the reports vividly convey the strong persisting barriers to communication these children experienced upon being thrust among strangers. Equally vivid are the reports of the impasse experienced by some in later childhood when parents urged them to be social successes, yet criticized and ridiculed any friend they brought home or told the child he was being exploited by his "friends."

In adolescence, it is the area of sex which presents unavoidable difficulties. In a close-knit family unit all vital feelings and impulses are supposed to be expressed in the family and to remain in the family; yet relating oneself to the members of the inside circle sexually is tabooed. For sex one must go to the stranger, the enemy. When affectionate bonds are reserved for the members of the in-group and jealously guarded, sex becomes a commerce with the enemy and is necessarily surrounded by anxiety, hostility, fear of being exploited. This state of affairs is well illustrated by two of the many jokes on the topic. A young man in considering marriage exclaims, "But how could I marry a complete stranger!" And another in the same situation says, "It is awful to think that I should have intercourse with the mother of my own children." The first quotation expresses the dread of the "outsider" which makes it impossible to establish a community with her; the second is a combined expression of the dread of incest and the feeling that sex is debasing and incompatible with affectionate regard which rightly belongs to the family. Thus the exclusiveness of the family may result in cases of "mother fixation," not always because the son's feelings toward her are more intense than is usual, but because, by definition, an affectionate tie to a woman is not feasible outside the family.

The difficulties created by an overemphasis of the family-strangers dichotomy are not limited to the sexual area; they can encompass all spheres of the growing child's life. The family is seen as giving affection and safety, but it is highly restrictive, providing no room for expansion. As the expansive urges grow, the outside world becomes intriguing and exciting, but it is felt to be cold and dangerous. "Remaining in the family" requires self-multilation. One must repudiate all strivings that would take one out of the family, must fear rather than desire success if it were to have this effect. This self-abnegation is greatly resented and spoils the existing relationship; the family unity is undermined. Yet moving out of the family, or anything conceived as such a move, exposes the person to manifold dangers. To the fear of the outside world is added the fear of retaliation, of abandonment by the family, and also guilt for disloyalty. One dreads disappointing the parents, making them suffer, perhaps even endangering their health, because of one's "selfish" wishes. When parents in fact adopt these attitudes, this conflict permits no satisfying solution.

Thus the image of the "stranger" with whom no understanding is possible, the residue and the symbol of the state of isolation, is seen to re-emerge at every stage of growth that demands forming new ties, ties with people who until now have been strangers. In a healthy development, this phantom, if it appears at all, is soon put to rest; it merely marks the transition to the unknown. In the neurotic development, the mythical stranger is a constant presence. This conception of the human world is masked by surface beliefs and adjustments, but in crucial situations it emerges as a strong dynamic factor which stunts the growth of the homonomous trend.

8. The Theory
of Universal Ambiguity

In Chapter 4, in discussing integration, I described how richness and range are achieved in personality through a multiple utilization of a relatively small number of components, through their successive reordering into a variety of patterns. Because of this mode of functioning, personality must be viewed as a multivalent, pluralistic organization. Such a description, however, is not sufficient since it side-steps the main issue. Man is to be understood not in terms of any specific traits he possesses, or any specific patterns they form, but in terms of the overall pattern that organizes these traits and their multiple interconnections. In the course of my work with neurotic patients I have been searching for a conceptualization of personality adequate for the practical tasks of education and therapy. The most significant general statement I am able to make as a result of this search is that while personality is pluralistic in the detail of its functioning, in its broad outline it is a *dualistic* organization

The Dual Orientation

There is no life course in which every developmental experience has been traumatic nor one from which all deleterious influences have been absent. There are both healthy and traumatic features in every child's environment and in his relations with it; the early attempts at relating oneself to the world succeed in part, and in part fail. As a result, the personality of the child develops simultaneously around two nuclei, forms two patterns. One of them may be underdeveloped but it is never absent. One pattern is based on isolation and its derivatives: feelings of helplessness, unlovableness, and doubts about one's prospects. The other is based on the confidence that a modicum of one's autonomous and homonomous strivings may be realized more or less directly. The overall system principle of the human personality, the guiding pattern of life composed of the two basic tendencies, does not change when the neurotic orientation comes into being. Whether in health or in neurosis, our life is guided by the same unalterable superordinate trends, autonomy and homonomy. But when two opposite sets of convictions have been formed about the nature of the world and the self, these trends function in a setting of very different expectations.

One outlook, while not indiscriminate optimism, reflects the confidence that the "supplies" for one's basic needs exist in the world and that one is both adequate and worthy of obtaining these supplies. The neurotic belief is that these conditions are not available or that they can be made available only by extremely complicated and indirect methods. Thus, in one way of life, the two basic human propensities function in an atmosphere of hope, confidence, trust, or faith, if you like. In the other, the propelling forces are the same, but they function in an atmosphere of diffidence, mistrust, and lack of faith. Phenomenological concepts such as hope, trust, and faith have not yet achieved a clear position in systematic theorizing, but no one can doubt that these states, as well as their opposites, do exist and are extraordinarily potent irrespective of whether or not they can be translated into current psychological concepts. Confidence and diffidence, conviction and doubt that human life is livable in this world, mark the "great divide," the point at which our path bifurcates and our life acquires its dual organization and its basic existential conflict.

The differences between the two ways of life, or the two "worlds" that are elaborated from the two nuclear convictions, have been stated, by implication, in the description of the main features of neurosis. They shall be briefly recapitulated here. The two patterns differ not only in their system principle but also in their integrational features. Although each can be tightly organized, the organization of the neurotic system bears the imprint of its origin in the state of isolation and anxiety; several of its features represent defects of integration along the dimensions of depth, progression, and breadth.

One of the two worlds is real, the other fictitious. This is not, strictly speaking, due to the truth or falsehood of the assumptions governing each system; both of them are expressions of faith and neither can be validly proved. But doubt and anxiety have the effect of making the images developed to elaborate or to disguise the basic neurotic assumptions ever more compelling and indiscriminate, so that reality easily falls victim to fantasy. In the healthy system, the basic assumptions do not call for disguises, and the confidence in one's ability to manage in the world as it is permits a realistic perception of the negative aspects of life.

The world visualized in the healthy pattern feels like one's home; it is rich in opportunities, lawfully ordered, and meaningfully related to the person. The world of neurosis is foreign and threatening, full of obstacles and dangers, lawless, capricious, a chaos rather than a cosmos. The consequences of this difference are many. In the "good" world it is possible and rewarding to pursue positive goals which one desires and enjoys; in the threatening world the main concern and joy must be to escape danger. The difference between working for and working against something is reflected in the fixed predominance of fear and anger in the neurotic as against the more positive feeling tone and the wider range of normal emotions. Communication and the absence of it are crucial for contact both with people and things. Love and community formation are easy in the one pattern, difficult or impossible in the other. In the healthy orientation it is possible to perceive wholes, to see things in a wide perspective, to receive impressions which point beyond the datum itself; continuity and intentionality make the world meaningful. In the neurotic orientation, the things and events of the world appear as isolated items or fragments. The long view is replaced by shortsightedness; the fresh outlook yields to a stereotyped and biased one. Impressions cannot be fully valued and enjoyed, because their pointing quality, their "message character," is lost; the result is a truncated experience.

The person himself is also transformed by the negative fantasies about himself and by assuming poses and characteristics that are not genuine to him and are meant to disguise his imagined lack of worth. While in the confident orientation the person feels, thinks, and speaks as he is and not as he is "supposed" to be, the neurotic, having settled for appearances, acts for the sake of effect. He is not in touch with his real wishes, and the main function of his thoughts and acts is more often to "prove" than to enjoy. Since the connection between the expression and that which is expressed has been multiply twisted, neurotic behavior has no depth; it is superficial and inexpressive. A vivid example of settling for appearances is one patient's boyhood memory of how frustrated he was when a swimming instructor wanted him to take his feet off the ground. The boy finally cried in exasperation, "But *it looks like* swimming with just my arms, and nobody can see my legs under the water." He was genuinely nonplussed when the instructor did not accept his solution. This patient's adult life was, to all outward appearances, filled with exemplary achievements. It was only in his sex life that he was faced with the insufficiency of merely "looking" successful.

Integration along the dimension of progression is also disturbed in neurosis. In the healthy orientation the means are an organic part of the total activity and are positively valued both as a way to the goal and in their own right as a part of a whole. In the neurotic system everything is a means toward some vague end which is secretly believed to be unreachable. Means activities are thereby devalued, and so is the present as such, because everything is merely preliminary. If the neurotic is not dreaming about some value lost in the past, he is constantly hurrying and expecting. The present is related to his future no more organically than the means are related to his goals or his personal trends to expression. Both in experience and in his actions the neurotic leads an impoverished disintegrated existence. Many of his actions conflict with his other impulses and take no account of the surrounding realities; such incongruous, disharmonious actions are necessarily self-defeating.

Personality as an Ambiguous Gestalt

In the psychoanalytic theory of complexes these interfering unconscious forces are not thought of as single repressed impulses; complexes are partial organizations. The hypothesis of duality which I propose extends the use of the organizational principle by assuming the existence, not of discrete complexes, but of more inclusive systems competing for influence on the person's conduct of his life.

We live, all of us, in two worlds, not in one, but we don't live in these worlds simultaneously. Health and neurosis are not segments of personality so that one might be neurotic in some aspects of one's life and healthy in others at the same time. The two patterns which are almost mirror reversals of each other, two alternate ways in which our basic trends can seek expression, are both total organizations. Health and illness are determined by the dominance of one of the two systems. When one system becomes dominant, it tends to organize the total field, the total life of the person, since every Gestalt tends toward a complete realization of its system principle. The healthy aspects do not remain healthy, and the neurotic ones do not remain neurotic when the opposite organization gains dominance. The parts in a system function as such not through their immanent qualities but through their positional values; they change their mode of functioning when they become parts of a different system. Health and neurosis are to be thought of as two organized processes, two dynamic Gestalts organizing the same material, so that each item has a position within two different patterns. There can be shifts between the two, lasting or short lived, in either direction, but at any given moment the person is either healthy or neurotic, depending on which system is dominant.

This mode of coexistence of the two systems cannot be represented by depicting them side by side or by picturing one as enclosed in the other (as complexes or repressed conflicts are sometimes represented). They coexist, as it were, within each other. The dynamic aspect of the relationship, the coexistence of two fields of forces, can be expressed through the following metaphor: If a straight elastic rod is bent to form a loop, it retains its resiliency, a molecular arrangement that will straighten it out again as soon as the constraining force is removed. While it is bent, two organizations are present: the one that keeps it bent and the one that could straighten it out. Depending on which system is stronger the arrangement of the parts will be straight or crooked. This metaphor expresses quite well the simultaneous existence of two competing dynamic factors and the primacy of the ever-present factor of health, but it does justice neither to the complex articulation of the two systems, nor to the all-or-none character of their dominance.

In these respects the dual personality organization is represented much more adequately by being likened to a visual *ambiguous Gestalt* of the kind you find reproduced in treatises on visual perception. In the one most frequently seen the spatial arrangement is such that the picture may be perceived as representing either a black vase on a white background or two white faces in profile, turned toward each other. The basis for both organizations is there, but only one of the two can be perceived at any given moment. When a shift occurs, what was seen as the figure becomes the background, and each item of the spatial arrangement acquires a new meaning as part of a representation of a different object; the two images never mix. Because of its dual organization human life similarly is an ambiguous Gestalt, each part process having a different function and meaning, depending on whether it takes place within the Gestalt of health or the Gestalt of neurosis. Everything in life has a double meaning—hence universal ambiguity.

The theory of universal ambiguity has far-reaching consequences for the theory and therapy of neurosis. It precludes the conception of neurosis as a rotten part of a healthy apple, or a limited segregated growth within the person, a plant that can be pulled out by the roots without disturbing or changing the rest of the personality. The neurotic person is neurotic throughout, in every area of his life, in all the crannies and crevices of his existence. Conversely, one cannot say that there is in anyone only an element or segment of personality that is healthy. One is healthy throughout and this health extends over one's entire existence, down to the most distorted forms of behavior and the most troublesome symptoms. The so-called "healthy core," the patient's real self, will not be found stuck away in some distant or hidden region of his personality; it is to be found right there, where it is least expected. Health is present potentially in its full power in the most destructive, most baneful, most shameful behavior.

As a boy, one patient felt compelled to drink his own urine. Later he managed, with the aid of a contraption of his own invention, the difficult feat of performing fellatio on himself. The most agonizing paroxysms of shame accompanied these revelations, which demonstrated his isolation, his morbid preoccupation with himself, and the fantastic indirections he felt were necessary to achieve gratification. Yet the same behavior expressed diverse "completion" and "fulfillment" motives: "I could have belonged in the family circle only if I had given up the right to be alone; still the circle had to be completed, so I made my own." These distortions also expressed the tendency to experience sensuality to its fullest and a determined wish to affirm his uniqueness in the face of tempting conventional compromises.

In an ambiguous Gestalt, the parts do not belong independently to one pattern or another. All parts belong to both patterns and have their function assigned to them by the currently dominant system principle. There is therefore no motivational force that the person has to discard in therapy. If the pattern of health becomes dominant, the problematic factors will find their places within it in a system-consistent fashion. I do not mean that, for instance, a neurotic headache as such can find a comfortable niche in a healthy organization. I mean that whatever attitude the headache is expressing will fit constructively into the healthy pattern, filling a vital role and not being merely tolerated, and then this attitude will not be expressed through headaches. One of the frequent obstacles to therapy is that the patient conceives of the process of getting well as getting rid of something within him. This is like tearing away a part of himself, and he cannot wish it wholeheartedly. Alternately he may conceive of the therapeutic goal as becoming reconciled to an irremovable handicap or defect and learning to live with it, not a very inspiring prospect. Both conceptions are based on the idea of a segmental disturbance which can be removed or kept but not changed. Viewing neurosis as an organization provides a basis for a different conception of therapy, which will be discussed later.

The dual organization of human life, with one or the other pattern predominating, is often obscured from view because it is overlaid with what might be called the surface or social personality. In this stratum some manifestations of the two basic patterns may form a spurious kind of apparent synthesis. This surface patterning of personality, however, can hardly be considered an organization in its own right. Even in many healthy people this phenomenal level is superficial and devoid of personal roots. Since it is determined largely by compliance or compromise with conventions, such patterning is sometimes almost entirely verbal or composed of routine actions. It serves as a front for others and in part for oneself.

For the neurotic, the existence of this superficial structure provides easy proof that his life is no different from that of anyone else and blunts the secret impact of his feelings of futility. He may climb on a streetcar like anyone else and, even though he feels pushed, competitive, and on the alert, he may carry on a "perfectly normal" conversation all the while with another whose outward behavior is no different from his. The blandness of this culturally accepted cover is in strong contrast to the strength and vitality of either of the underlying organizations. In almost all styles of psychotherapy the patient is encouraged to abandon the superficial level; that is why therapy is the situation of choice for observing the workings of the principle of universal ambiguity.

Shifts of Dominance

The dual patterning of personality cannot become clearly visible, even to observation that penetrates beyond the surface, as long as one system maintains a strong dominance. The coexistence of two incompatible all-inclusive structures can be clearly and strikingly demonstrated only when a shift takes place between two patterns both of which are well developed and strongly articulated—much as the visual ambiguous Gestalts are revealed only through shifts. Such dramatic, seemingly sudden shifts are rare, but they do happen. Foremost among them are the phenomena of conversion, such as religious conversions exemplified by the reports collected by W. James, those described in some case histories of Alcoholics Anonymous, and the less well-known, spontaneous radical changes which are not formulated by the person in religious terms. No less clear cut is the evidence provided by sudden sweeping personality changes after an accumulation of traumata or an accumulation of insights in therapy. Similarly, some cases of traumatic neurosis and relapse after successful therapy represent shifts from health to neurosis. Cases of hysterical dual personality, though not founded in the basic dual pattern we have described, also demonstrate the possibility of complex alternate organizations coexisting in the same person. Some people, in whom both the healthy and the neurotic systems are strongly organized, report vivid experiences of periodic change of mood and behavior, each mood incorporating one of the two basic orientations.

Shifts cannot be expected to occur if, or as long as, the nondominant pattern is underdeveloped and has a low degree of organization. Consequently the best opportunity for observation of shifts is afforded the therapist at that time in therapy when, the neurotic pattern having been weakened and the healthy one strengthened, both are approximately equal in strength and give marked indications of competing for the patient's allegiance. The strongest empirical support for the hypothesis of the dual organization of personality comes from the observations made at this stage of the therapeutic process. The dynamic effects exerted by each Gestalt as it struggles toward a complete realization of its system principle by eliminating or refitting system-inconsistent elements can be best observed at that time. The resulting shifts are well exemplified by the experience of a patient who visualized his former way of life as a Roman circus arena where he had become very skillful in avoiding the lions, and in nothing else. He felt that in therapy he had learned to spot and reach the exits from the arena, but once he was outside, the doors looked to him "just as inviting in a devilishly compelling way; from the outside they are not exits, they are entrances —and before I know it, there I am right back dodging the lions."

Universal Ambiguity

The ambiguity created by the dual organization of human life is reflected in the fact that, taken outside of its context, every item of human experience and behavior has a double meaning. Language sometimes assigns different terms to the two meanings and sometimes combines them under one term, but regardless of the verbal formulation and its evaluative connotation, the two discernible meanings of any human trait are commonly evaluated in diametrically opposite ways. In the chapter on homonomy we have discussed how the healthy wish to be needed, to be of help, acquires its neurotic counterpart in a compulsive assumption of obligations and how "love" can mean possessiveness. These examples could be multiplied. Dependence, though the term has taken on a pejorative meaning, actually is one aspect of every community formation, an expression of the homonomous trend. Only the dependence that expresses the neurotic feeling of helplessness, and consequently far exceeds the objective necessity for support, merits negative evaluation. Pride is highly thought of when it expresses self-respect and pleasure in real achievement; in some dialects, "proud" is the equivalent of "glad." Yet "pride goes before a fall," and Horney uses the term "pride system" to designate an essential component of neurosis. Submission and surrender both refer to a state of nonassertion of individuality, of losing oneself in something else, but the difference is momentous. One submits to the alien and becomes diminished through submission; one surrenders one's isolation to enter into a larger unit and enlarges one's life.

These examples do not imply that each personal manifestation has only two psychological meanings, only two fixed contexts. Since personality is a multiple organization, each item of behavior can serve as an expression of a variety of motives and be a part of a multitude of subsystems even within the same person. All these multiple meanings, however, are subsystems of one of the two major patterns. This grouping is not an arbitrary classification in terms of the "good-bad" polarity; rather the very fact that a linguistic formulation of any human phenomenon can be given positive and negative connotations reflects the ambiguity created by the dual patterning of personality. This ambiguity often functions as an obstacle to communication in the theoretical discussion of human issues. The participants may disagree because in using identical or similar terms they assign to them not only different but practically opposite meanings.

An instructive example of both the dual and plural meanings of an attitude for which our language has but one name is afforded by the analysis of curiosity as it appears in healthy and in unhealthy contexts. Normal curiosity arises from the person's wish to broaden out, to learn about people and things for the sake of increased mastery and participation. Neurotic curiosity has entirely different goals and an entirely different emotional coloring. In one of its forms it is born of a feeling of helplessness; one feels that one does not know how to live and looks enviously at others who seem to be "successful" at it. The purpose of watching them is to find out "how they do it" in order to copy their methods; one does this without any reference to one's own inclinations and competencies, so that the borrowed methods remain inorganic accretions. Success is viewed as being achieved by some trick, not as growing out of one's total conduct of life. Much of the popular "adjustment" literature capitalizes on this neurotic trait; one reads it not to straighten out one's life but to learn the "techniques." The goal of curiosity in this pattern is the appropriation of something belonging to others; it is a method of stealing and one goes about it stealthily. It may well happen that the patient attempts to "steal" something which he actually possesses without knowing it, but this does not change the meaning of his act.

A more striking form of neurotic curiosity is directed defensively and aggressively against the assumed dangerous world. One seeks to "dig up the dirt" to alleviate one's own assumed worthlessness through comparison with the shortcomings of others but even more to protect oneself by storing up ammunition for an attack. One is gathering information that can be used against others, whether or not one is aware of this goal. Some go about it quite openly and make themselves disliked by asking personal questions that are "none of their business." More often, however, even publicly available information is gathered stealthily, and the person may engage in fantasies of the type "if he only knew that I know," a kind of secret psychological black mailing. He feels both maliciously triumphant and extremely guilty and fearful for having broken into another's privacy and stolen his secrets. This aggressive pattern is an essential component of voyeurism. Yet, in a perverted form the normal wish for human contact is present even in this aggressive form of curiosity. In all such cases that I have known there was an enormous craving to be loved.

"Amalgamation"

When a healthy motive and a neurotic one, each occupying an important position in the system to which it belongs, are aroused or expressed by an identical or strongly analogous behavior pattern, the two meanings of this pattern may coalesce or amalgamate. The pattern can then no longer function alternately now as a part of one organization and now as a part of the other. When the pattern is being utilized in the service of the dominant organization, it activates the meaning which attaches to it in the latent one and an inhibiting stalemate may result. An example of such a situation is provided by some types of fear of success. This fear can arise from a variety of neurotic motives, such as the boy's fear that his father will punish his attempts to become an active adult male. These motives, however, can amalgamate with others having strong roots in the healthy organization. In certain contexts, individual success may be seen by the person as separating him from his "universal background" of which the parents are representatives, thus condemning him to an isolated lonely existence. If this meaning of success is prominent for the person, the force of the neurotic motives is increased by that of the healthy ones and, in therapy, the fear will not yield until *both* its roots have been laid bare. Amalgamation can also take place between two distinct neurotic meanings of a pattern. However, the strength and persistence of some of the most destructive damaging symptoms—of which fear of success is one —often have their source in the amalgamation of the two meanings that represent health and neurosis.

Such was the case of a brilliant and dedicated young scientist whose career was on the verge of being eclipsed when he developed a circumscribed inability to prepare for his doctoral examination. As a child he had suffered from a deep uncertainty about what was expected of him. His father seemed to wish only to be left alone by his son and punished all attempts to attract his attention. The boy embarked early on various research pursuits, an effective and creative way of cultivating certainty and courting expectations. These activities brought gratification and success, but they skirted the issue of the needs and expectations of the loved ones. As he put it, "It was all for *me*." The examination in which he had to meet the expectations of his teachers in order to obtain the degree, a confirmation of his "right to success," brought the issue to a head. The study block, while neurotically self-destructive, was expressive of healthy impulses as well. It reintroduced an element of uncertainty into a pattern that had become excessively centered on establishing certainty, and it covertly expressed his wish to give up his too willful control which permitted no sharing with others.

Defense Mechanisms as Types of System Action

The theory of universal ambiguity represents a radical departure from the customary ways of viewing neurosis and health. It requires a reappraisal and a reformulation of those major concepts which have previously proved useful in the study of personality dynamics, and it makes some of these concepts appear in a new light.

The point can be best illustrated by a consideration of the defense mechanisms. I see the defense mechanisms as processes taking place not between the conscious and unconscious, or between ego, superego, and id, but between the two major organizations of personality which struggle for dominance. The conflict of these two incompatible orientations, these two ways of adapting to life, is the basic conflict of human existence. Within this framework the processes referred to as defense mechanisms acquire a new significance. They are organizational devices, specific types of system action, through which each system seeks to complete itself in a manner consistent with its system principle and to maintain this organization, thereby preventing the alternate system from reaching a position of dominance.

This conception has two implications. First, it implies that the "defense mechanisms" have two functions: the internal organization of the system and its defense against the alternate one. Both functions can be fulfilled by means of one process. The organizing function is in the forefront when the given system is in a position of dominance; the defensive function becomes prominent when the two systems are in strong competition. Second, this conception implies an essential symmetry in the organizational-defensive maneuvers of the two systems; they maintain themselves and thereby ward off each other with identical or similar means. This symmetry is not complete, for several reasons. The system based on confidence, when it is securely dominant, can maintain this position with a minimum of special devices. It is a relatively self-consistent stable system. The neurotic system, with its double focus on fear and on hope, is not stable even when it is entrenched. It must continue to use many devices to achieve at least a semblance of consistency. Some of these defense mechanisms—those that result in a crass distortion of facts—are not compatible with the principles governing the system of health. Furthermore, the traditional formulation of some of the defense mechanisms obscures those components that are capable of functioning bilaterally, on behalf of either health or neurosis. Reformulations are required to make these components obvious. In spite of these qualifications the proposition stands that defense mechanisms are part and parcel of the dynamics of systems and as such are utilized both by the system of health and by the system of neurosis. I shall demonstrate this proposition with examples of two dynamic processes for only one of which a traditional formulation is available.

In the original formulation of *repression* certain impulses are considered to be made incompatible with the person's sense of self-esteem by parental reflection of socio-cultural sanctions and are therefore excluded from consciousness. According to my theory, the repressed is that which is inconsistent with the dominant organization, whichever it be. Repression remains a very useful concept, but it takes on new properties. It is no longer a one-way affair but a two-way affair. Not only the neurotic feelings and trends but the healthy ones too may be repressed, in this case by the neurotic organization. Both organizations are repressive, in the general sense of the term, because they are incompatible Gestalts, two total patterns struggling for dominance. If one system gains dominance, the other is *eo ipse* subdued or submerged, and this may take the form of excluding it from consciousness, i.e., of repression in the technical sense of the word. This conception is borne out by numerous observations that one can and does repress feelings and wishes that are in no way socially tabooed and are even considered laudable.

One of the mechanisms that come to light in analysis becomes very prominent at the stage when an intensive struggle takes place between neurosis and health. Like many dynamic devices, it has no traditional name. I would call it perversion if this term did not connote sexual perversions, which are unrelated to the process in question. It could also be described as annexation or *appropriation*.

Let us picture a patient who is considered a very warm-hearted person, and let us say that in analysis he discovers in himself a strong tendency to exploit people. He can then say, "My kindness is phony; when I get a person well buttered up I exploit him. I have no real warmth." He may, however, be wrong. His warmth may not be a pretense but a genuine trait that has developed within the context of the health system but is used at times within a neurotic context, for a neurotic purpose. Figuratively speaking, it is unlawfully appropriated by the competing organization and perverted to its uses. This process can take place in reverse as well. A misgiving about therapy frequently expressed by people who feel that they are creative is that they may lose their originality, that they will become flattened out and turn into ordinary John Does. Usually this does not happen, but such misgivings are not entirely unfounded; the energy of the tension created by the neurosis *can* serve socially valuable purposes. If it does happen, the question may be asked whether such an outcome is healthy or neurotic.

In the psychoanalytic literature this question has been much, and inconclusively, debated in relation to sublimation, a concept which can be made to coincide with *one* of the two directions appropriation can take. In terms of my theory, the neurotic pattern appropriated by the healthy system remains neurotic unless its inner structure is changed. Yet is is used for a good purpose. We do not have to assume that all philanthropists are sincere lovers of mankind. People do a lot of good in this world out of quite unrespectable motives. The neurotic's wish to escape from doubt and turmoil can on occasion facilitate constructive decisions. A striking example of a neurotically founded impulse being made to serve health is a suicidal attempt that turns into a plea for help. The very thought of suicide can serve as protection if the person feels that he can bear his suffering because he knows he can stop it at any moment.

I see appropriation, or "perversion," as a very important mechanism, and, like repression, it is clearly a two-way street. It is used to a different extent by different people; those who use it extensively are extremely confusing to others. When in therapy the submerged healthy pattern comes more and more to the fore and the two systems struggle for dominance, each appropriates features that belong to the other and utilizes them for its own purpose. Other methods by which each system maintains and perpetuates itself will be discussed in Chapter 9.

Id and Ego in the Light of the Theory of Duality

The hypothesis of dual organization of personality establishes a distinction which I consider more basic than the ones between conscious and unconscious or between id, ego, and superego. It cuts across the other divisions and seems to me to make for greater clarity, especially in ordering one's observations of the therapeutic process. Needless to say, the distinction between the conscious and the unconscious remains important; no adequate description of personality dynamics and of the process of therapy can be given without taking into account the consequences of vital processes reaching consciousness, or remaining unsymbolized. However, as I tried to show in discussing repression, the dynamic factors reside in the two systems qua systems; both of them are organizations of the total personality process and consequently both include conscious and unconscious factors.

With regard to the structural division of personality, though I can see good reasons to justify it, I have found that the more I made use in my thinking of the idea of dual organization, the less I had occasion to think in terms of id, ego, and superego. In therapeutic work it is a great advantage for the therapist to be able to talk to his patients essentially in the language of concepts in which the therapist actually thinks, even though translated into the vernacular. I have found that formulations based on my theory made very good sense to the patients, meeting, as it were, their own concepts. On the other hand, I have found the concepts underlying the traditional structural division to be useless in therapeutic conversation, and sometimes worse than useless.

In trying to see how the psychoanalytic concepts could be meaningfully fitted into the cross-cutting framework of my hypothesis so as to retain their theoretical usefulness, I did not have much success with the concepts of id and ego. Since each of the two systems postulated by me organizes the *total* content of personality, in each system id, ego, and superego would have to be present. Such doubling of concepts would make sense only if one could ascribe clear-cut differences to each of these three structures, depending on whether each forms a part of the system organized by the confident or by the pessimistic and uncertain expectations. This cannot be done in the case of id and ego without violating their conceptual properties. But if one does not change its properties, the concept of id is altogether incompatible with the holistic point of view. In thinking about personality in terms of its most general trends, which ramify down to specifics, I do not assign a special position to those functions that are physiologically fixed, and even less do I consider them the basis from which all other functions derive. These functions are dynamically important, particularly because of the absolute necessity of satisfying these vital needs, but still they are only a few of the many manifestations of personality. Consequently I can only think of the id as either this special group of functions, or as a totality of functions in a very primitive early state of organization.

The question of how the concept of ego could be related to my system is the most obscure. Ego seems to be, first, the embodiment of the organizational principle as such, the totality of the organizational aspects of all human functions. In this meaning ego participates equally in the two systems I postulate. Both the system of health and the system of neurosis can be strongly and articulately organized, and in both this organization functions also as a defense against the other system. On the other hand, the function of reality testing, also ascribed to the ego, finds a greater development in the system of health than in that of neurosis. Finally, as a source of motivation ego seems to embody the trend to increased autonomy.

Superego: Duality of Conscience

The concept of superego has a more concrete and coherent content; I can think of this structure as a special subsystem of personality without violating either the concept of superego or that of a system. Within the framework I have outlined, the concept of superego would have to be doubled, and I feel that there is a sound empirical basis for doing just that. There is a healthy conscience without which the person is sick, a psychopathic personality, and there is an unhealthy one which makes the person spend his life worrying whether he has stepped on the cracks in the pavement.

It seems to me that in the classical psychoanalytic formulation of the superego, the problem of the healthy conscience is not touched upon.

The superego appears as a central accident, a necessary evil; it is not inherent in human nature as such but is an extraneous result of social development, something required not by the individual but only by society. Actually it boils down to fear of punishment or ostracism. The assumption is that, except for this ever-present fear, everyone would break the Ten Commandments and obey only the 11th: Thou shalt not get caught. Even when the commands and the punishment for breaking them have been internalized, the superego still represents an external factor, the society as mediated by the parents; it is not an organic growth. In its extreme forms this kind of conscience, which flourishes in neurosis and is never totally absent in health, implies the conception of a power that represents the *mythical enemy*, an alien and arbitrary force, an irrational authority. The "superego rules" that emanate from this power become idols or frightening demons.

There is no doubt that fear of punishment lives in all of us and that many of the "moral principles" we feel to be our own originate in this fear, but that is not all there is to conscience. There is another aspect which does not depend on swallowing something that has been forced down one's throat by society, but expresses certain value attitudes inherent in human nature. I derive this factor from the trend toward homonomy, from the need to belong and to identify with persons, groups, or causes. Guilt generated by this conscience may be termed "real guilt." It is not fear but an emotional reaction to having acted against somebody or something with which one is genuinely identified; such an act of disloyalty is also an offense against one's own integrity. The pattern that underlies the experience of real guilt, in spite of the wide cultural variation of its content, is a universal expression of a universal human trend. When acceptance of the "superego rules" is founded in the homonomous trend, they function (no matter how nonsensical their content) as expressions of the person's own ethical attitudes, and any offense against them is guilt laden.

A patient told me of a childhood event about which he felt most ashamed and guilty. He was Jewish and lived in a neighborhood where he was exposed to some very painful scenes in the street. There was an old man in the neighborhood who made his living by teaching Hebrew and who was apparently intellectually limited or peculiar in some other way. He was the target of non-Jewish children who often made fun of him. Once my patient was caught in a crowd of these children as they were shouting, "Jew, Jew" and throwing stones at the old man, who was running away crying. My patient panicked and in his anxiety started running and shouting with the children. He was closely identified with the Jewish group and with certain features of Judaism, but on this occasion his fear

got the better of him and he acted against the things he was devoted
to.

This anecdote illustrates the central phenomenon of real guilt: the
betrayal of somebody or something one loves. This is also a self-betrayal, because one acts not in line with one's genuine values but out of
one's weakness, one's fear. Usually hate is also involved—in the case I
have described there was not only love but also anger against the
community which exposed its members to threat—but the presence of
a positive tie is the necessary precondition of real guilt. An act directed
against somebody who is an enemy, and nothing but an enemy, would
not arouse guilt. But real people rarely live up to the qualifications of
the mythical enemy. Even in those whom we hate we can usually see
something that represents a possibility for human contact, and we can
consequently feel a measure of guilt toward them.

Guilt based on love is radically different from guilt based on fear of
retaliation, but in many instances the two are so closely interwoven
that it is useful to have a term which covers the whole complex. Both
kinds of guilt feelings can be called superego functions; the term conscience, however should be reserved for the pattern which underlies
the experience of real guilt. To disentangle the different roots of guilt
feelings is not simple. In every course of therapy a great deal of effort
must be devoted to this task and to working out the problems of
conscience and guilt. Even if someone feels guilty because he engages
in masturbation, it is not enough to try and reassure him, e.g., by
giving him statistics of its incidence or other pertinent information.
The correct information should be given, and it does bring relief, but
that is not the end of the story. Before getting this information the
patient was convinced that he was doing something evil and yet he
continued doing it, so there is still the issue of guilt to deal with, the
issue of having acted against the wishes and beliefs of those whom one
loved.

In therapy it is necessary to disentangle the various aspects of guilt
because one cannot treat all guilt indiscriminately by assuaging it, passing it off as unimportant, or citing extenuating circumstances. We have
the double task of freeing the patient from pangs of "conscience"
which are ultimately based on irrational fears, and of awakening and
strengthening his real conscience, making him feel real guilt. This
second goal is fully as important as the first, if not more so. The
patient's insight, accompanied by a feeling of guilt, into the nature of
his neurosis as a self-betrayal and a betrayal of others is a necessary step
in the development of his motivation for reconstructing his life.

The Dual Source of Anxiety

In conclusion a word about the position of anxiety within the dual organization of personality. Anxiety arises not only out of the state of isolation but also out of anticipating such a state. Consequently anxiety will appear whenever the dominant organization is threatened with dissolution, regardless of whether the threat is directed against the pattern of neurosis or of health. This is not as paradoxical as it may sound, if one recalls that both systems aim at fulfilling the basic human trends and are perceived as ways toward that goal. Although only in the healthy pattern are human purposes actually being realized, the entrenched neurotic pattern nurses the dim hope that they may be realized yet. A threat to the position of dominance of either pattern by its underdeveloped or subordinated alter-system is a threat to the only known path away from isolation and toward fulfillment. Hence anxiety, though phenomenologically undistinguishable, can arise from either of the two opposite camps. Freud's hesitancy and change in his formulation of anxiety is significant in this connection: there is good empirical basis for equating anxiety both with the (transformed) repressed content and with the reaction of the repressor to the threat of the repressed.

Anxiety signals the existence of a threat to whichever system is dominant, and leads to the enhancement of its self-protective measures. Thus it serves indiscriminately as a safeguard of the status quo. Those for whom the dominance of the pattern of health has been a hard-won position often find that sensitivity to anxious feelings is the best sentinel against the re-encroachment of the neurosis and an effective reminder that only challenges husband confidence. When the issue is to exchange neurosis for health, little progress can be made if anxiety is quickly allowed to initiate defensive measures which serve to protect and consolidate the old pattern. To collaborate with anxiety in this case means to make our first enemy our last ally.

9. The Genesis of Duality

In the present chapter the genesis of neurosis, which was briefly outlined in Chapter 6, will be pursued more systematically and compared with normal growth in the light of the theory of universal ambiguity. We want to know how the neurotic organization issues from the original healthy one, reaches the position of dominance, and maintains itself in this position. The question of how this development can be reversed and the dominant neurotic organization can be made latent will be discussed in the chapters dealing with therapy.

Traumatization: The Formation of a Neurotic Nucleus

The formation of the neurotic pattern is initiated by traumatic circumstances or events. Here I shall describe the process of traumatization in a generalized way; some of the frequently occurring traumatic situations will be listed in the chapters dealing with the genesis of specific neurotic patterns. By trauma one usually means some harmful influence, a contravention, either in the form of a positive insult or of a deprivation. A contravention is indeed a necessary condition of a trauma but not a sufficient one. Since we constantly have to deal with a heteronomous environment indifferent to our needs, the whole course of life, starting with the process of birth, abounds in contraventions; not all of them by any means have traumatizing effects, even when they involve some suffering. Trauma is a biospheric event, an instance of interaction between the world and the organism, and it can be defined only in terms of its outcome; important is not what it is but what it does, and this is not easily predictable. An event must be regarded as traumatic if it has led to the formation of a neurotic nucleus. On the basis of retrospective studies we can formulate the conditions that seem to be necessary to make contravening events pathogenic. To summarize in advance the discussions that follow: *a trauma is a persistent interference with the person's basic pattern of life which cannot be managed by him in accord with this pattern.* It leads to a distortion of the healthy pattern and eventually, through a generalization of the experience, to the emergence of a competing pattern governed by diffident attitudes toward himself and the world.

To become traumatic a condition must be either persistent or repetitive—not a passing accident but a situation that does not disappear by itself and about which something must be done. A hungry child can resort to sucking his thumb or exhaust himself by crying until he falls asleep, but the condition of hunger is there until *adequately* dealt with. Second and most essential, a traumatic event represents an interference not with something minor but with some condition necessary for the unfolding of the basic pattern of life—the exercise of self-determination and the achievement of belonging. The threat must be felt to this pattern as such, or to a part so important in the total scheme that destruction of this part is equivalent to the collapse of the whole; this includes the vital parts of the environment, in particular the persons with whom the child feels he belongs. In each trauma an existential problem is involved, a problem resulting from the basic structure of human life and therefore recurring throughout life though in different forms at different stages.

If the child's life is to continue on its true course, the threatening situation must be somehow managed and changed. The all-important issue then is whether or not the child proves able to solve the problem within the framework of his confident attitudes without puncturing his image of the world as fit for life and his image of himself as valuable and fit for the world. His ability to assimilate the disturbing event in this way will depend both on the nature of the event and on the child's own level of development, in particular on his level of confidence in meeting new situations.

Early frustration, or insufficient gratification, of the child's vital needs—for food, warmth, comfort—can become highly traumatic precisely because urgent need for relief is combined with his inability to do anything about it. Even objectively harmless situations can become major traumas in the absence of ways to cope with them.

A case in point is the patient who in the first year of his life was traumatized by an attempted abrupt change from bottle to cup feeding and a prolonged struggle about it, which he eventually won by dint of a hunger strike. The attempt need not have been traumatizing if the child had previously learned in play to like and to handle the cup and had developed a greater reliance in his mother's ministrations, or if the mother had been less rigidly insistent on complete immediate change. As it was, this episode of panic all but destroyed his trust in his mother, perpetuated the fear of starvation, and led him to place all his reliance in an aggressive self-damaging struggle to wrench sustenance from a depriving world—the device that had "saved his life" on the early occasion when bottle and survival were one.

The fact that traumatization depends so much on the child's view of the event has important implications when the early traumas are reappraised in therapy. The child's interpretations are not arbitrary; if he is really not loved by his parents he is likely to feel, correctly, that they are neglectful or hostile. Yet his perspective excludes many factors, such as the objective necessities that determine the actions of adults, and drastic misinterpretations can occur because of this. In particular, the child's feeling that what was threatened in a given situation was a value for which there could be no substitute is open to later correction. There is no alternative for the basic human pattern as such, but there definitely are alternatives for the concrete items in which this pattern is embodied; these substitutes are easily accepted if they are felt to have the same meaning, the same positional value in the overall pattern. Among the most important therapeutic insights are the discoveries that "there was another way." What was threatened and had been stubbornly pursued ever since was not a basic irreplaceable value but a specific expression with a range of equivalents, different at different age levels. Such insights may go a long way in relaxing the neurotic's insistence on limiting the acceptable satisfactions to the particular ones that were threatened by the early traumatic events.

Properly seen a trauma is not something that happens once, leaves the person in a damaged state, and disappears from the scene. Not having been able to master the problem at the time, the person is still struggling with the traumatic situation or with the current situations that have some resemblance to it. His fixation on the content of the earlier levels is one of the factors that make these attempts futile. The neurotic problem is an unfinished business which in its neurotic formulation cannot be finished. For instance, attempts to satisfy an adult's needs for affection through oral activities are a forlorn hope. But futile as the struggle is, these repeated attempts express the hope that a solution of the existential problem is possible, that a "right," system-consistent answer can be found.

Generalization as a Precondition of Neurosis

It is implicit in the preceding discussions that no event can be considered traumatic unless its effects on later behavior are generalized beyond the particular situation in which they originated. Many situations that have frightened the child result in a persistent fear of objects connected with that situation—e.g., fear of dogs after having been bitten—without more far-reaching effects. Generalization is indeed a condition of traumatization, essential for the genesis of neurosis; it is involved both in the formation of the neurotic organization and in the shift by which it gains dominance.

Generalization is present whenever a single object or event is seen by the person as representative of a much broader condition or issue. Being let down by a person in whom one had absolute trust may destroy not only the specific belief that this particular person is trustworthy but also the general belief in the goodness of people. Still, an adult need not be completely overwhelmed by such an experience because he has some capacity to distinguish between the specific and the general. This is not the case with the young child whose experience is global and undifferentiated. He cannot make the distinction. The role of this cognitive incapacity in the genesis of neurosis can hardly be overestimated. For the child, the home and the people in the home are more than the representatives of the world; they actually are his *whole* world. The specific *is* the general. The consequences of this lack of differentiation are far reaching. Since the mother fills the world, her actions teach the child that such is life and such is the world. If he feels rejected, his feelings, translated into adult language, are not "my mother rejects me," but "God has forsaken me, humanity has cast me out." If he is hemmed in by taboos, he feels that the world is against him, that the exercise of his will is punishable as such. If traumatic experiences occur before the child's world has expanded and become differentiated, generalization is not something that happens after the event, separately from the cognition of the concrete situation. It is built into the experience and quickly leads to a pessimistic pattern of expectations not just with regard to the mother but to life as a whole—not a partial but a total pattern.

Negative experiences made in later stages need not have effects of the same size, because they are not always generalized and can remain partial patterns. Thus the presence of a destructive adult in a large family, if he is only one among many, need not determine the child's image of the adult world. As the child grows, his world expands to include much more than the early situations, but the early pattern still determines his total view of the world. In the advanced neurosis of an adult the early generalizations, as distinct from the later ones, may be recognizable in the patient's indiscriminate approach to all people and all situations with one emotional attitude, such as, e.g., "You have to take care of me."

This conception of early generalization is essential for understanding the conditions of success or failure of later corrective experiences and particularly for understanding the role of transference. A child who had felt rejected early in life may later develop a well-founded conviction that his mother actually loves him; this may improve their relationship but will not change his neurotic outlook, save perhaps in those infrequent cases where she has continued to be practically his whole world. Usually, as the person's experiences grow the mother becomes just one person among many, even though retaining vestiges of her previous significance. The acceptance by her as an individual cannot undo the rejection that came from her as the primal mother equated with the universe. Similarly, someone whose food intake was threatened early in life is not basically reassured by a later abundance of food; only a partial function is satisfied, not the all-inclusive one that was threatened. This incongruity is the basic reason for the failure of continued attempts to solve neurotic problems. In seeking the affection of a particular person the patient is driven by the hidden wish for reconciliation with the primal mother, for acceptance by the one who was all in all. His attempts may be frustrated by his ineffective approach, but even if the concrete goal is attained, the affection received necessarily proves to be that of one particular and imperfect person and leaves one's need unfulfilled. The patient may feel, "Is that all?" He may then embark on a struggle to make the relationship into something different, or else devalue it and renew his search. Sometimes the ideal of finding *the* one truly "representative" person is replaced by that of acceptance by "everyone"—an equally impossible plan.

Transference in therapy is to be viewed primarily not as an emotional mistaking of the therapist for one's real parent (though this also occurs), but as investing him with the significance of the *primal* parent, experiencing him almost as one's whole world. Transference in this sense is manifested less in the specific reactions to the therapist than in the overwhelming emotional importance which for a time he acquires for the patient. The patient's interpersonal experiences in transference—and only in transference—may have a powerful corrective effect because their all-inclusive, totalistic character matches that of the early traumatic experience. If the patient does not experience the therapist as representing the "world"—whose acceptance he craves —or if he succeeds in quickly divesting him of this function, he will be compelled to explain away or discard as unimportant the acceptance and care he has received, or any other potentially corrective experience he has had with the therapist. The specific as such cannot affect the general.

The Emergence of the Neurotic Organization

In cases of traumas that do not date back to a very young age, the shift of attitude which results from generalizing is sometimes remembered by the patient. His descriptions reflect an awareness of the sweeping character of the change: "At that moment something completely changed in me," or "The bottom fell out of my life," or "Something died in me." A single crucial event occasionally has this effect. Usually, however, there will have been a series of events of similar structure; they were disposed of as exceptions, as single instances without general significance, and have remained unassimilated within the existing personality framework. The experientially traumatic event does not have to be weightier than the ones that preceded it, but may be merely the one that finally tips the balance. Even if not remembered, the change is probably always sudden although its preparation may be a long covert process. Once the shift has taken place many little instances that previously went unnoticed are revived and become effective as being consistent with the new orientation. Of particular interest are the cases in which the episodes recalled appear to have been actually well handled and assimilated at the time and did not have any traumatic effects; but a later occurrence of a severe trauma of an analogous structure seems to activate their potentially traumatizing aspects, so that they *now* become pathogenic and contribute to the establishment of the new set. This is an example of how the present can change the past when a past event gains a positional value in a new system.

Whatever its antecedents and timing, generalization is a crucial step in the genesis of the neurotic orientation. It brings together the experiences unassimilable within the healthy pattern and, by providing a new system principle, combines them into a coherent system which can grow and develop as such. At the least this step marks the "great divide," the beginning of the ambiguous structuring of personality with concomitant loss of unity and wholeheartedness, even if the pattern of health remains dominant. The existence of the second pattern will make itself felt at times—through brief periods of unaccountable moods, or symptoms of "pressure" and "intrusion." At the other extreme, the neurotogenic influences may have been so strong that the neurotic pattern assumes a dominant position at the very moment of its emergence as an organization. The resulting change of direction in the child's development need not be clearly noticeable either to others or to himself. The fact that the child's conduct of his life is now governed by a new set of assumptions is disguised by his continued adherence to his old beliefs although they become less vital, lose their roots, and are increasingly segregated within the surface layer of personality, the realm of the public and the conventional. The child may continue, e.g., to adhere consciously to his old belief in the goodness of his parents, and, together with the adults, view as strange and merely accidental such symptoms as slips or "irrational fears," which manifest his opposite conviction.

Under the pseudonormal cover the dominant neurotic pattern grows parasitically, drawing on the energy provided by the basic human trends and slanting these trends according to the neurotic set of assumptions. Implicit fantasies elaborating these assumptions limit experience, make unrealities plausible, and increasingly falsify the person's behavior and outlook. Various solutions of problems are tried and fail or prove inconsistent with each other; the attempts at correction or harmonization result in new tensions and conflicts. This process of elaboration of the neurotic superstructure may or may not be clearly reflected in changing directions of behavior or in consciousness. Usually only some of its turning points emerge into awareness. The submerged healthy pattern has little chance to grow and develop even though experiences are made and stored away by the person that might reinforce it and restore it to dominance. The neurotic's "growth" is not a progressive organic development of personal dispositions. It consists in change and growth of defenses, or else takes place by inorganic accretion: by imitation, role playing, pretense, by "borrowing" without assimilating.

The Healthy Growth

Let us now return to the starting point of the neurotic development —the potentially traumatic event—and trace the process that results in the entrenchment of the healthy pattern. The potentially traumatic event is usually a situation new to the child, one with which he has not learned how to deal, but it is not necessarily unmanageable to him at his given developmental level. If the child has not been traumatized previously and his level of confidence is high, he will grapple with the problem, internally and externally, and may emerge with a constructive solution, eliminating the threat to his basic pattern of life. The healthy solution, as distinct from the pathogenic, does not result in a distortion of his image of the world. What is even more important, is that it permits the child to remain himself, neither undermining his positive self-image nor making him falsify his feelings and adopt pretenses; he need not resort to roundabout ways of making life appear possible. A difficult novel situation solved or assimilated in this way necessarily means growth, i.e., development taking place in a system-consistent fashion. Thus dangers and frustrations that have been mastered prove to have been challenges, stimulants of real growth, rather than traumas; even severe frustrations can have this effect. While it is important not to expose the child to overpowering situations, helping him to develop resourceful and confident attitudes is a better protection against traumatization than trying to eliminate all deprivations and obstacles.

Frustrations that have been assimilated constructively not only further the child's growth in general but also contribute to the shaping of his individuality. The selective development of one's potentialities is determined by environmental influences, by the person's significant experiences, and among these the disturbing experiences play an important part.

> Dr. Heiser*, in a book describing his adventures as a public health officer in various parts of the world, tells of the great flood that wiped out his home town and his family when he was still a youngster. Elsewhere in the book he acknowledges that, though many aspects of medicine attracted him, he was able to become truly enthusiastic only about activities designed to save lives on a large scale. The connection is obvious; the catastrophe of his youth did influence the conduct of his life, but it was handled constructively. Had he been unable to assimilate it, the same experience might have served to crystallize a destructive approach to life.

The constructive and the neurotic solution of the same situation often have elements in common. A person may have developed a great interest and aptitude for research because his childhood situation was a confusing one, and he had to search for order and clarity to free himself from the pain of confusion. The same situation might conceivably have led to voyeurism or to the general neurotic curiosity described in Chapter 8. Some theorists try to account for the common element of these solutions by viewing the activity of the scientist as a sublimation of an early voyeuristic impulse, which is assumed to be basic. In my conception the two solutions are discontinuous and radically different, because their common element, the wish to find out,

* V. G. Heiser, *An American Doctor's Odyssey*. Norton, New York, 1936.

has been organized by opposite sets of assumptions. While secret aggressive spying presupposes a hostile depriving world to be stolen from or combated, frank exploration has no anxious or hostile connotations and presupposes the person's right to know and competence to find out.

When problems have been solved consistently with the principles of confidence and self-acceptance that organize the self-system, these solutions do not result in distortions of the self, nor do they remain mere inorganic accretions. They result in a "skewing" of personality, which consists in the person's developing his perceptivity, thinking, and all his faculties in some directions more than in others. This creation of asymmetries, or gradients, serves to mobilize and direct the energy of the basic trends; the asymmetries constitute the person's individuality, his specific dynamics, and function as sources of powerful personal motivations. When the therapists talk about the "real self" of the patient, distinguishing it from his neurotic self and from his pseudonormal "surface," they usually mean something more individual than the basic human trends in abstracto and something more limited and tangible than the person's total constitutional potentialities which can never be fully known or actualized. The "real self" includes that patterning of personality which has developed consistently with the system of health; the particular features that have resulted from the person's dealings with critical situations form a vital part of this pattern.

The constructive and the neurotic solutions may coexist in the same person. He may, e.g., handle one problem constructively and succumb to another, or handle differently two aspects or two instances of a complex situation, thus laying strong foundations for the development of both his individuality and his neurosis. Probably, such is the case of people who are both creative and neurotic. In therapy, when the patient relives the old traumas he may discover and choose the constructive way of dealing with the situation, thereby reshaping his past and turning handicaps into assets. When this happens, his individuality, his specific asymmetry, is not changed, but it now stimulates and shapes constructive personal growth rather than the growth of neurosis.

If the healthy pattern has become securely dominant through a constructive handling of most of the early problems, the person's further development meets with no insurmountable obstacles. In the absence of major crises healthy growth proceeds through expansion and differentiation under the reintegrating guidance of the basic personal pattern; new subpatterns emerge and are made more perfect and complete through movements directed toward "closing the gaps." When the healthy pattern is dominant growth is self-facilitating and rewarding.

The prepotent attitude of trust makes the person expect, and consequently perceive, new opportunities for gratification and expansion. Favorable circumstances are system consistent; there is no reason to fear them as traps that may lull one into a false sense of security. Consequently one utilizes one's opportunities and accumulates fulfilling experiences which reinforce the original premises.

No major obstacles block the person's path from one developmental stage to the next. When new satisfactions beckon, childish things are willingly put aside after having been thoroughly enjoyed. No unfinished tasks or unsolved problems keep the person tied to the past. The present is fulfilling and the future is also likely to be so. The person feels both free to move on and eager to move. Life is not a static Gestalt that once completed might become tensionless and remain in that state; its overall pattern is one of a process. The trend toward increased autonomy implies infinite progression; the trend toward homonomy involves progressive widening and deepening of communication. The forms of social, interpersonal, ideological integration accessible to an adult embody this trend more completely than the forms typical of the earlier levels. Yet, maturity should not be made an ideal as such. Growing into full membership of one's society and culture requires a specialization of interests. Only too frequently this results in a narrowing of the person's field of vision to what is pertinent to practical action; he loses the openness to impressions that is the charm of the child. Still, in a healthy life the gains of moving ahead outbalance the losses, and movement does not destroy continuity. Since the changes are system consistent, the healthy person feels his life course to be unified and unambiguous. His life makes sense to him both prospectively—as he first expands, then focuses his activities—and in retrospect when he can feel he has lived fully and has made the most of his life.

Growth and Anxiety

The predominance of the healthy pattern does not eliminate all the crises and anxieties that inevitably accompany growth. Abandoning the familiar for the unknown always involves risks. When the changes are far reaching or precipitous, they are bound to arouse anxiety. The view that growth is inseparable from anxiety is shared by practically all thinkers who have substantially contributed to our understanding of anxiety: Kierkegaard, Goldstein, Rank, Fromm, and many others. The anxiety felt at the prospect of the dissolution of one's current mode of being has been related by some to the fear of final dissolution, of which human beings have the certain foreknowledge; since growth requires the breaking of old patterns, willingness "to die" is a precondition of living.

In my conception, the human fear of death is identical with the fear of not being able to live humanly, and the anxiety inherent in growth must be viewed in the same light. In breaking up the current organization of one's life, one faces isolation. What is unknown is alien, and the chances of relating oneself to this unknown through participation and mastery are less certain than in the familiar sphere that is being left behind. That is why in times of major changes, for instance in adolescence, the pattern governed by anxious expectations often comes to the fore, reviving both the earlier traumas and those past situations that now demand new solutions. These disturbances subside after the anxieties have been faced and new competencies and integrations achieved. Anxiety connected with growth becomes overwhelming only if growth requires total change, such as the breaking up of the entrenched neurotic orientation. Excessive fear of death is often a correlate of the neurotic fear of growth and change. Growth crises occurring within a firmly established healthy pattern are minor in comparison. Hope and the lure of the new outweigh the doubts, confident action reduces the risks, and if environmental conditions are also propitious, anxiety need be no more than transitory and slight.

Pseudogrowth

The neurotic finds himself in a very different position. The unfinished tasks, a constant source of tension, keep him glued to the past; one can move wholeheartedly into a new phase of life only after the current phase has been satisfactorily completed. Behind his defensive shell he fights the old battles of his childhood, over and over again, undeterred by repeated failures and seemingly oblivious of all the changes that have taken place in the meantime. In his anxious isolation from the world the neurotic feels the new to be utterly alien; expecting little good from himself and the world and valuing security above all, he is compelled to cling to the familiar. Unfulfilling as it may be, the familiar is an island of safety amid the dangers of the unknown. Life in the family may be far from happy, but at least one knows what to expect. To meet the developmental challenges adequately the neurotic would have to change radically, to break out of his protective confines. No wonder he dreads the crucial developmental changes.

This feeling is expressed and elaborated by the younger patients in different ways. They may feel that time and life are rushing past and leaving them behind, anxious and alone. They may be consciously afraid of proving inadequate in the adult's role, or they may rationalize their reluctance to grow up by viewing adult life as burdened with humdrum tasks and devoid of all joy. "What is there to look forward to? A nine to five job." "I don't want to be just a wife and mother and sit there like a lump!" In some patients the idea of growing up is closely linked with that of death, each developmental step, or each passing year, being dreaded as a step to the grave.

The neurotic's wish to stay as he is does not, however, remain unopposed. Like every human being he has the intrinsic urge to grow and expand. Nor can he completely ignore the social pressures that do not allow one to remain in swaddling clothes in an obvious manner. Caught between two conflicting forces, the person resorts to characteristic neurotic methods of dealing with his dilemma, methods which lessen the pressure but do not resolve the problem. Utilizing and reinforcing his pseudonormal façade, he goes through the motions of normal growth, but by using neurotic devices he robs the experience of its impact and goes through these changes unchanged. Outwardly, this person passes through the usual problems and activities of childhood, adolescence, adulthood—completes his schooling, chooses an occupation, may marry and have children—but all this remains somehow unreal and insubstantial, lacking in wholeheartedness and emotional depth. It is as if he were playing at all these roles, much as a child imitates adult activities in play.

The methods used to evade growth, to divest the new of its newness, vary in different types of neurosis, but they all have the same function and the same effects. The evasion serves to protect the person from intense anxiety, but it also gives a hollow farcical character to his whole life and is itself a source of anxiety. Patients often feel much younger than they are, not the equals of their contemporaries; they may feel old and weary and yet immature; they never feel adult. The patient vaguely feels that in acting as a doctor, or a lawyer, or the head of a family he is merely pretending and that his bluff may be called any time.

It is hardly correct to conceive of neurosis as a regression to earlier developmental levels; fixation is a much more meaningful concept. The neurotic has never progressed to the later stages, except in a peripheral, proforma fashion. The so-called regressive phenomena occur when the surface layer of pseudomaturity has been broken through, or peeled off, uncovering the underlying immature patterns and their specific contents.

The Maintenance of Neurosis

No matter how one explains the origins of neurosis, the central question for any theory that is meant to be used in therapy is this: how does it happen that the new experiences, the widening of the personal world, do not correct the early assumptions? Why is the new wine always poured into the same old skins? We need to understand this if we are to help to transform stationary life into forward-moving life. The basic reason, implicit in all the preceding discussions, is the holistic nature of neurosis, its character of a *system*. If only a limited item were carried over, one would indeed expect the early assumptions to be corrected and discarded as nonsense in the light of widened experience. What persists, however, is not a partial attitude but an overall organization of experience which, like all organized dynamic wholes, tends to grow and to become perfected in accordance with the principles of system dynamics. One can only "grow into" an established neurosis, not grow out of it. In the following paragraphs I shall specify this statement by reviewing the specific devices—many of them the familiar "defense mechanisms"—through which neurosis is maintained and perpetuated. Similar devices are used by the established system of health, with essential modifications due to the different framework.

The capacity for new experience, even in the most favorable case, is extremely limited since, in neurotic and healthy people alike, the new impressions do not fall on a *tabula rasa*. If anything new enters a system at all it does so in a system-consistent fashion, by occupying a position within it; this means that the new is either incorporated into the existing pattern or excluded.

This basic limitation manifests itself first and foremost in the *selectivity* of our attention and perception, which has been well studied in psychology. We register only a small part of our environment, and in this quantitative limitation selective principles are at work. We react to the elements that conform to our expectations, disregarding the rest. A person who is afraid of cancer or heart disease can truthfully say that they are on the increase, and can base this statement on what he has read in the papers or heard people discuss. Items that confirm and justify his fearful outlook are taken in, while those that contradict it are overlooked. Anyone who has done scientific research knows how keenly facts consistent with his pet theory are noticed. The excluded experiences are not annihilated. A new insight, scientific or personal, will revive a multitude of facts previously disregarded or forgotten that are consistent with the new pattern; one is surprised to find how much one knows. We all possess an immense store of unorganized experience, but our lives are directly affected only by what we organize. Consequently we do not merely imagine living in a certain kind of world but actually do live in it, and increasingly so, because what happens to us is apt to be determined by our attitudes. Since the world is a mixture of favorable and adverse conditions, we might say that everyone lives in the sector of the world that he himself has selected as fitting his predilections.

Selectivity, however, does not always suffice. The many experiences that contradict the system but are too striking to be simply disregarded are dealt with in one of two other ways, each of which has many subvarieties: they are either *transformed* so as to be more consistent with the reigning system principle or kept from becoming effective by *segregation*. Transformation is possible, because there is no fact in the vital sphere of personality except the interpreted fact. In particular, people's actions (including one's own) can be assigned different meanings depending on the interpretation of motives. In this way interpersonal events can be easily distorted to fit the preconceived scheme. Even impersonal events can be made to change their meaning. A pessimist may inherit a million and think only of the taxes and worries: the lucky ones, he feels, are those whose limited income or large family greatly reduce their taxes. Things may look fine, but, "Don't praise the day before the sun sets," "Don't forget what happened to X in a similar case." Through invention, rationalization and other devices, the persistent facts are twisted and transformed so that positions can be assigned to them in the existing overall pattern.

The second way to deal with a striking system-inconsistent factor is to eliminate it or at least relegate it to a peripheral region distant from the system's vital core. The term "segregation" can be used for both cases. A simple way to eliminate such a factor is to suppress it, to follow the ostrich policy, "I won't think of it." More radically, the same purpose is achieved by repression. In both cases "placing outside" means placing outside of consciousness. Some people are so afraid of not being able to deal with anything that may come up that they use this method at the least provocation; no wonder then that they are often helped just by daring to take a second look.

The differentiation of all experience into subject and object, with the line of demarcation permitting of no rigid definition, makes it fairly easy to get rid of an inconsistent feature by simply removing it to the other side of the line. A personal characteristic or an event can be placed outside the self-system by not being acknowledged as part of oneself or as a result of one's own activities, but referred to external circumstances. Externalization is not limited to negative features. One can keep unaware of one's hostility, or justify it, by seeing the other as the aggressor, one can blame one's failures on bad luck, but one can also preserve one's negative self-image by ascribing one's successes to good luck and one's acceptance by others exclusively to their kindness. Externalization or projection is especially conspicuous in psychoses, and not in paranoid pictures alone. When the basic organization of experience into subject and object is severely disturbed, even sensations produced by bodily processes can lose their ego reference and be attributed to external agents.* Within the neurotic organization, ascribing a larger than warranted part of causation to "fate" or to others serves to perpetuate the image of personal helplessness and an overpowering world.

Neurotic attitudes can also be maintained and defended by distortions in the opposite direction, i.e., by an overemphasis on the self as the source of events. We need only refer to the role played in the genesis of neurosis by the ascription of all "badness" to oneself for the sake of preserving the image of good parents. Within the established neurotic pattern spurious guilt feelings are often perpetuated by magnifying one's own part in the production of negative events.

Instead of being repressed or projected, a factor may be segregated and deprived of significance by being relegated to the periphery. A fact inconsistent with our theory can be regarded as an "exception," whatever that may mean. In the history of science many facts that eventually led to significant discoveries had been pushed aside for a long time and attributed to errors of observation, or to an uncontrolled variable, such as an impurity in a chemical substance used in the experiment. In the personal sphere, one may register a newly discovered aspect of one's competence with great astonishment, or be excessively touched by friendliness, thus confirming the *exceptional* nature of these experiences. Since emotions are evaluations, symbolizations of values, depriving a factor of personal significance is typically reflected in a lack of adequate feeling. Faced with a crucial personal issue, the neurotic says in effect, "Yes, it is there, but so what. It does not matter, I don't feel anything about it." Or he may invalidate some important personal resolve by deciding that since he can do it he need not try now. (This

* A. Angyal, "The Experience of the Body-Self in Schizophrenia." *Arch. Neurol. and Psychiat.* 34:1029–1053, 1936.

is the time for the therapist to ask, "If not now, when?" or in other ways to remind the patient that not an abstract issue but his life is at stake.) Another method of isolating a major personal issue is to shrink it into a localized item, e.g., into a circumscribed neurotic symptom. This method often backfires, because the localized issue may cause enough concern to make the patient miserable; the artificial reduction does not prevent it from swelling again to major proportions. Even so, focusing on an isolated issue, such as a minor habit or a minor physical imperfection, serves to deprive it of personal meaning and thus prevents it from threatening the existing orientation: it can be experienced as an outside factor or at least as a factor outside one's control.

To sum up, new experiences do not correct the neurotic pattern, because they are not given a chance to do so. The dominant pattern guides their selection and interpretation so that opposition is not heard, or is driven underground, or made ineffectual. With the alternatives thus disposed of, the neurotic pattern continues without competition as the only way of life vitally known to the person; the rest is hearsay, a dangerous uncharted territory.

The familiar way of life has its satisfactions. Although the assumptions on which the neurosis is founded would seem to make life unbearable, ways around obstacles have been developed, compromises and compensations that make life appear tolerable. The satisfaction of any need is pleasurable, whether it is healthy or not, and needs are determined by the structure of the system. If the essential issue in the system is safety, escape from danger is vital and pleasant, just as achievement of positive goals is pleasant in the other system. Whatever the neurotic may say, his pseudosatisfactions—the only ones he knows —are very close to his heart. Nor are they *merely* counterfeit. It should not be forgotten that the neurotic pattern can siphon off energy from the healthy pattern only because it is a derivative of the healthy pattern, and both are ultimately governed by the same basic trends. If the neurotic expressions of these trends are distortions of the healthy ones, they are also their distant approximations; a circumstance which is of major importance for therapy. The fact that the person is not fully aware of his neurotic pattern, which is obscured by the superficial, pseudonormal structure, also prevents him from perceiving the discrepancy between his life and his personal potentialities and, consequently, from realizing the magnitude of what is at stake. Change is therefore not recognized as an impelling necessity until the appearance of emotional upsets, unsolvable conflicts with the environment, or of painful and incapacitating symptoms. If the person's neurosis is stably integrated and he also maintains an external social adaptation through conformity or through keeping distance, he may be "successful" and "well adjusted" from the point of view of his culture though his life is crippled and dwarfed.

The Maintenance of Health

The dominant healthy pattern draws on the same organizational devices as the neurotic one, but the distribution and utilization of these devices are not the same. Selectivity is effective here too, and, as in neurosis, its power is great but not limitless. Not all negative features can be selectively excluded; blind optimism is not a part of the healthy pattern but a special defensive superstructure of the neurotic one. Although the healthy pattern carries within it the seeds of success, pain and disease will exist in every life as will frustration and loss. Injustice and ignorance are ubiquitous on the human scene and no one is insured against becoming their victim or their agent. System-inconsistent factors must be managed also by the pattern of health; the difference lies in the ways in which they are managed.

While in neurosis system inconsistency arouses anxiety, and must be speedily and summarily dealt with by denial, isolation, repression, etc., in health the inconsistency can be clearly perceived first. There is no reason for it not to be perceived when the system principle is confidence in one's own ability to live in the world as it really is. One can approach the disturbing feature realistically, explore it, and try to eliminate it or to make it as innocuous as possible. If one finds it to be of one's own making, one may seek to give redress to oneself as well as to others. Thus the incongruent elements can be transformed in reality rather than merely through fantasy and need not result in further inconsistencies and tensions—the difference between an apology and an excuse. In health, interpretations of other people's actions are usually closer to reality than they are in neurosis, but even when they are misconceptions, these interpretations have different practical effects; the response of a person whose neurotic attitude is misperceived as healthy by another may make this misperception true.

The distorting features of organizational devices are attenuated in the healthy pattern, so that we can call these devices "defense mechanisms" in one setting, "reality testing" in the other. Location within systems governed by different principles is what makes the difference between the mechanism of isolation and objectivity, between displacement and inventive thought, projection and empathy, suppression and postponement. When we say that the healthy person has a stronger ego than the neurotic, we do not refer to any inborn "strength" nor to a difference in intelligence or in any other partial function. The healthy person can "afford" a strong ego because he sees reality as an opportunity and a challenge rather than as a threat, and he meets challenges with confidence based on faith in himself. The same traits and abilities that are here successfully deployed to meet challenges are arranged into patterns of neurosis in the framework of diffident expectations.

10. The Pattern of Vicarious Living

In the preceding chapters we discussed neurosis in general. Our next topic is the variability of the general neurotic pattern, the ramifications that result in specific clinical pictures. Classification is always a problematic undertaking; whatever diagnostic categories one uses, one can rarely put a label on a given individual case without doing violence to it or neglecting some of its aspects. The majority of the patients seen in private practice today would probably have to be characterized as cases of "mixed neurosis." The label as such is of no importance in therapy; in fact, premature labeling can do harm. If, however, distinct clinical pictures can be shown to have also different dynamics, the identification of these patterns could yield valuable guidelines for the exploration and therapy of individual cases.

The Dimensions of Neurosis

Specific dynamic patterns are distinguishable in neurosis, but they cannot be viewed as forming separate, mutually exclusive classes in one or another of which all patients could be placed. I find it more useful to think of these patterns as dimensions of neurosis, i.e., as present in all cases, though in varying degree. If there should be, e.g., two or three essential dimensions to neurosis, one could characterize each case by finding its position on each of these continua. In some cases one dimension would be found to be the most prominent, in others all might be represented with equal strength. The term itself should not, of course, be taken literally; "dimensions" of neurosis are neither continuous nor measurable in the strict sense of the word. They are actually developmental sequences which include the causative factors, the dynamics these factors set into motion, and the manifold manifestations of these dynamics. Only insofar as each of these dynamic sequences can be more or less prominent in the development of a given case of neurosis can they be viewed as dimensions.

I have found it possible so far to identify two significant dimensions of neurosis, present in each single case; one of them is represented by hysteria, the other by the obsessive-compulsive neurosis. It should be noted, though, that the patterns I have in mind are not identical with the clinical pictures of hysteria and the full-blown obsessive-compulsive neurosis. These patterns can also be very prominent in cases where the specific clinical symptoms are lacking. I am not certain whether or not these two dimensions suffice for an adequate description of all cases of neurosis, but they are doubtless the most significant ones. I find that several clinical conditions not usually thought of as related either to hysteria or to obsessive-compulsive neurosis can be viewed as manifestations of one of these two basic patterns as I see them. Anxiety neurosis is not a dimension or a special type of neurosis; manifest anxiety comes to dominate the picture whenever the organizational and defensive devices used by the neurotic pattern break down. This can occur episodically in any type of neurosis. In this chapter I shall discuss the dimension related to hysteria, the one more thoroughly studied and better understood of the two.

The Classical Hysteria

If one opens a book on hysteria one can find a description of a clinical picture that in reality is quite rare. It is a condition characterized by conversion phenomena or by attacks of acute anxiety. The term "conversion phenomena," originally applied only to certain kinds of motor and sensory disturbances, is often extended today to cover a wider range of somatic symptoms; this extension is not entirely justified since somatic symptoms have a variety of origins. Originally the term was restricted, essentially, to motor disturbances, such as paralysis without neurological basis, and to certain sensory phenomena. The most frequent of these are anaesthesias, i.e., the loss of normal sensations of different kinds. In hysterical anaesthesias the distribution of insensitive areas does not follow the anatomical pattern of nerve distribution. Rather it follows some broad functional pattern, such as the hand and the foot in the so-called glove and stocking anaesthesias. There are other indications as well that no organic impairment is present. Besides conversion phenomena, the old pre-Freudian books describe a very dramatic symptom, the so-called grand hysterical attack. The patient throws himself back and forth in an arc, the head and the heels forming the end points of the arc, and thrashes about in a way superficially resembling an epileptic seizure. Charcot and his contemporaries talked about the grand attack as if it were a daily occurrence, but it is hardly ever encountered today. The grand hysteria has left the scene a long time ago. Sociological factors must have played a role here. Even in my youth patients with grand attacks were found in Europe only in small secluded communities and not in large urban centers; at the clinics we jocularly spoke of "peasant hysteria."

The conversion symptoms proper, such as hysterical blindness or hysterical paralysis, also are rarely seen today, but I think that these symptoms, unlike the grand attack, have not actually become less frequent. To account for their apparent decrease one must recall the historical development of the study of neurosis. Observations of hysteria were first made by physicians in an era when people came to them only with ailments that seemed to be physical in origin. A person who felt miserable but had neither physical complaints nor complaints about unusual experiences such as compulsions might have talked to a friend or a priest but would not have sought medical treatment. Consequently observations of the hysterical condition were focused on symptomatology almost exclusively, and, correspondingly, the goal of treatment was the removal of symptoms. Not until it was discovered that there was something much more important in neurosis than these circumscribed manifestations did people start coming with the disturbances that precede symptoms. This development which is fairly recent makes it difficult to assess whether there has been as much change in the phenomenology of hysteria as we now tend to assume. With many more people coming under observation today, the incidence of clear-cut hysterical symptoms may appear to be reduced merely because these cases form a much smaller proportion of all patients seen.

To describe adequately the dimensions of neurosis we have to deal not with symptoms in the narrow sense of the word, but with the underlying character neurosis, i.e., with the effects of the pathogenic factors and of the resulting implicit assumptions about oneself and one's world as they manifest themselves in personality traits, in the person's ways of dealing with the common problems of life. Viewed in this light the hysterical dimension is ubiquitous today, whether or not the specific symptoms have become less frequent. I shall describe its "pure form," i.e., the pattern approximated by people whose neurosis developed predominantly along this path. My observations have led me to subdivide the hysterical character neurosis into three categories, which might be termed *simple hysteria, hysteria with negativistic defenses,* and *borderline hysteria.* In my formulations of simple hysteria every clinician will recognize the familiar features of the hysterical character structure, but the situation is different in the case of the other two patterns. Neither of these two rather distinct clinical pictures, one of which is encountered quite frequently, has been explicitly related to hysteria; in my opinion, however, both show a typically hysterical dynamic structure.

Simple Hysteria

A particular form of neurosis can be best characterized by the method the patient uses predominantly in dealing with the problems of life. Although a person rarely uses only one method, his conduct of life has a characteristic style, a particular *leitmotif.* The cardinal method of adjustment in simple hysteria is the *method of vicarious living.* This method implies, on the one hand, a systematic repression of one's genuine personality characteristics and, on the other, an attempt to assume a substitute personality.

In earlier times when one spoke of repression one usually meant repression of single factors, e.g., repression of some tabooed impulse or wish or of a connection of ideas in the so-called complex. If one were to represent personality schematically by a circle, the repressed impulse would have to be depicted as a small, segregated area within the circle and the "complex" as a larger one. In the first case only one item of experience is repressed, one unassimilable idea or feeling; if it comes to the surface in some disguised form you have the hysterical symptom. In the second case, a more extended, more complexly organized area is repressed, which may give rise to a more complicated form of hysteria, manifesting itself in a variety of symptoms. The kind of repression I have in mind is a much more sweeping process, a wholesale indiscriminate discarding of not just some tabooed areas but of all one's genuine feelings, thoughts, and impulses. This situation may be represented graphically by two concentric circles whose areas almost coincide. The area within the inner circle represents the repressed original personality, the area between the two circumferences is the manifest "surface personality." This representation of the hysterical character neurosis is not limited to the spectacular cases of dual personality, which are quite rare. Each pronounced case of hysteria is a case of dual personality, even if the repressed personality is not well organized and not clearly manifest.

The three representations of the hysterical disturbance discussed in the preceding paragraph are not meant to stand for three different forms of hysteria or for three stages of its development from a symptomatic to a character neurosis. I believe that every hysteria *is* a character neurosis. Hysterical symptoms appear on this background; with their double function of expressing and suppressing the repressed content, they are specific manifestations of the split between the surface and the core personality. Therapeutic work on a focal conflict represented by the symptom may result in a general improvement when the character neurosis is not strongly developed, but this character structure is always there, if only in a minimal degree. The problem is simply to look further than the symptoms, and this is what in the past people were not trained to do; they thought not in terms of personality but in terms of illness.

In the following discussions we shall address ourselves to three issues: the origins of the sweeping repression, the methods of creating a substitute personality, and the ultimate effects of vicarious living on the patient's adaptation to life.

The suicidal repression of one's spontaneous nature is based on the person's hidden conviction that his naked self is unacceptable, worthless, and of no account; it must be hidden at all costs. How does a person arrive at such a conviction? Several kinds of experiences which frequently occur in the early history of these patients have the common effect of conveying to a child that the way he really is, the way in which he feels and thinks, is no good. These experiences are not specific to hysteria, and usually not one but several of them are present in the hysterical patient's background. I shall list some of the more frequently encountered ones.

Among the early situations most frequently uncovered in therapy are those that are apt to produce a sense of insignificance in the child, a feeling that he does not matter. Being belittled or disregarded, having one's wishes or contributions discounted, not being responded to by an emotionally withdrawn significant adult fall into this category. Although such situations doubtless are frequent, they are probably not as frequent as would appear from patients' reports for the following reason. As I shall develop later in detail, these people in adulthood invariably have a feeling that they are an empty shell, that they lack substantiality. Part of this feeling may be a direct outcome of the early experiences, but much of it is a cumulative consequence of the structure of the neurosis itself. These people feel empty because most of their real feelings are submerged and the surface personality somehow does not feel like an organic part of themselves—it is just a mask. "It is not," as one patient put it, "that I try to deceive. I am, myself, a walking deception." Because of this feeling of spuriousness, of lack of substance, the patients are likely to pick out from the past the instances when they were disregarded, treated like an empty space, told that they should be seen and not heard. Many of these experiences are factual, but the patients tend to select and overemphasize them because of their contemporary feelings of unimportance and vacuousness. For therapy this selective emphasis is of little importance and need not be taken up with the patient. It does no harm for him to feel that all the earlier experiences of being disregarded have contributed to the development of his present attitudes.

Another group of situations that occurs quite frequently and results in the child's developing a feeling of weakness or incompetence involves the oversolicitude of a parent. The parent is, for example, overanxious about the child's health, or too eager to protect him from all danger. A real or spurious overefficiency of the parent may have similar results. He or she appears as one who knows everything, can do anything, and this overwhelming superiority tends to belittle the child's own competence. Very often the parents are well-intentioned people, but by doing too much for the child they are telling him by implication that he—unlike other children—is incapable of handling things by himself. In other cases the parent tries to counteract his own feeling of inadequacy by stressing his superiority in relation to the child. In either case the child cannot escape the conclusion that he is weak, too incompetent to cope with a difficult and dangerous world, and must rely on parents for help and protection. The right to be oneself, to live one's own life, is traded in for safety. The child may also be intimidated if the parents always emphasize the dangerous aspects of existence.

All experiences which imply to the child that he is being abandoned can have far-reaching and traumatizing effects. Such feelings are aroused in the young child not only by permanent losses, e.g., the death or divorce of the parents or the departure of a loved nurse but also by temporary separation from the mother due to illness, work schedules, or the arrival of a sibling. As we learn from those of the patients' latent fantasies which tend to emerge in therapy, abandonment usually implies to the child his own worthlessness; he was abandoned because he was no good. In extreme cases the child may feel that there is something monstrous about him, that he should not have been born. He then has no recourse but to deny himself since he cannot live as a monster.

Perhaps the most widespread of undermining experiences that invite vicarious living are those that imply to the child that his parents or his teachers are not satisfied with him essentially *as he is* but want him to be different. This dissatisfaction can be conveyed in many ways: excessive criticism and punishment, ridicule, or unfavorable comparisons with others make the child assume that some basic defect in himself precludes his doing anything right. Too many "don'ts" make him feel that the things he most wants are forbidden and evil. He may secretly conclude that he is evil, and then attempt to escape this conclusion by renouncing the wishes he cannot have as a good child. The repression of the tabooed results. Since sexual impulses are among the most heavily tabooed it is not surprising that repression often centers on that area. Even more powerful are the effects on the child of being explicitly cast into a false role by the parents, and being faced with expectations he cannot fulfill without totally disregarding himself. The parent may, e.g., praise him as a diligent student, a scholar who has no interest in childish pranks and play, and thus give him a powerful motive to suppress his genuine wishes and to cultivate a false front. This bribing is the counterpart and the complement of the influences that result in repression; the parents ascribe to the child not just "purity from evil" but positive merits which are equally untrue. He pockets them, but he knows deep down that this self-image is false, that he is a fake. In measuring himself against the excessive parental expectations he secretly begins to feel utterly worthless.

In some instances all the circumstances of the child's life seem to conspire to cast him into a role unnatural for his age and temperament. This happens, for instance, when adult responsibilities are prematurely forced upon a child. If the oldest girl in the family has for some reason to take over the mother's role while still a child, she must, as it were, skip childhood. This means denying and discarding the genuine characteristics that are hers at that age. Another example of a situation militating against all the natural impulses of the child is a pervasive gloominess, a funeral-parlor atmosphere in the home. One would expect such situations to be rare, but they are found frequently in these patients' backgrounds. To be cheerful was considered, in one home, almost a sin and immediately brought a reprimand: "What are you laughing about, isn't there enough trouble?" Here again an attitude is forced upon the child that is foreign to him. It cannot be natural for him to be gloomy with such gloomy adults. Many other kinds of parental behavior reflect lack of understanding of children and of respect for their needs. Major traumatic experiences which are too terrible to acknowledge and sufficient in themselves to cause a deep and massive repression are relatively rare, but an accumulation of small daily occurrences which convey to the child that he is no good as he is can have equally far-reaching effects. Since parents' images of their children are biased by their own wishes and seldom coincide with what would come naturally to the child, it is not surprising that the hysterical dimension is practically a constant in the structure of neurosis.

Once the child has repressed his genuine characteristics, his real emotions and thoughts, he must create for himself a pseudopersonality in order to live in some way. By whatever method this substitute personality is built, it is a flimsy and vulnerable formation which, to be maintained, must receive constant validation from the outside. This is why, in vicarious living, relationships to people are of central importance, and why the patients so strikingly demonstrate the general human struggle for closeness, for acceptance by others. Yet they cannot accept affection, the thing they most want, as long as they have reason to feel that in wooing for acceptance they are selling a bill of goods—that it is the mask that is loved, not the person as he really is. The patient will therefore settle for a substitute, will seek the evidence of making some impression, even if it should be unfavorable.

We usually think of attention-getting as a secondary gain in neurosis, as the utilization for this purpose of symptoms or attitudes that originate in a different context. In hysteria, however, attention-getting has a central and primary function. The sense of not mattering gives rise to an urgent need to be noticed, to not be disregarded. Although being noticed is only the first step toward being loved, it is experienced by the patient as life-giving, as a confirmation of his existence. The deep sense of nothingness, of nonexistence is quite real in some of these patients; this feeling is the natural outcome of the wholesale repression of oneself and is only partly allayed or covered up by vicarious living. Since this basic uncertainty about one's existence is a notion contrary to common sense, the patient will not formulate it in these terms at the beginning of therapy, although he may complain of feelings of emptiness or of uncertainty about himself. At a later period, however, one may get striking formulations of this central theme of the mythology of hysteria. The patient may, e.g., observe for the first time that when greeted by acquaintances in the street he feels astonished, as if he did not expect to be visible to anyone. He is like the hero of Chamisso's story, the man who cast no shadow, a person so insubstantial that the sun's rays went right through his body. One of my patients flew into a rage every time someone did not hear what he had said and asked him to repeat it. Not to be heard meant to him not to be noticed, and this in turn meant that he did not exist. Once he told me that he had only two ways of meeting such a "slight": "Either I get so angry that I don't care what happens and blow up, or else I stutter, get anxious, and feel as if I were falling off the earth, as if I were disappearing or dying." The anxiety attacks of hysterical patients, their acute fear of death, erupt when their method of living is threatened and they are faced with the underlying feeling of nothingness.

The substitute personality which functions as a thin cover for this emptiness can be manufactured by various methods. The person may accept and cultivate the false role into which he was cast as a child or he may impersonate an actual person whom he admires. The surface personality may also be formed under the influence of some idealized conception, some image of absolute goodness which one tries to live up to; then one has to be perfect and without blame, disowning all impulses incompatible with the ideal. Often the substitute personality embodies a cliché of popularity that has the acclaim of society or of the group to which one belongs. In striving for this acclaim the person may discard all the individual characteristics that are his or her uniqueness and charm and become as stereotyped as the smiling girl on the billboard. Actual imitation is very frequent and may show itself in the therapy sessions. Often a patient can be observed to imitate the therapist's gestures or light a cigarette every time the therapist does. In fact the whole life history of hysterical patients is full of instances of imitation. It may also contain a great many changes since the patient may respond to new social situations by adopting new models, new ideologies, and even a new "personality."

There is one developmental stage in which the pattern just described occurs normally, namely early adolescence. The adolescent actually faces the situation similar to one the neurotic creates: something old is being left behind and something new is being formed. This situation of abandoning an old personality for a new one results in the adolescent's feeling that he is nowhere, that he does not know who he is. During this period of uncertainty when the adolescent tries to form a new personality, we find mechanisms at work that are similar to the hysterical ones, for instance, imitativeness. We all know what happens if a teacher with a tic is introduced into a classroom of adolescents. The adolescent may also try to form a new personality around some absolute ideal of behavior, resolving that he will always do this, or never do that. To live up to such an ideal of perfection may require an exorbitant amount of repression. In choosing a model or a friend the adolescent often favors people of high social status. Since he is uncertain of his own feelings and valuations his choices must be guided by public opinion, and he feels safest in allying himself with people of prestige. In all these and many other features adolescents present a picture similar to the hysterical one, but in the normal course of development this stage is outgrown as new feelings and situations become clarified and assimilated.

One of the most frequent forms of hysterical vicarious living, i.e., of living through something other than one's true self, is a specifically structured dependence on another person, usually selected in terms of strength and prestige. In this attachment, which is usually intense and tenacious, the other is needed not as one to whom to relate oneself but as one who will fill out the inner emptiness, the assumed nothingness. He is to lend substance and worth to the patient by teaching or guiding him, by giving incessant praise and reassurance, or by supplying the patient with opportunities to bask in the partner's reflected glory. It is then the other person who functions as the substitute personality, and the patient experiences him almost as part of himself. The continuous presence of the other is essential for the patient's existence; if it were possible he would not let him or her out of sight for a moment. Some of these patients, as soon as they are alone, feel as if they were dying; they have to keep the telephone going, have to be continuously in touch in order to feel that they exist.

This method of vicarious living often takes the form of obedient compliance with the wishes of the person who is essential for one's life. The same approach is used to establish new relationships; one seduces people to react to one as to a childish compliant person with whom all sorts of liberties can be taken. Occasionally the patient rebels against this self-denying compliance and tries to stand up for himself, but these outbreaks are seldom effective, being passed off by the other as a "bad day." Some patients attempt to bribe the other not so much by compliance as by active giving, by an overgenerous offering of personal services or presents. This apparent generosity hides the expectation of a return, a wish to obligate the other to give, and is often marked by unconcern for the real needs of the partner. In other cases active giving of any kind is strongly inhibited, as if the patient felt that giving was incompatible with his strong wish to receive, that if he gave he would not be given.

Compliance often goes hand in hand with cultivation of helplessness, which becomes to the patient a precondition of being loved, a legitimate reason for claiming attention and care. He clings to this claim even when it does not bring the desired results. This attitude expresses itself in invalidism, an insistence on being "sick," or in a constant wish to be the object of little services, or in a constant need to have someone listen to his complaints and offer sympathy and advice. In one way or another the patient manages to keep the other person preoccupied with himself.

In seeming contradiction with the patient's compliant and dependent attitudes, there is often also a violent impulse to dominate the other person. This impulse is not primarily an expression of the power motive, not a battle to decide who is boss; the need for domination stems from a real predicament. The patient's substitute personality, the person through whom he must live, remains external to him; he can leave and this would be disastrous. The patient wants to immobilize his partner out of dread that he or she may desert him and leave him with his nothingness. As a result of this fear he seeks to keep control over everything; nothing must remain hidden. The partner is not permitted any privacy, and his every thought must be known; if, e.g., the husband on coming home does not tell his wife everything that has happened at the office this is a major offense. The dread of losing the substitute personality, of being deprived of this symbiotic existence, results in an extremely possessive, devouring attachment which the patient may consider to be love.

Whatever form vicarious living takes, whether that of building up a pseudopersonality or of living through another person, this method does not, of course, solve the patient's problem. It results, instead, in a vicious circle. The more one lives vicariously, the greater the neglect of the genuine self and the more urgent the need for the compensating vicarious living. This still leaves the patient with a feeling of essential emptiness, the most common of initial complaints. Complaints about disturbed interpersonal relations are also prominent because of the frequent frustration of the patients' strivings to obtain the kind and degree of support they require. Other disturbances—not all of them mentioned by the patients—can be viewed either as concomitants of the pattern of vicarious living or as attempts to combat and disguise the emptiness in which it results. I shall briefly describe some of the most commonly observed manifestations.

The instability of the structure of vicarious living finds a striking expression in fear of exposure. This fear may be vague or painfully conscious, although the real reason of the fear is not clear to the patient. He is in fact afraid that his surface personality will be recognized as pretense and his inner insignificance exposed. This fear manifests itself in different ways. It may lead to extreme secretiveness, combined with a vigilant watching of others for signs of their response; secrecy may be maintained even about events that are a matter of public record and seem to be devoid of personal implications. A more frequent manifestation of the fear of exposure is a peculiar kind of shyness, an expectation of being ridiculed, which may hamper the person in the performance of any adult activity. It is as if the patient expected people to say, "What are you trying to do? Who do you think you are? You are incompetent, weak, a child, not an equal!" The guilt feelings of patients in whose neurosis the dimension of vicarious living is dominant usually have a similar structure; they consist largely of the fear of being exposed and shamed. The more genuine guilt feelings are suppressed, particularly by those whose pseudopersonality is built around some ideal of moral perfection and who therefore must maintain the fiction of being blameless.

Fear of exposure may also be the cause of a peculiar difficulty of communication encountered in some cases. Despite his disproportionate need to be heard and understood, the patient may make it extremely difficult for others to understand him by speaking inaudibly, by not staying with the topic, or in extreme cases by being almost silent or by talking merely in hints. He seems to live by the slogan: "Understand me without words." This may also have the function of testing the listener's interest and acumen. But this attitude, particularly if combined with the obsessive-compulsive uncertainty, may make the patient's hints so ambiguous as to defy a confident interpretation by even the most sympathetic listener, and this failure reinforces the patient's belief that he is not worth a serious effort at understanding. In some cases, before the person decides on entering therapy one has to allay his fear that his problems are insignificant and not worth the therapist's time and effort.

Various forms of work inhibition (a very frequent complaint of today's patients) derive from the dimension of vicarious living; they reflect the patient's uncertainty about his real self and his assumed roles. For example, the unconscious notion may prevail that to work successfully means not to be loved for one's own sake but only for what one does and achieves. Work inhibition also results when being helped is equated with being loved; not being able to work can serve as a demonstration of one's helplessness and an invitation to someone's constant concern and support. When this attitude is not too ingrained, as with some students in college counseling, a mere statement by the counselor that the student would be entitled to counseling help even if he were to get all A's serves to lift the inhibition. Many spurious conflicts arise if in the patients' perception various kinds of excellence, or various ways of obtaining recognition, are incompatible. Thus a girl who as a child had used scholastic success to compensate for her lack of personal popularity may still feel as an adult that professional success detracts from her femininity, and may sabotage herself for that reason. Very frequently work inhibition is used as a face-saving device; it reflects the fear of putting one's real self to a test after secretly concluding that one could not pass such a test. Finally, since hysterical patients need constant attention not only from others but also from themselves, they are sometimes unable to attend to anything that has no personal reference. Any attempt to concentrate on a book that deals with an impersonal topic may lead to restlessness or to falling asleep. Some of the hysterical patients are quick and alert in their thinking; they grasp new ideas very readily though often uncritically. In other cases the renunciation of one's own thinking leads to an extreme stereotypy of intellectual processes, a few conventional categories being indiscriminately applied to all experience. In judging others, the patients are often misled by their great need to find an ideal person, superior in every respect; they are apt to overrate people and thus to invite subsequent disappointments.

We have already mentioned the attention-getting propensities that aim to counteract feelings of nonexistence. Though these propensities are often inhibited by the person's fear of being "seen through," the wish to be in the limelight may be expressed in obvious ways, e.g., in eccentric behavior or attire, in telling tall stories, in falsifications and exaggerations meant to increase prestige. A similar function is served by the overdramatization and overemotionality that are almost proverbial for hysterical patients. It has often been observed that patients with a fully developed hysterical character structure, though they frequently advertise themselves as people of easy affection and warm enthusiasms, may actually be quite cold—indeed, within this structure they could not be otherwise. Their real emotions are neither expressed nor felt, and this lack of feeling adds greatly to their sense of emptiness. To cover up this void such persons try to conjure up emotions by making dramatic gestures and by building up sensational situations. In this emotional game they often give priority to their own suffering and to the tragic in general; this is worked for all it is worth. The aim, however, is not merely to impress others. The patients come closer to the truth of the matter when they tell the therapist that they do not mind unhappiness because when they are suffering they know at least that they are alive. Little is genuine in the emotional life of such a person except an immense reservoir of anxiety which feeds vitality into these artificial dramatizations.

This completes the description of what I call simple hysteria, or the basic pattern of vicarious living. Its main features are a massive repression of the original personality with consequent feelings of emptiness;

building up a pseudopersonality or attaching oneself to a substitute personality; a pervasive dissatisfaction with this solution and a continuing secret feeling of vacuousness; continual attempts to escape this feeling by a variety of devices, most of them aimed at getting some response from other people. While at its extreme this sequence may result in a greatly impoverished and falsified personality, in milder cases it permits a development of some assets, such as a high degree of empathy, sensitivity to human problems and to their expression in art. Acting, in particular, has a great attraction for some of these patients and they are often successful at it; their descriptions of how they feel on the stage suggest that they are able, under the cover of "performance," to feel and express some of their suppressed genuine emotions and thus to feel more fully alive while they act.

Hysteria with Negativistic Defenses

The second pattern of vicarious living shows all the typical features of the simple hysterical pattern, but in addition there is a strong outer layer of defenses consisting mainly of a set of negative reactions. This form does not look at all like textbook hysteria, and I do not think it is ever diagnosed as such. On first inspection it may seem to resemble the obsessional picture, but upon close analysis of the dynamic structure one finds beneath the defenses the picture of simple hysteria. I refer here to the type of person who behaves as if he were in constant danger of having his integrity violated. He is strongly resentful of any authority or coercion, which he may read into the most harmless and neutral of situations. He expects and often provokes opposition to his desires and rejection of his demands. He is often unreasonably resistant to any suggestion, negativistic, and argumentative. Often the expression by another of an opinion on the most trifling issue is perceived as opposition or even as a vicious attack on his person. He feels continuously pushed around not only by people but also by the ordinary demands of his work, by changing schedules, the slowness of the streetcar, the weather, the thousand little annoyances of daily living, which he takes almost as personal affronts. It is very difficult for him to learn from others because he resists everything that he suspects of being an attempt to change him. One can imagine the difficulty this presents in therapy. This defensive rebellion and negativistic attitude can dominate the picture to such an extent that it completely conceals the underlying hysterical method of adjustment.

The meaning of this negativistic façade must be understood in relation to the extreme suggestibility that is present in every form of hysteria. As a result of the repression of his spontaneous self and of the artificiality and rootlessness of the substitute personality, the hysteric lacks a firm inner personal stand. He is easily invaded by external influences, by other people's emotions; he absorbs everything like a sponge. The negativistic defense can best be understood as a defense against one's own suggestibility, against the threat of a complete loss of personal identity and integrity. The hysteric senses that he is in this danger, and he may learn to fight it tooth and nail. He has to say "no," for example, even before he has heard what you are saying, because he has learned that if he listens he may not resist. The temptation is extremely strong to fill himself with anything that comes along in order to get rid of the feeling of emptiness. This drive can manifest itself orally, in overeating, and in a variety of other ways. The cause of this indiscriminately absorptive adjustment can be projected outward and experienced as an external threat of coercion, as violation of one's person; fear of rape, for instance, often occurs in the fantasies of these patients. In fighting external influences the patients are fighting themselves; what they are doing with one hand they try to undo with the other. This, of course, does not help matters much. They may give in to others on issues that should be most essential for them and yet acquire a reputation for stubbornness by arguing about trifles.

The stubborn negativistic streak and some degree of ambivalence often present in this form of hysteria simulate an obsessive-compulsive personality pattern. The dynamic structure characteristic of the obsessive-compulsive neurosis, however, is absent, and therapeutic exploration brings to light the typical hysterical features. The ambivalence can usually be traced to the conflict between the wish for symbiotic attachment and the need to defend oneself against the influence of the same person. Although the patient wants to be led and to lean on the other, he also vehemently protests against "always being told what to do." After having made his whole existence dependent on the other he fights him, or rather he fights his own tendency to delegate to the other the right to live his life. The coexistence of these two opposed attitudes, the absorptive and the negativistically defensive, makes for protracted vacillations and tends to turn the relation to that most important person into an almost unending war. In the intellectual area the patient may show a peculiar mixture of extreme credulity and extreme skepticism.

The negativistic hysterical person defends himself not only against his tendencies toward vicarious living but also against his tendencies toward excessive repression. The defense against the repressive tendency manifests itself in a peculiar avidity which makes it difficult for the person to postpone the gratification of a desire or to forego opportunities to follow any casual impulse. Just as he fights against being influenced, precisely because he knows that he is tempted to be, he also dimly knows that he is apt not to do what he really wants to do. Then at some point this tendency may turn into its opposite as if the person were saying; "I must have what I want, nobody will tell me otherwise, nobody will cheat me out of this." Usually no one is telling him otherwise; he speaks, as it were, to his own repressive bent. He wants what he wants when he wants it, because he is afraid that he will repress his wish, fail to act on it, and get nothing. Before he develops this insistence on his every whim, he has had a long history of denying himself his natural justifiable desires. As a result he often gives the impression of being a spoiled child accustomed to immediate gratification. Actually this person lives according to an economy of scarcity. He has little hope for gratification, and his impatient "now or never" attitude is based on the feeling that there are too few opportunities left. The frustration of a wish or even a mere delay makes him extremely unhappy, as if he had lost his last chance. If he had to choose one of two pleasures, he may be miserable about having missed out on the other; in talking to people at a party he is plagued by suspicion that a much more exciting conversation is going on in another group. He cannot afford to miss any chances, and his avidity gives the impression of capriciousness and lack of discrimination. Promiscuity is one of the forms this indiscriminateness frequently takes. The underlying feeling, often not conscious, is "I have to do this right away or I shall give up." But in his conscious mind the person more often than not projects outward this obstacle that is in himself, blaming frustrating situations or depriving people. He is right only insofar as the tendency to repression may have developed originally in interaction with such people and such situations. But, as usually happens in neurosis, by projecting the conflict outward he can make the fantasy real. His own demandingness and impatience can eventually cause other people to become depriving.

In extreme cases the patient will insist that no person and no circumstances will be able to hold him back from acting upon any impulse that passes through his mind. He may indiscriminately resist any potential influence, feeling that everybody is making excessive demands and trying to violate his integrity. In such a person the underlying features of suggestibility and absorptiveness are not readily visible. If simple hysteria can be diagrammed by two concentric circles, the diagram for this form should show an additional layer over that of the surface personality, a layer representing a defensive reaction to the method of vicarious living.

Borderline Hysteria

The patients who comprise the category of borderline hysteria pose a diagnostic puzzle; they are often considered psychotic and yet they may make a fairly good external adjustment. Certainly they do not require hospitalization. In terms of our diagrams we cannot represent this condition by adding another layer to the structure; it is indeed an additional layer, an added complication in hysteria, but one cannot picture it as superimposed on the negativistic defenses. Rather it seems to be an elaboration of the substitute surface personality. In its pronounced form this condition is quite rare.

While the negativistic hysteric fights his primary hysterical tendencies, even if in a self-defeating manner, the borderline hysteric abandons himself to vicarious living with relish. This development may take place either at an early stage, as a sequel to the formation of the surface personality, or after a previous fight against vicarious living. Since elements of negativistic defense can still be found in most cases, I tend to believe that the borderline condition usually develops after a fight has been waged and lost. Whatever the temporal sequence, the patient now embraces the hysterical mode of living with abandon. The hysterical forms of expression are cultivated and cherished, the resources of imagination are mobilized and recklessly used to form and uphold a vicarious pseudoexistence in an almost delusional fashion. The delusion-like productions and the tendency to act them out are the most striking features in these cases. The person seems to take his stand on the side of his neurosis, to throw himself into it, and to derive a great deal of satisfaction from the products he creates. These fantasies differ from delusions proper by not having quite the same degree of reality value for the patient. They are part of the histrionics in which the actor becomes so identified with his roles that he almost loses himself in them. He does not, however, completely lose reality contact. The fantasies are acted out only where this can be done with relative safety.

The outstanding themes of these fantasies are love and personal importance or power, all of spectacular quality and of grand dimensions. This is as one would expect; the feeling of being nothing, which is the nucleus of the hysterical structure, is counteracted by the assertion: "I am the beloved person, I have extraordinary importance."

This feeling may take the form of preoccupation with famous personages. For example, a woman patient who was considered a success in her field, and who behaved quite normally in the occupational setting, came to my office one day and sat down in a dramatic pose. I asked her what the trouble was and she said with tears rolling down her cheeks, "I have to teach school while Rita Hayworth is going out with Ali Khan, and I assure you I am just as good as she is." Or something might happen in the British royal family and the patient would take it as her own personal problem, talking only about that situation and living it for weeks.

Characteristically the object of the patients' love fantasies is a real person but one who is most unlikely to respond, e.g., a happily married man, a Catholic priest, or a person whose social status is very distant from hers. It is an essential condition for the fantasy that one have very little chance to put it into reality. If some man makes a realistic approach to a patient who is fantasying about love, she becomes emotionally paralyzed, panics, and flees. Often these fantasies of love from a distance concern someone whom the patient has seen only once; she elaborates this meeting in her fantasies and comes to feel that the other person must know and share her feelings, "but of course he is a man of honor" and cannot declare himself for such and such noble reasons, although there is a deep secret understanding between him and herself. This reaching for an unattainable person suggests that the fantasy is an attempted solution of the oedipal situation, and usually this is the case. At the same time it is a protest against the outcome of the basic hysterical constellation, against the deep-seated feeling that one is unlovable and useless. The fantasy is also a refutation of the sense of emotional emptiness, as if the patient were saying, "Look how deeply I feel, how immeasurable my love is. I am not an empty shell. I am full of great emotion." This is in line with the observation that in these patients the typical hysterical exaggeration and dramatization exceeds all ordinary limits.

The other set of fantasies is concerned with power; these fantasies represent a protest against the feeling of personal insignificance. This protest may take varied forms. Frequently, it expresses itself in extreme demandingness, as if the patient had some sort of royal privilege to order people around and to be served by them. Occasionally power fantasies are couched in religious terms.

One such patient liked to think of God as an ally who would do anything to oblige her. She threatened her parents with destruction by the hand of God if they did not repent and behave well toward her. When her father died she announced this to me with a triumphant smile. She must have felt that God personally had avenged her wrongs. On the basis of these power fantasies the patient tries to dominate the therapeutic situation and the therapist. One patient discontinued working with a previous therapist after a stormy scene; she had aimed a loaded gun at him demanding that he promise to marry her. The patient who felt allied with God announced to me that she had started keeping a record of therapeutic hours, noting those in which I did fairly good work as against those in which I did poorly. She had decided that she would pay me only for the hours in which I did well. Later she decided that I was wasting her time when I did not do well and that I should pay her for these wasted sessions. At the same time she knew all this was playacting. She could get so angry that she turned pale and yet could still be aware of the spuriousness of her feeling.

Work with the extreme cases of this type is at least as difficult as the therapy of true psychotics. Fortunately such cases are rare, much rarer than those of relatively simple hysteria or cases with negativistic defenses. Consequently, as a group, they are less of a problem from the practical point of view, but for the understanding of the hysterical structure it is important to note the extremes in which this pattern can result. Still the condition is not to be viewed as a psychosis, because the fantastic private world of these persons usually does not greatly interfere with their routine daily activities. Even complex occupations and professions can be attended to, occasionally with remarkable efficiency. The near-psychotic existence may remain an isolated area, although the patient considers it the most meaningful part of his life, to be cultivated and cherished.

Vicarious Living and the Social Scene

The variants of the hysterical pattern that I have presented in a somewhat schematic way are observable not only in persons whose personality structure clearly falls into this category. In a more moderate degree hysterical features are present in all neurotic patients; they have been observed and studied for a long time. I feel, in fact, that the total development of the psychoanalytic theory of neuroses, from Freud's early writings to the post-Freudian schools, has been overwhelmingly determined by the hysterical model, with much less attention paid to the obsessive-compulsive dimension. Repression, for instance, which has come to be considered the basic defense mechanism, is indeed basic to the hysterical dimension but not to the obsessive-compulsive one. What the neo-Freudians say about alienation from the self actually applies to the hysterical structure, and the brand of negativism they occasionally describe is specific to this structure. In general, the characterizations of neurosis offered by Horney, Fromm, May, Riesman, et al., seem to refer essentially to the hysterical dimension. This is understandable; these authors have brought historical and sociological interests to bear on the study of neuroses, and the dimension of vicarious living can be safely described as the "neurosis of our time." These writers emphasize the power of the social standard, of the anonymous authority of the group in determining the person's behavior. They stress the conformist tendencies, the wish to fit in, to adapt, to lose oneself in the group.

I have chosen to stress the method of living vicariously through a symbiotic attachment to a particular person. This method is typical of the patients' more intimate relationships, whereas conformism is often found in their public behavior and superficial contacts. Conformism serves more than one purpose. Besides providing the person with some way of life as a cover for his nothingness, conformism insures the patient's acceptability and thus provides him with a substitute for belongingness. I have also emphasized behavior that seems to be the opposite of melting into the group, namely the wish to be noticed, to call attention to oneself by being different. The contradiction is only apparent, because both ways of behaving serve to protect the person against being isolated, being alone, which is equivalent to being nonexistent. One person can use both methods. In contemporary American culture, compliance with the group is reinforced by the high valuation placed on smooth teamwork. Recently, however, the compliant pattern emphasized by Fromm, Riesman, and others began to give way to the secondary type, the hysteria with negativistic defenses. The "rebellious hysteric" is already quite prominent both in therapists' offices and on the social scene. It is possible that he will soon become the dominant sociological type, the spokesman for the times. There are already some indications of this in the empty glorification of "existentialism."

In this context a word is warranted on Bohemianism, or its contemporary expression in the ideology of the "beatniks." I have described how some hysterical patients defend themselves against their pervasive sense of nothingness by declaring it untrue and invalid. The beatnik denies this tormenting basic assumption by making himself distinctive and noticeable, by not being a gray spot on a gray background; he refuses to be nonexistent for others. The psychology involved and often consciously professed by the beatnik is positively conceived. It is a justified protest against the leveling tendency of social conformism which threatens the extinction of spontaneous individuality; we know that Bohemianism flourishes most abundantly in times of particularly strong pressures for social and personal conformism. Rebellion against such pressures, against the annihilation of individuality, is the constructive aspect of this social phenomenon. The reaction of an individual beatnik may be viewed as pathological only to the extent that the danger of suppression is imaginary, an unconscious hypothesis based on a falsification of the realities of his life. Falsification may be involved in a misconception of childhood events (if, e.g., the mother's temporary absence was equated with abandonment), and it is definitely involved in all methods by which subsequent reality is shaped to fit the unconscious hypothesis and by which situations that support it are "invited." The healthy aspect is present in the beatnik's reaction to the extent that the threat of external suppression is objectively real in his present life and not merely a fantasy or a thing of the past.

11. The Pattern of Noncommitment

A Bird's-Eye View

It is generally recognized that the so-called obsessive-compulsive type of neurosis presents great difficulties in therapy. The results of treatment usually are less satisfying than in the case of hysteria. The reasons may lie in the greater complexity of this condition and in a dynamic structure especially resistant to change. It may also be true, however, that our understanding of this type of malfunctioning is faulty or incomplete and that a better knowledge of the processes underlying it would lead to more effective therapeutic procedures. My own clinical experience has led me to modify substantially my former views about the dynamics of the obsessive-compulsive condition. By viewing its phenomena from a holistic perspective I have arrived at conceptions of the etiology, dynamics, and therapy of this pattern that are more at variance with the current theories, including the psychoanalytic, than are my formulations of hysteria. I do not believe that the obsessive-compulsive pattern is more strongly determined by constitutional factors, or represents a more regressive condition than the hysterical dimension of neurosis. It is, however, a much more complex structure in which the basic premises of neurosis are elaborated in a variety of ways, giving rise to many vicious circles within vicious circles. The patient uses his, often considerable, intelligence to build and maintain increasingly fantastic propositions which, in extreme cases, may border on schizophrenic products. Yet the underlying pattern has a clear-cut outline which, once perceived, can be readily recognized in its diverse manifestations.

This pattern results in a particular style of living, broader than the specific clinical pictures to which the term obsessive-compulsive is conventionally applied, i.e., the dual symptom complex of obsessive thoughts and compulsive urges or actions and the constellation of order-liness, stubbornness, and parsimony which Freud described in his account of the obsessional or anal character. These character traits and the obsessive-compulsive symptoms proper are only partial expressions of an overall pattern which, despite its inherent distortions, is a com-plete way of life, a method of dealing with life's main issues. We shall call this particular style of living *the pattern of noncommitment*. The reasons for this choice of term will emerge from the discussion. Like the dimension of vicarious living, the dimension of noncommitment is hardly ever absent from any case of neurosis. Its extent, however, varies greatly, the cases in which it is strongly predominant resulting in a life style quite different from that of vicarious living. I shall try first to state concisely the salient points of this pattern, in a bird's eye view, as it were, of the nature and genesis of noncommitment. This descrip-tion should enable the reader to keep in mind the total picture when its separate aspects are discussed later in the chapter.

In describing the origins of the neurotic condition in general, I stressed the role of the experiences which suggest to the child that the world is basically hostile, that he cannot count on its good will and friendliness. My main thesis about the pattern of noncommitment is that it is the outcome of an abiding confusion as to whether the world is basically friendly or inimical. This painful state of uncertainty leads the person to respond to significant people with both hostility and love and results in an unceasing search for ways to dispel confusion and to gain an unequivocal orientation to the world. Nothing is more charac-teristic of the life of the "noncommittal" person than this constant struggle against confusion and for a clear-cut, reliable, unshakable atti-tude toward life, for guideposts and rules to live by. In some cases this futile, endless battle for clarity, for settling the doubt, leads to total incapacitation.

In the childhood of people who develop this pattern one traumatic factor always stands out: the *inconsistent behavior* of a significant adult or adults that made it impossible for the child to discover even moderately reliable ways of gaining acceptance (which a hysteric is usually able to do at the price of self-obliteration). The confusion created in the child's mind by these inconsistencies seems to be the central factor in the genesis of the pattern, whereas other traumata play a subsidiary role. In many cases of noncommitment early severe deprivations and assaults are in evidence; in others they are not, but the confusion-fostering factors are never missing. Whatever mistreatment the children suffered may have been "balanced" by parental behavior which tended to arouse love and admiration. Still, the child never knew whether he would be indulged or mistreated; the severity of punishment depended more on the parents' mood than on the nature of his misdemeanor. This situation tends to produce strongly contrasting images of a good world and a bad world, but permits neither to become stably dominant. Any event can reverse itself into its opposite. Thus "universal ambiguity" becomes a persistent experience for the child, the basic situation with which he must deal. It was, in fact, the exploration of the obsessive-compulsive dimension of neurosis that brought into focus for me the concept of the dual organization of personality on which my general theory of neurosis is based.

A good illustration of the factors involved in this special developmental sequence is the childhood of a patient whose life followed the pattern of noncommitment, although in adulthood he showed neither the obsessive-compulsive symptoms proper nor the classical earmarks of the obsessive character. His childhood memories revolved around his temperamental father who dominated the family and whose behavior toward his son was inconsistent in the extreme. In his good moments he was affectionate, played with the child and fascinated him with imaginative stories; he gave the boy the most exciting wonderful times. But during his unpredictable uncontrolled outbursts of rage, the father would beat the child mercilessly, making him expect to be killed. The child felt that nothing could stop him and that there was no escape. These episodes of violence created in the child an undercurrent of fear that his beloved father might turn into a raging enemy on the slightest provocation. Any sign of the father's anger turned this apprehension into panic.

In his fifth year the boy had a number of obsessive and compulsive experiences. The first he was able to recall was a painful fantasy about his father. While hunting in the woods he had been killed by a cunning, cruel bandit who then disguised himself as his victim by donning his clothes and also parts of his body, fitting, e.g., the father's eyes into his own face. The evil man came to the house and is now posing as father. This thought was not recognized as fantasy; it was rather an obsessive suspicion of a dreadful secret, with doubts about its truth and a torturing feeling of guilt for possible injustice in suspecting the father of being a stranger and a murderer. The fantasy dramatized the child's confusion as to whether he was living in a loving home or in a cruel alien world which merely masqueraded as benign. It was also aimed at dispelling his confusion about the father, whose behavior made him both God and devil, by the device of "doubling" him, splitting his image in two. But this solution, implying the murder and loss of the *good* father, was unacceptable and failed to allay the child's doubts.

The preoccupation with this fantasy culminated dramatically in an episode of a compulsive commitment to an irrational rule of behavior. The boy had previously engaged in mildly compulsive games, such as crossing the yard in certain specified ways. On this occasion, on his way to the house, he suddenly was impelled to swear solemnly that he would step only on stones, never on the bare earth. When there were no more stones in his path he was paralyzed. His parents called to him to come in, but he remained glued to the last stone. After an hour, to his inexpressible relief, he was picked up and carried in by his father who had finally realized the presence of an abnormal condition. The child felt that this action of the father freed him from his commitment. We can see in this episode a desperate attempt to overcome the uncertainty as to the course to take in a situation permitting no rational choices. By committing himself irrevocably to a rule of action he had tried to put an end to the tensions of confusion and indecision, hoping against hope that the chosen course would eliminate danger and hatred, and make the "good world" come true. The intensity of the committment, symbolized by the solemnity of the oath, was proportional to the confusion it was meant to dispel and to the intensity of the fears and wishes aroused by the images of the bad and the good world.

The patient remembered many other childhood situations resulting in confusion; in most of them parental inconsistency played an essential part. There was a strong taboo in the family against using even mild swear words, a prohibition strictly enforced by the father. The father himself, however, would frequently lose his temper and curse like a trooper. These outbursts shook the son profoundly even when they were not directed against him. He felt an acute vicarious guilt and was stricken by fear that his father would be condemned to hell. Sex was subject to an even stricter taboo. But the parents were careless, and on several occasions the child observed them in the act of intercourse. Again, an unresolvable contradiction: sex is one of the cardinal sins, but my very good parents commit it without compunction.

Occasionally these contradictions emerged into the child's central awareness. Once he overheard a family quarrel; the father had made an unwise investment or gambled away some money, and the maternal grandfather was upbraiding him. At one point the father said, "But you know that I live only for my family." The grandfather replied, "No, you live only for yourself." This remark had a profound effect on the boy. The father had deliberately cultivated the son's idealization of him, and the boy had been sure that his heroic, magnanimous father would unhesitatingly lay down his life for his family if such a necessity arose. Yet he was unable to dismiss the grandfather's accusations as untrue; they resulted in conscious doubt, which brought in its wake a great fear and torments of guilt for doubting his father's devotion and bravery. Similar shocks of recognizing one's worst unavowed suspicions in other people's statements are reported by many patients.

Once a severe trauma of confusion over inconsistency begins to sprout, it grows by feeding on episodes that may be relatively harmless in themselves but fit in with the central traumatic situation in that they contain elements of inconsistency. In the case before us, innumerable events reinforced the trauma. For example, when the child was in the phase of persistently asking "why," he was constantly put off with nonsensical jocular remarks. He took them at their face value and spent hours trying to figure out their meaning. Since they had none, he came to a conclusion that in adult terms might be stated thus: "Nothing is lawful or reasonable in this world; events are ruled by the caprice of unknown mysterious beings." This seems also to have been his answer to the central traumatic situation of his life. But the answer was not acceptable since it provided no basis for a meaningful life. The boy continued his efforts to make sense of seemingly chance connections, to gain clarity about the major issues of life. Once he and a friend undertook to test the existence of God by the success or failure of a prayer they offered that a certain plant should sprout overnight. During his adolescence periods of doubt or disbelief alternated with those of strong religious feeling. Much of his adult life was shaped by compulsive commitments; they substituted for real commitment, which was precluded by a strongly ambivalent image of the world and the concomitant emotional confusion.

In the etiology of noncommitment the traumatic situations are not always as extreme as in this case; the contrast is not as sharp. But most of the elements of the case I have used as a paradigm do appear in the childhood of these patients. The majority have suffered some drastic and capricious treatment at the hands of an adult who was also a source of affection. In many cases this adult possessed outstanding gifts or great personal charm and was much admired by the child. Mistreatment of the child may take the form of severe punishment, physical or verbal, administered either in anger or with sadistic overtones, of exploitation of the child for the parents' own purposes, of a marked emotional withdrawal, caused perhaps by the parent's depression, or a kind of negativistic domination, when the parent indiscriminately censures and forbids anything the child strongly wishes to do. In the last situation, the child learns to conceal his true wishes or even to ask for the opposite of what he wants; he is driven to the conclusion that the parent is basically against *him*, rather than against some specific behavior. Some patients remember thinking in earnest that the parents were going to kill them and plotting elaborate schemes of escape and revenge. In the childhood of some Jewish patients under the Nazi regime mortal danger and escape had been facts, not fantasies; others had suffered vital threats in infancy, such as near starvation resulting from neglect, or severe pain caused by some physical condition.

The conception of the world as a jungle, of life as a fight of all against all, is held consciously by many of these patients or is only thinly covered by a conventional veneer. The theme of sharp contrasts is often vividly expressed in the patients' early memories and dreams. One patient's often revived memory was that of his mother angrily chasing him out into the cold and telling him not to come back; when she later found him sitting on the doorstep she laughed and let him in and was gay and affectionate. The reverse sequence appears in his recurrent childhood dream; his mother would leave the room promising to return, and a monster would enter.

Confusion may be produced by a parent's radical or frequent changes of mind about the way to treat the child. It may be deliberately fostered in fun, such as telling the child that he is a foundling or that some cherished plan has fallen through—usually with the intention of pleasantly surprising him later. Some parents follow a policy of keeping the child uncertain about some hoped-for event until the last moment, either with a "we shall see" attitude, or with an exaggerated recital of obstacles or expenses. The happy outcome, needless to say, does not undo the uncertainty this has created. One patient remembers always feeling very uneasy when his father told him to close his eyes and open his mouth, even though it was invariably some candy he gave him. The refrain "I never knew what to expect, good or bad" goes through many a patient's report.

Confusion as to how to act is created by contradictory demands and by the parents' obvious failure to live up to what they preach. A mother may encourage her son to behave like a girl, even openly expressing her wish that he were one, only to call him a sissy when his behavior is mocked by other boys. She may demand that a girl be a social success and censure her for failure, yet constantly warn her against her friends as inferior or exploiting. A father may preach independence and strict honesty but cater to public opinion and cheat in business. The child's great need to see his parents as good and loving often leads him to dismiss the negative evidence. Yet most of these patients consciously struggled in their childhood or adolescence with alternatives such as these, "Is my mother's nagging really an expression of love and concern as she says or is she plain mean and hateful?" "Is my father so poor that he is forced to insist on my working, or to appropriate my Bar Mizva presents, or is he stingy or unwilling to support *me?*" "Are my parents truly religious or is it bigotry?" "Are they progressive and liberal, as they say they are?" "Do they deny me my wishes for some good reason or just to spite me?" "Do they mean what they say; do they ever tell me their true reasons?" Active attempts to test these alternate assumptions met with little success. Often the child or the adolescent was left with the feeling that the parents' irrationality precluded discussion. In their adult lives these patients are still struggling with the same issues even if no longer in relation to parents. Suspicion of people's intentions and motives, or the feeling that they cannot be fathomed, are essential components of their outlook.

In some cases traumatic inconsistency is created by the strongly contrasting behavior and the conflicting demands of the two parents or two other important adults. The child's conflict is heightened if there is, besides, serious marital friction or divorce, particularly if the two sides fight for the child's allegiance and revile each other. The child then is compelled to make one parent into an angel, the other into a devil. Yet the situation is rarely so simple as to make this solution satisfactory, and the child's confusion persists. Again, circumstances may force him to ally himself with the nonpreferred parent and to suppress his affection for the other. The majority of the patients showing the pattern of noncommitment had been greatly preoccupied at some time with the problem of which parent was right, which was wrong. Many other situations may create or intensify the trauma of inconsistency, such as early drastic changes in the situation of the child, caused, e.g., by changes in the family constellation or by reverses of fortune.

My basic thesis traces the pattern of noncommitment to the confusion arising from a traumatic situation of inconsistency. This thesis must be supplemented with two further statements concerning the mode of functioning of this pattern. Both pertain to the relationship of the two parts of the dual orientation.

It is characteristic of the noncommittal person that his loving impulses are much more deeply hidden than his hostile and supposedly tabooed impulses. His hostility is often manifested openly; when it takes covert forms it is readily brought to the surface in analysis. On the other hand, his friendly orientation toward the world is often deeply hidden. In therapy the patient may put up the fiercest resistance when this aspect of his personality is approached. At first glance, this situation appears paradoxical, and it has led to the assumption that excessive hostility is basic to this pattern. Yet there is a simple logic to cultivating the negative side of the dual orientation and suppressing the positive one. Given the uncertainty as to whether the world is friendly or hostile, it is safer to act on the negative assumption than to let oneself be lulled into a false security. One must constantly be on guard. The patients approach every new person with the hope that he will prove friendly, but with an even greater fear that he will not. They are astonished anew by every instance of friendliness. As some of them put it, it seems that to be reassured they would have to meet all the people in the world. The need to assume the worst and to cultivate strength and cunning lest one be destroyed by treacherous people or malicious fate is a variant of the neurotic "safety first" attitude which is deeply ingrained in the noncommittal person and to which he may even consciously say "yes" and "amen." Yet the device of giving greater weight to the hostile orientation, though it allays the sense of being helplessly exposed to danger, has pitfalls of its own as we shall see when we discuss the guilt feelings of the noncommittal person.

Equally important for the understanding of this pattern is another aspect of the relationship of the positive and negative orientations. Since love and hate are directed toward *the same* object, any significant situation may arouse two sharply conflicting attitudes. This circumstance, a source of puzzlement and torment for the patient, is the greatest paradox in the dynamics of psychological malfunctioning. It has been described in psychoanalysis under the name of ambivalence and recognized as particularly characteristic of the obsessive-compulsive neurosis. Ambivalence, as a rule, is viewed as resulting from a conflict between strong id impulses and a stern superego, and the intensity of the conflict is explained by constitutional factors, and/or by the regressive nature of the condition. In my view, the conflict, although it may indeed be experienced by the person himself as occurring between his moral principles and his frightening irrational impulses, actually originates in the radical split between the confident and the distrustful orientation. When the impulses that naturally follow from each take the form of obsessive and compulsive phenomena they have already undergone many changes and their origins may be obscured.

I shall refer to the simultaneous arousal of the two conflicting attitudes as *coactivation of opposite tendencies*. This mechanism plays an important role in producing the many inhibitions and distortions that encumber the patient's life. To give one example: the noncommittal person may yearn to express the tenderness he feels toward another but find it utterly impossible to do so naturally and directly; his favorite way out of this impasse is to make a playful gesture of aggression, verbal or physical, toward the person he likes. Sometimes this type of reverse reaction is understood and accepted by the other, but often the disguised message is not decoded and is taken at its face value—as an affront—to the chagrin of the patient. Phenomena of coactivation reveal not merely the presence of two opposite sets of attitudes, but indicate that they coexist in an indivisible functional unit. The most damaging consequence of this close linkage is that the strength of the aroused impulse tends to be matched by the strength of its opposite, and a stalemate results.

For purposes of presentation, the range of phenomena in which the noncommittal style of living is expressed, including both symptoms and behavior patterns, can be roughly divided into four categories: (1) symptoms and/or behavior expressing confusion, a divided mind; (2) symptoms or behavior expressing fear and hostility toward an assumedly inimical world; (3) expressions—usually indirect ones—of love and devotion toward the world guardedly assumed to be friendly; (4) techniques and maneuvers designed to dispel confusion and to establish a clear-cut orientation toward the world, a task they usually fail to accomplish. In the rest of this chapter these four aspects will be taken up separately; the self-concept of the noncommittal person will also be discussed. Since the parts of this tightly organized pattern have multiple functions, some symptoms or behavioral items will figure under more than one heading.

The Manifestations of Emotional Confusion

The confusion of a double-minded orientation is clearly expressed in pathological *doubt and indecision*. Let us examine a common example of this type of doubt: a person after leaving his house wonders whether he has closed the windows or locked the door or turned off the gas. He returns to check and finds that all these things had been done, but this does not settle the issue for him. As soon as he leaves the house, he is once more assailed by obsessive doubt and has to return and check. He may repeat this *ad infinitum*, until some other matter diverts his attention. This person is always able to find or invent reasons that help to maintain his doubt. Well-functioning people also have experiences similar to obsessive doubts. After sealing a letter one may doubt whether one has signed it or after throwing a letter in the mailbox, one wonders whether he has stuck on the stamp. These acts have the common characteristic of being semiautomatic, capable of being carried out while one's mind is elsewhere; since they require no strong personal involvement, they do not leave a clear memory image. The obsessional person has doubts about vital issues as well. An extreme example is a young patient who was tormented by uncertainty as to whether or not, in a state of perfect sobriety, she had been raped a few days ago.

The obsessional doubt has two main sources. To the first, the analogous normal phenomena give the clue; not having been fully involved in the act is one of the reasons of doubt. But in this case noninvolvement is not due to the semiautomatic nature of the act. The noncommittal person is unable to be wholeheartedly involved in anything. Because the double orientation of hate and love pervades all areas of his life, none of his actions is backed up by his whole personality, and he is to some extent uncertain about everything.

The second source of doubt also has its origins in the specific double-mindedness of the noncommittal person. The issues about which obsessional doubt arises often have connotations of danger and aggression either directly, as in the case of rape, or else indirectly: neglecting to lock the door may allow burglars to enter, failing to turn off the gas may cause a fire. Beliefs, as we know, are determined less by facts than by consistency with the person's overall outlook and orientation. Doubt concerning overt or covert destructive acts is not eliminated by facts or even by double checking the facts; the half belief persists because it goes so well with the general hostile orientation of the patient, the prepotent part of his personality. The noncommittal person doubts, first, because being divided within himself he cannot be wholly there in his actions, and second, because the nature of the supposed act or omission is consistent with his generalized hostility.

Akin to obsessive doubt is obsessive indecision. The latter is not an uncertainty about having done something or about having omitted something; it is an internal debate about whether one should or should not do something. There are always valid arguments on both sides.

A good illustration is the case of a young male employee in a public institution. There was a rule against taking food into one's living quarters. Once this man took to his room an orange served with his breakfast. Soon he found himself in a dreadful state of indecision. To return the orange would mean a humiliating admission of dishonesty; to keep it was a "crime." He spent days weighing the merits of each course without being able to choose between them. The problem was "solved" only when the orange rotted away.

Indecision occurs in noncommittal people not only in the form of symptoms but also as a style of life. The person may postpone and avoid all important decisions or he may radically reverse himself again and again on the same vital issue. When decisions are being pondered the range of possibilities is usually reduced to two opposites. The following example will serve as an illustration of reversals.

The patient had married with the understanding that his wife would continue to live with her parents for a time; he would stay overnight at her place for a few days in a row, then return to his own apartment and live practically as a bachelor. While this arrangement lasted (a period of two years), he tentatively separated from his wife several times only to go back to her after a few weeks, usually as soon as she would mention divorce. His indifference would then change to affection; he would become an ardent lover and would make concessions in order to keep her. After one of these reunions he went so far as to take an apartment for both of them, but after a few days his feeling toward his wife began to turn into dislike. He felt his marital status was endangering his cherished freedom and began a campaign of deliberately demonstrating to her his indifference and independence, saying little, eating and sleeping by himself, and occasionally spending nights in his old room; the patient hoped that she would take the hint and quit on her own. As soon as his wife announced her readiness to initiate divorce proceedings, however, his feelings changed and he embarked on a most skillful campaign of seduction. They spent a happy week together, after which the cycle started again.

Another phenomenon which directly reflects the presence of two conflicting orientations is *inhibition of action and emotion*. The longer a person lives within the divided pattern, the more previously neutral issues become enmeshed in the dual orientation. He moves, as it were, in a dense medium of inhibition, because almost anything he tries to undertake also activates the opposite tendency. One immediately thinks of work inhibition, frequently seen in students and other intellectual workers who can go through untold futile torment in trying to get themselves to work. I shall not, however, discuss work inhibition as such; although this problem is often based on the pattern of noncommitment, it usually involves other factors as well. I shall mention instead another kind of inhibition of action which seems to be specific to this pattern. The noncommittal person, when confronted with some simple task, like doing a small errand, or even with some routine activity, like shaving, may have the subjective feeling that the act is extremely difficult. He may find himself not only reluctant but virtually incapable of carrying it out. One of my patients liked to take notes on sheets of papers which he lined himself. As he set out to draw lines on a few sheets of paper, he was often assailed by doubt that he would be able to accomplish this task, which suddenly loomed gigantic. Analyzing the inhibitions of such minor or routine acts, one frequently finds that to do these things means to the patient being a "good child"; by willingly doing what he should he is showing his affection toward "the adults." This, however, sharply contradicts the person's coexisting hostile orientation based on his assumption that people are bent on his destruction. The strange difficulty experienced by the patient signals the presence of the confused dual orientation. We shall return to this particular mechanism in discussing the hostile orientations.

Because of the continuous pressure of counterimpulses, the noncommittal person puts more effort into his activities than they normally require; additional energy is needed to keep down the counterimpulse. Tension is the characteristic mental and physical state of these people and insomnia is a frequent consequence (in contrast to the excessive sleep requirements typical of the vicariously living person). The noncommittal person usually falls asleep not because he is sufficiently relaxed but as a result of total exhaustion. After a few hours of sleep his tension may wake him again, often in a disturbed mood and with the memory of a frightening or infuriating dream. When no dream is remembered, there may be a "free-floating" anger analogous to the free-floating anxiety; he may feel enraged without knowing why.

The habitual *state of tension* is not usually reflected in the patient's appearance, which tends rather to reflect his inhibited state. Superficially he may appear quiet, composed, and phlegmatic. The inner tensions are, however, perceptibly reflected in the state of the skeletal muscles, e.g., the patient may keep his teeth pressed together and grind them during sleep. As I have said, the noncommittal person in order to combat counterimpulses puts much more energy into his actions than is ordinarily required. This he also does with his muscles. He may notice muscular pain in his hand after driving because he grasped the steering wheel too hard. It is likely that the patient tenses not only the muscles required for an actual or imagined activity but also the antagonistic muscles which would be involved in preventing that activity. Strong muscular tension may be felt in many places: in the jaw, the neck, hands and feet, the small of the back. There is often a contraction of muscles around the shoulders and the chest wall, as though the person were holding his breath or drawing himself together in very cold weather. These sustained contractions often cause pain. The strong tension of the scalp brings on the "steelband" headache; occasionally there is a painful spasm in the anal sphincter; there may be muscular aches in many other parts of the body. It seems likely that the tensions generated by conflicting impulses also affect the smooth muscles of the internal organs. I have rather convincing evidence that spasticity of the coronary vessels and of certain portions of the gastrointestinal tract may be significantly related to the tensions characteristic of the pattern of noncommitment.

Inhibition of action sometimes involves speech. I do not refer here to stuttering or stammering, which are special issues, but to an impediment related to the cognitive aspect of speech. Some noncommittal persons speak haltingly because they make very long pauses while trying to find the correct word or they do not finish their sentences.

Sometimes this proves a serious obstacle to the therapeutic interchange. Interestingly, some of the most inarticulate persons are unaware of this handicap and believe that they have clearly communicated what they vaguely had in mind. This type of speech strikes the observer as being meant to conceal as much as to communicate, as if the speaker were unwilling to put his thoughts on record.

Psychoanalysis rightly places great emphasis on the *modification of emotionality* in obsessive-compulsive neurosis; inhibition induced by the coactivation of opposite tendencies is especially conspicuous in the emotional area, the original seat of confusion. Fear and anger inhibit love, and love, no matter how deeply hidden, does inhibit the unrestricted expression of hate and anger. The contradictory impulses, having become inseparable, function as a unit, increasing or decreasing together. As a result, the person may helplessly observe himself doing the opposite of what he wants to do, particularly in relation to the people who are of greatest importance to him. He may have a strong yearning for relatedness but find himself treating people, against his will, as if they were criminals. Unaccountable hostility against the sexual partner may be felt, paradoxically, after particularly satisfying intercourse. If the patient's fear of women is expressed in sexual impotence, he is most likely to be impotent with a woman he loves and potent with those to whom he is indifferent. The inhibition works in reverse too. One of my patients always lost the childhood fights with his brother who was no stronger than he. Even in the heat of battle he could not bring himself to let go and strike out hard, while his opponent missed no opportunity to hit where it hurt most. When outbursts of rage do occur—as occasionally happens in situations of relative impunity—they are often so excessive, so inappropriate to the occasion, that they seem insane. They are expressions of piled-up anger held back for a long time, the precipitating episode being merely the last straw.

The person is often agonizingly conscious that he is doing the opposite of what he meant to do. When his limbs become paralyzed, or his friendly remark turns into mockery, or his weapon falls from his hand, he knows what is going on but is unable to change it. The accumulation of such experiences gives rise to a complication which feeds new material into the same mechanism. The patient begins to anticipate a recurrence of failure. When he wants to stand up for himself and to express his anger, he is afraid he will not be able to be aggressive enough, that the wounding word he would like to hurl at his adversary will not come to him or will not pass his lips. He foresees that, as in the past, he will hurt and ridicule his enemy only in his fantasies when the opportunity for action is gone. If you ask a patient who hesitantly fantasies about revenge whether he is afraid to hurt his "enemy" (e.g., his parent), he may protest vigorously that he is, on the contrary, afraid of proving unable to hurt him.

Such anticipations add to the patient's troubles because, in the setting of his basic pattern, fear itself acquires a reverse motivational force. Normally, fear, disgust, and similar negative feelings lead to reactions of avoidance. But when opposite impulses function in coalition, one is compelled both to avoid what one is seeking and to seek what one wants to avoid. The greater the horror, the more compelling the urge toward its object; the patient rushes into the situations he abhors. This sequence is confirmed by the clinical observation that many obsessions and compulsions start with a phobia; first a fear of high places develops, then an urge to jump down. The fear that "it will happen again" is a potent precipitating factor in such symptoms as blushing, palm sweating, premature ejaculation, tears, dryness of the mouth, stomach rumbling. It is as if the body perceived fears as commands and desires as prohibitions; wanting to fall asleep becomes a signal for insomnia. If the person actively struggles against the thoughts or behavior he wants to avoid, the coactivation of the opposite impulses only intensifies his quandary. Compulsive habits, such as compulsive masturbation, can be tremendously intensified by fighting them. In treatment, reinforcing the constructive tendencies cannot be therapeutic in itself if coactivation of contradictory impulses is present; both sides are reinforced simultaneously. A state of lowered impulse tension, a relaxation of struggle, is needed to find the way out of the impasse.

Because of his inner confusion, the noncommittal person from the start cannot be wholehearted about anything he feels. The coactivation of contradictory emotions and their mutual inhibition can eventually get him to the point where the normal gamut of feelings is greatly restricted. No emotions, save anger and fear, are consciously experienced, let alone expressed; and even these may be felt as such only infrequently, more often taking the guise of a general vague discontent. The patients may appear to be basically bland or dull people although actually they are anything but that. They themselves may feel incapable of any strong emotion, and may even make a virtue of this lack by championing "objectivity" and "rationality." The emotions in obsessive-compulsive conditions are dissociated from the corresponding ideational content, a mechanism known as "isolation." The patient may retain or recover the memory of a traumatic event, but the emotion to which it gives rise is not felt. In treatment, the noncommittal person often speaks and theorizes in a bland detached manner about issues which should be questions of life and death to him.

Since emotions reflect an evaluation of *personal* relevancies, their suppression leads to an impersonal mode of experiencing. Vital thoughts and impulses, when they appear in the form of obsessions and compulsions, are not acknowledged by the patient as entirely his own; they appear in a depersonalized fashion, not as self-expressions but as intruders, something one is *compelled* to think or do. Neither the patient's logic nor his moral standards allow him to acknowledge full ownership of these strange, illogical, often terrifying thoughts and actions. In a way he is right, for such impulses stem from only one side of his doubly oriented existence and are genuinely opposed by the other. When a priest reading the Holy Mass feels compelled to intermingle blasphemous expressions with the sacred text, he indeed "should" not accept full moral responsibility for this impulse. He may be a sincerely religious man who, unknown to himself, harbors a hateful and rebellious orientation as well.

The Hostile Orientation

In therapy, the noncommittal person rarely shows strong resistance to revealing his hostile tendencies unless the hysterical dimension is also prominent in his neurosis. Indeed, the patient may be strangely eager to bring out these trends; occasionally he almost gloats over the glaring manifestations of his hostility. ("Let me tell you how I got even with X for what he did to me." "I was bitchy again to Y and succeeded in making her feel hurt and angry.") These patients feel at home with their aggression, which, in the world visualized in their prevalent orientation, is justifiable and the only safe course to take: "If people are out to hurt and destroy me, I have every reason to fight back." Depending in part on the nature of the early traumatic experiences, hostility may be anticipated in different forms: exploitation, physical assault, humiliation, withholding of love, or a general vague ill will. The patient's counterhostility also may take many forms, some obvious, some complexly determined and covert.

In some of the obsessive and compulsive symptoms the hostility is obvious, as for example in the compulsion to hurt, humiliate, blaspheme. More covertly, the hostile content typical of these symptoms takes the form of fears, as when a person, shortly after seeing a banana peel on the sidewalk, begins to worry that someone may slip on it and be fatally injured because he neglected to remove it. This hate-fear phenomenon very often appears in the form of magical thoughts, the patient feeling that by committing or omitting this or that banal act he might cause great harm to someone. For example, "If I don't touch the doorpost when I go through the door, someone will die." Besides reflecting hostile impulses and the guilt attached to them, this type of symptom reveals the patient's hidden conviction that he possesses some occult gifts that tremendously increase his power. The symbolism involved in these magic acts is varied, and their original meaning may have become lost for the patient.

For example, for one patient clearing the throat and blinking meant a very severe offense, and he took great care not to offend people in these ways. The throat-clearing proved to be a rudiment of the act of spitting in a person's face; blinking originally had the meaning, "If I close my eyes you are no longer there; I have annihilated you," and also "You are nothing; you are a nobody."

Noncommittal personalities often have great difficulty in looking into another person's eyes, a difficulty which is not exclusive with them, but which in their case represents the inhibition of an aggressive act; looking may have the meaning of hostile curiosity and is more likely to have this meaning to them than to others. One of my patients had the compelling urge to read surreptitiously the titles of the books in my bookcase. He felt as guilty about it as if he were inspecting the skeletons in the closet of my private life.

A striking instance of hostile voyeurism was a patient who used to peep at a woman living across the street from him and watch her undress. The woman was careful about her appearance and dressed very neatly. But when she was naked the patient could observe her secrets, some physical signs beginning to show her age. The peeping excited him sexually, but its greater emotional emphasis was elsewhere. Once he said "You cannot imagine the wonderful feeling of triumph I have when I meet her in the street dressed up so pretty, and say to myself, I know what you really look like."

Aggression in this type of curiosity consists in invading the cherished privacy of another. Even if the patient never uses his knowledge to the other's detriment, its secret possession gives him a reassuring feeling of power.

More obvious expressions of hostility are the lurid fantasies of revenge in which many patients indulge. They usually keep grudges a long time and may for years periodically revive fantasies of vengeance for a single offense. Even more characteristic of the noncommittal person is his destructively critical attitude, a continuous compulsive faultfinding. One patient, while riding on the bus to and from his work, habitually engaged in finding fault with his fellow passengers, thus working up a state of irritation: this one is the pushy type, that one a slob, the third a grabber of seats, or disgustingly fat, and so on. A related type of fantasy goes the fault-finding one better; the patient not only takes people apart but puts them back together correctly. He may, in imagination, straighten people's ties, get them to have a hair-cut, a shave, or to harmonize the color of necktie and socks, or get a neater crease in their pants. Some spend a great deal of time in these fantasies, which reflect also the compulsive orderliness typical of the pattern. The faultfinding and domineering attitude, if put into action, prove very trying to the person's family, friends, and co-workers. This behavior, which may be rationalized as concern for people's well being or morals, is the dominant component in the actions of some social or religious reformers.

More intriguing than the manifestations so far described—because they are dynamically more complex—are the expressions of hostility that can be summarized under the heading of spiteful disobedience, or the lure of the forbidden; they cover a wide range and have far-reaching consequences. The origins of this attitude can be readily traced through the history of the patients' implicit generalizations. The early traumatic situation of inconsistency involves the lack of any clear connection between the deed and its social effects, between crime and punishment; the irrational capricious authority appears liable to punish anything. The child develops the feeling that everything he spontaneously wants is forbidden and punishable (a feeling reflected in the adult joke that anything one likes is either illegal, immoral, or fattening). This leads to the conviction that, "The enemy is against me, against everything I want; he does not let me live." The internal response to this is, "But I shall live; I shall assert myself and destroy anything that hinders me." These generalizations result in a reversal from, "What I want turns out to be forbidden or bad," to "What is forbidden and bad is what I want." It is as if the person lost all discrimination as to what he really desires. In the heat of battle forbiddenness becomes the criterion of desirability. Every prohibition or moral sanction becomes a compelling incentive: to be bad means to survive as a free person; to be good means to knuckle under, to give up, to become a slave. Wanting the forbidden is an expression of self-assertion through opposition, a bid for existence and integrity; the more stamina a person has, the more obstinately he fights against personal annihilation, and the more severe are his symptoms. This fight which shows the patient at his worst expresses also his best. The brave fight he is putting up would be laudable, if the world were really out to destroy him, thus making opposition the means of survival.

It thus comes about that the patient's hostile impulses are not limited to aggressive acts proper, such as killing, hurting, depriving. Many of these impulses have as their goal the tabooed as such. The obsessive thoughts and compulsive actions focus on that which society or convention forbid: killing, cursing, stealing, incest, masturbation, perverse sexual acts, handling dirt, and the like. While the hostile implications are obvious in most of these acts, this is not true of all. For example, masturbation in itself, as an expression of the sexual impulse, has nothing to do with aggression; outside of the pattern of noncommitment it is often pursued with little guilt. Compulsive masturbation, however, is always an expression of hostility and has only an indirect relation to sex. It is a spiteful behavior, the sexual impulse lending itself well for the expression of spite because it is, or was at one time, very strictly forbidden.

What is true for masturbation is also true for anal and urethral practices; all of them involve spitefully doing the forbidden. Freud ascribes to anality a particularly important role in the dynamics of the obsessive-compulsive neurosis and for good reason. The great frequency of anal fantasies and practices in this neurosis is a fact, but, taken in their entirety, the clinical facts do not suggest to me the classical analytic formulation. I do not think the obsessive-compulsive neurotic is one who, after failing at the phallic level of development, regresses to the "anal level," i.e., to a stage at which excretory processes are assumed to be the chief source of pleasure and at the same time also the principal means of expressing anger. I doubt if the anal stage is biologically determined to the same degree as the oral and the genital stages. It seems to be to a great extent a cultural product, only indirectly depending on maturation. Until in toilet training the child is asked to comply with adult demands—often poorly understood and hence unreasonable—he has very little opportunity to learn about "good" and "bad," to obey or to resist, to feel guilt and shame. What is characteristic of the "anal" period is not any sudden increase in the pleasurableness of anal sensations as such but the first acquaintance with the ideas of good and bad, with orders and prohibitions, and the first real possibility of fighting the supposedly hostile surroundings. Thus badness becomes closely tied to excreta and the act and organs of excretion; spitefully doing the forbidden originally means doing the dirty thing. The intense fun children often have with anal play is due largely to the awareness that they are doing something against the adult.

It is no wonder then that many patients in whom spite has become a fixed attitude show a preoccupation with excretory functions and substances or are "dirty minded" in other ways. Anal functions are preeminently suitable for expressing spite; their prevalence in the obsessive-compulsive conditions requires no assumption of regression, a concept which I find of very limited value in general. The neurotic does not *progress* to maturity, except in a peripheral fashion; his progress is more apparent than real. Furthermore, there are many obsessive-compulsive cases in which the patient's prevalent mode of expressing anger makes use of impulses and images typical of the stages which, in the analytic scheme, precede or follow the anal. Biting impulses, e.g., are reflected in the habitual tension many of these patients feel in the jaw. In the case of one patient who was periodically overwhelmed by a multitude of obsessions and compulsions these symptoms hardly ever had an anal reference. For the most part he saw every elongated object—whether pencil or lamppost—as a penis and felt an intense urge to bite these objects and also to bite off people's heads. The chief obsessional fantasy of another was that his penis functioned as a sword; he spent hours imagining how he would wound one person after another or stab them to death. Psychoanalytic theory might view these variations as resulting from a mixture of impulses stemming from various stages of psychosexual development, including the early ones to which the patient has regressed. In my view all these symptoms are simply expressions of aggression, the choice of specific acts being determined by their suitability for the purpose—among other things by the fact that they are tabooed. The defiant connotations which normal sexual activities often assume within the pattern of noncommitment are made quite obvious in some cases by the patient's special preferences. For instance, one woman's sexual gratification was extraordinarily increased if the sex act was carried out in the most tabooed places (such as churches) or in places where the risk of detection was greatest (being masturbated in a crowded restaurant, having intercourse in the doorways of apartment houses).

The implicit invitation of detection, which is obvious in this case, gives us a clue to the meaning of one form of masochism, possibly the main type of masochistic satisfaction. The fantasy of being caught and punished, which often accompanies the anal activities of children, reflects the child's wish to make the adult angry; the angrier he is, the more gratifying the fantasy. The enemy's anger is proof that one's spiteful behavior has hit him where it hurts, and the intensity of his anger is measured by the severity of retaliation. In the real or fantasied sequence consisting of one's own anger, one's rebellious act, the anger of the enemy, and the severe punishment, all steps express anger and reflect the struggle the patient is engaged in. When the fantasy of being mistreated is in the foreground its link to the total sequence may be lost from awareness, but it is usually easy to recover from the overtones of anger and triumph. Sometimes the link is retained and elaborated, as when the imagery of being tortured forms a part of an explicit fantasy of heroic resistance to an overpowering enemy, often cast as a common enemy of the people with whom one belongs. The pleasure felt in the fantasies of being tormented, raped, degraded, torn to pieces is not pleasure in suffering as such; the mistreatment indicates the tremendous reaction of the enemy, proves that the blow has struck home. The attitude that makes a neurotic into a living accusation, of his parents or of the world at large, is another instance of this kind of utilization of suffering.

A different form of "pleasure in suffering," not specific to the pattern of noncommitment, arises not from hostility but from the wish to obtain compassion and affection through suffering, invalidism, the signing away of all pleasure. In my observation this is, paradoxically enough, also the ground from which sadism grows, both the sexual perversion and the nonsexual behavior displaying a similar pattern. The two main manifestations of sexual sadism are infliction of physical pain and immobilization of the partner, e.g., by pinning down or tying him or her. In the background of the patients who practice or fantasy inflicting pain, I have regularly found a traumatic situation focused on the figure of an unresponsive parent, usually the mother, sometimes perceived by the child as unfeeling, as a block of ice; after having tried all means at his disposal to obtain affection, or attract attention, the child despairs of ever penetrating this wall and receiving the desired response. In the light of this sequence, the deliberate hurting of the sexual partner seems to be an attempt to beat out a tangible unequivocal emotional response from the unresponsive "primal parent" whose image now stands for the world. In the background of the patients who display the second type of sadistic behavior or fantasy, I invariably find a great prominence of the fear that the parent will go away and leave the child. The child feels that the adult cannot be relied upon to stay or return and that nothing but forceful restraint could keep him or her. Outside the sexual sphere, the wish to obtain response, *any* response, is at the root of the deliberate and seemingly purposeless manipulation of other people's emotions in which many patients indulge: shocking them, arousing them sexually, puzzling or angering them, making them happy, making them laugh or cry. The wish to get a response from the partner and the wish to enslave him in order to keep him are combined in the Pygmalion theme. One aims to create another being (e.g., by teaching or curing him) who will love and revere the creator as no one else will. But since the anticipation of rejection remains, the patient soon begins to resent the efforts expended in "creating" the partner and to feel hatred and jealousy toward one and all—toward his "creature," all potential rivals, and even, in a grandiose fashion, toward all potential love objects who could love him but dare to prefer others. This anger and the cruelty and possessiveness to which it leads result from the constantly felt threat to the patient's attempt to create (in the person of the other) a world in which he would be affectionately wanted.

Let us return to the topic of spiteful disobedience. Although the temptation to violate taboos may result in much suffering for the patient, he is even more handicapped when actions that are neither basically hostile nor conventionally forbidden also get caught in the wheels of this dynamism. Obviously one can fight the enemy not only by attacking him or by doing the forbidden but also by passive resistance, by not doing what one is told or expected to do. This strategy is responsible for the patient's negativism and ungivingness and has other far-reaching consequences. I have mentioned, earlier in this chapter, a number of inhibition phenomena which express the emotional confusion, the double-mindedness of the noncommittal person; many of these inhibitions also express hostility in the form of passive resistance. This attitude of "insubordination" often manifests itself in resentment of all imposed obligations or of anything that even remotely resembles them. Here again a sweeping generalization is involved; connotations of arbitrary command and unwarranted imposition meant to limit one's freedom are read into all sorts of neutral and impersonal matters such as deadlines and timetables. A student may quickly lose interest in a book he has been reading when it is assigned in a course. He may find himself unable not only to complete his written assignments on time but also to benefit from any number of extensions: he is able to start working only *after* a particular deadline has passed and is compelled to stop when he is given another.

The most crippling manifestation of this automatic resistance arises from a phenomenological transformation of one's *own* plans and intentions; they acquire the character of imposed demands and are resisted compulsively. The person may have been genuinely eager to do a certain piece of work or to take a trip; he has planned the necessary steps, but the mere fact that these steps are necessary turns them into demands. He now feels *forced* to go through with them and consequently he will not, as if forgetting that the necessity is impersonal and that no one but himself is the source of these "orders." This sequence exemplifies one of the processes by which activities that serve as a means to a goal can acquire a negative character. The work inhibition of a noncommittal person usually follows this pattern. One patient, whenever he completed a job to his own and his superior's satisfaction, had a strange thought flash across his mind: "This has gone too far; you must louse up the next one." And invariably he did; much as he longed to do justice to himself in his work, the equation between doing well and yielding to "the enemy's" demands made him periodically stop working.

In conclusion, let us say a few words about *fears*, which are an inherent component of the person's hostile orientation, his reaction to a dangerous world. The fears of the patients are strong and numerous. They are articulated into the pattern of noncommitment in a number of ways. Here I want to mention one characteristic type of fear which reflects an essential aspect of this pattern, namely the fear of the irrational. As children the patients are excessively afraid of the dark, in which intangible and invisible evil forces seem to lurk, of ghosts, and of other uncanny matters. As adults they are often disproportionately afraid of drunks, insane people, wild animals, barking dogs. The common characteristic of these objects of fear is that they are beyond rationality; they cannot be reasoned with. This group of fears has a typical etiological background. When the father of the patient discussed earlier in this chapter beat him in an access of rage, the boy could see no reason for the severity of the punishment. His father appeared to him insane, an elemental force that knew no reason and no mercy. Instances of rage, cruelty, and drastic inconsistency are not as rare in the adult's treatment of children as one would like to believe. The intense fear of the irrational which such episodes instill in the child may be very difficult to erase and sometimes persists through life.

The Self-Image

The self-image of the noncommittal person shows a dualism comparable to the dualism of his image of the world but it is different in content. The patient oscillates not between considering himself a friendly or hostile person but between feeling himself to be worthless or valuable, a polarity which is usually equated in his mind with that of being weak and being strong. The all-important question is, "Am I strong enough or too weak to cope with the hostile world?" This centering on power, strength, control, and independence which is brought about by the predominance of the hostile orientation, is intensified by frequent humiliating experiences of inhibition and impotence. In his changes of mood the patient varies between the elated feeling of being active, competent, influential, capable of achieving anything he wishes, and the more basic and enduring feeling of being weak, frightened, stupid, confused, unable to work or to do anything else. In some cases the obsessive thought reflects the compensatory alternative in a near-delusional fashion, but usually the elements of grandiosity are only implied and the patient's dream is of achieving superiority, physical strength, beauty, riches, fame. Usually these dreams remain dreams, but sometimes real attempts are made by the patient to achieve some aspects of this idealized image, and they may be quite successful at times. One patient who suffered from the fear of being physically attacked persevered in a grueling program of training and became a good boxer.

Actually the patient's private answer to the question, "Am I any good?" is negative; self-derogation in these people reaches an unbelievable degree. Morally they feel essentially worthless. In struggling to salvage the image of good parents by finding some reason for the mistreatment they suffered at their parents' hands, these patients early arrived at the conviction that there must be something basically wrong with them, that they are monstrous or "subhuman" in some ways. The fixation of this attitude of self-blame is facilitated by a factor which I have not mentioned so far but which is frequently present in the background of people who show the pattern of noncommitment. This is the so-called self-sacrificing attitude on the part of a parent, the overt or covert emphasis on how much deprivation and suffering the mother is going through for the child's sake, what dire results his behavior, or even his mere existence, has had or may have for her. When the child is threatened not with punishment but with a parent's unhappiness, illness, or death—which is in effect also a threat of abandonment—the results for his self-image may be disastrous. He not only feels inadequate because he can never fulfill the obligations which the parental sacrifices impose on him, but he also feels selfish and ungrateful because he does not constantly strive to repay his "debt" and even resents the obligation. Such a person may develop, in addition, a strong wish for self-sufficiency and an exaggerated fear of hurting others. The resulting self-blame can go to spectacular extremes. A man whose mother has told him that his birth had deprived her of the chance to have more children conceives of himself as a murderer of hypothetical brothers and sisters. Although the feeling of being worthless, or basically perverse, may be rationalized in various ways ("I don't deserve to be happy because I am a homosexual."), essentially it applies not to any single act or defect but to the person himself: "It is just *me*."

As these examples show, the patients' self-loathing is often quite conscious in spite of their compensatory high opinion of themselves. In fact, the person's self-contempt is so fundamental, the despair about his value so deep, that even when the grandiose self-image is in the fore-front he does not really believe in it; it is mainly something he wishes others to believe. Having settled on living with his assumed worthless-ness, he only hopes to put up a good front, to appear strong and worthwhile to others, to impress and intimidate them. Whatever feel-ing of self-value the patient has is usually hedged with qualifications: "I would have promise and potential if I had not wasted them in a bad way of living; now that I know better it is too late. Right now my life is worthless, I cannot use my abilities, but some day a miracle may happen and my great hidden assets may come to the fore." But these flimsy consolations fail to allay his profound disgust with himself as he is. Even the assets of which the patients feel most certain, such as their intellectual powers, are not really felt by them to be valuable or to be their legitimate possessions. One student who prized intelligence above all and who, on one level, knew quite well that he had high intellectual gifts, still managed to focus his self-image on his *lack* of intelligence. He "reasoned," e.g., that were his IQ really as high as reported, he, being a year older than most of his fellow students, should have sur-passed them in scholastic performance to a greater extent than he actually had. A patient who freely professes his high intelligence, of which he has incontestable proof, when it is commented on by an-other, may feel uneasy and angry. He reacts as if he were being ex-posed as a fraud or as if the other had meant to say, "You have intelli-gence but nothing else." Given the patient's profound lack of self-respect, he can turn any evidence of his worth into its opposite.

The Loving Orientation

In the pattern of noncommitment the impulse to love is most deeply hidden and most difficult for the patient to accept. One patient told me "I can deal with hostility. I feel at home with it, but if I meet with friendliness, if I am touched, or almost touched, by something I am at a loss. I feel like a fish out of water." Tender impulses have no place within the framework of the hostile orientation; they would only be handicaps in this life-and-death struggle. Loving and wanting to be loved are considered weaknesses. It is more important to be feared than loved. If the patient's tender feelings are pointed out, he may criticize this as a "superficial interpretation." Affectional relationships are used as means for a show of power; it seems much more important to have the power to call forth feelings in others than to have feelings for them.

If one has suffered rejection, feeling angry and indignant about it is much preferred to feeling sad and thus acknowledging the loss or lack of something valuable. "I have learned to lose my temper and to get relief in this way. I can accept violence in myself, but I cannot accept sadness; sadness spells doom." Revenge may be accepted as a necessary "settling of accounts," and the patient's only fear may be that some weak feelings might interfere with his or her scheme: "I want to see him once more and slap his face, but I am afraid that if he acts miserable I might become sympathetic instead."

Yet side by side with the hostile orientation there exists in the patients a perception of the world as friendly toward his wishes and as offering opportunities for both mastery and communication. This is the more covert orientation, the patient's secret even from himself. It appears in much more disguised forms than the hostile orientation. If this is not the case, if the positive orientation to the world is as strong and well organized as the hostile one, we have the case of tortured natures. Such persons do not develop the features typical of noncommitment, and their lives, though full of inner struggles, can be productive and meaningful. In the case of neurotics, the fact that the healthy orientation is largely submerged and hidden from view can easily lead to the conventional conclusion that the peculiar duality which is obvious in the obsessive-compulsive phenomena expresses a conflict between two neurotic impulses rather than between a neurotic and a healthy orientation. However, at least four distinct groups of phenomena typical of the pattern of noncommitment indicate the presence of an orientation toward the friendly world.

In those cases of neurosis where obsessive-compulsive methods are prevalently used, severe *guilt feelings* are always present.They appear either openly or as compulsions and obsessions with a special content: doing penances, compulsive handwashing and other purification rituals, various forms of magically undoing what has been done. The phenomena of reaction formation in which hostility turns into friendliness can also be viewed as expressions of guilt. All these phenomena of atonement are usually interpreted as arising from fear of retaliation. It is indeed natural that hostility directed toward a powerful enemy should arouse fear of reprisal. Beyond this fear there exists, however, a deeper source of the guilt feelings and of the compulsive phenomena originating in them. This deeper source of the sense of guilt is the hostility directed against a possibly friendly person. The patient discussed in the introduction was not concerned as a boy with what his father would do to him if he knew his thoughts; he was horrified at his own meanness in having had such thoughts about one who perhaps dearly loved him. When aggression is felt to have been directed against a loving person, the fear of punishment, if it does arise, comes about through this sequence: "For such meanness I *ought* to be punished. Therefore I will be punished, so I am afraid of being punished." This is not the fear of the enemy—external or internalized—which is a part of the hostile orientation but the fear that derives from guilt.

The prevalence of guilt feelings in obsessive-compulsive patients proves that besides the hostile and hated world there exists for them also a world that is loving and beloved. It exists, not besides the hostile world, but within it; it is the very same world, the same people, that evoke the hostile and the friendly orientations. The mythical enemy is not a clear-cut enemy; there is always the possibility that he might be a friend. This confusion is a source of pervasive guilt because the friend is punished together with the enemy. One incurs no guilt in fighting an enemy who is out to destroy you, but what if your hatred and vengeance are directed against friends? This is biting the hand that feeds you. This source of guilt is so obvious that it takes a preconceived notion of human nature to derive the feelings of guilt simply from a sadistic superego. Guilt incurred through confusing friend and foe is what creates and maintains the patient's image of himself as perverted and morally worthless.

The guilt is often felt consciously, but it is seldom felt in its full impact or placed where it truly belongs. The impact of the correctly perceived guilt is dreaded in anticipation as the final proof of one's basic depravity. As one patient put it; "I don't want to *feel* guilty, but what if I should find out that I *am?* Then I would either have to feel guilt or rationalize it away." And the patients do use various methods to avoid the full impact of guilt. They may displace it from its source to some less weighty matter or erase the emotion resulting from the knowledge of being at fault, thus depriving the event of personal relevance. A man who in an affective state had committed an act of violence at first felt some guilt but later declared the episode closed. When he appeared in court he felt detached "as if the person they want to punish is not *me* any more." Many patients feel no guilt toward those whom they have mistreated and are only dimly aware of having caused suffering; some, although realistically certain that the victim will not strike back, have nightmares that give evidence of what they expect. The missing guilt feelings make themselves felt as fears.

The second group of phenomena suggesting an orientation toward a friendly world comprises the acts or fantasies that express a *wish for subjection*, usually in a compulsive form. One chronic obsessive-compulsive patient told me, "I have an intense desire to be kneaded, to be clay in a potter's hand." There are compulsive urges to be a follower, a slave, to swallow the penis of an admired man, to offer oneself as a passive sexual object, to conceive a child; in treatment the patient may feel an urge to accept anything the therapist says, to tie himself to him by an enslaving bond. These phenomena, often characterized as masochistic, are usually interpreted as propitiation, as efforts to divert and soothe the anger of a hostile agent by voluntary obedience. They can indeed serve the function of self-protection, but it seems to me they express something more than saying to an enemy: "Don't hurt me. I will do anything you want; only spare my life." In feeling these urges the person seeks to love and to be loved, even if he visualizes love as an undifferentiated state of commingling or blending with the other. The wish for union, in whatever form, is directed not toward an enemy but toward a friend or a potential friend. No matter how it is perverted, this urge has its roots in a trusting attitude to the world.

The fact that the contents of the submissive compulsions and wishes are usually primitive does not change their general meaning. On all developmental levels the natural response toward a friendly world is to seek to establish communion with it. This tendency to community formation will express itself through whatever material is available, through the concerns and activities that fill the person's life at a given stage of development. It may express itself through the imagery derived from oral activities, in the wish to swallow the object or to be swallowed by it; penetrating and being penetrated are the active and passive phallic ways of establishing union; from the stage of toilet training comes the idea of union through obedience. All these primitive wishes are frequent phenomena in the obsessive-compulsive pattern. Their predominance stems in part from the circumstance that the issue of community formation had become problematic and difficult very early in life, and in part it reflects the fact that the imagery stemming from vital functions remains concrete and potent through life.

The friendly orientation to the world is also expressed, timidly, in a kind of *abstract idealism:* devotion to science, art, humanitarian goals, a general concern for human welfare. This concern is schematic and abstract. It usually results in the person's loving humanity in general but fearing and hating the next fellow. The person harboring such attitudes appears hypocritical to those who realize that he does not practice what he preaches and that his abstract benevolence is often contaminated with aggressive power-seeking impulses. Though there is good reason not to take the idealistic attitude of the noncommittal person at its face value, I think one cannot in justice dismiss it as completely ungenuine. More likely, the person does feel the need of a constructive relatedness to people but is too fearful or hostile to act accordingly when he finds himself face to face with them. His constructive urges can be more safely and comfortably expressed in abstract impersonal pursuits. The neurotic uses often made of these inclinations are perverted uses of something valuable and genuine. The same holds true of the patient's religious feelings.

The *image of a worthwhile world*, of "a scheme of things in which I can be of use," besides being postulated in these general idealistic interests, appears also in the patient's private fantasies. Most patients have a conception—sometimes recurring in dreams, or as a dim memory image—of some wonderful world in which at some time, in some way, they will lead a happy existence. The conception is nebulous, but the patient's associations suggest that it refers to the unknown world of healthy living. In spite of its vagueness this image exercises a dynamic pull which, however, serves only to reinforce the patient's neurotic attitudes. He feels reluctant to commit himself fully to anything in the present so as not to forfeit some future opportunity for this unknown happiness. Sometimes the good world is imagined to be in some distant place. This notion, confirmed by the relief some patients feel when away from the tasks and relationships of their daily lives, gives rise to the frequently encountered dreams of travel. To a patient who was planning a stay in Europe, "Italy stood for paradise; in going there I would wipe the slate clean, drop my phony ways, and lead a genuine life."

The four groups of phenomena I have described are not the only manifestations of a hopeful and loving orientation to the world occurring in the pattern of noncommitment. In fact most of the patient's neurotic pursuits can be viewed as efforts to make this hoped-for community come true, and if need be to wrest it from the world by force. Some patients lead, self-protectively, an almost hermitic existence; they deny their need for love and strive, instead, for complete self-sufficiency, freedom and independence. But the majority do get involved with others. Typically, however, all attempts to establish and maintain close loving relations with people become perverted by anticipation of harm and the resulting aggressive maneuvers until hostility is uppermost and determines the long-range results. The orientation to community, having lost its roots, appears only as a conventional veneer or as a means of self-justification.

The unceasing search for a loving partner, when it turns into the wish to "at least" prove one's power to evoke emotions, may result in a series of seductions and abandonments. Once the heat of the search is over and the need to get a response has been gratified, the "loved one," who had been "invented" rather than discovered, may be experienced almost as an object. The patient notes that he knows little and cares less about the person with whom he had been so intensely involved. The tenderness the patient felt and expressed is forgotten; or it may appear to him in retrospect to have been unreal, a deceptive trick on his part. He must then either view himself as a fraud or devalue the partner as undeserving; usually at different levels he does both. Guilt and fear of being shown up as a fraud may combine with the wish to relieve suffering and to meet the other's needs. These confused motives may make the patient commit himself to a relationship he no longer values, though it may burden him with insuperable tasks. Such commitments, however, result not in closeness but only in further frustration and anger; the patient withdraws from the partner emotionally even if he continues to serve him and goes his own way. If he persists in trying to make the partner into the boundlessly loving person he feels he needs, these attempts soon deteriorate into hostile criticism, possessiveness, domination, or a cat-and-mouse game of alternating approach and withdrawal.

Given such outcomes, the patient's pervasive sense of guilt remains the only unmistakable manifestation of his loving orientation toward people. In positive form this orientation can appear only in fantasy or in relation to abstract pursuits. No snowballing fear and hostility are provoked by the other's response to the patient's ambiguous and paradoxical ways when the "other" is not a human being with his own foibles and liable to be angered or hurt. The need to lessen the other's reality in order to establish a relationship devoid of these risks is reflected, in childhood, in the creation of imaginary companions—in adulthood in the limitation of one's relations to superficial or professional ones. Some patients can work well in therapy only if they view the therapist not as a real person but merely as a "therapeutic role"; they feel freer to talk to this impersonal entity. Others communicate best in writing.

One patient who, after a difficult start, was obliged to discontinue therapy, both to her regret and relief, asked her therapist whether there was not a substitute for talking intimately to a real person. Could she imagine someone understanding, with whom there was no need to pretend, and talk or write to this imaginary person? In church she had tried to talk in this way to God, and found that this greatly helped to clarify her thoughts. She was reaching out for communication with an unambiguously loving parent whom she had never experienced and despaired of finding in a real person.

Methods of Dispelling Confusion

In the noncommittal pattern confusion is the constant state, more painful than anxiety which becomes acute only rarely. Anything would be better than perpetual uncertainty; in fact the patient may experience relief when he learns the worst. "When my mother told me—not in anger this time—that nothing I could do could please her or distress her, I knew it was a moment of truth. I felt very calm, almost relieved, and now all decisions are easy."

In trying at all costs to gain clarity or at least to reduce the painful tension of doubt, the patients use many methods, all of which fall short of their mark. Their everyday thinking, feeling, and acting is shaped to serve this function; the obsessive-compulsive symptoms proper are also aimed, ineffectively, at dispelling confusion. It is as if the person kept asking himself; "How should I think to find out how to live?" "How should I act to be lovable?" The pain of confusion stimulates thinking. In searching for clarity the person practices and develops his intellectual faculties. These may be used for creating fantastic and farcical structures or may be wasted in endless ruminations, but they can also be utilized productively. The basic dilemma of the dual orientation cannot be resolved through thinking alone, no matter how correct the conclusions. But the fact that the patients' thinking has this purpose helps to explain the tremendous value they usually give to intelligence and their great reliance on it. Most patients insist on the strength of their intellect, even if they cannot think of any other personal assets.

One can view the devices used by the patients as having four main objectives: to reduce confusion by making clear-cut divisions, to achieve a synthesis of opposites, to evolve rules to live by, to override confusion. I shall give some examples for each category.

One way of dealing with the confused image of the good-bad world is to *divide it sharply in two*, ascribing goodness to one part, badness to the other; one can then respond to them differentially. In the perception of a noncommittal person the here and now is frustrating and threatening, but he also vaguely envisions, at least while he is young, some remote paradise in the future. Applied to people, the division results in clear-cut doubling, as if the parent, e.g., were present in two editions, good and bad—the loving father and the murderer posing as father, the "day mother" and the "night mother" that took turns with the child in one patient's dream. The image of the bad parent often forms the content of obsessive thought. The child who fantasies that he is adopted and will sooner or later be reclaimed by his loving and exalted true parents is also "doubling." The two images may be embodied in two real people, particularly if their characteristics fit them for these roles: the good mother and the bad stepmother, the bad father and the good uncle. Drastic reversals may occur when someone previously cast as good is suddenly proved "bad." In therapy both images are projected on the therapist, whom the patient wishes to be good and friendly but suspects of being secretly inimical. This fear makes him watch the therapist sharply to catch his unspoken thoughts.

The device of doubling has the effect of undermining the patient's adaptive thinking; the rift it creates in his world is difficult to bridge. In searching for clear distinctions and easy rules, the patient increasingly indulges in either-or thinking which oversimplifies and violates reality. Schematic absolutes replace realistic discernment which could lead to dynamic adaptation. This kind of thinking results, among other things, in obsessive purism or in a preference for extremes; these may take the form of rigid insistence on lofty, unadulterated principles of performance or conduct, either in general or in some specific area. Such extremism can then be used also in the service of neurotic fault-finding. But, with rare exceptions, the method of dividing or doubling fails to dispel the patient's confusion and to give him reassuring certainty. Unlike the hysteric who, by suppression and exaggeration, can easily make things look black or white, the noncommittal person rarely succeeds in his desperate struggle to achieve a lasting separation of his two orientations. Again and again the positive and the negative images are blurred or reversed; the two items embodying them can shift positions in no time at all, sometimes in the course of one statement, only the polarity as such being a constant. Instead of black *or* white, everything eventually is black *and* white. The two colors neither separate nor blend and never form a differentiated series of grays.

Instead of forcibly dividing the confused world image in two, one can try to make it consistent by synthesis, i.e., by *reconciling the opposites*. Within the comprehensive framework of a system both may, for instance, be shown to emanate from one and the same principle. This method of dealing with confusion leads to a search for laws and regularities, for explanations of what seems to be chance, for ways to reconcile what seems to be mutually exclusive. Many noncommittal persons apply their intellect to such ordering, system-building pursuits quite productively—in scientific work or in other areas where ordering complex material is of the essence. The urge to ferret out all the "buts," to know both sides of every story, can be an asset in many contexts. Indiscriminately applied, the device of overcoming confusion through order can lead to pedantry and to obsessive disfunctional orderliness.

Within the obsessive-compulsive symptoms proper, the wish to preserve both sides of the dilemma and to combine them in an orderly fashion is reflected in the widespread use of ordering devices, such as numbers. If one can think of no other way of ordering a multitude of items, one can always count them. The same attitude is at the bottom of the patient's insistence on symmetry. Symmetry, in fact, is the basic pattern of obsessive-compulsive symptoms: doing and undoing, approaching and withdrawing, sinning and expiating. In many compulsive acts and rituals the idea of re-establishing balance is conscious and symmetry is an explicit requirement. In some touching compulsions, having touched an object to one's right one must touch one to his left or the right and left hands must be used alternately. Sometimes the alternating preference for the right and left hand was clearly related in childhood to some conscious "balancing intention," such as doing justice to both of the warring parents.

The wish to find guidelines through the maze of confusion leads the patient to search for something stable to believe in, and particularly for safe *rules to live by*. Not knowing which way to turn, he may try to evolve a master plan for his life, some comprehensive program or project or commit himself to a life situation offering such a program or one which at least channels his life: get married, join a political movement, enlist in the army. (The wish for belongingness, for giving himself to people or causes, also plays a part in these commitments.) On a smaller scale the patient keeps devising ritualistic rules for meeting specific situations. These rules may be quite rational, as, e.g., the self-given order to smile when talking to people or always to prepare one's statements in advance. But since they have the rigid form of "always do this" or "never do that," they suppress the person's spontaneous responses to the situations he meets causing his abilities to shrink through disuse. The patient may come to his therapy session with his plan for the hour all made: "Let's take up where we left off." "There are three things I want to discuss." He may object to the therapist's bringing up something new or talking at all. The "program" he has prepared has to be gone through first. In thinking of the benefits to be gained from therapy the patient may pin his major hopes on learning some foolproof rules of behavior, some slogans that work, as it were, by themselves.

Regardless of their specific content, most of the compulsions represent magic rules for warding off harm and insuring the fulfillment of wishes. The child who is unable to discover the conditions under which his parents are good to him resorts to inventing such conditions himself. Their original content may or may not be related to some behavior assumed to be "good" or expiatory. It may later undergo many changes, but the function remains the same. "If I eat no sweets, if I don't step on cracks, if I remember to count backwards every time I count forwards, etc., etc., all will be well and I shall be loved." These magic rules may remain slight or episodic, as they do with normal people; it is well known that omens and superstitions flourish in situations of danger and uncertainty, e.g., among war pilots. In the noncommittal patient they can become a complex dense net of compelling prohibitions and orders in which the person is caught to the point of incapacitation. Yet his goal had been to find simple rules to live by. The wish to simplify one's life, to free it from all superfluous detail, is one of the motives also for the hermitic existence which some patients lead and others dream of.

The method of making sharp arbitrary divisions is sometimes combined with a species of desperate dogmatism which arbitrarily *overshouts doubt*. People who succeed with this method have in some aspects a superficial similarity to hysterics. They see everything sharply as black or white and unhesitatingly divide people into sheep and goats. They perceive no possibilities or probabilities but only truth and untruth. They can sell convictions to themselves and to others; they often make eloquent teachers. Such persons stand by their convictions firm as a rock but at times make a complete turnabout and stand equally firm by their new convictions. In this way they escape paralyzing doubt and ambivalence and give an impression of clear direction and strength. The danger with this type of adjustment is the possibility of a severe depression which typically shows a strong admixture of anxiety; abnormal states of elation may also occur. As long as reality remains sharply split into two polar categories, and the person can stand in the middle and respond to them differentially, all is well and orderly in his surface universe. But if one side of the picture acquires undue prominence, his sense of proportion is suddenly lost and an affective reaction ensues. Still, while it works, the method of counteracting obsessive doubt with dogmatism helps the person to escape from the torment of confusion and futility and may enable him to achieve a better level of practical adjustment.

In conclusion, I shall outline the overall method of dealing with the demands and challenges of life which I had in mind when choosing a name for *the life style of noncommitment*.

Human life means change and growth, but the neurotic, much as he would like to move forward, is unable to do so. He is held back by the unresolved issues of his past and the fear of losing the few satisfactions he has by venturing into the unknown. Therefore, he invents methods of evading growth that would meet, if only in an unreal ephemeral way, both his own wishes for expansion and society's demand that he progress and mature. Noncommitment is one of these methods. This method of evasion consists in saying "yes" and "no" at the same time. The person undertakes a new course of action, and by doing so says "yes" to it; but he does not commit himself wholeheartedly, and so, by implication, negates it. As if continuing childhood play at adult activities, he does not earnestly reach out for the real thing. He may appear to go through the normal developmental stages and outwardly act his age, but his actions and relationships lack reality. He refuses to take responsibility in the sense of identifying himself with his actions and saying unequivocally, "Here I stand." The person is always eyeing two possibilities, choosing a little of both, but neither completely. In this way he turns his life into a farce and deprives himself of real fulfillment. He usually feels that in avoiding commitments he leads a brave fight for personal freedom, but since he does not use it when he has it, the fight turns out to be a fight for freedom to sit on the fence.

Avoidance of wholehearted commitment is most clearly evident in the relationship with a partner of the opposite sex. The compulsive search for the partner or the assumption of external responsibilities is the "yes" of the dilemma; the "no" is expressed in the equally compulsive flight, external or internal, lest the relationship become unqualified and thus binding. This "yes-but" attitude can be found in all spheres of the patient's activity. Avoidance of commitment may also appear in the guise of inability to choose between two potential partners or two fields of work, or between different groups that claim one's allegiance. The crux of the problem is not the characteristics of the competing objects but the person's inability, based on his abiding confusion, to give himself without reservations to any person or cause.

12. Comparison of the Two Patterns and Implications for Therapy

The Salient Features of the Two Patterns

Before discussing the major points to be kept in mind in treating hysterical and obsessive-compulsive patients, I shall review the salient features of these two patterns of life in order to sharpen them by comparison. In reality there is no clear dividing line between the two; both dimensions are present to some degree in every instance of neurosis, although the way in which they are articulated and combined varies from case to case.

The view of the self as weak and unlovable in an overpowering inimical world is common to both patterns. Because of differences in the original traumas (possibly interacting with some little known constitutional factors), this crippling basic assumption is elaborated in different ways.

The hysteric sees the world as frustrating or *depriving;* he is afraid that his positive desires will remain unfulfilled; he sees himself primarily as unliked and unlikable; his central goal is to gain friends. The obsessive-compulsive views the world as *threatening;* he is afraid that he may lay himself open to a destructive attack by an enemy; he feels weak and defenseless, and his most urgent goal is to develop superior strength in order to fend off the enemies.

The central neurotic strategy is focused on one or the other of the two poles of the personal world. The vicariously living person concentrates on the *subject pole;* feeling empty and worthless, he sets out to change or "create" himself—through imitation, by living up to some borrowed standards, or by allying himself with a valued person—and

190

to restore his self-esteem by obtaining attention and approval. The noncommittal person concentrates on the *object pole* of the world; the hostile world must be forced to yield the satisfaction he craves. The hysteric, who represses all tabooed impulses so as to remain good and blameless, insists, in effect, that *he* must be perfect; the obsessive-compulsive insists that the world must be made perfect. Thus the main issue on which neurotic maneuvers are centered is, in one case, the person's own assumed inadequacy, in the other, the assumed hostility of the world. In one pattern the most painful emotional state is the "anxiety of nothingness" which results from self-obliteration and may appear as fear of death or of fatal disease. In the other case, the worst pain comes from uncertainty about whether the world is good or bad and the resulting emotional confusion. Thus hysteria highlights the existential issue of death, of *cessation of individual life;* the obsessive-compulsive neurosis—focused on the polar opposites of good and evil, love and hate—highlights the *ambiguity of human existence.*

As a result of his basic confusion, the noncommittal person suffers from guilt feelings arising from his *hostility* against those who possibly love him and whom he possibly loves. These guilt feelings increase his need to maintain the image of the hostile world so as to justify his own hostile actions. Guilt feelings also perpetuate his extremely derogatory image of himself which, unlike the negative self-image of the hysteric, is usually close to awareness and is not counteracted effectively by the compensatory grandiose one. The vicariously living person has a less serious problem with guilt feelings. In his case they are centered on the issue of *pleasure* and sometimes amount to little more than the fear of being found out in pursuing satisfactions assumed to be forbidden or selfish. Little guilt is felt about hostility, even when its level is high, because it is not in the focus of the neurotic dilemma and strategy. The genuine guilt feelings that appear during treatment refer primarily to the betrayal and falsification of oneself. The range of feelings in general is restricted in both conditions, but while the obsessive-compulsive just lacks feelings, rejecting as "weak" particularly the positive ones, the hysteric attempts to fill out his emotional emptiness by trumped-up, unreal emotions.

Personal development, which results from meeting life's challenges and dealing with them, is precluded by the isolation and anxiety inherent in both neurotic patterns. Both may be viewed as methods of evading personal growth while giving the semblance of maturing, and at the same time as methods of denying responsibility for one's conduct of life. Since the "I" of the vicariously living person is not his real I, he says in effect, "*It was not I who did it.* I was told to do it, I did what was expected of me, or what everyone does." The noncommittal person avoids responsibility by not taking a stand, by saying "yes" and "no" at the same time, by not being wholehearted about anything he does. In merely going through the motions, he deprives his acts of reality and is saying, in effect, "It was done, but it was not real. *I did not mean it.*"

The function of interpersonal relations is different in the two patterns. For the vicariously living person people are of the utmost importance as models for imitation, sources of guidance and approval, or partners through whom one can live. The desire for "life-giving" human contact and for dependence on others is intense and usually conscious. A "strong" partner is usually preferred. The patient is apt to cling to the relationship and may become dominating and possessive out of dread of being deserted and left with one's nothingness. If separation has to be accepted, it is most important to counteract its effects on one's self-respect by proving that one is innocent, that one did not deserve abandonment.

The noncommittal person, believing that he cannot gain acceptance, rejects this wish as a sign of weakness. He wants to be strong, self-sufficient, and free; other people mean very little to him in the long run, and he avoids commitment by withdrawal. Such a person tends to choose a "weak" partner, one who will see him as strong and who can be counted on not to revolt too soon against his ways. Besides, only those who seem needy, handicapped, starved for affection, offer the promise of being satisfied with the little he feels he can offer. Even so, he is compelled to woo the object of his choice with explicit or implied promises which he knows he cannot keep; he lives in dread of the moment when he will be called to fulfill them.

In some respects the needs typical of the two patterns both contrast and dovetail. Contrasting personal preferences, e.g., for leading and following, teaching and being taught, doing one's own work and assisting others—when they are organized by confident and self-confident expectations—can result in harmonious teamwork. But the rigid neurotic absolutes permit no adaptive interpersonal integration. The dovetailing features of the two patterns can attract two people to each other but cannot insure lasting satisfaction. The relationship dissolves or deteriorates into mutual enslavement. The hysteric's need for constant attention, praise, and support, and the wish to assure these by controlling the partner, clash with the obsessive's need for independence and personal freedom. If the demand for excessive guidance and help is met by the "strong" partner, this perpetuates the other's helplessness and brings no reward to the giver who is accused of selfish domination if he is not accused of callous indifference. Such accusations hit the noncommittal person in his weak spot. Because of his proneness to guilt feelings he can be bullied into doing almost anything, and the partner may instinctively capitalize on his handicap for making him undertake increasingly burdensome obligations, which in turn increase his resentments. No matter how unjust the specific accusations or how deliberately used for exploitation, the noncommittal person does have good reason to feel guilty since his inner detachment, his refusal to share with the partner, confirm the other's hidden feeling of being utterly worthless. This guilt may prevent the noncommittal person from dissolving the relationship: to do so would mean to deliver the final crushing blow of rejection, the force of which he knows all too well from his own experience.

If in one of the partners the healthy organization becomes dominant, the neurotic features of the interaction can be partially redeemed within the healthy pattern. At its worst the neurotic partnership may result in two neuroses being integrated into a new unit as self-perpetuating and self-enhancing as an individual neurosis. Since each of the two members functions as a part of the other's neurosis, a part which remains outside the therapist's office, such a stabilized organization can put serious obstacles in the way of therapy.

Therapy of Hysteria

Hysteria has always been considered relatively easy to treat. In part this opinion was based on false assumptions, namely on equating the illness with its symptoms. The typical hysterical symptoms can be made to disappear very rapidly with almost any kind of therapeutic approach, including direct suggestion. But this quick "cure" seldom lasts. The symptoms reappear, and even if they do not this is only a minimal gain. If the underlying hysterical character structure has not been modified, the person is still engaged in a complex and unproductive mode of living which brings little satisfaction and may get him into all kinds of trouble even in the absence of symptoms. On the other hand, if in working on symptoms one goes beneath the surface and uncovers some at least of their roots, the gain may be substantial and more lasting.

Chances for success in treating the hysterical character neurosis are highest for simple hysteria, although in some cases extreme anxiety about any dislodging of the "false front" presents a serious obstacle to treatment. In particular, those patients whose pseudopersonality is formed around some absolute ideal cannot bear to appear less than perfect. The slightest criticism is a threat to the whole structure and may lead to its collapse. These difficult cases, however, are balanced by those patients who blossom forth in a spectacular way once the relevant dynamic factors are touched upon. In some of them, very primitive urges may be uncovered once the artificial surface personality has given way. This probably indicates that excessive repression had set in quite early, so that many functions were prevented from maturing; what breaks through at first may be infantile. This, however, is a transitory phase and nothing to worry about; the important thing is that genuine feelings and impulses of whatever kind should come through and be recognized by the patient as his own. They may be primitive, but they mature quite rapidly once this area has been opened. After all, the person has been growing, even if only peripherally, "in secret," and he catches up very quickly once the contact with himself has been established. Some cases of simple hysteria show this rapid development in therapy and within a short time achieve substantial and enduring results. Such cases contribute to the opinion that hysteria is easy to treat, but they are by no means the rule. Most character neuroses of long standing show some complicating developments, and time is needed to work them out. Yet it remains true that patients who show the pattern of simple hysteria are in most respects "good patients." They are usually very cooperative, take therapeutic work seriously, and are eminently capable of insight and of experiencing emotionally the significant personal issues that analysis brings up. In working with them, however, one must guard against certain pitfalls which may result from their suggestibility, their wish for guidance, and from their tendency to dramatize.

In trying to help the patient to strengthen and shape his relatively undeveloped healthy personality, the therapist must resist the temptation to teach these extremely eager and teachable people who quickly discover what it is that he wants and act it out most convincingly. If he is not careful, the therapist may unwittingly meet the patients' need for a great teacher at whose feet they can worship and thus increase their dependency and play into the hand of the neurosis. When an adult patient acts toward the therapist like a helpless little girl, I do not assume a corresponding tone but treat her respectfully as an adult woman. To react to the healthy aspect of the patient rather than to his neurosis is one of the many ways available to the therapist for stimulating and furthering the patient's growth without falling into didacticism.

A serious problem arises if a patient who has a strong tendency toward dramatization makes the process of analysis a part of his or her neurosis by turning it into a hotbed of emotional sprees. He not only relives the emotional issues of his past that gave rise to persistent fantasies but makes them the main content of his present life, failing to gain distance and perspective. He neglects to add to each exciting discovery that it is sheer fantasy, very different from the present reality, and to draw conclusions from that. Thus analysis itself becomes a fascinating vicarious existence, much more important to the patient than the rest of his life, and termination becomes a thorny issue; getting well and settling down to ordinary life is felt to be an uninspiring prospect.

Hysteria with negativistic defenses also has a good prognosis in therapy, but the presence of an additional layer in the neurotic structure creates additional difficulties which may require a longer time to be worked out. The nature of these difficulties should be obvious from the nature of the defenses, which are directed against any interference from outside; as long as these defenses are strong, the patient is not easily accessible to therapy. Many of the patients who at some point in their lives develop strong defenses against their own malleability harbor a hidden belief, based on early traumatic experiences, that they have been maliciously and deceptively kept from the "good things" of life (such as sex and closeness with people) and that they have been made into something they are not by selfish and arbitrary parents. If at the time of entering treatment these patients have not yet made these beliefs explicit to themselves and still deny themselves needlessly, feeling that the good things are not for them, they often make rapid progress in therapy. What they seek from the therapist is a confirmation of their sneaking suspicion they they *do* have the right to enjoyment, and they respond promptly to his implicit reassurance. At this stage, before protections against "foreign influence" have been erected, the therapist has a chance to ally himself directly with the patient's genuine impulses and thus create a sound basis for the subsequent work. These are the relatively simple cases which conform to the frequently described classical pattern; the self-limiting values taken over from others are only lightly held by the patient and can be easily discarded in therapy.

The situation is different if the patient comes into therapy after having discovered the "deception" by himself and having broken through the inhibitions that kept him from enjoying life—even if he has done this in a rebellious and anxious fashion, whistling in the dark as it were. One might expect therapy to be easier after the patient has gained these insights, but in fact treatment at this point is often extremely difficult. Feeling that the early "deprivers" succeeded for a time in dominating and deceiving him by taking advantage of his trusting nature, he is strongly determined that this should never happen again, bent on preventing history from repeating itself. This creates a great deal of suspiciousness, of resistance to therapy, as well as a tendency to dominate out of fear of being dominated. In addition, since the first compliant phase has not been adequately worked through and resolved, the remaining uncertainty about "friend or foe" creates some ambivalence and guilt which makes the clinical picture shift toward the obsessive-compulsive side. The resulting obstacles to learning in therapy require careful handling by the therapist and take a long time to be understood and overcome. In these patients the neurotic's usual defense of his dominant pattern of life is compounded by a passionate indiscriminate resistance against anybody or anything at all.

In cases of borderline hysteria the obstacles to therapy are almost insurmountable because the gratifying fantasy holds sway. Tendencies in this direction are found also in patients with negativistic defenses. In some of them the wish to dominate and mold others—e.g., to convert the therapist to their way of life, or to their religion—has a function that goes beyond that of defense through offense. To create a world congenial to the patient's desires and ideas in which he could live comfortably is a positive alternative to having to fight tooth and nail against a world that would arbitrarily change him. This alternative is reflected in the patient's tendency to divide the world sharply into two camps: people who understand and love him, who are of his own kind, and the selfish arbitrary opposition. To maintain this black-and-white picture the patient resorts to the most fantastic distortions of reality, creating people who love him deeply and making devilish characters of others. In "borderline" patients this omnipotent fantasy celebrates its triumphs; the patient's full alliance with his illness is the malignant feature that makes the prospect of real therapeutic success more than doubtful. I myself have worked with only a few of such cases, and on the basis of my experience I feel that one can be satisfied if one succeeds in helping the patient to keep his fantasies within limits and to curb his tendency to act them out in potentially deleterious ways. The prognosis is better in the case of those patients in whom this pattern is not yet stabilized.

Therapy of the Obsessive-Compulsive Neurosis

The dimension of noncommitment presents greater difficulties in therapy than the dimension of vicarious living. Obsessive-compulsive neurotics probably make up the bulk of those patients who fail to be substantially helped by therapy, sometimes with a succession of therapists over many years. In my experience, one can work with these patients successfully, provided one adapts the procedure to the special features of their pattern and learns to avoid certain pitfalls. One of the requisites is the therapist's willingness to make use of methods other than interpretation and generally to counteract the trend toward purely intellectual discussions. These patients, because of their detachment and their high valuation of the intellect, readily substitute abstract theoretical formulations for personal insights and convictions; whether or not these formulations are correct, their therapeutic value is usually nil.

The difficulties that require special attention and handling arise from three interrelated sources: the extreme self-derogation of the patient, his despair about himself; the coactivation of opposite tendencies, which may result in extensive blocking; and the pervasive guilt feelings, which work against any radical improvement in the image of the self and of the world.

As long as the coactivation of impulses works full time, very little can be achieved in therapy; every strengthening of constructive, healthy impulses is matched almost automatically by the strengthening of the opposition. Something must be done as early as possible to weaken the bond between the two components of coactivational units, particularly if the tensions and inhibitions resulting from their struggle have become wide-spread and incapacitating. A good inroad for attempts to relax the tension of the opposites is afforded by those situations in which the fight on one side is carried out consciously—fight against an obsessive thought, or a compulsive act, or an inhibition of action. Since this struggle is deliberate and usually viewed as a realistic necessity, the patient can check it if he becomes clearly aware that it merely adds to his predicament. With a patient who was tormented by obsessive fantasies of jealousy and a desperate struggle against them, my offhand suggestion not to fight them happened to strike home and marked the turning point in his treatment. There is room for this kind of direct attack on some particularly disturbing or incapacitating symptoms, but essential relief can be expected only if the patient succeeds in transforming the specific suggestion into a general attitude, a conviction he can securely hold as his own.

This process is well described in the following letter written by a patient: "When you first suggested to me the slogan 'Easy does it' as a way out of my terrific feeling of strain, I felt it would reduce me to complete inadequacy. My slogan for many years had been, in effect, 'What do you mean you can't do it? You've got to do it even if it kills you!' But by that time the evidence was clear that my straining had brought me to the crippled state I was in. As I began to understand and practice the heretical idea of doing things within the limits of ease, I began to find here and there that it worked, and my confidence in it began to grow; gradually I realized the great value it had for me. For instance, I used to prepare even for petty routine situations by anticipating what might happen and thinking of what I would do if it did. As I started controlling this and crossing my bridges when I came to them, I found that I was able to see the novel aspects of the situation and to deal with them in a way I could never have anticipated. Similarly, as I gave up writing down everything I had to remember, I found that my memory worked all right. But even more important than these specific dividends was the resulting general feeling of confidence in myself, the recognition that I had reason to repect and trust the natural workings of my mind and, more generally, myself. Perhaps giving up straining is a way of finding yourself; to put it in an oversimplified fashion—you are what comes easy and natural."

Relaxing, giving up the struggle, is an important precondition of change; it can usher in a shift from the neurotic to the healthy organization. We shall encounter this phenomenon on a larger scale when we discuss some crucial stages of therapy.

I am convinced that one of the main reasons of failure in the therapy of the noncommittal pattern is our incorrect or inadequate approach to the problem of guilt. One cannot deal with guilt feelings therapeutically by merely trying to assuage them or by pointing out their fantastic nature. No matter how exaggerated or displaced they may be, and how destructive their consequences, they usually have a basis in real guilt, in a betrayal of one's own actual or potential loyalties. Such feelings are evidence of the patient's submerged healthy orientation, and should not be dismissed as mere neurotic distortions. I shall return to the problem of guilt when I discuss therapy (see Chapter 15). Here I shall only describe one mechanism, typical of the noncommittal pattern, by which guilt accumulated in the course of a neurotic life can cause the patient to persist in his fearful and hostile attitudes and thus become a formidable obstacle to change.

There is one way of hushing up guilt feelings in which precarious self-justification is achieved at the price of increased hostility. The situation is familiar from everyday life. A does some injustice to B, perhaps merely out of thoughtlessness or ignorance, and then discovers the true facts. Now A must either admit his mistake or, if he is not ready to face his guilt, find more fault with B to prove himself right. The belief that B does not deserve any better protects him from the pain he would feel at having hurt an innocent person. This is often the main function of the excessive faultfinding I mentioned before. The patients themselves may be dimly aware of this, noting, e.g., that they feel glad when someone has wronged them because then they can vent their anger without guilt; they may reproach the therapist for being irreproachable. However, the method of silencing guilt by stepping up overt or covert aggression only results in more guilt which has to be countered in the same way, so that both guilt and hostility increase in a vicious spiral. Like a little lie bolstered by bigger and bigger lies, the situation can snowball until the person is buried under a mountain of guilt and has no way of getting out. At the same time the tender impulses are pushed away farther and farther; feeling them means risking to find out that one has been hostile toward a person one loves.

The patient's guilt feelings cannot be dealt with fully as long as his extreme self-derogation persists. Because of his complete lack of self-esteem, no interpretation should be given that can be used by him to confirm or increase his feeling of worthlessness. Interpretations that imply the deep-seated or instinctual nature of the patient's destructiveness fit only too well into his own neurotic mythology and increase his despair about himself. Consider the dream with which one patient responded to his first contact with psychoanalytic literature. He dreamed that he was due for an appointment in a shack bearing the sign "Bestial natures corrected," but he was not sure if the last word was not "castrated." In making his comments the therapist must keep his manner free of any implications of superior knowledge or of demands the patient cannot fulfill at the time; either can increase his feeling of inadequacy. But these precautions, important as they are, do not suffice to alleviate the patient's basic self-contempt. In fact, even noticeable improvement in his way of managing situations will not alter his entrenched negative self-image. One patient remarked, e.g., that he knew he had changed because people remarked on this and responded to him differently but that he himself felt no difference: "My concept of myself lags way behind my behavior."

To make a change possible, the first task, after the exploration of the patient's psychological situation, should be to uncover the constructive roots of his behavior, including the behavior he himself abhors most. In working with noncommittal patients a safe rule to follow is that the task of uncovering the latent healthy pattern should have precedence over all the other tasks that must be accomplished in therapy. Until this is achieved in some measure the patient will view even his constructive behavior as resulting from reprehensible motives. In one such instance, when the therapist remarked that other motives besides the neurotic ones might have been involved, the patient reacted with a strong surge of hope: "If I only knew that there is some good in me I would not mind facing all my neurotic attitudes and working on them."

If one fails to help the patient discover a firm personal basis for self-esteem, the treatment will be unnecessarily prolonged or end in failure. Without this preparation the patient has only his neurotic pretenses to fall back on under stress. When he realizes that he cannot pretend to the therapist, that he is unmasked, his conclusion must unavoidably be "My therapist thinks I am worthless. I knew it all along and now I am sure. There is no hope; I am beyond repair." If he brings out these feelings, the therapist has another chance and can correct his mistake. But it may happen that the patient does not voice these feelings and, his hopes dimmed, goes on with the treatment in a halfhearted fashion. He no longer believes that it will help, but he sees no other source of help either, no alternative he could try. So, feeling utterly lost, he keeps going to his sessions, without enough hope to motivate him to work on his problems; he just lets himself be exposed to therapy. Or, the patient's belief that the therapist does not think much of him, or actually despises him, arouses anger mixed with grandiosity: "I will show him! He will be sorry when I show the world who I am!" And he goes about "showing him" in his habitual neurotic fashion. In this way the therapeutic relationship may become another personal failure, confirming the patient's negative conception of himself and of the world at large.

Part Three

Treatment

13. The Holistic Approach to Interpretation

The Holistic Approach and the Focus on Specifics

After some years of experience every therapist evolves a conception of what is going on in his patients and between his patients and himself, even if this conception remains unformulated or is, in part, a "borrowed Bible." I believe it is to the advantage of our work to formulate a theory of treatment as explicitly as possible, even though it must be kept flexible. The holistic approach postulates that man is to be understood not in terms of specific functions or traits, but in terms of the broad system principles which organize these traits into a hierarchy of systems and subsystems. According to my particular conception, personality viewed in its broad outline is a *dualistic organization;* any personal trait can function as part of the organization of health or of that of neurosis. Viewed in greater detail, it is also a *pluralistic organization;* each concrete item can function as part of a number of subsystems of the two major organizations. The discussions that follow should demonstrate how these theoretical assumptions color and define, or redefine, our conceptions of the day-to-day therapeutic enterprise. The theory of the dual organization of personality, of "universal ambiguity," is especially pertinent to the next three chapters, in which I shall give a generalized description of the total course of therapy and the handling of its typical stages and turning points. In this chapter I shall deal with the holistic method of viewing and organizing the information obtained from the patient, with emphasis on the pluralistic aspect of personality organization and on the initial exploratory phase of the treatment.

In describing the genesis of neurosis I have tried to show how single traumatic occurrences are generalized into a set of diffident and pessimistic expectations which are then elaborated in various ways and organize all future experience. The therapist is thus confronted not with a number of specific disturbances caused by a number of specific traumatic events, but with a complex *system of generalized attitudes* of which the patient himself is not clearly aware and which he cannot communicate directly and quickly. How should the therapist approach the scattered information received from the patient in order to respond to it in therapeutically effective ways?

The fundamental implication of the conception of neurosis as a system is that significant change can come only from above, from the larger whole and not from the part, from the general and not from the specific; in other words, it is mediated by *holistic insight*. The desired changes do not take place piecemeal, first in one small item, then in another, until they accumulate to the point where they make a practical difference. Changes of major importance take place in attitudes of broad scope; the broader the attitude, the wider the therapeutic effect.

A major change may be explicit and conscious. In some cases one can trace both its gradual preparation and the final precipitating experience. This is not true of all cases, however, since vital attitudes are not identical with conscious sentiments, and their shifts are not always reflected in awareness. One sometimes observes striking and extensive improvement, the roots and circumstances of which are hidden from both the patient and the therapist. In some exceptional cases awareness of processes that underlie change may be lacking almost completely. One of my patients, a successful businessman referred because of a psychosomatic problem, seemed incapable of any psychological understanding; to my invitation to talk about his life he kept replying "What is there to talk about? If I have a stomach-ache, I have a stomach-ache." He talked only about external events. When I tried to point out their personal implications, he listened as a student might listen to a difficult lecture, but it was obvious that he did not understand what I was talking about. Some of it nevertheless seemed to penetrate, bypassing awareness as it were, and to produce effects that testified to changes of attitudes. But this is an unusual case. The general point I want to make is that in many instances what we observe are the radiating consequences of changes of a broader scope which themselves have escaped observation.

On the other hand, an improvement achieved in one specific item rarely lasts because of the pull exercised by the superordinate dynamic pattern. We cannot expect to eliminate the symptom unless we facilitate the resolution of larger neurotic subsystems to which it belongs. At one time nailbiting was treated by immersing the fingertips in a bitter fluid; this was supposed to remind the person not to bite his nails when he inadvertently started to do so. But fighting an undesirable habit every time the temptation arises requires extraordinary effort, and still the struggle remains largely futile. Some patients try to use partial insights gained during treatment in a like manner, resolving that in specific situations they will remind themselves of that insight: "This may have been necessary when I was a child, but not any longer." "Remember, he is not your father." Yet when the occasion arises, they often forget, and if they do remember, this does not lessen the struggle. These formulations are in fact mistaken. The early significant experiences were not with the patient's father as seen by him or her today, but with the "primal father" who stood for all men. Reference to the father is therefore less relevant than would be the registering of one's attitude to men or to people in general. This method of exploiting partial insights is essentially useless. It fails to increase the patient's trust in himself; his freedom is, in fact, reduced if he has to watch himself at every step as if he were an unreliable servant. Significant changes cannot be enforced on the behavioral level. Effort is certainly required to bring about change, but not the effort of forcing or suppressing single manifestations of general attitudes. When holistic insight leads to changes in broad attitudes, the details of behavior fall into place more or less automatically, without excessive expenditure of effort, even in areas that have not been worked on in therapy at all. One changes significantly in one's roots, not in one's branches.

The implication for the therapist is that interpretive work should focus on the broader attitudes indicated by the totality of reported and observed items and not on single items or symptoms. By focusing on specifics we actually play into the hand of the neurosis, since the patient himself may resort to the method of focalization to make the real issue inaccessible to awareness.

A patient who came to me after an uncompleted analysis with another therapist had an aversion to birthmarks. If he discovered a spot on a person's skin—and even a tiny freckle was a "birthmark" to him—he would have nothing to do with that person. He told me pathetically but with poorly veiled triumph that all the previous interpretations, such as a possible connection between a birthmark and the color of the nipple, had failed to solve the riddle. This man in his daily life showed an unusual degree of neurotic faultfinding and spent a great deal of time "digging up dirt" about people. He would quickly find some defect in any person, idea, or cause to which he felt attracted, and this made them completely worthless to him. While he was greatly concerned with the hidden significance of birthmarks, he was not at all concerned about the obvious destructiveness of his life. He saw his urge to find fault as a valuable critical talent.

Another patient was greatly annoyed at noisy people with "no consideration" for others. He often fell asleep with his own radio on, but he was upset and angered if a neighbor quietly played his radio at night. His former analyst had suggested that this was a reaction to an early experience, or fantasy, of his parents having intercourse in the next room, an interpretation which had no effect on the symptom. When I suggested that it might be just another instance of his compensatory feeling of being someone very special to whom great respect and consideration were due, this clicked and proved helpful. As he later told me, this interpretation also increased his faith in both me and himself since we had proved able to work fruitfully with the evidence of his current feelings and observations instead of having to rely on theoretical clichés and on reconstructing events he could not recall.

These examples should not be construed to mean that I am against genetic interpretation as such. Genetic insights are indispensable, but their significant function is not the tracing of separate histories of specific symptoms. Aversion to birthmarks may or may not be founded in some early experience connected with the breast; a general attitude can, as it were, pick up along the way the details through which it can express itself. If there was an early event that gave rise to the aversion, its reconstruction or reliving by the patient would be of value only insofar as it made plausible and vivid to him the traumas that had initiated his neurosis as a whole. The exact genesis of a particular symptom, though it can be an object of intellectual curiosity, is not a promising road to therapeutically effective insight. But if used as a clue to factors relevant to the patient's current life, the symptom can lead to the discovery of personal attitudes that have an important position in the structure of his neurosis. Pointing out such attitudes is the best antidote to the tendency to think in terms of isolated problems. As one patient said in retrospect about an early interpretation of this nature, "I can see now that this started me thinking about myself instead of about my 'medical problem.'"

Most patients accept the holistic interpretations quite naturally; in fact, they do not become actively curious about the genesis of their neurosis until they have become at least dimly aware of the nature and extent of their neurotic predicament. Exceptions are found among those who have had treatment before or have read on neurosis and therapy. Some of these sophisticated patients assume that nothing but the excavation of the past can have therapeutic effects; they hope for some "archaeological find" to bring about a miracle. One has to make it clear to them that if the issue were only in the past and not alive in the present, no amount of exploration of childhood could yield practical results.

Emphasis on broad attitudinal trends does not imply neglect of the individual patterning. It is true that one must bring to the patient's awareness the attitudes common to all neuroses: pervasive fear, hostility and anticipation of hostility, self-derogation, the lack of genuine fulfillment, the distortion of external and internal reality. But one must never lose sight of the fact that these attitudes are elaborated, interconnected, and implemented in individual ways. Unless these individual patterns are given full weight, the patient will not recognize the general attitudes as his own and will not be able to grasp the pervasive common denominator of his current mode of living. It will help the therapist to keep in mind the characteristics of neurosis as such as well as those of its subpatterns so that he can recognize them in each individual case. Still, he should not use short cuts; he must work in terms of the evidence provided by the patient himself and beware of discarding anything that does not fit his own preconceived notions. Only in this way can he let the individual person come fully into his own. If the therapist regards the patient as just another instance of a theory, he forfeits his own chance to learn something from him.

The therapist must also resist the temptation to locate quickly causal connections and causal chains in the complex web of neurosis even when this looks deceptively simple. Hardly anything in neurosis is connected in a straightforward cause-and-effect fashion; the processes are circular, and "effects" and "causes" easily trade places. One cannot form an adequate conception of the complexity and variety of neurotic organizations if one considers merely their starting points and their outcomes and tries to connect them directly. Both the nuclear traumas and the neurotic symptomatology have only a limited range. It sometimes seems incredible that a single problem area, e.g., the oedipal conflict, can give rise to such multiform developments, and, on the other hand, that such a wide range of different failures of integration can find expression in one and the same symptom. The traumatic causes and the neurotic outcomes show only limited variations from case to case, but between them lies the individual neurotic creation with all its complexity and variety.

The Finding of Syndromes

The first step toward discovering the idiosyncratic variants of neurotic attitudes is to reduce the vast array of symptoms, peculiarities, and other manifestations of neurosis by grouping them into larger units or syndromes. This procedure of gathering single items into larger units as instances of the same theme is not arbitrary classification. The syndrome, we assume, is more than the term means literally, namely certain items running together. The fact that they run together may indicate that they belong together within a larger dynamic unit and therefore may serve as signposts to the broader prepotent attitudes of the person. Thus a tentative gathering of single items into syndromic units is a form of interpretation that gradually reduces the diversity of the material, tests hunches and hypotheses, and prepares the way for further interpretations. Holistic interpretation leads from specific items to syndromic units and through them to personal attitudes of wider scope.

To illustrate the point that a single symptom can be interpreted only as part of a syndrome, let us examine *premature ejaculation*, a clear-cut symptom and a very frequent disturbance of the sexual function. On the face of it, this phenomenon is a short cut, an abbreviation of the normal process. With this in mind one may wonder whether it does not represent a precipitous rush to the goal of need satisfaction, and one starts looking for evidence of the same trend in other contexts. In many cases this hypothesis is confirmed. One may notice, e.g., that the person cannot tolerate hunger; barely registered, it takes on an urgency that must be immediately relieved, the alternative being a generally disorganized state. Thus in many cases the approach to the symptom must be through the syndrome of *generalized impatience*, of inability to wait. Studying the symptom in conjunction with other manifestations of the same attitude will be more illuminating than studying it in isolation, but we must know the signs of the syndrome to be able to decide whether the symptom conforms to the pattern.

The term "inability to wait" is misleading. All of us learn to wait in the sense of living through the time that elapses between the appearance of a need and its gratification. We may be eager to get an answer to a letter, but we can do nothing but wait; the question is *how* one waits. A person who is comfortable in the present and fairly confident of the future is satisfied with having done whatever was possible at the time toward the achievement of his goal. The pressure of need is temporarily abolished leaving him free to turn to other concerns. In contrast, the person who is "unable to wait" is actively engaged in waiting or, rather, in time-consuming futile efforts to make the expected event come about. Waiting for a kettle to boil, he must watch it continuously, as if to help it along. If he is waiting for a letter, he will go to the mailbox repeatedly, even when, as he knows, no mail could have been delivered. He engages in elaborate fantasies about how exactly the expected event will take place. His current activity is disrupted by these futile efforts; he is in fact so busy waiting that he has no time for anything else. Or he looks for ways to "kill time" to relieve the pain of waiting.

This generalized impatience can have various meanings and roots. Contrary to popular opinion, "spoiling" the child by quickly granting most of his wishes is hardly a major causative factor in itself; even the most indulged child has ample opportunity to learn to cope with unavoidable delays. Spoiling, however, can be traumatic in conjunction with some anxiety-producing factors, such as initial denial of wishes followed by their gratification if the child insists strongly enough. This pattern emerges from many a patient's childhood memories. Probably the most important traumatic factor is the abrupt deprivation of something very essential, such as occurs, e.g., when abrupt weaning leads to virtual starvation. The impatience and the panicky leap to the end of the process are based on the principle, "Get it while the getting is good." In fact, when frustration of a vital need is involved, a panicky grab for the supply that threatens to disappear is a natural reaction, more adaptive than, e.g., attempting to deny the frustrated need by developing an aversion to milk or by becoming a poor eater in general. Other protections against the recurrence of the trauma are hoarding and similar measures to insure supply; elaborate fantasies about growing foodstuffs, hunting, or fishing may be pursued with great diligence and be a source of great fascination. Several such methods can be used by the same person; when they are carried over to the handling of needs other than the one originally frustrated, their expressions are legion. (In premature ejaculation itself, the method of rushing to the goal may be combined with that of reactive rejection of the threatened gratification and with fantasies such as the harem fantasy—about continuous abundant supply.) If the patient is found to use many such methods, the probability is high that his disturbance dates back to an early frustration of a vital need.

The same conclusion cannot be drawn from generalized impatience alone. This syndrome is found quite regularly in that variant of vicarious living which is characterized by negativistic defenses against one's own tendency to repress or suppress genuine wishes. The patient's feeling that a vital satisfaction is threatened and must be grabbed quickly need not be an upshot of a similar early frustration; it can also stem from his having too often and too easily given up, or "lost," his own wishes. Linking premature ejaculation to the broader syndrome of impatience is only the first step in mapping out the position of this symptom within the neurotic organization.

If the syndrome of generalized impatience is not in evidence, the therapist must look for another syndrome of which the symptom might be a part. A second group of factors with which premature ejaculation is commonly found to be homologous involves not a fear of frustration resulting in a panicky eagerness but a series of other fears which may center on intercourse itself. Here the person's situation is comparable to that of a soldier who, to reach safety, must cross a strip of land under enemy fire. The strategy is "Get through as fast as you can." Fear of sexual intercourse has many varieties, some of them extremely common: fear of doing something forbidden and punishable, occasionally connected with the fear of detection; fear of harming or debasing the partner, sometimes with the hidden desire to do so; fear of being damaged, depleted, or made ill; fear of being swallowed up, of losing one's independence; fear of experiencing pleasure; fear of not being able to satisfy the partner, thus breaking implicit promises; fear of asserting oneself as an adult; fear of a recurrence of failure, which in itself invites failure. The presence of these factors can be deduced, first, from certain features associated with the symptom itself, e.g., the thoughts that precipitate it, and, second, from the recurrence of similar fears in situations other than the sexual one, i.e., from the presence of a homologous syndrome. I shall take up in detail some of the syndromes which these fears indicate.

(*a*) The fear of doing something prohibited and punishable, while simultaneously pressed toward gratification by natural impulses, is found to lead to the symptom only infrequently, except when the risk of detection makes haste a realistic necessity. This particular fear is more likely to lead to disturbances of the sexual function other than *ejaculatio praecox*.

(*b*) The fear of hurting or damaging can occur as a primary attitude or in a reactive fashion. In the first case, we find the symptom embedded in a syndrome of fear of hurting women, especially of hurting them sexually. The fear may have its origins in actual observation of sexual acts when one was young enough to perceive them as violence; or the child may have overheard the mother objecting to intercourse or asking the father to be "careful." The facts of menstruation as observed by the child may also give him the idea of the woman having been wounded and so may accounts of the pain and danger of childbirth. In one case there were memories of numerous illegal abortions which repeatedly placed the mother's life in jeopardy. In this context, and particularly if the mother emphasizes her sacrifices for the children, a tendency develops to view her every illness or suffering as a consequence of these sacrifices or of childbirth as such. The total syndrome is centered on the extreme vulnerability of the other person, with emphasis on women, and is marked by feelings of inordinate obligation: fearing the worst for the women to whom one is related or close; assuming all women to be frail, easily hurt and damaged; being unable to stand the sight of their tears or to deny them anything. Such people can be dominated by the threat of another's suffering more than by any other threat or method of domination. A man who holds this attitude is at the mercy of the masochistic woman who suffers on the slightest provocation. To such a man, her behavior is comparable to throwing herself in front of a moving car, forcing the driver to stop. It allows no freedom of movement to the partner who has the choice of being either completely dominated or extremely cruel. Most frequently he chooses the first, for dread of burdening his conscience, and he cannot even express his resentment of the situation because this would defeat his purpose of not hurting. He must repress his anger; the fear of hurting or damaging the woman is then reinforced by his reaction to his own repressed hostility.

(c) The symptom itself may originally have an aggressive component, an urge to frustrate the partner. Thus the same symptom may express two contradictory purposes: to rush through the process that may be dangerous to the woman and to take revenge for the frustration by disappointing her. In the cases with which I have had close acquaintance the linkage with the hostile impulse seemed to be a secondary development; that the abbreviation of the sexual act had a frustrating effect on the partner seemed to be learned and utilized after the symptom had developed.

Another group of components is indicated by an excessive reaction to the observed response of the partner. It is well known that sexual excitation can be heightened or reduced by the intensity and quality of the partner's response. The stimulation and joy one experiences is enhanced by the excitation and joy of the partner. In close homonomous integration the main element in this added satisfaction is pleasure in the partner's pleasure; the other component, which can degenerate into mere feats of prowess, is pleasure in one's own potency, a pride in how intense an enjoyment one is able to give. The partner's lack of response takes away these satisfactions and may diminish the pleasure. In premature ejaculation, however, the reaction to the partner's response is not merely exaggerated but paradoxical. In a large proportion of cases (not in all) no precipitate reaction takes place even after prolonged genital stimulation as long as the man feels that the partner is not responding fully, that she will not, e.g., agree to actual penetration. In this situation he reacts to the stimulation provided by intense sexual play quite normally, but as soon as the woman indicates her readiness for intercourse, or gives other signs of a strong response, this triggers off the precipitate reaction. Following this clue and looking for homologous syndromes, one may find a fear of being swallowed up and losing one's individuality, but still more frequently one finds that the person responds with fright to emotional demands made of him in any situation. I shall discuss only the latter fear, which occurs in two closely interrelated syndromes.

(*d*) The demand implied in the woman's sexual desire will be frightening to the man if he feels inadequate, unable to give what is wanted and what he himself wants to give. (A generalized ungiving attitude is not typical of these cases; I found it more prevalent among the few cases of retarded ejaculation and of the so-called psychic aspermia that I had a chance to observe.) A late cause of this fear of inadequacy is founded in experiences with the symptom itself and the subsequent anticipation of repeated fiasco, sometimes reinforced by scorn and blame from the partner. There are, however, earlier causes of feeling panic stricken when faced with an emotional demand. In some cases there are indications that this fear is rooted in very early experiences of rejection by the mother, with an obscure feeling remaining that rejection was somehow deserved, that there was an insufficiency in oneself. This feeling gives rise to the assumption that one is unable to satisfy rightful demands. The early traumatic experiences resulting in these assumptions are very rarely recalled, but they are strongly suggested by the syndrome of excessive apprehension that one's tasks will prove to be beyond one's power, that one will break under the burden and leave untended and dissatisfied a great many people who depend on one and who will scorn and hate one for letting them down.

(*e*) Overlapping and interwoven with this pattern there may be a larger syndrome, an aspect of the neurotic's sham existence typical especially of the pattern of noncommitment. The person lives, as it were, on overdrawn promises, and consequently on borrowed time. Feeling weak and worthless, having no hope of being accepted for what he is, for what he can do and give now, this person makes excessive commitments and promises for the future and then lives in fear of the day of reckoning. The "promising young man" who always remains just that is a case in point. The promises need not be made explicitly; they are more frequently mere intimations and hints, but they are meant to get across to the other and usually do. As soon as the promise is taken seriously, the patient begins withdrawal maneuvers in order to avoid the payoff. Ironically, the promises are often unnecessary. The person may be accepted for what he is, but this he cannot believe; he feels that he would have to make superhuman efforts to hold the other's affection or respect.

In the sexual area these attitudes are very clearly expressed in courtship. There are constant allusions to boundless, undying love, hints at passion barely controlled, implicit promises of unheard-of imminent pleasures. Usually, however, there are also obstacles that loom large and may frustrate the carrying out of one's desires; this part prepares the withdrawal. Satisfaction in creating belief and desire in the other person coexists with a dread of destroying the illusion and the wish to contrive an ending before the decisive test. Most of these courtships come to nought. When such a man is finally in a sexual situation, the first show of intense desire on the part of the woman is perceived as a demand to "deliver the goods." It is no wonder, then, that he goes into a panic, and leaves the scene, as it were. The conception of woman which develops within this syndrome is that of an insatiable creature whose only true interest is an unceasing passionate search for sexual pleasure.

The example of *ejaculatio praecox* demonstrates that the same disturbance may have very different meanings in different patients. In the same person one symptom can also be a part of a number of syndromes or trends and can be fruitfully approached now from one perspective, now from the other. The analytic concept of overdetermination of a symptom or act, i.e., the presence of multiple meanings and motives, refers, in fact, to a general feature of personality organization present both in neurosis and in health. The multiple meaning of all human expressions does not entitle the therapist to consider all conceivable interpretations of a symptom equally valid, but it does imply that more than one interpretation of a given phenomenon can be correct. Once interpreted, a fact should not be put aside as a riddle solved; it should be reinterpreted when evidence for a new context has accumulated. The new interpretation does not make the old one wrong, as some patients tend to assume. In tightly organized neurotic structures new meanings may keep emerging in the course of treatment; the most persistent symptoms are probably those that have strong roots in several significant syndromes. They will not subside until all of their roots have been laid bare.

The Methods of Exploration

What can the therapist do to facilitate the discovery of syndromes? He must, first, insure a sufficiently wide range of material by inviting the patient to extend the field of discussion. Starting from the problems initially presented, the field must be broadened to include other areas of the patient's present life, his past history, childhood, and those mental states that are not given serious attention in everyday life, such as dreams, fantasies, seemingly random or inconsequential thoughts. From the start, the process of data-gathering should be oriented to the next step, that of finding connections and syndromes. The patient must experience the facts he reports not in isolation but as parts of a whole; this can only be achieved if the focus is kept steadily on his *present life situation.* Only if this is done will the sessions be vital, not just an hour from four to five, unrelated to the rest of his existence.

It is up to the therapist to emphasize the current relevance of all topics discussed. When the patient relates facts of his childhood, the therapist may respond, e.g., by stressing the emotional potency of some of these events and remarking that they probably made a difference in the patient's later life, perhaps even in his present condition. Although the connection is not yet clear, the patient can realize that the past is not past but still alive in the present, and he can learn to think of it as of "the childhood that is still in me." Similarly, dreams and fantasies should not be left in some remote corner; even when he cannot understand a dream, the patient should begin to think of it as something that *he* dreamed, that reflects *his* current concerns, not just a funny dream but his life. Freud recommended that to facilitate integration of different areas, the therapist should make references to reality if the patient keeps talking about dreams, and vice versa, and similarly with the past and the present. The patient will not follow these shifts and cross references willingly; he dimly senses that the broader view of himself at which the therapist aims will cause pain and make him question his established way of life. But there is no substitute for this course. Unless the focus is kept on the vital issues of the present, the whole process of finding facts and connections will be futile and will result only in stillborn ineffective insights.

Listening to the patient during the period of exploration, the therapist should pay particular attention to details that do not seem "quite right"—that seem out of proportion or out of keeping with the rest of the story. There may be contradictions or inconsistencies in what the patient says; a reported reaction may seem exaggerated, inappropriate to the situation, or different from his other reactions to comparable events. Many of these observations can be shared with the patient right away, and their possible relevance indicated. One can convey to the patient that behind the inconsistencies, the seeming lack of logic, there may be some other type of coherence, some meaning which, if discovered, would make these contradictions understandable. The assumptions that would make the story consistent can be tentatively spelled out. If, e.g., the patient reports having fainted after slightly cutting his finger, clearly he reacted as if to a much more painful and threatening event; one should go as far with pointing out such implications as the patient can follow at the time. The therapist should keep his eyes open for similar idiosyncrasies recurring in other contexts: in different stages of life, in different areas, in fantasies, and dreams. This careful observation will eventually lead to the discovery of repetitive patterns imbued with personal meaning. The rigid use of these patterns in inappropriate situations, in spite of their failure to achieve the desired results, marks them as neurotic devices; their content provides clues to the elaboration of the neurosis in the given individual case.

To trace this elaboration it is essential for the therapist to learn to see patterns, to discover syndromes in the material itself, without the guidelines of theoretical preconceptions. This ability has to be trained, much as the ability to use the microscope; a schooled eye sees what an untrained eye does not. Specific directions are of little help in this training. Progress in this, as in other therapeutic skills, is achieved less through learning technical tricks than through cultivating certain attitudes and mental habits. The habit needed for perceiving syndromes is the habit of divided attention. The therapist must learn to listen to the patient both for *detail* and for the emerging *whole;* he must constantly interrelate the two, hear the dream as a whole, the therapeutic hour as a whole, and keep in mind the whole formed by the patient's present and past. This habit will develop naturally if the therapist assumes that a coherent story will be told, that there will be a connecting theme to the hour. This method of listening is not equally rewarding in all situations. If the story told by the patient is continuous and coherent even on its surface, there is less chance to learn from it what the patient does not clearly know than there is when his communications are jumpy. In the last case one obtains material comparable to the kind one hopes to get when one formally instructs the patient to associate freely; the sequence will be more revealing than in a well-organized presentation.

The method of interrelating separate items can be utilized in various ways. If a dream one is working on does not yield its meaning easily, there is no point in spending time on a device that is best used as a short cut. More often than not the meaning of the dream becomes clear, if the therapist listens, from what the patient says afterward. Similarly, if the patient is unwilling to stay with an issue and changes the subject, the chances are high that he will soon be talking in a different form about the same issue. One can also bring together what is separated in time by tracing the carry over from one session to the next. If some detail of the hour, or its emotional coloring, appears puzzling, unrelated to the session's main content, it pays to check on the possible relationship of this material to what transpired in the preceding session.

The therapist who develops the habit of constantly relating single items to general patterns will reap the benefit of improved memory; organized material is remembered better than unrelated detail. If he learns to see connections quickly, on the spot, he will also have a good chance to make interpretations when they count most. If the therapist pieces the parts together only in retrospect, he will have to wait for a good opening to communicate the whole to the patient, and the timeliness of the interpretation may be lost. During the session one responds mainly to single items, leaving comments on the total story (if it does emerge) for the end of the hour, provided there is no special reason to postpone the interpretation. Such a conclusion of an exploratory session is natural and satisfying for the patient. He is pleased to be shown how much he has said in the hour and the arbitrariness of the end is mitigated.

The initial sessions during which the patient and the therapist size up each other present special problems. At this stage incautious interpretations may do great harm. It took one young man five years to give therapy a second try after his strongly felt religious commitments were interpreted in an early session as possibly playing a defensive role in his life. Sensitivity to the patient's attitudes and concerns will also enable the therapist to make correct decisions on matters other than interpretation. He may, for example, in one case take the initiative in discussing the details of the symptoms, thus showing that it can be done with propriety; in another instance he may refrain from such initiative, thus showing that therapy will not involve humiliation. In neglecting to avail himself of his early impressions, the therapist may miss an opportunity to say or do the one thing that might cause the patient to give this new person in his life a high degree of confidence and candor.

One patient in the course of several sessions never permitted the therapist to get a word in edgewise. This man had previously worked with therapists who apparently had let him monopolize the sessions; he had been helped very little. After the trial period the therapist agreed to work with the patient on the conditions that he was *not* to associate in the sessions (as this apparently served to disguise his problems), and would agree to be interrupted at any time by a given signal so that the therapist could comment. Tears came to the patient's eyes as he said, "I don't know how you knew it, because I didn't know it myself, but I think I have been hoping all my life to find someone who would understand me enough to say 'shut up.' " After that, therapy could start and proceed, although information about the childhood situations which explained the patient's reaction came only months later.

One can vary one's approach to fit individual needs if one does not rigidly insist on the "proper procedure" to which the patients must conform or be deemed untreatable.

Interpretations, at all times, should be adapted to the patient's current state of insight and to his tolerance of anxiety; they must stimulate his thinking and not be overly threatening. As a protection against errors in timing, interpretations may be offered tentatively and dropped without further argument if they find no response; debates have no place in therapy. To insist that the patient see a connection which is obvious to the therapist may merely make him feel that he is stupid; there is no point in shaming the patient by demanding something he cannot do. It is important to avoid any comment that could be taken as censure, ridicule, or invasion of privacy. For instance, no reference should be made during the initial period to the patient's facial expression, gestures, or mannerisms. The therapist's comment must be limited to what the patient himself designates as a proper topic by putting it into words. The patient's self-image, in particular, must be treated with care; in the early stages of therapy any imputation of negative traits to the self is to be avoided. What is difficult and what is easy for a patient to take depends to a large extent on the dimension of neurosis that is predominant or is to the fore at the time. If the hysterical component is dominant, the person's ideal is to be all-loving and accepted by all; hostility is then difficult for him to recognize. Conversely, an obsessive-compulsive patient, if his aggressive impulses are overt and are equated with strength, will find it very difficult and upsetting to recognize his gentler impulses. If the therapist has identified the pattern, he can shape and time his interpretations accordingly. The therapist's procedure should never appear strange or mysterious, nor should the patient ever be given grounds to believe that the therapist is keeping something from him. Telling the patient the reasons for certain questions and comments will help to prevent their misinterpretation as criticism or as an expression of esoteric knowledge; this may preclude starting a chain of neurotic reactions which jeopardize or slow down progress.

It is essential that the patient participate actively in the interpretive process. If he assumes the passive attitude of a pupil or the detached attitude of an observer, he will not get insights. The notion that the therapist is the only one to gain understanding should be discouraged from the start. If the patient hands material to the therapist with the implication that "This may help *you* to find out what ails me," he should be made to realize that the therapist's "findings" as such will not help him, and that he himself can find answers only if he starts wondering and asking questions.

The therapist should try to get the patient involved. The way in which he himself goes about making interpretations should be aimed at this. Instead of proffering a formulation, he would do well to put the elements of the picture before the patient by restating various things he has said, perhaps in a different sequence and with a different emphasis, so that the patient can see for himself what is implied; only if this fails should he offer his own formulation. Sometimes the therapist may choose to wait for a great deal of evidence to accumulate. Instead of using up his ammunition, he waits until he can make the interpretation compellingly convincing. Other times he may state his hunches as hunches and leave it to the patient to test their validity; the method that most stimulates the patients' own thinking is the best. If the patient rejects or "forgets" a valid idea and later discovers the same connection by himself, he is better off for not having accepted it passively. When he takes the therapist up on his interpretations, subjects them to scrutiny and testing, and actively seeks their larger implications and possible cross references, these are signs that insights are in the offing.

The atmosphere most conducive to a successful exploration of the patient's personal patterns is that of a common enterprise, the patient and the therapist looking at the facts together in as open-minded a way as they can and trying to make sense of them. The spirit in which the therapist conducts this enterprise affects not only the development of insight but also the patient's confidence in his ability to get at the truth. The neurotic distrusts this ability and with good reason. His intellectual processes, no matter how highly developed, are too often used in the service of the opposite goal, that of distorting or camouflaging the real state of affairs. He may feel unable to think clearly, to grasp what is essential, or to penetrate below the surface of things. Some patients come to feel that in psychological matters there is no such thing as truth, that it all depends on the viewpoint; they feel there is no way of telling whether a statement is valid—at least they know of no such way. If the therapist gives interpretations dogmatically, with an air of superior wisdom, the patient's weak confidence in his own experience is further undermined. He may try to silence his doubts and to put all his faith in authority. As one much-analyzed patient put it, "I came to feel that my concern with evidence was merely neurotic resistance and that my salvation lay in fitting myself to the interpretations."

A therapist who holds the conviction that the patient is the one who knows the truth about himself, and with help will be able to find it, has the opposite effect. His interpretations will take full account of the patient's observations; his assessment of the evidence will be shared with the patient; he will not fall back on theoretical clichés, try to gloss over difficulties, or attempt to force certainty in other spurious ways. Such behavior will convey to the patient, more effectively than words, the therapist's confidence that the confusing and contradictory picture can be disentangled through their common effort. The patient's active participation in sifting and weighing evidence, in testing and discarding hypotheses, are steps toward the rehabilitation of his intellectual processes. Practice in distinguishing rationality from rationalization raises his faith in his own intellectual competence. In therapy we need practices just as much as insights. A therapist who is aware of their value will find ways to use to the best advantage the opportunities for practice provided by the process of a shared pursuit of insight.

As a result of the process of exploration, the patient's self-understanding will grow, but this will not, in itself, induce change. Intellectual insight, which is simply a statement of facts and their connections, has only an indirect bearing on motivation for change; because the patient now sees the situation differently, his feelings about it also may change. Gaining insight, important as it is, particularly in the first half of the therapy's course, has the function of paving the way for the more dynamic processes which alone can displace the entrenched neurotic pattern from its position of dominance.

14. Demolition and Reconstruction

An Overall View

In human personality, as in any ambiguous Gestalt, two major organizations compete for dominance: that of health and that of neurosis. Both patterns seek to realize the general human tendencies toward mastery and participation. Whereas the health pattern is based on confidence that these can be attained more or less directly, in the neurotic pattern these trends function in a context of doubt that human needs can be fulfilled—except, possibly, in some tortuous ways. This pattern can be viewed as a distortion of the primary one or a distant approximation of it. In the neurotic person the secondary organization has gained strong dominance; the function of therapy is to reverse this development and to restore dominance to the primary structure, thus reducing conflict and ambiguity and enabling the person to become more unified and wholehearted. This at least is the goal to aim at whenever possible. In some cases one cannot set one's sights any higher than elimination of the most noxious features of the neurotic pattern; the patient's approach to life is not basically altered but it will cause less damage and suffering to himself and to others. This minor repair work is not to be belittled, since it can make a major difference to the patient, but neither "adjustment" nor alleviation of pain can be viewed as primary goals of therapy: like sedatives in physical illness, they make the patient feel better without making him well. In some circumstances sparing the patient pain may even preclude achieving in treatment all that might have been possible.

Which is the road that leads from neurotic illness to health? Of the various things the therapist does, what is effective and what is not? Good descriptions of total courses of therapy could help to answer these questions and enlarge our knowledge both of the essential requirements of treatment and of the errors that can prolong or wreck it; there are, however, not very many of those. Some authors bypass these issues, stating that the methods of treatment follow directly from our knowledge of the dynamics of neurosis. This is true as far as it goes, but there is more to therapy than the mere application of psychodynamics; clarifying its other aspects could save us much fumbling.

In Chapters 14, 15, 16 I outline the unfolding of the therapeutic process from start to finish as I have observed it in those cases where therapy was aimed at a radical reorganization of personality. This reorganization has two aspects: the weakening of the neurotic pattern and the strengthening of the healthy one. The course of therapy can be roughly divided into *three major periods* according to the relative strengths of the two patterns. During the first period, when the *neurotic pattern is dominant,* the preparatory explorations described in the preceding chapter lead over into two kinds of processes: the gradual recognition by the patient that his neurotic way of life is destructive, and the gradual discovery of the healthy factors buried within the neurotic pattern. During this period, the first process is usually more prominent than the second, since therapy starts with neurosis having the upper hand, while the healthy pattern has to be laboriously unearthed and grows only slowly. Changes in the strength of each of the two patterns over the whole course of therapy can be represented schematically by a descending line (neurosis) and an ascending line (health) which converge, cross, and diverge. The gradual equalization of the strengths of the two patterns achieved during the first period ushers in the crucial stage of therapy—*the struggle for decision,* when the patient wavers between the two ways of life that claim his allegiance. In favorable cases this strenuous stage results in a shift of dominance from one pattern to the other; in our schema this shift is represented by the point of intersection of the lines, although it usually involves many movements back and forth over a period of time. During the terminal period of a successful therapy, the *healthy pattern,* now *in ascendance,* grows rapidly and the patient begins to master the difficult art of staying well.

Since processes of different kinds run parallel or interweave in all stages of treatment, it is impossible to describe the course of therapy coherently in its chronological order; the discussion must move back and forth between earlier and later events. The simplified schema of the time sequence offered in the preceding paragraph will serve as a rough frame within which to place the descriptions of the various therapeutic tasks and of the factors that help or hinder their accomplishment.

The Task of Demolition

As every therapist knows, the neurotic person does not, as a rule, seek treatment because he has recognized the unwholesomeness of his conduct of life. When he comes to you, you can safely assume that he is completely dominated by the neurotic pattern, which is an all-inclusive organization with its own motivational forces, desires, hopes, and fears forming a closely knit whole. He cannot break out of this enclosing circle, nor does he want to. The patient comes to the therapist because some of the consequences of his way of life are painful; he feels anxious, he has distressing or handicapping symptoms, he is frustrated in various ways or finds himself trapped in some messy situation. He suffers and he wants to get rid of the pain. In fact, if we want to spell out what he expects from therapy, it is not that the patient wants to be helped to change the self-defeating methods with which he pursues happiness; he expects to be taught how to succeed with these methods without suffering painful consequences. Only in the process of therapy does it gradually dawn on him that much more is involved than he had bargained for. One might say that the patient wants to learn how to sin without being punished. In this he is like the pathological drinker whose wish is not to give up alcohol completely but to become a "moderate drinker," which of course is impossible for him.

If the patient has some secondhand knowledge of how therapy works, he may give a sophisticated formulation of his purpose in coming, but this can rarely be taken at its face value. One patient, for instance, told me, "I am like a six-cylinder automobile running on only four cylinders, and I want to run on all six cylinders." This sounds constructive, but the question is where he wants his six cylinders to take him. Perhaps he wants to achieve more because achievement keeps in check all kinds of doubts he has about himself; or he may want to function on all six cylinders in order, as one patient put it, "to be in such a position that nobody could touch me." The patient's initial statement of goal cannot be constructive. Being a prisoner of his neurosis, he cannot even wish the right way. He can wish only within the framework of the neurotic organization and pursue only neurotic goals.

A great deal of work has to be done before the patient can be mobilized for the process of change. His reliance on the neurotic pattern of living has to be broken and the latent healthy pattern has to be unearthed and cultivated before it can be restored to its rightful dominant position. This second task, the revitalization of the basic personality, which is too often neglected in therapy, is fully as important as the first. One cannot just demolish without giving the person something else to turn to. As the task of demolition proceeds, the patient will clutch at his neurotic hopes as a drowning man clutches at straws; he will not let go until he feels there is something solid that he can quickly grasp with his other hand. The work of demolition will be discussed first, but in practice the two parts of the therapeutic endeavor must go hand in hand.

As the exploration of the neurotic patterns progresses beyond the initial stage, the therapist can no longer limit himself to formulating the patient's general attitudes, their genetic roots, and their multiple interconnections. He will use every opportunity to bring to the patient's awareness the consequences of these attitudes, in an attempt to make him face in earnest what he is doing with and to his life. There are reasons why this is necessary. The neurotic places all his reliance in the complex methods he has developed for dealing with the problems of life even if they have failed hundreds of times. His failures do not convince him that he is on the wrong track; he clings to the belief that his methods need only to be improved, or that they would work if only the situation would change, or if other people would change. He finds some explanation of just why things went wrong and tries again and again: "This time it must work!" Like a gambler who keeps "perfecting" his system, the neurotic is able to sell himself all sorts of fantastic notions about why his method has failed and how it can be improved. If he is intellectually gifted, he can produce the most fantastic elaborations.

The punishment these methods bring goes unheeded. Though he does not think much of himself and will admit all kinds of shortcomings, both real and illusory, the neurotic usually has great confidence in one thing: his ability to extricate himself from any mess he gets himself into, which he sometimes ascribes to skill, sometimes to luck. The frustration and pain the patient has suffered are quickly forgotten, and he may feel that he has succeeded so far. Actually, half of his life may be spent in getting into tough spots and the other half in skillfully extricating himself from them; life may seem full of excitement and challenges as long as he does not realize how little he gains and how much he loses by these monotonous exercises. One young woman who had badly damaged herself through a repetitive pattern, recently told me; "You know, somehow I always come through all right; I never get hurt." One does not want to cause pain needlessly, but this woman has to learn, and one has to help her to learn, that she *does* get hurt, and already has been very badly hurt.

It is the therapist's job to show and to emphasize, in the face of the patient's evasions, the hopelessness and futility of his way of life. He will do it gently at first, with a light touch, later more forcefully, but constantly gauging how much the patient can stand at the time. He must also take care not to throw out the wheat with the chaff. The healthy nucleus present even in the most destructive manifestations of neurosis must be protected, not damaged by rough handling. By asserting or implying that the patient's behavior is "nothing but" neurotic, one undermines the total person, not merely the neurosis. But while exercising this care, the therapist must constantly aim at showing the patient that his neurotic ways just do not work, e.g., that he never does and never will obtain from people the response he truly desires by forcing himself on them, or by cultivating helplessness, or by any other neurotic device. In the first approximation, the therapist should convey to the patient that, basically, he wishes for the right things but, because of his false assumptions, uses methods that are doomed to failure. This unmasking of neurosis has to be done in hundreds or thousands of concrete variations all converging on one point. One of my patients compared me to a bulldog who takes care not to hurt but never releases his grip; and indeed the therapist must exercise stubborn persistence to counter the patient's persistent defense of his way of life. The tenacity with which these realizations are fought off is truly impressive but need not cause discouragement; in fact, it is an encouraging sign. Even though the patient is defending a distorted version of himself, his fight for self-preservation has a healthy source. If he shows stamina in standing up for his neurosis, he will show stamina later in standing up for his health. But neurosis is a powerful adversary, and the therapist must be cocky indeed if he expects to lick it easily, e.g., using only one fixed method or a narrow range of therapeutic devices. Much persistence and ingenuity are needed to use every opportunity to the best advantage. Only when every avenue of escape has been sealed off is the patient forced to admit defeat and to give up hope that his neurotic ways may succeed.

Important as the therapist's role is in preparing this event, he is powerless to bring it about. The established pattern of neurotic living will not yield to detached thinking, generalizations, and explanations; only experiences of shattering power can effectively combat it. The neurotic structure melts in the fire of an intensive and persuasive emotional experience. At the core of this experience there is always profound despair. The patient's hopes of succeeding in the ways with which he is familiar have been shattered. He sees the utter futility of his accustomed mode of life and does not know any longer which way to turn. He feels hopeless, utterly ignorant of life and of how to conduct it. Seeing no future ahead of him, he hardly cares whether he lives or dies. The work of demolition culminates in the bankruptcy of the neurosis, which the patient experiences as his own total bankruptcy.

This description may sound exaggerated for various reasons. It may be that I witness more dramatic happenings in therapy than some other therapists do because of my style of working. I shall return to this later. Mainly, however, this description overdramatizes by telescoping events that may be spread over a long period of time. In some cases, the experience of "bankruptcy" does occur in a massive dramatic fashion. In other instances it does not, but if one has an eye for it, it is recognizable when it comes in small doses. These, taken in their entirety, have the same loosening effect on the neurotic structure as do the more spectacular forms. The experience may also be hidden or displaced by other phenomena so that one barely sees it even when watching closely. This is the case, e.g., if the constructive part of the personality grows and develops very powerfully right from the start; the bankruptcy of neurosis need not be shattering when the hope for something else is clearly there. Nor does this experience occur if the treatment is aimed only at some minor changes within the dominant pattern. But with severe neuroses, if one aims at a fundamental cure, there is no other way to recovery than the way that leads through despair. Much as one would like to lead the patient gently over the hill to a better form of living, this is usually not possible. A sweeping experience of bankruptcy must come if the person is to break out of his neurotic enclosure and take a chance on a different mode of existence which at first is unfamiliar and frightening. It is essential for the success of therapy that the therapist recognize this despair for what it is, i.e., not just another manifestation of neurosis, but *the* crucial step forward, a fruit of his work. When this experience comes he must not stand in its way.

Unless all the therapeutic tasks of the period preceding the crisis have been properly accomplished, despair may be replaced by depression, a possibility to be kept in mind. If the patient has strong depressive trends, one should not let despair develop until one has done much work on the healthy pattern and until the patient has built up confidence in the therapist's unconditional support. Unlike despair, depression has a tenacious quality and indicates that a profound attachment to the neurosis still exists. The depressed person says, in effect, that doom and disaster are inevitable, that he is a complete failure, completely worthless, and that in this way he does not want to live. Severe depression, with its danger of suicide, can usually be avoided, but even a slighter depression implies an unwillingness to consider alternatives to the threatened neurotic pattern. The patient proclaims, as it were, that his way is the only way, that he does not want to play the game differently. This is an indication that some obstacles to change still have to be worked on and removed.

In contrast to depression, the despair which marks the crucial point in therapy passes into a stage that can lead out of neurosis. After the acute emotions have subsided, the patient may feel empty, passive, and numb. There is no point in further scheming, in trying to meet situations in his usual ways. It is a state of insensibility where nothing can help or hurt, and it contains also an element of impassive acceptance of the existing state of affairs, an acknowledgment of its factuality. This emptiness, this emotional and volitional neutrality, is a momentous advance along the road to recovery; the inertness of the neurotic organization provides the ideal conditions for the emergence of the basic healthy pattern, which up to now has been held in check by the neurosis. Both in therapy and outside it, significant new experiences are often facilitated by the state of passivity and blankness that results when the person feels completely beaten or completely taken out of his usual life.

> This may be exemplified by a minor episode of "despair" in the therapy of a young girl who was engaged in frantic attempts to please and captivate men. On this particular occasion some external obstacles prevented her from going through her usual compulsively elaborate ritual of beautification before going out on a date. Ordinarily, since she placed her main reliance in her looks she would have canceled the date, but this time her initial panic changed into weary indifference; she met her escort, feeling that, since she had no chance of impressing him anyway, it did not matter what she said or did. Instead of tensely planning her remarks, she listened and responded in a relaxed fashion. After a while she realized with astonishment that, for the first time in her life, she was having a genuinely good time on a date.

Weightier experiences which have the same pattern appear later in therapy. When the passively receptive mood flows from sweeping despair, from the feeling that one cannot move *anywhere* any more, the door is opened to new experiences emerging on a larger scale and leading to widening perspectives. In such cases, the experience of despair may mark the transition to the terminal stage of therapy.

For this positive outcome more is required, however, than the "demolition work" that brings about the experience of bankruptcy. This experience loosens the structure of neurosis but does not in itself show a way out. If the patient is not adequately prepared for the crisis, he will not profit from it and may not even reach the crucial stage. The growth of the healthy pattern must have progressed to a point where a new hope can replace the crumbling hopes of succeeding in the old way. Equally important is a previous working through of the powerful obstacles to change that make the patient cling to his neurosis. While the core of the experience of bankruptcy is despair, associated with it are other forbidding emotions: specific fears, intense general anxiety, and an acute sense of guilt. Anxiety and guilt must be faced before the crisis can reach its culmination; it is the therapist's job to prepare the patient to face and handle them as the crisis approaches. Let us then retrace our steps and consider the reconstructive aspects of the therapeutic work before we discuss the intense struggles that surround the crisis.

The Task of Reconstruction

I believe that we do not sufficiently emphasize the reconstructive aspect of the therapeutic work, perhaps because we mistakenly equate it with the imposition of our own values on the patient or because we expect him to take care of it by himself. In the classical Freudian analysis, for instance, it seems to be assumed that once the unhealthy elements of personality and their origins are discovered and worked through, the healthy forces will automatically assert themselves and take over. This happens to some degree in most cases, but to leave it to chance is to underestimate the power of neurosis. We fail to do all we can if we do not foster the reconstructive process as deliberately and systematically as we pursue the work of demolition. I consider the two tasks equally important. In my work, over the total duration of analysis, more than one half of the time is devoted to reconstruction. Work on this task must begin early in therapy. While the patient is completely caught in his neurotic existence he has neither the possibility nor the wholehearted desire to find his way out. Even when he starts wishing for change, he merely wishes that he could *wish* to change. He is like the man who wanted to learn to like spinach, but had this misgiving: "If I learn to like spinach I shall eat lots and lots of it, and I hate the darn stuff!" The patient cannot lift himself by his own bootstraps. To lift a weight one needs a fulcrum, a point outside the object. It is a major part of the therapeutic task to build a fulcrum for and with the patient from which the neurosis could be lifted—a base of operations outside the neurotic organization.

Some therapeutic procedures are not specifically aimed at this task yet make contributions to it. Loosening the neurotic organization by giving the patient some insight into it serves also the cause of reconstruction. The process of gaining insight has one important curative aspect that is not often discussed. To gain insight means to look *inside* the functioning of one's unhealthy pattern. While doing this, one stands *outside* one's neurosis; one gains an outside vantage point. This is not just a play on words. At the moment of insight one sees one's neurotic problems in perspective, instead of being entirely buried in them. The therapist, by holding up a mirror to the patient, enables him to take a look at one or another neurotic feature as something partly extraneous to himself. As soon as the patient recognizes it as his own, he also gains some distance from it. Every time an insight is gained, the patient's foothold outside the neurotic entanglement is slightly enlarged; a small addition is made to the structure that will eventually provide the leverage for lifting the burden of neurosis.

This, however, is not enough. Potentially, the main anchoring point is the person's own healthy self, still encysted in the neurotic structure. It must be brought to light, often a laborious process, and made an object of insight in its own right. Because repression and other defense mechanisms work in two directions, the patient resists the unearthing of his healthy features as much as he resists the deep probing of his neurotic pattern. Trusting feelings may be suppressed as exposing him to danger; personal competence may be sacrificed to the goal of being accepted as a helpless child. Interpretation and related procedures must be put to work in two directions in order to uncover the deeper features of both patterns. Discovering them is essential. Not much is gained therapeutically if the work of reconstruction is confined to pointing out and stressing those aspects of the patient's functioning that are least distorted by neurosis. These relatively unproblematic assets are not unknown to the patient but are usually peripheral to his deeper concerns and have no effect on his self-concept.

The essentially personal healthy features exist not beside but *within* the neurosis; each neurotic manifestation is a distorted expression of an individually shaped healthy trend. The distortion must be clearly seen and acknowledged, but the healthy core must be found within the distortion itself. Suppose a woman patient complains that she is a poor housekeeper, unable to cope with her work, and exploration uncovers an attitude of protest against the feminine role which she conceives of as inferior. The therapist will, of course, analyze the sources of this misconception to enable the patient to correct it. It would never do, e.g., to leave her with the childish belief that she is essentially lacking because her sexual organs are different from those of the male. But regardless of the origins of her devaluing notions, insofar as she rejects the inferior role for herself, even at the cost of denying her sex or having to admit her incompetence as a woman, she expresses, in an unhealthy fashion, a basically healthy trend. No analysis of neurotic behavior is complete until this behavior has been traced back to its healthy source. The realization that in a wrong way he has been fighting for the right purpose lessens the patient's feeling of shame and gives him courage to continue his self-exploration. Thus the "destructive" and the constructive parts of the therapeutic process presuppose and further each other; this was clear to the patient who said that she knew she was making progress in therapy because the more she improved, the more clearly she realized how sick she was.

Actually, "demolition" is not an entirely fitting description of the first part of the therapeutic work. Therapy neither eliminates what is there nor creates anything new in the person. It prepares a rearrangement of his inherent traits. No personal characteristics are destroyed when their neurotic meanings and uses are discovered and the origins of the distortions understood. They will eventually find their place in the pattern of health when alternative constructive solutions are found to the early traumatic situations which twisted them out of shape. Therapy is not surgery but a gradual transplanting of the patient's attitudes and traits from one pattern to the other; the analysis of the healthy core of a given behavioral item serves to convert it back to, and to anchor it in, the latent system of health.

As the work of rehabilitation proceeds, the patient's fear that the vaguely hypothesized goals of treatment might prove beyond his capacities or alien to his tastes may be partly allayed. It begins to dawn on him that these goals are to be found right under his nose, carrying the reassuring smell of selfhood, and that he also possesses many skills —though misapplied so far—that can be used in reconstructed living.

Consider the young man who emerged from some traumatically deceptive childhood situations with remarkably uncompromising standards of truthfulness and integrity which, in the neurotic system, were used to force others to redress his old grievances. Once the healthy and neurotic roots of this attitude were disentangled, he realized that he still could and would adhere to these standards, making them eventually his firm undoubted possession. The same patient showed oddly reversed attitudes in his search for love and for employment. He approached each potential partner with the explicit expectation of being accepted, because "I deserve it, it would only be just, right and reasonable," denying in effect that the other person's needs and tastes had anything to do with the outcome. In seeking employment, though he greatly wished his gifts to be recognized and rewarded, he behaved with a degree of modesty that belied his unquestionably superior qualifications. In neither area did his approaches produce the desired results. As their roots and functions were clarified, the patient realized that to improve his chances he would merely have to switch the behavior patterns he already had at his disposal.

Such tentative realizations of his real resources will stand the patient in good stead later on, when he will have to face the bankruptcy of his neurotic style of living.

Analysis of dreams offers ample opportunities for uncovering healthy trends. Every dream has many meanings; it kills not two but five or fifty birds with one stone, so that the therapist always has some choice of what to interpret. As therapy progresses, manifestations of hopeful attitudes become more pronounced and more obvious to the patient himself.

The following dream illustrates this. A patient dreamt of walking in a forest on a road overgrown with grass. At the end of the road he saw lumber stacked in an orderly way, and found that it was good sound wood. It seemed a pity to let it go to waste; he wanted to salvage it, but as he approached the logs he became frightened that the whole pile might topple down on him. So he decided to go into the village and let the people know; maybe he could organize a campaign to salvage the wood. The patient's associations made clear that the wood represented himself: good material, at present inaccessible, but which might be recovered in some way. This prospect aroused some anxiety, and there were other neurotic elements that could be pointed out, but the best use to be made of this dream at the time was to emphasize its predominant aspect, the patient's growing awareness of his potentially valuable self.

Even when one of its meanings is more pronounced than any other, every dream faces the interpreter with some choices—whether to emphasize the neurotic or the healthy elements, whether to bring out the transference aspects or to keep quiet about them. The decision must not be arbitrary. If he violates the material, the therapist will very soon notice that things do not go well in the sessions. The situation cannot be forced; rather it must be diagnosed from minute to minute. Dreams similar in content may have very different meanings in different contexts or different stages of therapy. For example, a dream that depicts the patient as reaching his goal may be a primitive dream of wish fulfillment, i.e., a childish desire for a short cut that would bring him there or an indication that the patient is actually getting ready to take important steps toward health and that therapy is approaching completion.

Having obtained a picture of the dynamics of the patient's neurosis, and some clues as to how he will feel and act when the neurosis is on the run, one must continuously gauge the state of therapy, extrapolating from its past course to the present moment. Where do we stand? What has been done so far? What is being worked on now? The answers to these questions help the therapist to decide how best to interpret whatever the patient brings up, including his dreams. If one always stresses the positive aspects, the healthy trends, he risks slipping into a Pollyannaish optimism which is no help at all. The distortion of the healthy trend is there; *this* is the problem, and as long as the distortion exists one must keep pointing it out, even if the patient sneaks it in, in some disguise, inbetween positive manifestations. There can be no general rules as to when the healthy and neurotic features should be emphasized, but if the therapist realizes the importance of the reconstructive aspect of his work, he will be sensitive to the situations that are propitious to it.

Beyond being a mere interpreter, the therapist exercises an important influence on the progress of recovery through his attitude toward the patient, the spirit in which his interpretations are given and the whole treatment is conducted. These are not matters of technique; respect and care cannot be conveyed by tricks, nor by direct verbal protestations. If these attitudes are present, they will manifest themselves in a variety of ways, such as paying attention, not being annoyed by accusations, catching and freely admitting one's own mistakes, developing attitudes that train one's memory for what happens in therapy. If one remembers clearly what the patient said a year ago, this is proof that one really cares. The cultivation of attitudes that enable the patient to move forward in therapy and enable the therapist to keep increasing his understanding and skill is the condition *sine qua non* of the therapist's work; the only valid proof of his helpfulness is that the patient has been helped.

From the beginning of therapy to the point at which it nears its end, the unrealistic aspect of the patient-therapist relation is quite strong. Transferring onto the therapist the image of the "primal" parent, the patient sees in him alternately the mythical enemy and the answer to his wish for an all-giving magical helper. This intensification of his neurotic fears and hopes can be very fruitfully used for exploring and demonstrating to him his particular version of the mythology of neurosis. But the realistic aspect of the relationship, determined by the real characteristics of the two people and the purpose that has brought them together, is also there from the start and offers rich opportunities for the work of reconstruction.

Since the neurotic person is wearing a mask and constantly dreads detection, he feels relief when he succeeds in revealing himself to another as he is, or as he believes he is, and discovers that his fears were much worse than the actual experience. The effects, over a long range of time, are not limited to catharsis. The patient reveals to the therapist many aspects of his life about which he feels guilty and ashamed. In addition, many hitherto unknown roots of his actions are discovered which are most unflattering to him. The patient notices, however, that the therapist does not blame him; he gradually notices also that the therapist's acceptant attitude is based neither on blindness nor on moral indifference. The therapist takes the unhealthy attitudes of the patient seriously, and in some ways more seriously than the patient himself, because he perceives their destructiveness more clearly. If he continues to value the patient as a person and to show him sincere respect, the patient gradually becomes aware that the therapist sees in him, despite all his shortcomings, a likeable and worthwhile human being. Thus it begins to dawn on him that there is something within his own self that is different from his neurosis, something that stands outside his destructive way of life. The presence of the therapist as a real person is perhaps the most important point of anchorage outside the neurotic way of life that the therapeutic situation offers the patient. For the therapist to try to remain a *tabula rasa*, eliminating entirely the human aspect of the relationship, is to cast away a most valuable means of helping the patient back to health.

15. The Struggle for Decision

Before a patient admits the bankruptcy of his neurosis, he usually goes through a difficult and stormy period, sometimes quite long, marked by intense guilt feelings and severe anxiety and fears. In order to reach and pass the critical point of despair he must first deal with these feelings.

Guilt

That guilt is a weighty issue in the therapy of neuroses is widely recognized, but I think we still do not fully appreciate the magnitude of this factor. Many therapists regard guilt feelings as an entirely negative feature, i.e., as neurotic symptoms to be removed or relieved. This I believe to be the basic mistake responsible for many of our failures; assuaging guilt does not resolve it. Guilt can become an insuperable obstacle to progress if it is not dealt with adequately. Since this requires several steps, the topic of guilt should be opened as early as is feasible.

One should certainly try to remove those guilt feelings that originate in an assumption of responsibility for events over which the person has no control. Consider, for instance, the patient whose mother died in childbirth and who harbors guilt feelings about it: "I came into the world through the death of another." Such feelings should be analyzed as fantasy productions since no true guilt is involved. However, such simple and straightforward situations are rarely, if ever, found in the analytic work. In most instances, therefore, it will not be enough for the patient to realize the illusory nature of his guilt. To some extent this applies also to those guilt feelings that have their origin in the fear of punishment for violating orders and prohibitions which were later internalized but which still remain foreign bodies within the patient's own pattern of values. This development is described in the psychoanalytic theory of the superego formation. When such fear-guilt is present in relatively pure form, the patient's recognition that he does not actually hold these imposed views tends to dissipate his guilt feelings or to change them back into fear of external punishment or social disapproval. These fears can then be tested for their current reality value. But such pure cases are rare and that is why, in most instances, the repudiation by the patient of his earlier standards, and the recognition of the harmlessness of his "sins," do not free him from guilt feelings.

The focal problem is *real guilt* as defined in the chapter on universal ambiguity, i.e., the person's emotional response to having acted against not just some externally imposed standards but against his own genuine loyalties or against people to whom he related not merely with fear but with love. Recall the Jewish boy who, in a moment of fear, joined the crowd of children deriding an old Jew and later felt this to be one of the most shameful episodes of his life. He felt he belonged with the Jewish people, and in his panic he had gone against this genuine loyalty. To feel guilt about such violations of homonomous bonds is part and parcel of healthy human functioning. If a patient has betrayed his own values, or caused or intended harm to a loved person, he is not helped in the long run by the therapist saying or implying that it is foolish to feel guilty about it—because that is not true. Although the neurotic puts his guilt feelings to very destructive uses, in essence they are outgrowths of his basic strivings for belongingness and autonomy; as such they must be utilized for reconstruction, not summarily discarded. Real guilt has to be faced in a much more meaningful and vital way than by denial or by making light of it. Only a confrontation with it can help the neurotic to transform his partly irrational guilt feelings into a healthy conscience. Guilt feelings represent the key to effective self-control.

Since the neurotic falsification of life always results in self-betrayal and in shortchanging others, guilt is always present but it is never in the open. When manifest guilt feelings are minimal or absent, the therapist's first task is to bring them to the patient's awareness by utilizing the indirect indications that both reveal and disguise guilt. Some of the most common disguises are certain brands of fears, symptoms or behavior patterns that have the function of "undoing" the acts leading to guilt, protestations of perfect goodness and innocence, distortions of reality systematically aimed at minimizing own guilt, or lack of emotional response to instances of obvious factual guilt. On the other hand, conscious guilt feelings may be present and even prominent, but on the surface they rarely refer to the actions or attitudes that caused the real guilt. This guilt, of which the patient is aware only dimly or not at all, is usually camouflaged by the manifest guilt feelings, often exaggerated or irrational.

This close interweaving of real and spurious guilt is understandable, particularly in the light of the early origins of guilt feelings. The discrepancy between the external commands and one's own genuine values may be small, and the distinction is not always easy to make. The basic human strivings must be embodied in concrete values, and these are usually formed by the child in accordance with the suggestions and opportunities offered by the culture. Even if some of the parents' demands represent a severe and unreasonable violation of the child's natural impulses or individual preferences, they are more often than not accepted by him not purely out of fear but also out of love. Consequently, if he later discards or modifies his false standards, the issue of guilt for their violations is not *ipso facto* resolved; it remains true that he had acted against the beliefs and wishes of those he loved. Still, it is important to distinguish between guilt based on fear and real guilt deriving from the violation of homonomous bonds since their different implications require different handling. For example, the severity of guilt feelings about early sexual activities varies widely depending on their personal meaning. If they were pursued primarily for pleasure, guilt resulting from the violation of parental wishes may be minimal; it certainly never reaches the magnitude of guilt that is in evidence if an early fight with the parents had fashioned the sexual activity into a secret means of expressing spiteful disobedience. This kind of guilt is not easily dispelled by later reassurance about sex.

Once guilt feelings have been brought to the surface, one must disentangle their various roots and meanings in order to locate the real guilt. Often guilt is displaced from its true source to some insignificant neutral event or minor offense, which the patient brings up as something he feels terribly guilty about. Such exaggerated feeling is actually a defense, a denial of guilt. The patient cannot help realizing, however dimly, that the trifling nature of the thing he feels guilty about makes his guilt ridiculous, and this realization partly cancels the feeling; he can be guilty, tongue in cheek, so to say, or can even cherish his "guilt" as a sign of a sensitive conscience. The use of guilt feelings for keeping up the pretense of being a moral person perverts them to serve the neurosis; instead of being a spur to action and change they become means of preserving the status quo. While the healthy person displays the constructive sequence ("I did it. I regret it. How can I do better next time?") the neurotic behaves as if merely having guilt feelings settled the issue. He can use them in fact as an argument against settling anything: "I have spoiled everything. What is the use of trying; I can never live it down." Before these attitudes can be changed, the sources of real guilt must be discovered beneath the patient's exaggerated guilt feelings or other disguises of guilt.

I shall not discuss the various means of uncovering real guilt, but I want to take up one type of camouflage that is both very common and quite difficult to deal with, which was described in the chapter on the obsessive-compulsive neurosis. To avoid feeling guilty about his treatment of people, the patient continuously finds fault with others; the underlying idea is that if a person is a louse he deserves nothing better than the treatment he gets at the hands of the patient. This method of maligning the victim only increases the patient's guilt, which then must be counteracted by ever more vehement deprecation of others. People who use this method extensively can make their life miserable by being chronically enraged, but they have no overt guilt feelings; understandably, they live in terror of guilt.

> One of my patients, who had always frankly feared and disliked his incalculable and vengeful father, spent a major portion of his day in pursuing, with passion, critical and hateful thoughts about practically everybody. This quasideliberate cultivation of hatred turned out to be an attempt to silence severe guilt originally felt in relation to the split-off positive image of the father, which was absent from the patient's emotional awareness; he was able to acknowledge his father's positive features only in an abstract cold way. In the patient's adult life this guilt was augmented by his active mistreatment of people who had meant him well. Like many other patients of this type, he would become upset by every instance of positive interaction with others; his state became worse whenever he met with kindness, since this greatly increased his guilt. Yet he never *felt* guilty until he developed this feeling in therapy.

In my experience, it often pays to explore for the presence of this mechanism, particularly in cases where a steady, high level of hostility is combined with a conspicuous absence of guilt feelings. But these are not the only cases where this pattern may occur. The structure of the situation is the same in some cases where the predominant emotion is not anger but fear. If the patient is scared of practically everybody, constantly anticipating insult, exploitation, or other assaults, by implication he accuses his fellows of faults or crimes and proclaims that they deserve no better than they get. This mechanism may also be present in patients whose hostility or fear are less constant and conspicuous. The function of open or hidden aggression as defense against guilt is an aspect of neurosis that is easily missed, because hostility can usually be quite plausibly accounted for in other terms. Still, within a complex neurotic structure hostility, like any other attitude, can be put to a variety of uses, and these sources of reinforcement must not be neglected. Disregard for them may have led to the assumption of regression in the obsessive-compulsive neurosis as an explanation of the high level of the patient's hostility. In my observation this mechanism is often responsible for the patient's stalling in therapy. In many analyses there comes a time when one is puzzled as to why the patient is not more advanced than he is. He has been working well, gaining insights, yet he does not show any improvement, in particular no diminution of hostility. A frequent reason is his unwillingness to face the guilt which his hostility is masking.

If the vicious circle of mutual reinforcement of guilt and hostility is to be broken, its existence and meaning must be brought to the patient's awareness; but since he cannot tolerate guilt this is a slow and difficult process. One gets a lucky break if some extreme manifestation brings home to the patient that he has a stake in maligning others and in hanging on to his anger.

> One of my patients, on waking up on a Sunday, said to himself: "My wife won't get me my breakfast; she knows how much I enjoy it; it is my best meal, and I can't take time for it on weekdays. Once a week she could get it for me, but she won't." He spent half an hour working up bitterness about it. Then his wife called him to breakfast; she had prepared exactly what he had wanted, but he was so angry and upset that he was unable to eat any of it.

In this instance the patient could not help but start wondering, since in reality his wife never neglected his breakfast. More often, however, the accusations have some basis in reality, and their extravagance can be recognized only gradually from their frequency, from their disproportionate intensity, or from other indirect signs. If the exaggeration is pointed out to the patient, he may easily come to feel that the therapist does not understand the situation or disbelieves his report. Therefore, instead of trying to interpret ambiguous situations, the therapist would do well to wait for his chance. When some episode brings out the pattern in a clear-cut fashion, the patient himself may start noticing it in more complex situations as well, for which others are partly responsible. Gradually he realizes that he has blamed them more than they have deserved. Eventually his defensive anger will subside, permitting the guilt feelings to emerge into consciousness.

The therapist's efforts must be aimed at placing all guilt feelings where they belong, i.e., locating the real guilt which must be faced and not minimized. This requires careful preparation because facing guilt can be shattering. As discussed in the chapter on noncommitment, intensive work on guilt should not be attempted until a partial uncovering of the healthy pattern has lessened the patient's self-contempt and provided a matrix within which real guilt can be placed.

The therapist's initial reaction to the patient's guilt feelings is properly one of reassurance, expressed preferably by implication only. Attempts at direct reassurance at this stage suggest a lack of regard for the patient's intense feelings. But if after hearing his anxious confession of guilty feelings or fantasies, the therapist remarks on some detail rather than on the "crime" itself, he effectively conveys to the patient that he is neither shocked nor greatly interested in it, that it is an everyday sort of thing. This reassurance will clear the way for the expression of other guilt feelings, some of which can be shown to be illusory or based on fantasy or misinformation; providing correct information has a place in this context.

Once the real guilt is out, one must help the patient to realize that in the given situation, particularly in his childhood, he could not have helped acting or feeling as he did. Next, the healthy core must be uncovered within the very feelings and motives that led to his guilt— the struggle for survival, or integrity, or belongingness that was at the basis of his action. Only such anchoring of the patient's guilt in his healthy pattern can enable him to face the facts squarely, and to feel their impact, without feeling crushed. Yet this rehabilitation of the patient's past is not the last step in dealing with guilt but merely a preparation for it. If he is left with that, he is not freed from guilt and he is likely to seek escape from it in self-pity and self-justification.

In the course of his analysis the patient learns a great deal about the factors that have forced his life into unhealthy channels. He will recall and re-experience the frustrations inflicted by the circumstances of his early life and the severe blows helplessly suffered at the hands of others. These insights can be misused and perverted; they then serve as resistance against getting well and actively reordering his life. The patient draws from these insights the half-wrong conclusion that others alone are the cause of his troubles: "I am innocent; others made me what I am. Others should take over and shoulder the burden of my problems. It is the therapist's job to get me well." In placing on someone else the whole responsibility for his neurosis or its cure, he is avoiding his own responsibility and thereby losing the chance to reclaim his life as his to direct.

Wallowing in self-derogation is no more constructive than shifting responsibility. In this case the patient says in effect, "I am no good. I am rotten to the core. There is no hope for a person like me." This is equally irresponsible in that it leads to dodging change. Taking responsibility is very different from looking for excuses and from unproductive self-blame, but the falsity of the either/or perspective—I am either guilty or innocent—is not readily obvious to the patient. He finds it difficult to grasp the idea that he has had an active part in the conduct of his life, even if there were good reasons for his developing as he did, and that now the responsibility is increasingly his. To put it plainly: the patient is not guilty, because he did not know any better. Now that he knows better, he cannot keep dodging responsibility. If he cannot get beyond self-blame or self-justification, he must be helped to realize that his guilt is in the present not in the past. As long as the patient continues the mode of life that has led to guilt in the past, he is bound to feel guilty.

To take responsibility means to acknowledge, simply and frankly, the part one has played, and still is playing, in all of one's actions and in one's self-destructive mode of living. By admitting this to another, the patient discards his false front and moves beyond the confines of anxious secrecy. This is a momentous step forward; he could not have taken it without some confidence that he can live differently in the future. The therapist must stand back and simply accept the patient's acknowledgment of responsibility. Both interpretation and reassurance are now out of place. When the patient has taken this step, he is ready to deal with his guilt. There is only one way of dealing with guilt—to regret it. This means sorrow for the harm that was done and the constructive actions left undone: for the chances that were never taken, for the adventures missed and perhaps no longer possible, for having shortchanged those who loved or needed one and tried in vain to come close and to be helpful. Beyond the regrets it means turning one's back on the neurotic pattern, with a strong desire to discard it and to live in a different way. When the patient begins to react to the destructiveness of his conduct of life with strong feelings of regret, the neurotic structure starts to give.

If in the earlier part of the therapy the patient has not been prepared for facing his guilt in this way, he will be unable to deal with it in the crucial period when despair mounts and the scope of guilt feelings widens to include the whole neurotic mode of life. The burden of guilt will then be a powerful obstacle to change. Sometimes an impasse is created, or aggravated, by a species of circular thinking which more often than not is implicit and has to be brought out by the therapist. It arises when the patient starts envisioning the possibility of change, and it goes something like this: "If I get well, I shall avoid the actions that previously led to harm. But if I can do that, then in the past, too, my destructive behavior was not unavoidable; if I do things differently now, I *could* have done so in the past." The past faults are then felt to be unforgivable and the guilt over them irremovable. But if a person is hopelessly sick and unable to change, he cannot be held responsible for anything he has done. So the patient remains in the helpless state; he does not dare to move because he is unwilling to shoulder the burden of guilt for the past. And thus it may happen, if the therapist is not careful, that the patient's first significant advance into health not only ends in retreat but becomes an obstacle to future advances.

Anxiety

Long before reaching the point of despair, the patient seems to sense what is lying ahead. Reluctant to plunge into this devastating emotional experience, he fights it off as long as he can and approaches the crisis with great anxiety. The anxiety felt when the neurotic structure begins to crumble is often diffuse and pervasive; it is a response not to a circumscribed danger but to a threat to one's very existence. Neurotic life, the only one with which the patient is familiar, is equated with life itself. Painful as this mode of existence may be, he has at least survived so far and has always hoped to do better with it in the future. As yet the patient sees no alternative. Any non-neurotic satisfactions he may anticipate at this point are shadowy at best, often no more than hearsay; the familiar neurotic satisfactions have much more body to them. Small wonder that when his neurosis is threatened the person feels that everything is falling to pieces, that he is about to dive into nothingness, that he is dying. Parting with neurosis feels like parting with life. And indeed one could say, paraphrasing the Gospels, that the patient can gain a new life only by losing his life as a neurotic.

If the loss of neurosis is equated with losing some cherished values, anxiety may be more focused and less overwhelming, but it still has a wide scope. As the patient approaches the point of crossing from neurosis to health, he is assailed by many doubts. "If I let myself trust and like people, will this not make me defenseless, weak, spineless, a doormat? If I worry less and drive myself less, shall I become lethargic, lose my ambition, end as a bum? Will the sources of my creativity dry up? Won't the new life be dull, deprived of the excitement and of all the pleasures my old ways provide? Don't I have to give up a great deal for something very uncertain, perhaps undesirable?" The non-neurotic attitudes may be looked down upon, e.g., as moralistic, humdrum, or as romantic adolescent ideals. But once new satisfactions beckon, the patient may feel not only anxious about losing the old ones but guilty of being disloyal to his neurosis, to the values—no matter how distorted—that have been his for a very long time. His dreams may depict him resisting some alien power—Nazis, Communists, foreign invaders—and refusing to sign a confession or to change his credo even if resistance may cost him his life. The prospect of giving up his neurosis is experienced as a threat not to his life but to his integrity; it is a self-betrayal to be resisted at all costs.

At a later stage the patient may experience specific fears which cause him to delay the moment of decision even after he has clearly seen the way that could lead him out of his narrowed existence or specific predicament. For those patients who have been building castles in the air and living on promises, this requires piercing many bubbles and getting out of the debt they have incurred by overdrawing their emotional bank account. Suppose the patient has realized that to put his life on a healthier basis he must take certain steps that will cost him pain: he may have to eat humble pie, incur someone's anger or scorn, or lose valued associations. These obstacles loom large for the neurotic because he usually has an excessive fear of pain, the exaggeration deriving from the significance a specific pain has for him. For example, being physically hurt often stands for being killed. Having to admit that one has been at fault is not a calamity for a self-confident person, but for the neurotic, in whose system compensatory pride is a crucial element, losing face is disastrous. He feels that the loss is total and irreversible, that he can never face people again. Therefore, on realizing what painful steps he must take to put his life in order, he will search for other ways; having failed to find them he may still cling to the hope that he might.

> One of my patients, when he had already discovered the course that would lead him out of his predicament but was reluctant, as he said, to "wade through the mud" of pain, anxiety, and shame, had the following dream. He was walking and came to a short stretch of road which led directly to his destination, but it was under repair and full of muddy holes. The workmen had put up a sign, *Shit Street;* the patient was not sure that any other road led to the place he was going, but still he decided to try another one. If it did not lead to his goal, he would return and take the muddy road—maybe.

Fear of pain causes the patient to hope that luck or a clever but still neurotic maneuver may yet open a way to escape. These preposterous hopes are discredited in therapy, as they are also discredited, one by one, in his real life. Indeed, if some "lucky break" does occur, it can cause a therapeutic setback since it may greatly strengthen the patient's hope of succeeding in his old way.

Dealing with anxiety and fear in ways that permit the patient to move forward is a constant problem in therapy. During the crucial period we are now discussing, the patient may derive some support from his hope that a better way of life may prove feasible, but at this point the hope is too slight to dispel anxiety. In observing patients deal with anxiety, one finds that it can be dissipated in two diametrically opposite ways; though both involve going through the experience of anxiety rather than warding it off. One method is to explore the seemingly dangerous situation and prove it innocuous. The child is afraid of the witch he saw in the basement, but when the light is turned on he sees that it is merely a broom; the horse afraid of shadows loses its fear after having been forced to cross them. In all therapeutic and educative procedures, ample use is made of this method of "unmasking the bogeyman." The patients are encouraged to put their fears to the test, first in anticipatory thinking and eventually in reality. This method, however, is of little help at the time of the approaching crisis, because what is feared here—the total change, the unknown—is all-encompassing and too vague to be put to a limited test. The other way of shedding anxiety is to become convinced that the dreaded event is unavoidable. This seemingly paradoxical effect follows from the fact that anxiety always presupposes some doubt and some hope; once one realizes that the feared event is inevitable, one is no longer anxious. When anxiety is dispelled by losing the hope of salvaging the neurotic pattern, the way is clear to the crucial experience of despair and the subsequent reconstruction.

The Culmination of the Struggle

If the healthy pattern has gained sufficient strength before the time of the crisis, the state toward which the patient strives will have some specific content instead of being completely vague. The patient can then fight for his health in a deliberate goal-conscious fashion. At this stage the battle is most intense. The threatened neurosis attacks its host with all its weapons; after each defeat it entrenches behind more formidable defenses. New symptoms are to be watched for; it is not uncommon for accident proneness to appear at this stage, or for somatic symtoms to develop, even if the person never had them before. Somatization removes the conflicts from the psychological realm where they can be made accessible to observation and consequently represents a strong line of defense.

Early in his work Freud noticed that toward the end of therapy there is a recrudescence of the entire symptomatology, as if the therapeutic work had been for nought. Such flare-ups are precipitated by the approaching separation from the analyst, but on closer observation a similar reaction is found after each decisive step forward in therapy. While the person is reaching toward health in a goal-conscious manner he may be assailed by temptations of the old ways, by acute anxieties, by accidents and somatic symptoms, or he may make "slips" that have serious practical consequences and which may disarrange his life for a long time to come. These disturbances may not yield to analysis or to any of the ways of managing that the patient has learned in therapy. In this situation some patients, after realizing what is at stake, resort to a painful but effective method of passive resistance. They just keep on their course, not allowing themselves to be deflected from it by the onslaught of the neurosis. One patient spent three days sitting in his armchair gritting his teeth and holding on to the chair. Later he called this period his "stint in the wilderness," likening it to a similar "stint" described in the New Testament. This kind of passive resistance requires courage; it can hardly be kept up for long unless it is reinforced by some new rewarding experiences.

The quality and intensity of anxiety, guilt, and the other phenomena just described indicate that during this period a fierce battle for dominance is going on between the neurotic and the healthy organizations; by comparison, the earlier encounters appear as mere skirmishes. In the course of this struggle, dominance will be seen to shift from one system to the other from week to week, from day to day, and sometimes —in the session—even from minute to minute. It is during this phase that repressed memories and fantasies are most likely to be recalled. The theory of the dual organization of personality offers an adequate explanation for this. It does not seem very plausible that repressed memories should emerge at a given time merely because a particular trend of associations has, more or less fortuitously, led to their hiding place. Rather they are recalled when the patient is ready, or almost ready, to deal with them as he was not able to do within the framework of the neurotic system. This happens when the alter system has developed sufficiently to provide a new framework within which the item in question can be assimilated in a system-consistent fashion; it is then and only then that the repression is lifted.

One young woman's symptoms and trends of thought suggested that she had witnessed parental intercourse at an unusually late age, but her repeated efforts at recall yielded only an isolated image of her father's face with a "funny grin" on it, and her associations failed to confirm our hypothesis. It was not until she began a determined struggle to discard her general attitude of secretiveness and to become more open and confiding that recall followed a repetition of a recurrent childhood nightmare. On awakening from this dream (in which her house was being bombed and she could not reach her parents) she first thought, hazily, that the situation was not quite so dangerous. Then she remembered vividly the crib in which she slept in her parents' room until the age of six, and "saw with my own eyes where that image came from." "No wonder I remembered his face," she said, "they did it sideways." This was followed by a flood of other memories. If one observes carefully the conditions under which repressed items emerge, one will usually find that this is facilitated by a concerted bid for dominance by the alter system.

Another phenomenon observable during this period is the appropriation by each competing system of intrinsic parts of the other, which it perverts to its own uses. This method of defense and offense is a constant element of the therapeutic process, but it becomes especially conspicuous when the struggle is most intense. Any progress toward reconstruction may be followed by an attempt to utilize the gain for neurotic purposes. For example, a patient who for the first time in his life was able to admit to a friend that he had been at fault, was at first genuinely pleased about it; but at some point this pleasure turned into pride, and the new experience was thus made to serve the old attitude. He now felt that his humility made him vastly superior to others! Increased self-confidence may also be used to pursue a neurotic interpersonal pattern more effectively; a retiring boy or girl who merely dreamed of collecting scalps now goes ahead and does it. At this point of "success"—unless earlier work has provided a basis for seeing it in perspective—the patient may decide to leave therapy while he is ahead. A very common example of "perversion" is the patient's use of new insights as weapons against his family and friends.

In the sessions the patient's remarks may start as an expression of one pattern and mood and end as that of their opposites, even if their substantive content is identical and the patient himself is not clearly aware of the change. Difficult as it may be for the therapist to respond to these mixed expressions adequately, it is important for him to follow closely these repeated reversals. The neurotic pattern will return again and again—a wolf in sheep's clothing—and must be unmasked anew every time. The patient will not admit the defeat of his neurosis as long as a single loophole is left.

The period of struggle, with its upsets and anxieties, puts great demands on the patient. To deal with them he may and should use everything he has learned in therapy; much, however, depends on sheer courage. The passive resistance to anxiety, described earlier in this chapter, is certainly a manifestation of courage. Other manifestations of growing courage are a new readiness to express anger, an increased willingness to make choices, and the deliberate decision to throw one's weight on the side of the healthy pattern.

Expression of anger, particularly toward the therapist, is generally considered therapeutic because of its cathartic effect and because it gives the patient a chance to test the therapist and to learn that he does not strike back. These effects are often present but not invariably. An outburst of anger may leave the patient merely ashamed if he sees how unreasonable it was yet gains no new insight into its origins and meanings. Nor is anger constructive when the patient clings to it stubbornly and no change follows the repeated release of hostility. However, in many patients who have never dared to express anger openly and directly, venting it is an expression of growing self-respect and courage and as such is a positive action. The anger may be misplaced, the patient may be fighting windmills, but at least he is fighting instead of giving in to anxiety. One of my patients who had been timidly picking his course through life expressed this clearly when he said, "I don't care what happens; I refuse to live on my knees any longer." Graduating from a state of fear to the expression of anger is a step forward, though the patient may still have a long way to go.

A similar shift to a more self-confident attitude is reflected in an increased willingness to make choices. Faced with an important issue, such as marriage or a new job, the neurotic often procrastinates because he fears that a poor choice would be fatal. He grossly overestimates the importance of making the "right" decision, because he assumes that he is incapable of influencing and changing situations and feels at the mercy of circumstances, of good or bad fortune. Because of this the patient exaggerates the potentialities of the situations and builds up unrealistic expectations. He may, e.g., place a tremendous burden on marriage by expecting it to solve all his problems. Only when his self-reliance increases does he realize that the choice, though important, is not all-important. Whatever he chooses, a great deal still depends on how he will handle the situation; he can make it much better or much worse. The one really important choice, he gradually discovers, is what kind of person he is going to be. Some patients manifest their growing faith in their potentialities by consciously siding with the healthy pattern, throwing in their lot with it, so to speak; more will be said about this in the next chapter.

The therapist, in accompanying the patient through this stressful period, has many specific tasks, but probably more important than these is the encouragement his attitude conveys. At least that is what patients say in retrospect. "The biggest help when the going was rough was to sense your confidence that I could make it." No less important —in this phase as in others—is the therapist's part in creating a setting that awakens the patient to the vital significance of what is being transacted in therapy. Whether or not the patient will experience every phase of therapy in its maximal impact depends in part on the therapist. The nature and style of his interventions increase or diminish the depth and vividness with which the patient experiences the despair caused by the bankruptcy of neurosis, the drama of the struggle for decision, and the beckoning of new satisfactions in the reconstructive phase of therapy.

The Drama in Therapy

I want to disgress here and discuss the drama in therapy. I once conducted a clinical seminar with a group of young therapists who were still being supervised in their work. During the year their supervisor left, and they had to carry their cases by themselves. They were capable people, but inexperienced and therefore very cautious. This is as it should be, but what happened when they were left to their own resources was that the zip went out of their work; it became lifeless. Such work, no matter how "correct," is useless because thoughts in themselves are ineffectual; only emotions, the primal evaluative experiences which tell us in the strongest language what is or seems to be good or bad for us, can motivate us for action and change.

Whatever else the therapist does, he must see to it that the sessions do not drag and become humdrum; there is nothing worse than a sleepy therapist listening to a sleepy patient. A sense of vitality should pervade the therapeutic hour from beginning to end; the session should be maintained at a high emotional pitch, and it is up to the therapist not to let the patient remain neutral. If to some insight which should have a resounding emotional impact, the patient responds by remarking, e.g., that it is "interesting," the therapist must do all he can to make him realize that it is much more than that. To this purpose it is necessary to dramatize. The language one uses is an important factor; it should be pictorial, the more concrete the better. The patient's own expressions that have proved to be highly charged with emotion can be revived where appropriate, or the therapist himself must provide such expressions. If, for instance, the patient has dreamt of a lion, there are associations about lions that can be used to help the emotional implications along: a beast of prey, the king of the desert, his courage, his ferocity, his roar, his fangs, his shaggy mane. One must give pictures, because the unconscious speaks in pictures and will most readily respond to its own idiom. Discussions conducted in generalized abstract terms are more apt to kill feelings than to evoke them. I do not mean that the therapist should be an actor, though I was accused of being one by a patient who said I should be given an Oscar. One cannot create feelings in another by a premeditated procedure. That is, in essence, deception; it may seem to work for a season, but in the long run it will fail. The therapist should not "put on" but he should be very much "with it." He must dramatize to help the patient recapture the sense of the true drama of being alive, of which his neurosis has robbed him.

To keep the sessions at a high emotional pitch is actually congruent with reality since vital issues are being dealt with. A person is spending a great deal of time and money on treatment; in his life much depends on whether or not he gets well. We have one hour; there will be others, but still there are only so many of them. Imagine a busy person making all sorts of arrangements to fit in his therapeutic appointments, rushing to be on time, and then spending the hour yawning and feeling bored. Of all falsifications of reality this is one of the most fantastic. If the therapist keeps in mind that this person's happiness and future are at stake, that the person himself is at stake, he will find means to make the sessions vital, and his dramatizations will be realistic. When one dramatizes realistically in this sense, many emotional implications which would otherwise remain hidden come out strongly and make their impact. For this reason I may witness more drama in my work than a therapist who does not share this conviction and fashions therapy into a detached diagnostic procedure or a humdrum quest after "better adjustment."

Keeping centered on emotional significances is strenuous and at times difficult. Suppose one has a patient with a penchant for long silences; trying to make him speak is like pulling teeth. Finally, the therapist himself is reduced to silence. But he can be silent in different ways. If he can meaningfully appraise this particular silence, the therapist is *actively* silent. He realizes what is going on, though he may say only a few words at long intervals to convey something of it to the patient. Both his remarks and silence may be telling the patient many things: "I understand. You feel you have nothing of value to say. What is on your mind is too painful to tell. You don't believe I could understand you—nobody ever did. I offended you when we had that misunderstanding—we are not on speaking terms today, you are just too deeply hurt." The silence may have a hundred reasons, but if the therapist guesses the correct one, he has done a lot, even if he has said only a few brief sentences during the hour.

Therapists vary in their ability to inject a sense of drama into their work, or, rather, to bring out the drama that is inherent in therapy. It is useful to have some degree of dramatic ability, but this is not an absolute must. Every therapist who is keenly aware of what neurosis does to the patient's life will develop his own style for conveying to him that something very important is going on in the sessions and that we are not here to twiddle our thumbs. If the therapist himself is not alive to this, or lets himself be diverted from his central task by a search for specific connections, or by fascinating discoveries, he is not functioning as a therapist.

16. The Shift toward Health

The General Course

The neurotic pattern has been weakened in the course of the struggle, and the pattern of health can start gaining ascendance. Some turning points stand out in this process. The struggle may culminate in the experience of profound despair in which the defeat of the neurosis is implicitly admitted; a period of "emptiness" may follow, the neurotic pattern remaining inactive. A different type of shift is experienced by the person who gets a clear view of both sides while the struggle is still in progress, decides where he stands, and deliberately throws his weight on the side of health. The decision, which is not as detached and explicit as it may sound in this description, may follow the patient's facing of his guilt, his taking courage to express his anger, or any other vital experience that drives home the difference between neurosis and health. In most cases "turning points" occur more than once. Frequently there is no single massive experience dwarfing all others; rather, a number of minor ones, spread over a long period of time, turn the person around as it were, so that he is now facing away from neurosis and toward the goal of health. At this stage this goal may be only dimly perceived; the patient has yet to take decisive steps toward health.

The negative experiences that have been undergone during the struggle provide one kind of motive for moving ahead. If his sense of bankruptcy is strong enough, the patient may plunge into the unknown even without any great trust in it, feeling that nothing can be worse than the state he is in; this may be experienced almost as a suicidal step. Some degree of negative motivation is indispensable for crossing the bridge from neurosis to health, but negative motivation alone is not sufficient. If the patient is to keep moving forward, he must be supported by the positive motivation provided by new, rewarding experiences. The emergence of such experiences is what characterizes the terminal stage of therapy; once the grip of the neurosis is broken, the work of reconstruction that has been carried on all along starts bearing fruit. The patient begins to reach out from the enclosure. New experiences, never envisioned before, lead to new perspectives and possibilities, which eventually "seep down" and become organized into a new image of the world and a new system of personal attitudes. In the optimal outcome, the patient becomes identified with the new outlook solidly and permanently. More often than not, however, the problem of keeping well remains with the patient even after the termination of therapy.

The Emergence of the New

"Starting anew" after the neurosis is largely defeated seems hardly possible to the patient because of what he considers a realistic assessment of facts: since it has always been this way it must continue this way—a kind of statistical proof that change is impossible, which reinforces the dire expectations typical of neurosis. But this proof is invalid since the patient's sample of past experiences has been biased through his selective perception and his distortion of "facts." Given this systematic error the past facts prove nothing, but the patient's experience as yet contains little else. The implicit expectations of people in the patient's milieu are an additional obstacle to change. It takes an extraordinary person not to be influenced by the consensus of his culture about what is possible and what is not; innovators and reformers are rare. For the patient who is not yet certain of his new self, the conservative expectations of others are a powerful influence. Those who know him are only too likely to feel that "The leopard cannot change his spots" and to take his attempts at change skeptically; this has a very demoralizing effect. If the patient nevertheless keeps to the new course, his sincerity and persistence will eventually force the others to revise their expectations, and in turn these new expectations will support him in his new course. But in the initial stage the patient, weighed down by his own conservatism allied with that of others, finds himself in a situation where he can say sincerely that only a miracle could help him. And he is right; no one gets well without a miracle—in the sense not of a supernatural event but an event outside the established system, impossible and unthinkable until then.

Typically the patient starts experimenting very cautiously, sampling what is outside his usual way of life without entering into anything that is radically new. He may let himself get into a situation that gives him a taste of what it is like on the other side or he may find himself acting in unaccustomed ways. He may, for instance, for the first time in his life, take the initiative of approaching someone he likes, speak up in a group, agree to take charge of some undertaking, or accept a compliment without embarrassment. Such minor deviations from his established pattern may seem accidental, but they never are; they testify to changes prepared by a great deal of work. Still, the preparation may have been insufficient for the patient to benefit from these slight experiences. A patient who for the first time in his life calls up a potential friend is taking a chance, but he may still feel shattered by any semblance of rejection and be discouraged for a long time from trying again. He feels he has learned his lesson. This proves that the constructive step has been premature, and it is well worth noting that premature moves sometimes reinforce the neurosis. If the patient realizes this, he has a better chance of avoiding this pitfall. Had the time been ripe for the step, the patient might have realized the major significance of his novel act, apart from its outcome. Opportunities for such realizations are bypassed if the novel acts or feelings go unnoticed, are interpreted away as situationally determined, or as merely surface appearances—according to the patient's or the therapist's habitual frame of reference. The experience is then registered as a feeble exception and is eventually forgotten without having had an effect. Yet such experiences can generate revolutionary insights if their significance is appreciated. It is the therapist's responsibility to see to it that they are not aborted by inattention or lack of preparation. Experience in itself is no teacher, one can learn from it only after having become teachable.

> Some patients become so expert at excluding novel experiences that they can remain insensitive to them for a long time. One of my patients clung to her pervasive mood of cautious annoyance long after she had seen through the neurotic dynamics. One day I asked her whether there was not even one little corner in her life that was not filled with frustration and gloom, and this simple remark sparked an experience that was a real eye opener. She suddenly saw that her view of her life was both narrow and untrue; she had not dared to admit to herself and to others the new satisfactions that were coming her way.

When the new experiences start "coming through" they often seem to the patient nothing short of miraculous; new worlds are opening up. Some of this may take place in thinking. For instance, the person thinks of ways to handle a certain situation and suddenly sees an alternative: "It can be done that way too—in fact this is the obvious way, why didn't I think of it before?" He may then act on the thought, even if

with doubt and trepidation. Acting "out of character" may also over-
take the patient unawares as it were. In either case the experience,
if properly assimilated, can become a wedge into a wider range of
possible feelings and actions.

> After two years of treatment a young man brought up in an emotionally
> constricted home was bogged down in the project of expressing his hostil-
> ity on every possible occasion. One day a friend while working with him
> in the garden lost a penknife he had borrowed from the patient a few
> minutes earlier. The friend said he felt like an ass, and the patient, in one
> of his customary outbursts, replied, "You should feel like an ass, because
> you *are* an ass." On this occasion, however, proving that he could vent his
> anger was not the end of the story. When after an unsuccessful search the
> friend said that he had to go home, the patient, to his own amazement,
> answered warmly, "That's all right Jim; no need for both of us to look.
> I'll find it." What amazed him was the realization that "I had really
> forgiven him and he knew it. It was weird. I felt closer to him than ever
> before." After this experience the patient changed his goal from proving
> that he had overcome his anxiety-filled past to exploring and developing
> the full gamut of his emotional resources.

The type of insight that is involved in the discovery of new potentialities is perhaps best described as *growing faith*. Later, when the new
ways of feeling and acting have repeatedly brought rewards, their
feasibility and effectiveness become obvious. But before this happens
the patient must act on faith, accepting something he does not fully
know. The kind of faith I have in mind is not the "blind" faith based
on authority or on one's own wishes and fears but the faith of widening vision. The neurotic's range of vision is restricted; he wears blinders and can believe only what he sees. Therefore few alternatives exist
for him, and he behaves as if he had no choice. When this person starts
dispensing with his blinders and looks beyond his habitual range, he sees
at first only indistinctly; this makes his perception different from
knowledge and akin to faith. Rather than revealing clearly articulated
detail, the new vision is an experience of an enlarged horizon. The
patient comes to feel that what he previously took for the whole world
was just a small corner of it.

The opening of new vistas which follows the kind of event that
"just does not happen in my life" is sometimes accompanied by a
feeling of miraculous newness which may extend to situations unrelated to the specific event. The patient may experience a sharpening of
all his senses; he sees, hears, smells things as he never did before. As he
walks in the street the houses and trees look peculiarly pleasing and

new, as if he were seeing them for the first time. Occasionally a patient describes such a change in perception when neither he nor the therapist can see any reason for it. It is safe to assume in such a case that something significant has happened and it pays to search for it in recent events.

The Identification with the New

The gradually accumulating new experiences, especially if recognized and responded to by the therapist, become convincing invitations to a permanent change and may result in a radical reorganization of the patient's modes of feeling and acting. What is the factor that operates in this reorganization and insures the stable primacy of the healthy pattern? I have come to think of it as identification; whether or not the patient's insights and struggles will result in lasting changes of real consequence depends on whether he identifies with the newly emerging pattern of health, i.e., redefines himself in terms radically different from those of his neurotic self-concept. Psychological facts necessarily involve a subjective or creative element; they fill reality with personal significance. When we identify something as useful or harmful, loving or unloving, difficult or easy, beautiful or ugly, we experience these qualities as *essential* components of the object, not just accidentally associated with it. In this way we do not merely register features of the biosphere but also potentiate them, i.e., increase their effective reality. It makes a difference whether we view someone's friendly or hostile behavior as being essentially his—he *is* a friend or an enemy—or as merely accidental; he just happens to be in a bad mood, but basically he is friendly. How we identify others has consequences in reality, not only in our feelings, but the consequences are much more far-reaching when the process is applied to the self. The self is the part of the personal world whose qualities are most amenable to potentiation, to being brought into effectual active existence. In the process of therapy the patient's former self-definitions are loosened, and the rigid segregation of the conscious self from the total self is partially overcome. This extension of intrapersonal reality presents him with a wider choice of characteristics on which to base his self-definition.

If the patient, having recognized his neurosis, confronts it in all earnestness as the central issue of his life, he is provided with a strong motive for throwing in his lot with the newly discovered alternatives. The act of reidentification then results in a new self-definition, one that implies capacity both for autonomous expansion and for homono-mous integration. This act results also in the determination to adhere to the new self-definition.

To clarify what is involved in identification we may take as a con-crete example any patient whose main problem is either some compul-sively self-destructive act (e.g., pathological drinking) or some self-destructive form of paralysis (e.g., chronic work inhibition). What-ever else happens in therapy, recovery must include the solution of this focal difficulty; in this respect it is not hard to determine who has and who has not been cured. Consequently such cases present good oppor-tunities for learning what differentiates those permanently cured from the rest.

The difference does not lie in a speedy and complete disappearance of the neurotic urge. Those who are "cured" report, rather, a growing ability to nip each rising urge in the bud. An emerging individual urge can be combated only while it is barely forming. If one goes along with it even for a short stretch, the battle is lost; nothing can stop the urge until it plays itself out, i.e., until the Gestalt achieves closure. Efforts at forceful suppression are ineffective or short-lived. The urge soon surges up with renewed force. What seems to be needed to deal effectively with neurotic urges—be it an urge to take "just one drink" or to stop working—is a kind of preconscious vigilance which allows one to detect the urge at its very inception, so that a countermove can follow instantaneously. In these cases noticing is acting, and this inter-nal move dissipates the Gestalt just beginning to form.

In exploring the antecedents of patients' capacity to maintain this high level of vigilance, one often discovers a prior act of reidentifica-tion. In some cases this act does not reach the level of consciousness or it is not retained in memory, and can only be inferred from the fact that the patient no longer resorts to his former neurotic devices, though he may struggle and flounder in pursuing his new course. Often, however, the momentous step of giving allegiance to the healthy pattern is remembered and reported. This act is never de-scribed as a forceful assertion of will power; it is very quiet, seemingly effortless, and not at all dramatic. Its concrete content varies, but the experience has two distinctive features. The first is finality. As long as this quality is lacking the patient is merely playing with the idea of change; he does not burn his bridges. One of my patients at this stage dreamt he was holding a pack of cigarettes. He had recently given up smoking, and in the dream he said to himself, "Why should I carry these around with me? Well, I don't smoke any more, but just in case . . ." And he put the cigarettes back in his pocket. In the act of reidentification, by contrast, the decision is made once and for all. It is not "I will give it a try," "I will start tomorrow," or "I can do it when the breaks of the game are with me." It is simply "I do" or—in the case of discarding an urge—"I will not." The stand is unqualified and final.

The second characteristic of the act of reidentification is that the affirmation is made not about how one will *behave* but about the kind of person one will *be*. Drawing on the reports of reformed alcoholics one finds that they differ from the short-lived conversions in that the habit was given up not merely because of its specific deleterious effects; a broader change of attitude has rendered the habit incompatible with the dominant system.

> One member of Alcoholics Anonymous, an unskilled worker, described the change in these terms. "It is a change you can hardly explain. Everything is altogether different now. I do think of all kinds of things where I did not think at all. When you're drinking you don't think; you just react. I did not even use to think of repairing the roof when it leaked—now I keep my house fixed. When you've got your own mind, you think altogether different, because you got a chance to think. Now I am kind of interested in public affairs. I think about labor situations, and I am trying to think about religious situations. I am getting so I think about lots of things in life."

This man now feels that drinking is inconsistent with his self-definition as a rational and responsible being—no longer a thoughtless fool blind to the consequences of his actions. Only a change in the superordinate pattern can insure lasting change in details of behavior.

Re-identification is an inner movement. It cannot be directly induced from outside. The preceding struggle for decision and the emerging new experiences are its preconditions but are no guarantees. Sometimes the process may be initiated by a conscious act of will in choosing one set of alternatives. This observation is worth emphasizing. Will, i.e., government by the conscious self, has long been in disrepute among psychologists and not without reason. Its assumption of hegemony over the total self results in limitation and distortion. There is not one of us who has not willed himself to be less, or other, than what he ideally could have been. When the conscious self is severely limited and rigidly segregated from the total self, many of its attempts at governing fail; this is reflected in the neurotics' complaints about their weak will. But when this segregation is partially overcome, the potency of the will grows. It is worth noting that acts of will can on occasion provide leverage for momentous inner shifts. It would be of the utmost practical importance to learn through what concrete steps patients arrive at the decision implied in the act of reidentification, and what the therapist can do to help them take these steps.

The patient's new definition of himself does not cut him off from his past history, but it changes his perception of his past. He has to settle the past by getting reconciled with it before he can proceed in the new way. This is the theme of those impressive dreams, sometimes signaling the end of therapy, in which the patient vividly re-experiences himself as the child he was, yet as having benefited from what, as an adult, he has learned in treatment.

> In his next to last session, a patient brought in a dream in which he was pruning a forest of trees to see more clearly a distant house on a hill, and also to make it easier for a little boy with a clubfoot to get around and to have some fun in life. The early period of his treatment had been devoted to analyzing unfounded fears of homosexual and other "monstrous" or crippling predispositions, but during the months preceding the dream we had dealt mostly with his determination to develop his own growth potential and to resist his tendency to make decisions in terms of external appearances. Remembering that he was an expert in landscaping, I asked the patient what the purpose of pruning trees was. He replied: "Well appearance, of course, but basically to get rid of the dead branches that prevent a tree from growing the way it wants to, to free all of its resources . . . I guess the tree is me." In this dream the patient's past, present, and future were seen from a new vantage point.

With time the new self-definition and other explicit formulations of the new outlook on life recede into the background of consciousness. The struggles that have been lived through are also partially forgotten, especially by younger patients. A few years after the completion of therapy some of them are quite vague about the nature of their past difficulties. But this "forgetting" does not mean that the therapeutic achievement has been lost. The new organization of the personality brought about with the aid of conscious processes does persist; it is the patient's self-consciousness that is gone. He now pursues the healthy course with less effort and self-concern.

The Task of Staying Well

A deeply resonant experience of reidentification is the crowning achievement of therapy. It insures an ideal outcome since it enables health to become "second nature," effortlessly and stably maintained. But the ideal is not the rule. For the majority of patients, the task of recovering falls into two parts: getting well and staying well. I think we pay too little attention to the second part; we should be honest enough to admit that relapses—both during treatment and after its completion—are almost universal. It often happens during treatment that after an important insight or a significant experience, the patient improves markedly. Sometimes improvement is so great that he could be considered "cured," if only it would last. Even granted that not all problems are solved, why the relapse? Why is it that the patient cannot stay at the level he has reached and go on from there?

When such temporary improvements occur early in therapy, one can always assume that some of the strongest underpinnings of the neurosis have not yet been loosened, so that the improvement lacked a firm basis. It is useful to gain understanding of the experiences that have caused a shift toward health, so one can provide more of them for the patient, and it is useful to explore the causes of relapse. With the neurotic organization still powerful, the gain is often lost by being placed in its service. It is as if the patient were at a loss about what to do with his newly found competence and were reduced to using it in the pursuit of his old goals. He may, e.g., lose a substantial gain by deciding to test it and to prove himself in a difficult situation, which he deliberately seeks out, or by using the gain to assert his superiority over a rival. A thorough discussion of these goals can prevent some of the losses, which also underscore for the therapist the importance of preparing the patient in time to make constructive use of his gains. But when relapses occur after a successful completion of an extensive analysis, an explanation that invokes the persisting strength of the neurosis does not seem equally valid.

Perhaps the reluctance of some therapists to admit the prevalence of these setbacks is caused by conceptions of illness and therapy which dictate a pessimistic view of relapses. If neurosis is seen as a focal disturbance or as a malignant growth to be removed by therapy, a relapse indicates that it has not been completely extirpated and that another operation is necessary. One tends to assume implicitly that the factors involved in getting well and in staying well are the same; a relapse then would mean that the recovery had been imperfect. An astute observer could have predicted that it would not last. This is not entirely in accord with observed fact. There is a positive correlation between the degree of improvement and its durability, but it is far from perfect. Both to subjective and objective observation many improvements later followed by relapses seem as good while they last as the more enduring ones; conversely, improvements that are far from perfect may prove to be lasting.

Within the framework of the theory of the dual organization of personality, the occurrence of periodic relapses is understandable—is, in fact, to be expected. Since in therapy the elements of personality are not removed but merely rearranged, it is hardly astonishing that under certain conditions the neurotic pattern can once more gain a position of dominance. If we discard our perfectionistic attitudes, such shifts are no cause for pessimism since they, too, are reversible. The healthy pattern may reappear in full vigor even without any additional help. If the healthy state of a patient formerly entrapped in his neurosis is interrupted only by infrequent and brief relapses, we need not minimize the success of therapy. Yet it is important to increase our understanding of the nature and causes of these shifts. A relapse may not only interrupt the patient's healthy functioning or delay its stabilization; it can also undermine the healthy pattern by insidiously perverting it to neurotic uses, and thus reduce its chances of regaining dominance. Perhaps it is even more important to explore the factors that make for resiliency, the characteristics that enable the person to make comebacks after relapses. The patient's degree of resiliency may determine whether he will lead a self-destructive existence, with only infrequent flashes of healthy conduct, or lead a healthy life, in spite of occasionally falling into self-destructive ways.

It is widely agreed that relapses may be expected to occur when some current situation in the patient's life reproduces the central traumatic experiences of his past. The reactivation of the trauma may also reactivate the neurosis. Precipitating factors of this nature are frequently found in sudden dramatic relapses, and uncovering them often results in a quick comeback. However, it would be a mistake to assume that all relapses follow this pattern.

Overpowering experiences and debilitating conditions need not be present; the vicissitudes of daily living tend to gnaw insidiously at the pattern of health. Continued contact with people to whom one had been tied in a neurotic relationship represents a continued threat to the new attitudes, which may also wear off in routine dealings with people who assume that the patient's new conduct is merely a hypocritical pose. The patients whose social contacts drag them down find it easier to hold on to their new orientation while they are alone or in a new environment: in the early morning, in the evening, on vacations. But even impersonal and unimportant daily routines, such as driving to work or having a drink before dinner, may undermine the patient's new attitudes, simply because they have for a long time been parts of the framework of his neurosis. This is not to say that he drove to work or brushed his teeth "neurotically," but he did it daily for a great many years while leading a neurotic existence. These actions may exert a magnetic pull on the total pattern of which they used to be parts. The recently discarded, but long familiar, period of reverie may slip in after the familiar drink, making him forget his intention to work or to write a letter. Thus the constructive orientation is lost inadvertently and almost unnoticeably. The neurotic pattern may reinstall itself through a series of small steps, and a long time may pass before the person realizes the change.

During the relapse the formerly established healthy orientation is unavailable to the patient. He may grope for it but have difficulty in recalling its tenets or he may recall them as mere words, no longer alive and moving; he may feel that he knows them, but he just does not care. The patient makes a comeback by re-establishing contact with the healthy orientation; its reappearance proves that it has not been lost. It is my hypothesis that resiliency, i.e., ease in making comebacks, depends not on the relative strength of the healthy and the neurotic organization but is a function of the degree of communication existing between different regions or systems of personality. At present, psychological theory can say little about this important feature of personality structure. We can, however, describe one type of experience occurring in therapy which might be considered a manifestation of this structural feature.

Discussions in therapy are centered on the individual person's neurosis and health, but some patients have a knack for acquiring knowledge far beyond this limited topic; between the lines of the therapeutic dialogue they read the therapeutic orientation. For example, the patient not only comes to view his specific ailments within the larger pattern to which they belong but he also learns that all specific ailments may be viewed in this way. He discovers, as one patient put it, that the emotional ills and symptoms are like annoying children. "They can wreak havoc on your peace of mind, yet you just can't beat the little devils. The trick then is not to deal with them at all but to take them to their parents." During the phase of struggle a person can learn not only that the period of darkness was followed by dawn but that one will always see dawn after darkness—if one knows how to stay awake, how to sweat out anxieties, how to convert guilts into responsibilities. Thus the patient comes to generalize from the specific lessons of therapy to unknown problems in the unknown future. He learns to tell when he is caught in the squeeze of two neurotic impulses and how this feeling differs from those which signal larger conflicts between his neurotic and his healthy self. The person becomes sensitive to widening vistas and to other harbingers of personal growth and does not discard them as anomalies and trivia. He can learn the many languages of his self and can also learn how to learn them; thus he can be prepared to learn new ones. A patient who has learned all this may be expected not to be helpless if he has a relapse. It would be very useful to us to know just what facilitates such latent learning and the growth of resiliency in general and in what ways the therapist can promote it.

Perhaps the strongest protection against future relapses is the sense of humility which the patient may develop when he admits the bankruptcy of his former ways and discards his neurotic compensations and pretenses. Horney,* in her last book, called the totality of neurotic attitudes the "pride system"; one could rightly call the healthy organization the *humility system*. It may sound exaggerated or outright false when a member of Alcoholics Anonymous who has not touched a drop of liquor for years still refers to himself as an alcoholic. Far from being insincere, this self-evaluation is literally true and is the best protection against relapses. When an alcoholic proudly proclaims that he "has licked the habit for good," the time is not far off when he will go on a binge; *mutatis mutandis*, the same is true for neurosis.

To remain well, the patient must recognize that his neurosis has not been erased once and for all when health got the upper hand. Though it is a bitter pill to swallow for a patient who has hoped for a golden era, he has to learn that recovery means no more than this: the strength of the neurotic pattern has been reduced, and he has learned how to live in a wholesome fashion. But the potentiality for his special way of malfunctioning always remains with him. It is immediately activated when the patient succumbs to conceit, pride, or self-centeredness and retreats into his angry anxious isolation. This realization can help the patient to deal with relapses, resisting the temptation to indulge in self-blame and to work up a feeling of helpless and final defeat. Such demoralization is the worst consequence of relapse since it reinforces the neurotic pattern and all its vicious circles. If the patient accepts his fallibility, he can, instead, gently call himself back to where he was before, and can even learn and benefit from the relapse if he succeeds in detecting its cause.

* K. Horney, *Neurosis and Human Growth*. Norton, New York, 1950.

17. Insight

The preceding descriptions of therapy were centered on its course as a whole. I shall now review some of the part processes of psychotherapy: insight, resistance, reviving the pattern of health, and the patient-therapist relationship—dwelling particularly on the aspects of these topics that in my opinion have not been adequately covered in literature and which require further clarification.

Insight is a therapeutic factor of prime importance, but we all know that not every insight has therapeutic effects; an insight emerging as a great revelation may yet prove just another "false hope." The problem is to determine what characteristics or dimensions insight must have, and/or what other processes must accompany or follow it to make it therapeutically effective, i.e., capable of initiating significant personal changes.

Definition

Definitions of insight vary from the very narrow to the very broad; some limit it to a particular content; others accept insight as "real" only if it has brought results, thus in effect equating it with the sum total of the processes needed to produce change. To confuse matters further, the term "insight" is applied both to single instances and to the total continuous process of acquiring self-knowledge; in either case the emphasis may be either on the process or its product. This semantic hodgepodge impedes the advancement of knowledge. For the purposes of this discussion let us define insight as both increment of knowledge and the total resulting knowledge of personally relevant factors. These may be single facts, relationships between facts, or complex patterns of relationships. This definition is broad but not as all-inclusive as some; in accordance with the general psychological usage, insight is here defined in purely cognitive terms. I find it convenient and clarifying to view insight as a multidimensional phenomenon varying not only in content but also in such characteristics as degree of completeness and clarity. To describe an insight adequately, all these dimensions must be stated.

Insight can be assumed to go through a process of growth. In the course of therapy it changes and expands in content; from a fragmentary perception of single connections here and there insight grows to include the complexly interlinked, total pattern of neurosis. In the dimension of clarity, any single insight can grow from a vague possibility, through increasing plausibility, to be as "clear as a bell." If we conceive of insight as growing from feeble beginnings to maturity, obviously its effectiveness must depend on its developmental stage. A "young" insight provides little dynamic leverage; we cannot expect it to move mountains. But we need not therefore discard it as useless. It may pave the way to further discoveries. A true insight is followed by many others, though not always at once; there may be a period of incubation. Any immature, budding insight, if patiently fostered, may well prove an important step toward the ultimate goal of therapy. Although the fully ripe insight ready for use may appear suddenly, impressing the patient as an instant revelation, a great deal of work has usually gone into it. Maturation of insight may be viewed as a process of successive approximation of the state of complete self-knowledge, although this state is never achieved.

New Facts

I have made my definition of insight sufficiently broad to include not only the discovery of connections and patterns but also the discovery of previously unknown facts, external or internal. Newly discovered facts, interpreted in conjunction with those already known, can result in important insights into relationships; taken by themselves, they are only potentially valuable material.

One source of new facts is the recovery of repressed memories. This source has been overemphasized and overvalued in classical analysis, possibly because the condition initially studied was simple hysteria, in which such recovery occurs fairly frequently. The emergence of repressed memories is a spectacular event which usually has important effects, but it is neither common nor a therapeutic "must"; many patients go through analysis successfully without experiencing it even once. More frequent than full-blown memories are hints from which one can infer the nature of some early events, and one can work with these constructs quite profitably. Equally common are memories which, without being repressed, have not been in use; the patient suddenly recalls an experience he has not thought of in a long time. Rich sources of "new facts" are dreams, fantasies, and other brands of seemingly inconsequential thought. Thus the knowledge of personally relevant facts grows to greater completeness through the recovery of repressed and suppressed memories and, to a much greater extent, through recognizing the importance of many items of one's experience and behavior to which one previously paid little attention. The enlarged field of factual information provides material for insight in the precise sense of the term, i.e., the discovery of relationships and patterns.

The holistic approach is sometimes misinterpreted as a demand that one study the total personality, in the sense of not omitting a single detail; *everything* must be included. This, of course, is a gross misunderstanding. "Holistic" refers to the nature of the concepts used, and these aim at the essential, not at "everything." Obviously, it is neither possible nor necessary for therapy to discover all there is to know about the patient, and the question naturally arises of how far the fact-finding and the elaboration of relationships should be pursued: just how much insight does one need? One might say that as many facts must be gathered as are needed to discover significant personal patterns; and at least as many of the specific patterns must be explored as are needed to lay bare the patient's basic assumptions. This formal answer, however, provides no guidelines to an economical gathering of therapeutically pertinent knowledge.

How much factual knowledge one needs is one part of the question about the essentials of therapy that systematic research may help answer. There can be little doubt that only a portion of what we do in therapy is necessary and effective. By varying the amount and kind of facts collected in the exploratory stage of therapy, we could learn the effective minimum; this knowledge would help eliminate much waste of time and effort. It might also be feasible to conduct a similar program with regard to insight proper to determine which connections and patterns it is most important to discover. In the absence of such established guidelines I shall try to indicate the types of insight that in my experience are necessary for success, or more exactly, for bringing the patient to the crucial point when he is ready to grapple with the issue of change. When this point is reached, insight gaining has served its purpose and is no longer essential. The last stretch of therapy consists not of learning more about oneself, but of a struggle to discard the old attitudes and to find out how one can live in a different way.

Types of Insight

Insights can be divided into two groups: those pertaining to the genesis of the neurosis and those pertaining to its present structure and functioning. In the early days of psychoanalysis great emphasis was placed on the early origins of neurotic disturbances. Analysis was assumed to be the deeper, the more complete and effective, the further back the symptoms could be traced into the pre-oedipal phases. This assumption presupposes a one-to-one causal relationship between the early events and the present, disregarding the complex neurotic structure the patient has built up in the meantime. It also presupposes that clarifying the original cause will automatically eliminate the effects, an assumption which has proven untenable. In my conception, in the temporal Gestalt of a life, "causation" works back and forth, and the present can change the past; the future is influenced by the past as the past is *now*.

Important as the *genetic insights* may be, emphasizing them at the cost of holistic insight into the neurotic character structure would be a grave error. Only insight into his current mode of functioning can mobilize the patient's motivation for change; the genetic insights themselves can be vital only if the patient as he knows himself now can identify with the child he was. If one were to limit the field of therapeutic exploration either to the patient's childhood or to his present, the present might well yield better results. Fortunately, in long-term therapies no such choice is necessary. Genetic insights are indispensable, and not only because by showing the varying elaboration of the neurotic pattern over time they contribute to holistic insight; they are invaluable because they demonstrate how the pathological originates from the healthy. This, to my mind, is the most important function of genetic insights. Showing the patient that his deviant development is a natural response to the traumas incurred during the period of infantile dependence—which are often the fate of the young of the human race—makes his self-concept lose the quality of monstrosity and reduces his feeling of utter difference and isolation. The patient sees that, in entering the path of neurotic development, he could not have helped to feel and act as he did. By linking the patient's neurotic present with his past as a child with whom he can sympathize, genetic insights quickly lead over into the constructive phase of the therapeutic work; they reduce shame and guilt to more realistic proportions. At a later stage, a repeated review of the early traumatic situations may also bring the insight that they did not have to put a stop to a confident pursuit of basic satisfactions; viewed from the vantage point of a later developmental level other paths were available.

When the patient enters therapy he is entrapped in a complex neurotic structure which has developed over a long period of time. The first task of therapy is to loosen this tightly knit fabric by broadening and deepening the patient's understanding of his neurosis. This goal is achieved primarily by the uncovering of unconscious fantasies, or *implicit assumptions about himself and the world*, which, unknown to the patient, determine his attitudes and manifest themselves in repetitive behavioral patterns. The totality of these assumptions are the blueprint of the patient's neurosis. These fantastic concepts have to be laid bare and their origins and interconnections traced. The main function of intellectual insight is to create order in the picture of the complex operations that lie between the origins and the outcomes of a neurosis. This requires grouping the observed facts into syndromes and deducing from these syndromes the underlying basic assumptions, a process I described in Chapter 13. Here I need only reiterate my conviction of the importance of *holistic insights*, i.e., of insights into attitudes which affect large areas of the person's life. The realization of their scope also is important. The patient will have had glimpses of his attitudes, let us say of his fear of exposure, but the impact comes only when he realizes that his total experience has this *Leitmotif:* "My life is built on shaky foundations." The germinative nature of such insights is clear from their effects. When one of them makes its appearance, many instances of the same general principle occur to the patient that were never discussed before. The already explored symptoms and syndromes gain a new meaning, and facts previously viewed as separate become connected as instances of one superordinate pattern; in general things click and fall into place.

Insights into more specific personal patterns also are indispensable since they uncover the concrete elaboration of the patient's neurosis, but they do not attain mature status until the specific patterns are seen as rooted in the general ones—in the patient's basic personal axioms. When this happens, a limited therapeutic effect is sometimes achieved at once. The realization that a specific fear or concern symbolizes a wider and different one may reduce its intensity, even while the general concern still persists. But some other specific concerns may develop. Attempts to translate partial insight into behavior will meet with the resistance of the unresolved general attitudes, and the improvement will not be lasting. Durable significant changes can come only "from above," from changes in attitudes of wide scope. Holistic insights have a prime importance as mediators of lasting therapeutic results.

To become ultimately effective, insights into the broad features and the detail of the contemporary neurotic pattern must be supplemented by other kinds of insight. The elucidation of the patient's neurotic assumptions must be accompanied by some realization of their invalidity. Little is gained if he sees clearly that he expects ridicule from everyone he meets but continues to feel that his attitude is justified by facts. Compensatory fantasies developed to conceal the basic neurotic assumptions, e.g., grandiosity masking impotence, must also be given their share of attention as must be the devices used to make all these contradictory attitudes appear consistent with each other. The patient must be confronted with all the inconsistencies and conflicts inherent in his style of life. The delineation of the mechanisms by which the neurosis maintains and defends itself is an inherent part of the analysis of the neurotic structure. Most important of all, the patient must realize, repeatedly and in concrete detail, how destructively his neurotic attitudes affect his whole life. Although this may be obvious to the therapist it is far from clear to the patient. In fact his unwillingness to admit it may blind him to the simplest causal connections between his actions and their consequences. Changing this blindness to clear sight is one of the main tasks of therapy. As the work of demolition progresses the patient must discover the pervasiveness of his neurotic mode of living and realize that he is cheating himself out of life. This realization serves to counteract his tendency to believe that, apart from some specific complaints, he is pretty well off as he is.

I have emphasized, throughout, the necessity to supplement the analysis of the neurotic structure with insights into individual *potentialities for healthy functioning;* this task is too often neglected and left to itself. Yet the weakly developed healthy pattern may be buried as deeply as some of the roots of neurosis, and the patient may strongly resist its being brought to light. When some of his genuine constructive potentialities are pointed out to him, the patient feels this to be an undeserved compliment; he may view the comment as a therapeutic trick or may conclude that he has succeeded in deceiving the analyst. Opportune occasions therefore must be found for such demonstrations, e.g., moments when some genuine feelings break through or are close to the surface.

> One young woman came to the session shaken by the realization that some people she knew were genuinely fond of her. She felt that, being incapable of affection, she herself had nothing of value to give them; while saying this she started crying bitterly. I asked whether it seemed likely that someone who could feel such grief over her inability to give affection was basically cold and unloving, and she admitted, relaxing, that there must be more in her than she knew.

It happens that after a constructive insight has filled the patient with new hope, he promptly forgets it. A day or two later he may have a vague feeling that he had made a great discovery, but for the life of him he cannot remember what it was. The pattern of health is being held down by the dominant pattern of neurosis.

Insight into the existence in oneself of submerged healthy potentialities must be accompanied by at least a glimpse of their possible actualization: things can be different from what they are now. This liberation from slavery to established "facts" in a significant area of one's life may be experienced as a real illumination and may change one's expectations of the future, thus paving the way for behavioral change. Changed expectations are not limited to one's own conduct. Insights into constructive possibilities may refer also to other people, situations, the laws governing interpersonal relations; through such insights the patient's neurotic image of the world as totally alien and hostile is transformed into a more positive and discriminating one.

I have discussed insights into the neurotic and the healthy personal features separately, but that is an artificial separation. Not only do the two kinds of insight interlink in reality: explicitly relating neurosis and health is in itself an indispensable kind of insight. I am referring to the discovery of the *healthy roots of the neurotic trends,* i.e., finding health right inside the neurosis. Such discoveries make it possible to transplant personal traits from the neurotic pattern to the organization of health. This reduction of neurosis to health occurs through the demonstration of the original healthy intent in specific types of neurotic behavior; the methods of pursuing the goal have been twisted out of shape by the patient's false assumptions. Thus the neurotic trends of bullying, domineering, or toadying may actually be roundabout methods of forcing acceptance from an assumedly hostile or indifferent world. A special instance is the amalgamation of a neurotic and healthy trend. Thus in the fear of success the neurotic components may be amalgamated with the wish to preserve one's belongingness with others or not to disadvantage them: "I am prettier and a better student than my sister, and our parents always praise me and criticize her; if through therapy I should become socially successful as well, I would deprive her of the only asset which she feels is hers." When both the neurotic and the healthy meanings are represented by the same symptom and activated simultaneously, the strength of the symptom is nearly insuperable and is ascribed by the patient to the strength of his neurosis. Insight into this constellation counteracts this assumption and makes a great deal of difference for the patient's self-esteem and his outlook on the future.

A different case is that of a personal asset developed within the framework of health but later perverted into the service of neurosis. The patient can do something well: conduct research, make critical appraisals of other people's work, write or enjoy poetry. He discovers in analysis that these activities form an inherent part of his neurotic pride system, that he uses them for self-glorification, and he jumps to the conclusion that they are nothing but that. This, however, is most unlikely. If he can write good poetry even occasionally, something more than self-glorification must be involved. The therapist then has to step in and salvage the good component by differentiating it from its neurotic misuse. The patient may also have attached a negative meaning to a healthy personal manifestation simply because of ignorance or misinformation, much as a child ignorant of some of the phenomena of sexual maturation may interpret them as symptoms of illness. In such cases the correct information is all that is needed to free the neutral or positive act of its unjustified negative connotation.

As therapy proceeds another kind of "double-barrelled" insight must make its appearance; the patient must become aware that he is reluctant to give up his neurosis and afraid to take a chance on his health. This realization is another component of the fully developed state of insight. It enables the patient to understand and weather the ups and downs of the period of struggle. As a last item on this list, the aspect which I call *identification* must also be present in all developed insights —genetic or systematic, negative or positive. The patient must feel that his past, his actions, his fantasies, feelings, and potentialities are not merely "there" but are "his." They do not belong to a child whom he barely remembers, or to neurotics in general, or to an "interesting case" he can cleverly discuss, or to his superego, or to his illness seen as detached from himself. Insights of this type consist not of emergence of new content into consciousness, but rather of new or old content being included in self-consciousness, of the patient's owning to it. Unless he admits to the ownership of all his experiences and actions, both neurotic and healthy, he will have no basis for a later responsible choice between neurosis and health.

To illustrate this discussion of various types of insight, I shall describe a burst of insight which occurred early in the therapy of a young man who had entered treatment because of feeling depressed at times and feeling inhibited in his attempts to form intimate relations with women. He ascribed this difficulty to the effects of early parental teachings about sex and vacillated between minimizing his handicap and suspecting himself of incurable homosexual leanings. He was at a loss to see how therapy could help him and was actually afraid that it might harm him. His feelings about men and women proved hard to clarify. Though there were many hints of early confusion and strain in his relation to his parents, his need to protect them from criticism partly blocked the genetic avenue of approach.

After having extended the field of exploration to other topics, the therapist began pointing out to the patient that his pessimistic expectations were not limited to the therapeutic enterprise and to his heterosexual future but recurred in a variety of situations. The patient opposed to this his optimistic belief that he could get all he wanted through unremitting effort and hard work. He was, in fact, certain that once he had satisfied his need for emotional security by finding a suitable mate and could turn all his energies to the pursuit of success, a brilliant future and even fame were assured; he knew he would not settle for less. The patient seemed little impressed by the therapist pointing out that in view of his hopelessness about finding a mate this certainty was spurious, and that his belief in the efficacy of a hard fight was belied by his own experience of getting the least done when struggling hardest; nor was he open to the suggestion that he relax his struggles and see how he fared.

Still the patient seemed intrigued with the notion of his pessimism and his grim struggle. During the next weeks he occasionally returned to it, discussing e.g., the relative advantages of an optimistic and a pessimistic outlook and expressing confusion about his own. At the same time his behavior in the sessions showed a slight change. He permitted himself some pleasant daydreams about a former girl friend, and he became more receptive to the therapist pointing out some positive feelings toward others in the actions and wishes he himself had thought of as "purely selfish." Next came the realization that he was deeply discouraged and desperately lonely. This was the patient's first strong emotional experience in therapy, and after it he became more alive in the sessions. He surprised himself by working for a whole day without any struggle and effort; the work simply held his interest. At this point a situation arose at the patient's place of work which provided him with an opportunity to experience his submerged feelings. He spoke with strong emotion about promises broken by the management and about hopes of fair dealing coming to nought.

After this session the patient had a "revelation." First he re-experienced an intense wish for fame, but this time he noticed, with some puzzlement, its complete emptiness. The activity that would bring him fame did not seem to matter. He escorted to a party a girl who had just broken with her boy friend, and he was repelled by her flattery, her attempts at seductiveness, and her expressed gratitude for his kindness. He felt used and exploited. Then in a flash came a string of insights: "Fame stands for affection. I want it because it is free of exploitation. If I were famous, people would expect no gain from me but would admire me for myself; only it wouldn't be really myself, they wouldn't even know me. What I really want is affection, someone accepting me for what I am. I want it for itself, not as a stepping stone to glory. But I am afraid to trust affection; I always believe I am being used, not loved for myself. It is not my parents' teachings that keep me from women; it is my own mistrust, part of my pessimistic outlook. Perhaps my parents did use me; I always had to be a credit to them, their perfect creation. They probably loved me, but the messages I got from them were confused."

These thoughts were followed by a rush of memories of interpersonal situations that had disturbed the patient for a variety of reasons. Now he realized that their common denominator was his suspicion of being used and that in some instances it was not justified. He emerged from this torrent of new thoughts feeling that he was now ready for friendship with a girl and was able to find and recognize genuine affection, but he also had a budding doubt about being able to reciprocate fully. "Now I begin to wonder how much affection I myself can give. I know this is not yet the solution of my problems, though it almost feels that way. If I were at all mystically inclined, I would call it a supernatural revelation. I see now that there is something going on in therapy that makes the answers come as if by themselves; there is no use struggling for logical formulations. I probably wasted the first weeks in trying to give a perfectly coherent report of my life and my problems."

This example, though necessarily streamlined, illustrates many types of insight and many of the points made earlier: the period of incubation, the facilitating effect of discovering healthy feelings, and in particular the function of the developing holistic insight—the beginning realization by the patient of his pervasive pessimism. In the chain of discoveries representing the result of two months' work, specific insights mesh with the general, parts of the neurotic pattern are seen as distortions or disguises of one's real desires, identification is clearly present and so is a glimpse of possible causes and future changes. The experience also opens a new perspective on therapy and, less happily, on the aspects of the self that may emerge within this changed perspective. Not much has been seen yet, and the patient is right in mistrusting his feeling that the task has been almost completed. Later, the discoveries just described became a starting point for the development of further insights.

Self-knowledge grows only slowly to include all the aspects discussed, and many valid insights seem to get lost on the way. This need not astonish us. At almost every step the process of learning that goes on in therapy meets with resistance, i.e., the opposition of the threatened dominant pattern. Many budding insights come to nought precisely because they are correct and therefore alarming. But let us assume that insight has grown to full maturity in all the aspects we have specified. Is this all that is needed? If self-knowledge is complete in content, well structured, and clear enough to be held with conviction, does this insure its therapeutic effectiveness?

As a cognitive phenomenon, insight is merely a statement of facts and of their connections; in itself, it has little motivating power. A patient can see his personal patterns clearly and discuss their antecedents and consequences intelligently without the slightest change taking place. Insight presents the patient's life situation in a new light. What matters is how he responds to this changed view of himself and of his situation. Every therapist knows all too well that there is a world of difference between a patient's gaining an insight and his responding to it. Lack of a commensurate response or a grossly misdirected or perverted response are unfortunately quite common. Only a certain kind of response can make an insight vital and ultimately effective.

The Vitality of Insight

A popular terminological distinction is that between *intellectual* and *emotional* insight; only the second is supposed to be therapeutically effective. This distinction certainly aims at something essential. Intellectual interaction is often the starting point of therapy, but one hopes that it also has strong emotional overtones. Cognitive processes as such can remain divorced from personal reality; a full experience of an important personal issue must include, besides thoughts, the evaluation of personal relevance. Emotions grasp vitally that of which thoughts are merely a pale reflection; they are concrete value experiences and thus are the springs of our actions. Insight can pave the way to change only if, seeing the state of affairs differently, we also come to *feel* differently about it. Realization must lead to evaluation. But there is still the question of just *how* we feel. The term "emotional insight" is too vague and general. It could apply, e.g., to the feeling of excitement or elation about having made an important discovery; such feelings have little therapeutic value and may even hinder progress if "discoveries" come to be the ultimate goal of the therapeutic process. But even if one defines emotional insight more precisely as an emotional reaction to the *content* of the newly emerged insight, the question of the nature of emotion still remains to be answered. Suppose the patient, on discovering some component of his neurotic pattern, reacts with a feeling of unbearable humiliation or self-loathing. This reaction can only cause a setback in therapy and often indicates that the therapist has pressed the issue prematurely or has failed to prepare the patient for facing it by doing some reconstructive work first. Rather than fostering such emotions one must try to reduce them by interpreting them as stemming, ultimately, from the patient's false, derogatory self-image.

It is misleading to ascribe therapeutic value to emotional responses *as such,* because in human personality we are dealing with a dual organization and consequently with two sets of emotional experiences: one expressing the basic pattern of health, the other that of neurosis. When neurotic pattern is dominant the patient's emotions are almost entirely determined by it. He values and desires what is required for the maintenance and completion of this pattern of living, abhors and fights off all that is contrary to it. In therapy the patient has to express these neurotically founded emotions, but this proves productive only insofar as it clears the way for other feelings or results in further insights, e.g., if the patient starts wondering why certain events anger or please him out of all proportion.

Real progress is in sight when the patient starts responding to insights in an increasingly adequate manner, no longer rooted in a hopelessly negative image of himself and the world or in the fantastic assumptions meant to ameliorate or disguise it. This means, e.g., responding to his isolation from others with sadness, loneliness, or longing rather than with humiliation at being rejected or pride in his self-sufficiency. Progress means responding to real guilt with regret; feeling horror, rather than self-loathing or indifference, on realizing the monstrosity of what he does with his life; responding to a glimpse of his constructive potentialities with pleasure and hopefulness rather than with fear or exaltation. The change in the quality of feeling may be gradual and the difference not always clear-cut. It is most important that the therapist catch the fine nuances distinguishing the new from the old and that he respond to the new. The healthy feelings, whether happy or unhappy, must be welcomed, not interpreted. If the therapist fails to notice the change in the patient's feelings—e.g., from falsified unproductive guilt to genuine regret—and continues to interpret or assuage them, he impedes the patient's progress.

Insights accompanied or followed by a strong and appropriate emotional response—one might call them *vital insights*—have the best chance of becoming effective, at once or in time. However, such a happy turn of events does not always occur. The experience may lose its vitality and deteriorate into a purely intellectual insight; nor is this the worst that can happen. An originally genuine experience can be absorbed into the neurotic pattern thus strengthening the very organization one is trying to weaken. The emotion may be periodically revived only for the sake of catharsis of a temporary and questionable nature, the patient showing no inclination to move beyond these outbursts; floods of totally useless tears can flow in therapy. Consider the strong, genuine emotions of anger, grief, indignation, and compassion that the patient may feel on discovering how harsh, cruel, and confining the circumstances of his childhood had been. Such emotional experiences may provide a basis for gradually redirecting one's life into more venturesome paths. But they may also be used by a patient who tends to avoid responsible independence to justify those very attitudes —of self-pity, of blaming others for his troubles—which serve to perpetuate his misery. This point needs stressing. Strong upsurges of emotion, particularly of rage and hatred, are only too often considered an unqualified boon in therapy; this is a widespread professional superstition. When a person who has harbored and dreaded such emotions reaches the point where he can fully feel and express them, this experience has a tremendous potential value but it cannot be taken as a finished accomplishment. Little is gained if such an experience results merely in the "freedom" to be constantly enraged. A strong emotional experience can lead either to progress or to greater entrapment in the neurosis. The therapist is well advised to watch the patient's course so he can warn him in time of the wrong turn he may be taking and thus save much confusion and delay.

Emotionality, or vitality, of insight is a necessary but insufficient condition for its becoming therapeutically effective; even vital insights are not directly responsible for significant reorientation. The goal of therapy is not the gaining of insights to be laboriously applied from moment to moment, but the formation of new attitudes, i.e., of sets that automatically determine perception and action. Insight gives us the knowledge of all the attitudes potentially available to us, but the personal moves required to choose and form new attitudes are radically different from insight. These moves have been described in Chapter 16. After recognizing his problem in its entirety, the patient must confront it as the central issue of his life; he is in a crucial predicament and something must be done about it. Following a period of struggle and despair, he arrives at a decision which means a shift in identification, and he now identifies himself with the emerging pattern of health in a manner that permits no qualification and second thought. These steps are prepared but not produced by insights, and although they may be foreshadowed or tried out on a small scale early in therapy, they can only be taken in its late stage. Analysis with all its detail is merely preparatory and it does not have to be complete. When the patient is ready to face the issue of his basic orientation, he has had enough analysis. This central neurotic issue—the choice between trust and distrust, between stagnation and movement—is decided in a global manner. The therapist must facilitate these internal moves not only by fostering the growth of insight but also by methods aimed more directly at preparing the patient for change: keeping a constant focus on his present life; periodically inviting the patient to review the goals of therapy and noting their change; maintaining a high emotional tension in sessions; helping the patient to abstain from isolating and perverting his gains, helping him to plan how to put them to use. The therapist will find the appropriate means if he keeps the therapeutic process focused on the central issues: the patient's predicament and the need for change.

18. Resistance

A General View

The patient's maneuvers to obstruct therapy can be collectively called resistance. Two opposite forces operate in the patient during treatment: a tendency toward reconstruction and a force which strongly opposes radical changes. Resistance is not just inertia; it is the active self-defense of the neurotic pattern. The great resistance to progress encountered in therapy is in fact one of the bases of my conception of personality as a dual organization. In this formulation, resistance is directed not merely against the uncovering of the content that is unacceptable to the superego or conflicts with reality; nor is it limited to the form which was the first to be noticed in analysis, namely, resistance against yielding up to consciousness what has been repressed. It resorts to many devices and is directed against any exploration and discovery—including that of the patient's constructive potentialities—that threaten the neurotic organization.

The strength of resistance varies in the course of treatment. It does not uniformly decline; the change from neurosis to health is not a smooth process. Each decisive step forward is followed by a flare-up of resistance, and its intensity grows with the progress of therapy. As long as the therapist's interpretations touch merely the periphery of the neurosis, things may move along briskly, but when the core patterns are approached, the neurotic pattern will not take the threat lying down. The patient's resistance reaches its height during the "struggle for decision," when it is directed against facing the bankruptcy of his way of life and against being plunged into despair; it is the life-and-death struggle of the neurosis. To understand this is of great help to the patient as well as the therapist. The suffering caused by the recrudescence of the neurosis can be better tolerated when the disturbances are viewed as hopeful signs; real progress has been made and the defeat of neurosis may be close. In contrast to the useless suffering that unavoidably accompanies neurotic living—whether the pain is suppressed or magnified and neurotically misused—the anguish of the struggle is a concomitant of reconstruction and as such can be accepted; this suffering is not for nothing.

Though the therapist must constantly deal with the patient's resistance, he should not view it merely as a hindrance or an implacable enemy of progress. The neurotic pattern feeds from the same sources as the basic healthy one. Therefore the strength of resistance is also a measure of the patient's personal strength. As long as he identifies with neurosis resistance is both self-protection and self-assertion, even a defense of integrity; it becomes a matter of honor to be loyal to one's neurosis. Resistance is the therapist's ally in that it protects the patient from the possibly shattering impact of premature insights. It also has other uses. The patient's specific ways of resisting insight and reorganization in therapy are intensified versions of the devices used by the neurotic pattern to deal with what is inconsistent with its system principle; the same defenses are prominent in the patient's life. If he miraculously succeeded in suspending resistance to therapy, he would leave essential components of his neurosis and, potentially, of his health outside the therapist's office. The therapist then would be deprived of his best opportunity to observe at first hand and to point out to the patient the devices he uses to perpetuate his neurosis.

Resistance in general is best dealt with by insight into its presence, nature, and cause, but the therapist cannot expect to promote such realizations by merely calling the patient's attention to the presence of an obstacle to insight and progress. When the patient is told "You are resisting," he is apt to feel unfairly accused or to assume that the therapist is annoyed with him. This remark is never well received and is often taken as an invitation either to obey or to engage in a battle of wills. Suppose the patient resists the therapist's formulation of an unconscious factor abundantly indicated by evidence. Instead of telling the patient that he has been repressing it, the therapist might as well give a more detailed and relaxed explanation, for instance: "The evidence of your dreams, actions, etc., points to the possible presence of such and such a factor; it might or might not be there. But if it is there, don't you see how much it would be at variance with all your present wishes, ideals, and goals, with everything you hold dear? So it is quite possible that you cannot become clearly aware of it because it is in opposition to everything you want and believe." Such an explanation, which implies a temporary acceptance of resistance, lays the groundwork for understanding its function as the defense of the dominant pattern.

This frame of reference facilitates the spotting and understanding of specific methods of resistance. Consider, for example, the method of *misappropriation*, or perversion, i.e., misusing an insight, or any other step forward, for neurotic purposes. If the patient has assimilated the idea of his compulsive defense of the status quo, such instances can be met with a direct, well-documented interpretation of the mechanism in question. This mechanism may become immediately evident to the patient from his own experience—some patients in fact discover it by themselves. Once grasped, the notion of "misuse" can be actively applied by the patient to check on his course, helping to dispel confusion and leading him out of many blind alleys. The patient may learn, e.g., to catch those moments when a new insight leads over into unrealistic elation, becomes a weapon against others, or a block to further progress. Thus one patient refused to move on to other topics, insisting that he must first assimilate perfectly the lesson he had just learned. The notion of defense by misuse of gains is readily acceptable to the patient because it implicitly recognizes his health as well as his illness.

But it is necessary to start dealing with specific resistances early in therapy before it is possible to establish this general framework. One can profitably approach some of these methods by focusing on the mechanisms which the patient brings up as complaints, i.e., as handicaps in his daily life. For example, complaints of poor memory invite an exploration of the nature of the forgotten topics and the circumstances and results of forgetting. Simultaneously the therapist can start bringing to the patient's attention all instances of "forgetting" topics from session to session or within the hour itself. Sooner or later the patient himself will start noticing how difficult it is for him to hold on to a gain, e.g., to recall an important insight, or at least to recall it vividly. These shared observations can then be combined with those reported by the patient for an initial elucidation of the function of forgetting in his life and therapy.

Once the patient sees his defensive maneuvers as something other than irremovable defects of memory and intelligence or equally unaccountable and unchangeable character traits, he can recall them from limbo and recognize them as his own acts. The therapist can further this by changing the wording from passive to active; e.g., when the patient talks of becoming confused, the therapist can ask him to what purpose or by what means he has confused himself. The patient's dawning realization that much of his energy is expended in blocking or altering his experiences may increase his motivation to explore and modify his defenses. He cannot fight them head on, but if he is looking for means to speed up progress he can learn, for instance, to notice when the course of his thoughts and feelings suddenly stops and changes. In this way he can do something toward identifying and eventually bringing under partial control the blocks he is placing in the path of insight.

The progress that follows is slow and discontinuous. Even a modification of an established partial pattern that leaves the total neurotic pattern unchanged meets with resistance; opposition becomes intense when material pertinent to the more central subpatterns is being explored. I mentioned previously (in Chapter 15) that repressed memories do not emerge until the patient can afford to remember the event, i.e., until he is able to deal with the repressed issue constructively. This statement can be generalized: resistance in any form against any insight will weaken only when the insight becomes assimilable within the developing new framework. Sometimes the therapist makes a certain interpretation repeatedly and the patient gives indications of having grasped it. But then a time comes when the same suggestion strikes him as a highly significant discovery. The patient asks the therapist why he never told him before. On previous occasions the insight obviously did not "sink in," but in the meantime a transformation has taken place or become imminent so that now, in the changed context, this particular insight has become system consistent.

Some Special Forms of Resistance

In this section I shall describe some common forms of resistance and some methods of dealing with them. The neurotic organization has many ways of defending itself against penetration by system-inconsistent factors. They can be eliminated from consciousness by repression or suppression, removed from the self by externalization, or incorporated into the system after having been adapted to it by distortion. In another group of processes the incongruous factor is retained (overtly or covertly) within consciousness but is not incorporated into the total pattern; various methods are used to weaken its impact and to relegate it to the periphery. Let us concentrate on the processes in the last category, which I believe are encountered more frequently than they are discussed. First, however, a few words about *externalization,* i.e., the ascription of internal events to environmental sources.

Externalization has a special place among the various modes of resistance. As long as the patient sees the source of his troubles exclusively in other people or in external circumstances, no sound basis for therapeutic work exists, and interpretations are accepted with great difficulty. Uncovering other modes of resistance can be postponed without detrimental effects, but externalization cannot be left untouched if the patient is to move beyond merely expressing self-pity and blaming the world. This stand must be tackled from the very beginning and worked on until the patient at least partially abandons it. In the initial stage it often helps to get the patient to understand that if some sources of his trouble can be found in himself, there is greater hope that the difficulties can be worked out. Granted even that circumstances are mainly to blame, if he can identify his own contribution, no matter how small, there is a chance that a change in himself will either improve matters directly or enable him to change the circumstances. If the patient feels strongly that only external changes are needed and he has some plans for bringing them about, e.g., by moving to a new place or a new job, therapy is best postponed until he has tried out this method. If an adult considers entering therapy merely to satisfy a worried relative or to "learn about analysis," he should be discouraged from doing so. There is no basis for therapy as long as he himself professes to be satisfied with his life. If the person actually does need help, the necessary shift of attitude may occur even during the discussion of the issue or he may return later, this time admitting his own need and wish. One can begin working with a patient who, while professing some need for personal change, merely wishes to learn how to go about changing another. By the time this intent has been made explicit, sufficient material about the patient may have come to light to make him modify his initial goal. It is well to remember that these patients may have great difficulties in accepting any interpretations that place them in an unfavorable light and to prepare them by doing some reconstructive work first. In cases of persistent externalization only limited therapeutic goals can be pursued.

In the methods of resistance to be described next, the inconsistent feature is not excluded from the system; instead it is made ineffective and thus innocuous. One frequent way of achieving this effect consists in *devaluing or making unreal* some progress made or an insight achieved. It happens occasionally that during the therapeutic hour the patient has a stirring emotional experience; it surprises him as being outside his usual range of emotions and makes a strong impact. A day or two later you may find that the patient has managed to dilute the significance of the experience. He feels as if he had been on an emotional spree and had talked himself into imagined emotions. The whole episode appears to him exaggerated and artificial. A very similar process may take place after the patient has gained some new insight, e.g., has recognized a current pattern of behavior as a repetition or continuation of his response to some situation in childhood. In the next session he tells the therapist that he had been exaggerating the similarity or that he did not tell the truth about the childhood episode, although he cannot say exactly what points he falsified. Relating the present to the past now seems to be purely theoretical, the connection remote. He is no longer convinced that such early experiences could still be active in him.

Both variants of this phenomenon are a kind of "Indian giving," of giving and taking back. It serves no purpose for the therapist to oppose directly the patient's changed perception. He can explore the patient's way of explaining the change and make explicit the fact that what he originally felt as a step forward has been canceled by it. Beyond this the therapist can convey to the patient his assumption that the alteration is not permanent, going so far in some cases as to sympathize with him for still having to devitalize his experiences. In other words, the therapist must not allow the alteration in the patient's memory to cause a similar alteration in his own.

Another mode of resistance is the use of *jocularity* as a way of "debunking" and neutralizing important insights; by adopting a playful attitude one avoids the impact of thoughts and events that could be sobering. This systematic use of humor is to be distinguished from an occasional tense joke intended to mask or master an upsurge of anxiety. Such occurrences have no untoward effects and usually call for no comment. The patient himself is partly aware of the function of his strained humor. He may later express his appreciation of the therapist's understanding in *not* having laughed at the joke or reproach him for having been fool enough to do so. But as a systematic method of devitalizing serious issues, the use of humor is a powerful weapon of neurosis. It is a brand of cynicism, but its destructiveness is hidden behind laughter and false enjoyment; this makes it very disarming in everyday life. Such a form of defense is the more devastating in that it undermines a very resilient component of anyone's system of health, the true sense of humor. The patient can easily convince both others and himself that he is demonstrating his ability to see things in their true proportions and to take a joke on himself when he talks flippantly about some neurotic problem of his that is far from being resolved.

One patient, when he started realizing how he had been disclaiming responsibility for serious interpersonal troubles he has been actively caus-ing, dreamed of himself as a little baby bird watching a battle of many armies from a high tree. He knew the war was over him, and he won-dered innocently how a small harmless creature like himself could have unloosed such strife. Instead of feeling the impact of this formulation, the patient merely enjoyed its humorous aspect. He joked about himself pleasantly as the innocent little bird, yet his destructive behavior continued unchanged.

Jokes about one's neurotic pretenses can be genuinely funny only when the humorous perception embodies *effective* insight; to joke is to relinquish pretense by admitting it. The use of humor for perpetuating neurosis is one of the most striking examples of "misappropriation," by which a component of health, originating in the basic organization of personality, is diverted to the service of the dominant pattern.

Since the sense of humor can be relied on to stimulate system action in the Gestalt of health, the therapist, once he is no stranger to the patient, may safely meet this form of resistance head on. By calling its bluff the therapist appeals, as it were, to the natural loyalties of the sense of humor. There is nothing funny about neurosis; no one knows this better than the neurotic himself. If he is capable of humor, he is not likely to feel humiliated if one reminds him of this fact point blank. The rare patient in whom the defense of neurosis through humor has become compulsive can benefit from noticing that the therapist feels no need to share in his compulsion, although he is tolerant of it and may feel compassion for the patient who has to use this device.

The patient can avoid facing important issues by the diversionary method of *focalization*, i.e., by concentrating on some minor point. A broad issue loses its vital significance by being shrunk into a small item.

> One of my patients was greatly concerned with the fact that during urination he would, for a second, involuntarily tighten his sphincter and a few drops of urine would land on the toilet seat. He would spend the whole hour discussing whether he urinated more freely today than yesterday, while his whole life was a mess and his total behavior lacked freedom. Finally I asked him to consider whether his goal in therapy was to put his life on a sounder basis or to become a perfect marksman.

Reminding the patient of more vital issues does not work equally well when the topic he focuses on is not really trivial. For example, the patient may be preoccupied with the issue of homosexual feelings to the exclusion of everything else, bringing up no material that could throw light on their meaning and origins; this effectively blocks progress. The therapist may have to bide his time until he succeeds in picking up and demonstrating to the patient some other personal problem on which he might prove willing to work. The issue of homosexuality might eventually be approached by this detour. This issue, like any other, can have a variety of personal meanings wider than the specifically sexual. It may express confusion about oneself, a reluctance to make choices or to give up anything, a wish to be different, or a suspicion of some basic "wrongness." For many patients in our culture, "homosexual" stands for all that is despicable. Working toward holistic insights is the best way of countering the "focalizing" brand of resistance.

The patient can take the wind out of the therapist's sails by *eagerly agreeing* with everything he says. By this tactic he manages to keep the therapeutic venture on a superficial level; nothing that is said means very much. When this method is pursued by intelligent patients it can be very disarming. It would be a mistake to try and discourage this type of resistance by deliberate unkindness. These are precisely the patients who wither and withdraw before any indication of misunderstanding. One way of countering this method is to diligently run down inconsistencies. After all, if the patient has enthusiastically agreed with opposed hypotheses, the possibility may at least be entertained that the desire to please interferes with his thinking.

The patient can also prevent the achievement of clarity by creating a general *atmosphere of confusion* which counteracts the process of integration. He does not hear, or mishears, what the therapist says, forgets what has just been said, or cannot understand it, or he understands but has no reaction. He does not know what he thinks of it; he feels nothing; nothing seems to matter. In the midst of a discussion of a critical issue the patient starts yawning and suddenly becomes tired and sleepy. The resulting confusion is the muddy water in which the neurosis can have good fishing. The best approach to this form of resistance is to draw the patient's attention, at a timely moment, to the fact that it is nothing less than his whole life that he is taking so lightly.

Another method of resistance consists of attempts to make a kind of *intellectual game* of the analysis. For a patient of good intellectual capacities it may become fascinating to find out what is behind this and what is behind that and what the connections are in between; the whole procedure remains remote from his life and his actual problems. If one allows the patient to go on in this manner, he will gladly offer rewards and bribes. He compliments the therapist on the progress made, finds that this hour was much better used than the last, when clearly both have been fruitless. The entire analysis takes on the complexion of a fool's paradise. If the therapist points out to an intellectualizing patient that recognizing his feelings may be more important than developing theories, the patient may counter this move without modifying his mode of defense. One of my patients picked up a remark of this kind and used it for a time as part of his resistance. Whenever some mild pressure was exerted to make him turn to important matters or an interpretation was offered that he did not like, he would remark, "Yes, I can see it, but just in an intellectual way, so it is not important." Occasionally a dramatic interpretation can succeed in overpowering the patient's intellectual resistances, disarming him before he knows it. If the patient seems particularly gratified by genetic interpretations, which absolve him from guilt, this offers a clue to how best to deal with his resistance in the long run: look for the sources of real guilt.

The six varieties of resistance described in the preceding paragraphs have the common effect of devitalizing insight and experience and of turning therapy into a game or a humdrum routine. They are typical of the dimension of noncommitment, the style of living that deprives life of substance and meaning by turning it into make-believe. To counter this trend in any of its expressions one can, on rare occasions, remind the patient of the fact, surprising to him, that therapy can fail—not to frighten him, but to prevent him from jeopardizing it by turning it into a game. He must realize that it is his life he is playing with.

The last form of resistance to be mentioned here consists in bogging down in *transference*. This type of resistance is often observed when intense positive transference develops rapidly from the start. Such patients begin to feel, sometimes after only a few weeks, that they are deeply in love with the therapist. The original purpose of the meetings is almost forgotten, and the chief issue is whether or not the analyst reciprocates the feeling. Reluctance and disinterest meet all attempts to analyze the transference aspects of these emotions. To the patient they are a realistic issue; the problems that initiated the analysis become unimportant by comparison. Patients rationalize this situation by maintaining that they can get well only if they get some concrete proof of reciprocation. The neglect of the therapeutic purpose makes this behavior immediately suspect; there may be other meanings involved, but it is also a form of resistance. In my experience, if this attitude persists it usually indicates an underlying structure of borderline hysteria. In these cases the therapeutic goal usually must be restricted to strengthening the patient's ability to maintain contact with reality. This the therapist does also in meeting the transference resistance. He simply goes about his business of giving the patient his complete attention in the sessions but does not yield to any requests for special favors.

There are many other methods patients develop to deprive the therapeutic process of vitality. The general background from which these methods arise might be called, for lack of a better term, *halfheartedness*. The patient wishes to achieve new goals and at the same time dreads success, so he is compelled to undermine his own efforts. Or he may reject making any effort at all, expecting therapeutic results to drop into his lap. The therapist will somehow do the job without help from the patient or even in spite of his subversive countermeasures. The patient may wish and strive for change but not expect it to happen: "If things have always been this way, why should they ever be different?" This halfheartedness which precludes an integrated striving is an inherent characteristic of the neurotic condition. Giving up neurotic satisfactions means giving up the only ways the person knows of pursuing the basic human goals; he will not give them up until new ways emerge or until despair makes him take a chance on the unknown. Wholeheartedness will replace conflict only after the patient has made the crucial step and has identified himself firmly with the basic pattern of health.

19. Reviving the
Pattern of Health

The Real Self

I have stressed throughout that unmasking the patient's neurosis must go hand in hand with uncovering his pattern of health. Probably most therapists foster health intuitively, perhaps viewing what they do as "support"; yet this part of the therapeutic enterprise has been pursued much less systematically than the analysis of the neurotic structure. This is a task for the future. Here I shall point out some of the obstacles in the path of this endeavor, suggest ways in which existing therapeutic techniques can be made to serve this goal, and speculate about the possibility of developing new ones.

I believe that one of the obstacles to the therapists' fostering of the healthy pattern has been the lack of conceptual clarity about what it is that they want to foster. I am not referring to a lack of general agreement on the criteria and indices of mental health. I feel that this agreement is quite high among therapists, regardless of whether they spell out their criteria or refer merely to personal growth or self-actualization in order not to violate by definitions the person's individual pattern of health. What I have in mind is the lack of clarity about the conceptual locus of this pattern within the framework of personality theory. It must be defined as distinct not only from the given person's neurosis but also from the basic trends common to all human beings. The concepts of ego or ego strength cannot be used to define the pattern of health. These concepts lack reference to concrete individuality and, if spelled out for a given case, cover only the preferred types of system action, i.e., organizational devices that can function in the service of neurosis as well as of health. The notion of the "conflict-free ego-sphere" * comes closer to the requisite, but I doubt if in a fully

* H. Hartmann, *Ego Psychology and the Problem of Adaptation.* International Universities Press, New York, 1958.

285

developed neurosis such areas can be prominent or, in fact, completely free of conflict. More likely, the involvement in the neurotic system is a matter of degree and progresses with time. Even if such isolated areas should exist, they could not be equated with the person's total pattern of health to be resurrected in therapy.

In the schools of therapy other than psychoanalysis, the idea of a personal pattern of health is often referred to by the term *real self*. Yet the term is rarely defined or clearly distinguished from related concepts, such as the self-system, the total self, or the conscious self. When definitions are attempted they lack the degree of specificity necessary for tying them in with the conceptual framework of a personality theory. Thus Horney defines the real self as "that central inner force, common to all human beings and yet unique in each, which is the deep source of growth." * The lack of a clear definition contributes to the aura of mystery surrounding the concept of real self, and this leads to its rejection by many and leaves the reconstructive aspect of the therapeutic work without a firm foundation in theory.

In terms of my system, the nuclear organization of the real self is that patterning or shaping of personality which has taken place consistently with the principle of confident self-acceptance that governs the basic system of health. One can call this self real, because its formation did not require negation or distortion of the child's essential wants but required merely their organization and channeling; this patterning involved no falsification of feeling or commitment to pretense. Still, the real self is not a preformed mystical entity originating entirely within itself. Environment enters into its formation by determining the selection and the shaping of the person's inborn potentialities. All relatively direct ways of pursuing mastery and belongingness developed by the child in an atmosphere free of threat contribute to this healthy nucleus, and so do his constructive, system-consistent solutions of difficult or threatening situations. The neurotic nucleus, on the other hand, is the precipitate of unmanageable traumatizing situations which undermined the child's confidence in his ability to relate himself to the world through mastery and participation and which increased his anxious isolation.

When the neurotic organization becomes dominant through a generalization of the diffident expectations, the nuclear organization of the real self is repressed and submerged, and its components become part

* *Neurosis and Human Growth.* Norton, New York, 1950, p. 17.

and parcel of the neurotic pattern which now starts to grow and develop. The attitudes and the habits of action in which the real self used to express itself may be retained in the surface layer of personality but, no longer being rooted in a vital organization, these attitudes now function as mere pretenses, not to be taken at their face value. Thus what once was a genuine smile, an expression of pleasure, turns into a strained social grimace. Yet beneath and within the neurosis the nuclear real self survives; it has a potentiality for growth which can result in the reorganization of the total personality consistently with this basic pattern. If such a shift does take place and the pattern of health becomes securely dominant, the concept of real self, with its emphasis on the first word, becomes largely superfluous. For a person who is stably identified with this pattern, it is equivalent to the simple unqualified self.

This formulation should make obvious why therapeutic work on the pattern of health must include much more than "giving support"; all devices of the uncovering therapy must be utilized to make its existence first plausible, then obvious to the patient. The healthy pattern must be sought and uncovered, not within the pseudonormal surface personality where its vestiges serve merely to disguise the neurotic assumptions, but within the depth of neurosis itself. Only when the destructive and self-destructive attitudes—masked, e.g., by excessive altruism—can themselves be shown to be distortions of healthy trends is contact with the real self established; one gets to it by going through the neurotic attitudes, not around them. Tracing manifest disturbances to the unacceptable motives generated within the neurotic framework takes one only halfway toward understanding them. This partial understanding fills the person with shame and guilt, which in themselves are not conducive to change. Real understanding traces the neurotic manifestation all the way back to its healthy sources. When the neurosis is discovered to be an approximation or a twisted version of health, the patient's outlook becomes hopeful.

The various types of interpretation that contribute, directly or indirectly, to the discovery of the pattern of health have been mentioned in different chapters; they are summarized in Chapter 17, which deals with insight. Here I want to discuss the methods of eliciting *experiences* that could lend support to these interpretations and make them meaningful for the patient. This presents problems, particularly in the early stages of treatment. Thoughts, feelings, and impulses stemming from the pattern of health rarely come to the surface, and when they do they are not recognized as such. Patients whose neurotic patterns have been partially unmasked may become very distrustful of themselves. They feel deprived of all criteria for distinguishing illness from health, and verbal pointers are of no avail until some concrete experience comes to serve as a reference point. When the therapist tries to introduce to the patient the idea of the real self as distinct from his basic neurosis and also from pretenses, roles, and false fronts, he finds in him very little resonance to such distinctions. The patient will ask what this real self is, what its attributes are; to have such a better self would be just too good to be true. If he grasps the idea of following more closely his genuine impulses and desires, he may be afraid that all of them will prove offensive, unacceptable to himself and to others, as the unmasking work has led him to expect; or he may want to be told what these impulses are, what it is that he really wants. If the patient attempts to follow the suggestion that he feel his real feelings and thus listen to his real self directly, he will complain that when he listens he does not hear anything or hears only the voice of neurosis, and how is he to distinguish between the voices of neurosis and of health?

At this point a convincing discovery of the elements of the real self becomes a crucial task; this task is not readily achieved by interpretation, i.e., by the therapist making inferences which become increasingly plausible when they are seen to fit more and more instances. Plausibility can set the stage, but it does not substitute for experience. Eventually experiences may emerge. I spoke earlier of those "fortuitous" perceptions and actions which place the patient for a time "miraculously" outside his habitual realm of existence. But why must we leave this largely to chance? We cannot create experience, but we should be able to develop some practices that would temporarily relax the grip of neurosis and create a frame of mind permitting the unexpected to come up or enabling the patient to see in a clearer light what happens to come up. To do all we can to awaken the real self is not a superfluous "luxury," and not just a means of speeding progress, though even that would make the undertaking worthwhile. These measures may spell the difference between failure and success of therapy. To quote Horney, "Serious doubt may arise in some cases whether this most alive source of energy is not altogether dried up or permanently immobilized. In my experience it is the better part of wisdom to suspend judgment. More often than not, with sufficient patience and skill on the part of the analyst, the real self does return from exile, or "come to life." * I do not believe that in working with neurotics such tentativeness of judgment is called for. If the conditions

* *Op. cit.,* p. 173.

of early development were such as to preclude, or almost preclude, the formation of even a nuclear healthy pattern, a more severe disturbance would have been the result. We can confidently assume the continued existence of the real self, but the possibility to reach and mobilize it may depend on the means at our disposal. The experience of failure which comes to all therapists underscores the urgent need for actively developing such means. Patience on the part of the therapist is not enough; his skills must include more than proficiency in analyzing the neurotic structure.

Reaching the Real Self

An opportunity for contact with his pattern of health naturally arises in therapy if the patient is able not merely to report but actually to *relive his childhood experiences* with their original emotional coloring. The wider the range of memories that can be revived in this way, the greater the patient's chance to actualize a mode of experiencing not yet distorted by neurosis. If the therapist supports the patient's assumption that in talking about his childhood he is to focus on traumatic events, many such opportunities may be lost. Memories of unproblematic harmonious situations should not be excluded from the review of childhood; the message they carry should be heard. Sometimes the child's genuine feelings are recoverable only within a small special area. He does not remember how he felt about his human environment or about himself as a child, but the memory of a loved pet, or of his loss, brings up strong feelings of affection, loneliness, grief. The review of traumatic situations can also serve to establish communication with the real self if the original emotions accompanying them can be resurrected. This, of course, does not always happen at once. To one patient, e.g., an early episode of getting lost on a beach was a lark, until it suddenly re-emerged in memory as a terrifying experience. Early fears and angers caused by parents' behavior are sometimes recovered in similar ways. The patient can genuinely sympathize with these feelings, and their nature and intensity make obvious to him why his later development had to take a deviant course; this review may also provide a glimpse of alternative solutions.

A revival of his childhood experience takes the patient back to the springs not only of his neurosis but also of his health; this source of experience and insight can be tapped fairly early in therapy and used for laying a foundation for later reconstructive work. But to recover oneself in one's early past is not enough. To realize that his real self has survived the neurotic development, the patient must discover it in his present as well. This is not simple; since the pattern of health is held in check by a complex net of operations, his current experiences contain little that is genuine.

Sometimes the inhibiting neurotic mechanisms can be relaxed by *direct suggestion*, if the patient's own active efforts can be enlisted for the task. This condition can be met if the patient is suffering as a result of the tension produced by neurotic conflicts and if he has realized, beyond a doubt, that his efforts to fight the inhibitions head on only increase the tension. In such situations patients may eventually respond to comments of the following kind: "Always having to put your best foot forward—what a strain! Do you really want to go through life that way? Never take yourself for better or worse—let the chips fall where they may—and never find out if being yourself might not be much happier and better?"

> The patient whose letter was quoted in Chapter 12 is a case in point. By learning to abstain from driving himself in his work and from laboriously planning every simple action, he not only reduced the painful physical symptoms of tension but also discovered in himself unexpected resources which gave him a feeling of getting to know and to value his formerly submerged real self. Another patient felt that he had to smile at people when meeting them or taking leave of them whether he felt like it or not; since he rarely felt like it—or did not know it when he did—his face usually felt stiff, and he suffered agonies of worry about whether he would be able to smile when he must. When he decided to stop forcing himself and tried greeting people without smiling, he at first felt very hostile and guilty, and was certain he would be rejected by all. But he found that people usually did not seem to notice, and he gradually realized that the world did not cave in when people did not smile at *him*. "Oh, did I feel liberated, what a burden lifted from me!" Relaxation of compulsive controls provides the patient with a chance to experience genuine feelings, e.g., those that underlie a genuine smile, and to learn to distinguish their "feel" from that of a conventional gesture turned compulsion.

With patients whose emotions are not, or no longer, completely submerged or falsified, a sensitive *recognition of all their feelings by the therapist* can do much to increase the patient's differentiated awareness of his mental states. Because of this greater differentiation, and also because the therapist naturally resonates to genuine undistorted feelings, this process also furthers their growth. This is one reason why reflection of feelings advocated and practiced by Rogers *

* C. R. Rogers, *Client-Centered Therapy*. Houghton Mifflin, Boston, 1951.

and his followers often proves so effective in bringing to light the patient's real self; although, in entrenched neurosis, such shifts toward health are likely to be short lived if they are not preceded and supported by a working through and weakening of the neurotic pattern. Probably the most constructive factor in Rogers' approach is the therapist's attitude of "unconditional regard" for the patient which is effectively conveyed through the acceptance of all his feelings. The therapist's relationship with the patient is a source of significant experiences and, potentially, one of the most powerful means of reviving the real self. I shall return to it in the next chapter.

The *technique of free associations* used in classical psychoanalysis may at times serve similar goals, although it was devised for another purpose. The rationale of free association is the assumption that contiguous ideas, though they may seem unrelated, are connected with each other through some unconscious idea; if they are reported without restriction, the unconscious ideas can be inferred from them. An alert observer may then skillfully convert "beating around the bush" into "calling a spade a spade." Many analysts have discovered that the inferences drawn from the patient's associations may highlight healthy attitudes and feelings as well as neurotic ones. But the method can also be used for bringing the patient in touch with his real self in a more direct way than through inference. The instruction to tell "everything that comes to your mind" not only serves to preclude hiding things from the analyst; it also trains the person to notice everything: pleasant and unpleasant, realistic and fantastic, serious and childish, significant and insignificant by conventional standards, fleeting images, feelings and thoughts that appear in the margin of consciousness and usually disappear without leaving a trace. Such practice, by widening the patient's access to his inner processes, may lead him to discover offshoots of his pattern of health and to differentiate them from those of his neurosis. By centering the instructions on noticing rather than on telling all, and perhaps combining this with some relaxation-inducing measures, one can adapt this technique for creating a frame of mind favorable to the emergence of new experiences of every kind, the tabooed impulses being only one set among many.

The *state of relaxation* is an organismic phenomenon, a state of the total organism; while its most clearly observable facet is muscular relaxation, it also includes a certain state of mind which can be utilized for therapeutic purposes. In the standard psychoanalytic procedure relaxation of the muscles tends to be favored by the patient's recumbent position. Relaxation, however, might be induced more systematically and in ways which take into account the nature and requirements of the different stages of the therapeutic process. For this purpose we must distinguish and study in greater detail different types of relaxation. The type of relaxation favored by the recumbent position is advocated by such systems as Jacobson's * and is used in inducing hypnosis; this is *flaccid* relaxation, loss of tonus, a state comparable to paralysis. The psychological correlate of flaccid relaxation is the erasing of tension; it is a neutralizing state which seeks to stop, to silence. What is usually silenced is a great deal of defensive, angry, fearful, compulsive tension. The muscular tension resulting from inhibited actions is relaxed: the tightness of the clenched fist or jaw, the tension of facial muscles. Flaccid relaxation, however, is not the only form of muscular relaxation. There is also *tonic* relaxation, tension without inhibition, i.e., without any contraction of antagonistic muscles. The subjective sensation is that the whole body is as one piece, energized, without strain, poised. In this type of relaxation the recumbent position is not essential and probably not preferable; it is a state of readiness for action that is strikingly different from the unorganized state of tension resulting from conflicting, mutually inhibiting impulses to action or expression.

The psychological correlates of these different muscular states closely parallel the conditions typical of the different stages of therapy. The state of unorganized tension expresses fear, anger, defensiveness, conflict, pretense, i.e., the features typical of an entrenched neurosis. In the early phase of therapy, where the main aim is to achieve insight into the structure of neurosis, we may do well not to discourage the patient from expressing his neurosis through the language of the body and to attempt relaxation only occasionally. The observation and report by the patient of his various tensional states can provide useful additional data. A patient who rejects the recumbent position may find out, if he occasionally tries to lie down, what anxiety or what fears are aroused when he abandons the position of tense watchfulness. The state of flaccid relaxation corresponds to surrender, self-abandonment, admission of failure, i.e., the states of mind which often result from facing the bankruptcy of the neurosis (no longer the struggle to get rid of the old but willingness to drop it). At this point in therapy, flaccid relaxation may well be encouraged in order to facilitate these experiences; techniques for this are available.

The state of tonic relaxation, harmonious tension, corresponds to the emergence of the real self. It is characterized by a feeling of ease, by the disappearance of obstacles to thought, perception, feeling, will, and

* E. Jacobson, *Progressive Relaxation.* University of Chicago Press, Chicago, 1938.

by awareness of the availability of resources. Unfortunately we are not equipped with techniques that could support these experiences through inducing tonic relaxation. Occasionally this effect can be achieved by suggesting to a frantic, harried patient that he try to do things within the limits of ease, allowing more time for each job and eliminating unnecessary concerns and self-demands that only interfere with performance. "Let go, let God" expresses this idea in religious terms. For those patients who are able to make them their own, slogans such as "Easy does it," or "One thing at a time" can work wonders; at the least, they provide the patient with the experience of occasional harmonious functioning. Similarly, some patients can learn to desist from endless rumination of minor decisions once a trial has given them the experience of making effective snap judgments or otherwise functioning mentally in an easy harmonious fashion. Like any gains, these new experiences can be perverted and used to reinforce the neurosis; instead of taking "Easy does it" as a way of doing things, the patient may use the slogan to justify making no effort, i.e., as a way out of doing.

It is possible that we may yet develop, or adapt to our purposes, practices that facilitate the states of harmonious functioning through inducing muscular tonic relaxation. The experiences of those active in the field of physical training could help us in this task. One of my patients, a student of dancing, once performed a dance step in my office. This was the best way she could find to characterize the state of mind that was emerging at that stage of her therapy, namely, letting go of the equilibrium of a previous position and simultaneously being all energized and prepared to land in a new one. She called it "taking a chance on movement," and I know of no better description of the state of emerging confidence in one's newly discovered real self.

The real self can also be approached through the medium of *imagination*. The neurotic's interaction with the real world is patterned by his false assumptions which are in turn supported by the resulting vicious circles. Loosening the ties to this known "reality" clears the way to a different solution of existential problems, more consistent with the person's real self. Tentative alternatives, premonitions or memories of a different mode of existence, may appear in the patient's dreams after they have revealed the depth of his despair and run the gamut of neurotic pseudosolutions. Such alternatives can also be gleaned from the themes of elaborate fantasies which represent attempts at solutions of earlier problematic situations that have proved traumatizing. In people who have not succumbed to neurosis, the adolescent fantasies and activities organized by the problematic and challenging episodes of earlier development are the precursors of realistic deliberate planning or of a less conscious formation of a design for one's life.

A woman (not a patient) had had to come to terms in her childhood with the death of her only brother, which occurred at a time when there was a good deal of rivalry between them. She successfully cultivated both "feminine" and "masculine" activities and traits, and in her adolescence she composed (in imagination only) an autobiographical novel. The heroine of this fantasy left home disguised as a man and obtained training in her father's field of business. Then she became, unrecognized, her father's valued helper and continued in this role until falling in love with a young man made her reveal and resume her feminine and family identity. In her later life, this woman enacted the theme of restituting the lost son to the family before fully coming into her own as a woman, though for a long time she was not aware of the connections of her adolescent fantasies with earlier and later events of her life.

In neurotics the constructive elements of problem solutions attempted in fantasies are submerged and replaced by the neurotic alternatives, but they can be revived and salvaged. Jung and his followers have made effective therapeutic use of induced fantasies and of interpretation of patients' artistic productions; there is no reason why such devices could not be planfully used in other systems of therapy. I have, with very rewarding results, experimented with inducing states of light hypnosis in some patients for the combined purpose of achieving relaxation and facilitating the production of fantasies. For a period of time the patient spent the major part of each session in this state, dreaming aloud, as it were, while I occasionally made a comment or asked a question; during the rest of the hour I discussed his experience with the patient, who was now in his normal state.

One such series was carried out with a patient whose rigidity and anxiety made him practically mute in regular sessions. For several hours his fantasies depicted him wandering aimlessly in desolate empty cities. His attempts to enter empty houses met with passive and active opposition from inanimate objects and even from parts of his own body; occasionally he had to hack off a foot stuck in a hole or a hand that could not be made to release its grip on a doorknob. He felt no pain and no emotion. Later the patient started glimpsing single human figures in the distance, but they disappeared when he approached. When he finally reached them, the attempted handshake would turn into an iron grip and soon all that remained of the other was a dead gripping hand. Many sessions passed before the patient was able to visualize fighting an adversary who was and remained human and whole and to feel anger in fighting. At the end of four weeks of hypnotic sessions he managed to get out of the dead city into a pleasant country with houses here and there. He was walking purposefully toward his own home, still quite distant, and he felt sufficiently relaxed to take in all he saw and to stop for brief chats with strangers and friends of his childhood. He experienced real joy at the sight of trees and flowers and in the sensations of sunshine and fresh air, first with wonder and disbelief, then with increasing calm and acceptance. From this point on the patient was able to talk and to express some feelings in sessions, and therapy was continued through the usual means of dialogue.

Imagination can also be stimulated by "borrowed" images. Some therapists suggest reading to the patient, and many patients can quote instances of personal insights having been mediated by something they read in psychological literature. Often these insights pertain to the workings of neurotic trends, but occasionally the thought that strikes the patient is pertinent to his grappling with the concept of real self. One patient, puzzled about how she could be anything but her familiar unacceptable self, happened to read the celebrated passage in William James in which he expresses his conviction that human beings draw only on a small fraction of their mental and physical energies. This thought, and the examples quoted by James of people occasionally performing seemingly impossible feats, made instantly plausible to her the notion of a less limited self and brought up memories of certain moments in her own life when she felt and functioned harmoniously, when her experiences were truly fulfilling. Another patient reported having first realized that expression of anger can be both justified and constructive when she read the episode in Tolstoi's *War and Peace* where Natasha's indignation is aroused by the sight of wounded soldiers pleading in vain for transportation, while carriages are being loaded with her family's belongings. Natasha rushes to her parents ". . . afraid to weaken and to lose her charge of anger," and by attacking them with it quickly achieves her purpose.

World literature is replete with passages highly relevant to the patient's struggle and search. Reading them could afford true experiences to those who are becoming receptive to them. This will not happen, however, if the image or the thought is enjoyed merely as a work of art, as uplifting poetic fiction which one dismisses upon returning into the everyday world. Imagination can become a dynamic force only when what is imagined is perceived as real; this means that, to be effective, the meaning conveyed by a work of art must be taken not as poetry but as simple down-to-earth truth. Strong aesthetic experiences are often described as fascinating and exciting, but those that prove therapeutically effective can be more aptly characterized as sobering; they are statements of unquestionable facts.

Some of the experiences discussed above fall into the category of *peak experiences*, described under this name by Maslow,* or at least approximate them. Such experiences of exceptionally free and harmonious feeling and functioning, of life fulfilled, occur, in some degree, in the lives of most people, both healthy and neurotic. It would be quite important to explore the possibility of their therapeutic utilization. In my conception these states are outstanding examples of the "complete" experiences which contain, distinctly, all the characteristics human experience can have. Such states of completeness are rare. Our everyday mental states are, if not twisted and deformed, at least impoverished, probably as a result of their partial segregation from the vital subsystems of personality; they are segmental, truncated experiences. Peak experience, being complete, clearly shows the homonomous aspect, that of relatedness or "part-ness." Its object—e.g., in the aesthetic experience, or that of love—on the one hand possesses a distinct uniqueness and individuality; on the other it points to something beyond itself, a sphere of life of which it is a participant and a manifestation. In peak experiences the heightened feeling of self is combined—paradoxically, it may seem—with a feeling of unity with the world: the segregating barriers fall.

We do not know enough about the conditions that precipitate peak experiences. In therapy, insights sometimes take this form, and other kinds of peak experiences may occur in or out of sessions. Patients' reports indicate that these experiences are often preceded by a state of tensionless emptiness which in turn occurs after an intense inner struggle has been given up, e.g., when one has accepted defeat, or given up an ambition, or when external events have suddenly eliminated a goal or a source of anxiety, thus making striving superflous. A peak experience may provide a clue to the strivings and fears the elimination of which made it possible. Like other exceptional events, it can serve to clarify the nature of a patient's neurosis. In the present context, however, we are concerned with utilizing these exceptional states for the work of reconstruction to which they would seem to lend themselves naturally. In the literature on inspirational states and in some other accounts of peak experiences, great claims are made for their effects. During these states of clear vision and thinking solutions to one's problems may be perceived, psychosomatic healing may take place, or there may be a radical shift of orientation. I have no doubt that such instances can be documented, but it is equally clear that in very many cases peak experiences—which typically appear rarely and last only a short time—pass without any effect on the person's life.

* A. H. Maslow, *Toward a Psychology of Being*. Van Nostrand, Princeton, 1962.

They remain only as objects of longing or as treasured memories of the high points of life.

Perhaps these states can bring vital answers—beyond mere intimations of what life at its best could be—only if the struggles which precede their appearance represent a quest for such answers, as is the case in the "struggle for decision" in therapy. Unless there is a real need, an open Gestalt that seeks closure, the experience, striking and fulfilling as it is in itself, remains an isolated incident, no element of which can be incorporated into one's everyday life; one simply goes back to "business as usual." We have much to learn about peak experiences: their differentiation from some brands of psychotic experiences which subjectively appear very similar, their different contexts and the preconditions of their occurrence and of their dynamic effectiveness. Should we at any time incorporate similar exceptional states into the therapeutic process—e.g., through the use of consciousness-expanding drugs—I believe that patients would have to be prepared for them just as they must be prepared to make effective use of insights. Preparedness is present when the open Gestalt of a wish has been filled in with all the detail that the person can deliberately contribute, so that it is now nearer completion and seeks closure with greater energy. Speaking concretely, to be prepared means having a real need for new answers; it means expecting them and knowing concretely how to put them to use, the *right* use, and realizing clearly that one might be tempted to put the experience to neurotic uses. This is like snatching the gift of health and trying to profit by it on the wrong side of the divide. Exceptional experiences, by virtue of their very exceptionality, are segregated from one's everyday existence. Unless they are integrated with the pattern of health, the very fascination they arouse can divert the person from the task of reorganizing his life, making him substitute for it a pursuit of states which are and will remain exceptional.

Whatever methods the therapist may use or suggest to the patient to support his search for his real self, the enterprise must be experimental in nature and the final choice and action are the patient's. We can do a great deal toward preparing the patient to benefit from experience instead of discarding or perverting it; we can do something toward putting the person in a frame of mind conducive to real experience, and we should learn to do more. But when all is said, the "inner movements" by which experience is used to establish new attitudes cannot be specified and taught; everyone discovers them for himself.

Many other techniques for establishing contact with the real self and mobilizing its energies can be discovered in the teachings of various religious groups: meditational exercises, silence, and a wide range of other practices. It would be worthwhile to explore the possibility of adapting some of them to psychiatric uses. My own experimentation in this area has been too limited to enable me to make any concrete suggestions. Instead, I should like to outline the difference between the religious and the psychiatric conception of the self which I think helps to explain the advantage of the religious approach in devising techniques for reviving the real self.

In studying various religions I have found striking similarities between the contemporary psychotherapeutic approach to mental illness and health and the religious approach to the central issues of human existence.* There is, however, one point at which psychiatry and religion have always sharply diverged. It concerns the concept of self. From the psychiatric point of view, the real self is something that differentiates one person from all others and which grows according to its own inherent nature, whereas the neurotic self develops by arbitrary impositions and pretensions. One can find corresponding conceptions in many religions, but here the similarity ends. According to the current psychiatric orientation, the self, whether neurotic or healthy, begins and ends in the individual. Therefore we run into difficulties with anything that does not seem confinable within these boundaries. For example, one's loving relation to others transcends these boundaries, but we place it back within them by stating that to love is in the nature of the human being; thus love is regarded as a phenomenon which begins and ends in the individual.

Phenomenologically, however, the real self is not experienced as strictly immanent. In contrast to the narrowed and walled-in neurotic self it is open to the world; it is experienced as a part of larger meaningful wholes. According to religious conceptions, the self is a finite distance on an infinite line. The life of the person is a temporally limited segment of something that runs "from everlasting to everlasting." Religion considers that the neurotic self results from an artificial separation of this finite segment from its infinite context, to which it really belongs and in which it should "move and have its being." Many religious practices are aimed at facilitating the experience of transcendence, at opening the person to the infinite meaningful world.

The difference between the religious and psychiatric points of view is probably irreducible, but the holistic orientation provides a framework for the phenomena of transcendence without recourse to metaphysical assumptions. Within the person each process or structure is

* A. Angyal, "The Convergence of Psychotherapy and Religion." *J. Pastoral Care,* V, 4:4–14, 1951.

part of a larger one; an act has meaning as the expression of a motive, and the motive is a part of a whole structure of motivation. When we study one subwhole, in isolation, our knowledge is not complete because the structure is not complete within itself; it points to a larger whole. Similarly, the person is a whole, but the person as far as he is known to us is not complete. As part of a whole he must be larger than we know him, so our knowledge ends with an openness, a door to a larger context. A living person is an open Gestalt, and all we can perceive of an open Gestalt is a series of pointers to the ways in which it will seek to realize itself further. In contrast to the isolated neurotic self which is increasingly narrowed, the real self can grow—and it grows not only by increasing the sphere of its domination. By becoming a part of increasingly larger wholes, the person gains a larger territory in which he can feel at home.

20. The Patient and the Therapist

The Basic Therapeutic Orientation

Since the therapist has the dual task of demolishing the neurosis and fostering health he must be sensitive to the manifestations of both patterns. Other things being equal, the best therapist is the one who facilitates the expression of the full range of the patient's potentialities, the worst as well as the best, and makes all of them dramatically vivid to him. But acceptance of the total range of personal phenomena means neither indiscriminateness nor neutrality. The assumption that the therapist can work outside any value orientation is a fiction based on a confusion between specific conventional or individual value systems and their common core of universal human strivings. Trying to "adjust" the patient to some conventional values or to convert him to one's own is certainly not therapy. On the other hand, no one could be a therapist who did not place a high value on every person's chance to pursue the common human goals in a direct untrammeled fashion. It is this value that motivates the therapist's efforts to restore the patient to health; accordingly, he must actively dislike the anxiety which is at the basis of the neurosis as well as anything that produces unmanageable anxiety. While knowing the force of an entrenched neurosis he must be convinced, in a sober nonsentimental fashion, of the primacy of health. This conviction is the source of his confidence that the patient's life can be liberated from its unsound context and made concordant with the basic organization.

It is of the essence that the two aspects of the therapeutic task be performed in conjunction; if they are separated, the patient does not get the full benefit from either. What he is deprived of is the chance to discover health within the neurosis itself, a most potent means of rehabilitation. It is not easy to describe in psychological terms the therapeutic attitude corresponding to this integrated approach, which addresses itself simultaneously to the patient's initial duality and his progressive unification. I am struck by the observation that the attitude and the approach correspond almost point by point to the concept of forgiving as it is understood both in the religious context and in human interactions. Real forgiveness, obviously, means more than merely refraining from retaliation or a superficial "Let's forget it"; saying that no harm has been done would be meaningless, because harm has been done. In the act of forgiving, the unhealthy, ill-motivated behavior is straightforwardly recognized as such yet is not regarded as expressing the person's basic nature and wants. Forgiving has a negative and a positive aspect; it is both unmasking and rehabilitation. One forgives in the sense of discarding a fault, letting the other give it up, as if putting aside a mask and at the same time revealing the person's real essence and worth. In this sense the therapist's efforts are experienced as forgiveness by the patient and they facilitate self-forgiveness, although the forgiving is not a single dramatic act but a laborious item-by-item translation of neurotic traits into healthy ones.

The attitudes of the therapist that patients value most are founded in this orientation. Foremost among them is the therapist's confidence in the patient's ability to come out all right. This confidence effectively counteracts the patient's fear that the conditions needed for this will not be fulfilled and that unshackled human existence is not for him. We know from everyday life that when we are anxious about something and discuss it with a friend, we often draw courage from our friend's confident *attitude*, as distinct from his arguments or proofs, and our courage is not always short lived. One patient, in panic and despair, poured out her troubles to a friend whose outlook was genuinely hopeful. A week later she told me "I was able to fill myself with her confidence and to function all right waiting for you to come back." This familiar experience points up a remarkable fact, namely that a deficiency in one person's psychic functioning can at times be compensated for by the presence of this factor in another. This process cannot be adequately described in terms of individual functioning, e.g., as the patient's response to a set of stimuli presented by the therapist's behavior; it must be conceived of as an interpersonal or group process.

Many observations bear out the fact that in some regard the participants of the therapeutic situation actually function as one unit. I have often observed that when I am in a good resilient frame of mind my patients become more productive and in general work better in their sessions. This observation was confirmed in private conversations with other therapists. The difference does not seem to be due to what the therapist says; his mood is unwittingly picked up by the patient from his facial expression, posture, tone of voice. Conversely, the therapist's bad frame of mind is reflected in the poorer use the patient makes of the hour. It may also happen that the therapist starts the hour in a discouraged mood and the patient, by bringing in something hopeful, lifts him out of it. The conclusion is inevitable that to become a better therapist one has to become a better person. Given equal skill and experience, the therapist's dominant frame of mind will largely determine whether or not the treatment will be successful. The argument is still heard occasionally that only the therapist's "scientific" skills, and not his personality, are important in therapy; that is merely a convenient fiction which can blind the therapist to some of the most important processes that go on in the sessions.

Transference

The relationship between the patient and the therapist has two aspects: the *transference* and the *real relationship*. Both components are active agents in therapy but they have different functions. Loosely used, the term transference covers a wide range of phenomena, from the universal tendency to respond strongly to the long-familiar values to the extreme distortions of all interpersonal experiences perceived almost entirely in terms of old or fantasied ones. In therapy we mean by transference proper an unrealistic image, or images, projected by the patient on the therapist and on the therapeutic situation as a whole. These projections reflect, point by point, his neurotic assumptions and his way of coping with interpersonal issues. In comparison with the patient's everyday life these features may be thrown into strong relief since the situation is focused on him, revives his vital experiences, and dispenses with the conventional props that support his pseudonormal functioning.

One usually thinks of transference as projection on the therapist of the images of the early significant figures and of the emotions aroused by them. Thus the therapist is seen by the patient as father, mother, older brother, etc., in either the wishful or the feared variants of these images: positive and negative transference. However, within these projections different layers and aspects must be discerned. The great intensity transference can reach is not due to an emotional mistaking of the therapist for one of the family members as they were experienced in the later stages of childhood, after the child's world had differentiated and expanded to include many people. This powerful transference arises from investing the therapist with the significance of the *primal parent* who, at an early time, was the child's whole world. The totalistic, all-inclusive character of the early experience is matched by the quality and intensity of the transference feelings. For a time, the analyst acquires a tremendous importance for the patient, who feels that acceptance or rejection by this one person can make or break him. In interpreting these phenomena it is often more profitable to refer to the patient's hopes and anxieties about the total human world rather than to his feelings about the primal mother; this image and this response are usually only inferred, not remembered, although they can be relived in transference.

The phenomena usually subsumed under transference are not limited to the projection on the therapist of parental or other prototypal images, or of the generalized expectations directly resulting from these images. The patient's approach to the therapist reflects also those methods of dealing with people that are the end results of a complex developmental sequence of neurotic maneuvers, and that have no one-to-one correspondence with the patient's early experiences. The therapist will be cast in the roles presupposed by these methods as one to be humored, bribed, dominated, opposed, disparaged, etc., depending on the patient's repertory and his elaboration of the neurotic trends. The complexity of the transference phenomena demands that the interpretation be varied accordingly and not limited to a monotonous reference to parents. The therapist will refer now to concrete figures from the patient's childhood, now to the general tenets of his world view, now to specific assumptions in which this view is embodied.

The strength of the transference can be reduced or enhanced. The therapist remaining entirely impersonal and neutral is supposed to enhance the transference. The patient is provided with a blank screen on which he can project, unopposed, his biased perceptions and sentiments; this at least was the early psychoanalytic conception. Alexander and French * suggest that the therapist can try to counteract transference by deliberately acting in a way diametrically opposite to that of the patient's significant parent. To my mind both of these methods are questionable since they demand that the therapist behave in an artificial way. In the long run such behavior is bound to undermine the patient's uncertain trust in his sincerity, a trust which is furthered by the therapist's simple straightforward ways; such ways indicate that his feelings are clear, not divided or confused. In the regular course of therapy, transference is effectively reduced by repeated interpretations which place the patient's emotional reactions back in the context in which they belong and thus detach them from the therapist's person; this reduction, however, takes place slowly. Transference is only partially

* F. Alexander, T. M. French, et al. *Psychoanalytic Therapy*. The Ronald Press, New York, 1946.

under the therapist's control. It results from the patient's way of functioning and forms a prominent part of the therapeutic relationship from the beginning until close to the end, when neurosis recedes into the background.

The great emphasis psychoanalysts place on working with transference is fully justified; its presence is a great asset. Not only does positive transference provide leverage for the patient's efforts; transference, both positive and negative, is an invaluable aid in the main job of the first phase of therapy, the work of preparation and demolition. Since it mirrors and objectifies the neurosis, the transference relationship can be used to explore, demonstrate, and loosen the neurotic organization, showing it for what it is. It is often said that recovery takes place through the neurosis being transformed into a transference neurosis and then resolved as such. Accordingly, the identification and handling of transference phenomena are among the therapeutic procedures most systematically taught and most widely understood.

The Real Relationship

Transference is only one aspect of the therapeutic relationship, and demolition is only one aspect of therapy. Some therapists try to eliminate the genuine human aspect of the situation by making themselves maximally neutral in order to throw the transference into the highest possible relief. They are acting on the assumption that the corrective processes will follow more or less automatically from a convincing demonstration of error. I do not share this assumption. Changes of attitude are not brought about by interpretations, but they can be facilitated by a different form of communication, that of *concrete vital experience*. Such experiences can be mediated by the relationship between the patient and the therapist; to eliminate this relationship is to throw away the most valuable aid in helping the patient back to health. Indeed, I find the real relationship fully as crucial in the reconstructive aspect of therapy as the transference in the demolition work of the early phases. The therapist cannot limit himself to working with transference because he has an even more important function to fulfill. To free himself from neurosis, the patient must have an anchor outside the neurotic system. The therapist serves this function by allying himself with the patient's as yet undeveloped real self and also by representing the outside world, the other people, not only as they appear in the world of neurosis but also as they are in the world of health. Though the therapist stays close to the patient through all his neurotic tribulations, he remains outside the patient's neurosis, and this is one of his most important functions. But to use his vantage point fully, he must permit himself to be human and not limit himself to the role of neutral observer.

The double function of the therapist as expert promoter of insights and as a source of genuine interpersonal experience was succinctly stated by a woman patient during one of her last sessions. "It is amazing how the problem I had before I came has become a different problem, and yet it's the same. Before I started therapy I felt bad because I couldn't have my period. Now I feel bad when I can't be a woman . . . There are two separate relationships here. In one you're the doctor and I'm the patient, and I've gotten lots of help as a patient, and I can feel it. In the other it's person to person, and it's there that I've opened up with someone for the first time, and I feel valuable, like I have a capacity, something to offer. . . . I don't think I could have done without either one. On the doctor-patient side I have the *idea* that there is nothing wrong with me, that I'll be all right, but it's only an idea. So I could still really be fooling myself. But on the person-to-person side I can imagine how it could really be between us. Of course with you it can only be imagination, but this is not the point, the feeling is general; there is no fooling around about it, I *know* I'm a woman."

Let us define the patient-therapist relationship realistically. Two human beings gradually learn to know each other in a specifically defined situation. One of them is seeking to obtain help through the other who accepts the responsibility of service in this most important undertaking. The therapist is defined as one who wants to help and is competent to do so, which means that he knows ways of helping without humiliating. While the transference aspect depends on the patient's way of functioning, the quality of the realistic relationship depends overwhelmingly on the therapist—on how he functions as a person within the framework of this situation. To fulfill his function, he must *be* a person of sympathy in his relation to the patient, and all his reactions and actions must be guided and informed by a genuine desire to help; otherwise he would be merely paying lip service to the definition of the therapeutic situation. Other feelings and attitudes toward the patient can develop within this framework, but sincere sympathy and helpfulness are the minimum and the essence; without them there is no recovery.

Adherence to the definition of the therapeutic situation is, as we know, the best method for keeping the transference neurosis within bounds and the therapist's best protection against transference demands. The patient's fantasies constantly clash with reality because the therapist cannot pretend to be a father, a mate, or a pal. An important part of therapy is the agreement that there shall be no pretense. But since pretense is basic to the neurotic way of life, the patient has many frustrating moments because the therapist confines himself to his realistic function. Frustrating the transference wishes cannot and should not be avoided. It can be compensated for, however, by unrestricted giving: by the therapist's unflagging interest and attention, a sensitive recognition of the patient's feelings, by remembering detail, by discovering and frankly admitting his own mistakes, by meeting some of the patient's unexpressed wishes and needs, by not making demands the patient cannot fulfill and not humiliating him in other ways, by showing an appreciation of the power of anxiety underlying the patient's resistance and seeing the person behind the neurosis.

These are some of the ways in which the therapist's basic attitudes can be manifested, but the concrete manifestations cannot be standardized or planned in advance. A therapist who does not choose to be detached is frequently faced with decisions that have to be made on the spot. He must, of course, keep watch over feelings of his own that could mar his therapeutic attitude, but to make the correct decision he must take account of other factors as well. At a given stage of therapy, keeping in mind the states of the transference and real relationship, how personal can he afford to be with the patient, and personal in what ways? It takes a great deal of experience and judgment to know how far he can go safely for both parties and constructively for the patient.

Certain ways of being personal are excluded by the nature of the situation which must remain focused on the patient; those of the therapist's needs that are unrelated to his job of helping the patient must not occupy the center of the scene. There are times when telling the patient of a personal experience can be of great help, but this must not be used too often. Only a fine line separates a story told for the patient's sake from one that satisfies the therapist's own needs. If he discovers that neurotic attitudes have been activated in him by contact with the patient, he must deal with the countertransference and correct the mistakes he has made without burdening the patient with his troubles. But within these limitations the therapist still can be himself, with his true attitudes and his individual characteristics. He can be gentle or firm, humorous or forceful—always, of course, gauging the patient's state to make sure that this glimpse of himself will not be untimely. The same personal facet may be reassuring or challenging to the patient in one stage of therapy and offensive in another. A gentle approach may be necessary at first, but when the patient gets stronger he may feel belittled by being handled "with kid gloves" and respond

better to a more forceful approach. Difficult as the handling of transference is, fostering the patient-therapist relationship in beneficial ways
is an art requiring even more alertness, patience, and skill. The therapist will find the effort worthwhile if he realizes that his ways of
interacting with the patient immeasurably influence the therapeutic
outcome.

Developing the Relationship

One may ask whether the patient is able to perceive the therapist's
true attitudes until his neurosis and transference have subsided. To
some extent he does perceive them from the beginning though his
perception may be peripheral and uncertain. Above all he is apt to
perceive, and exaggerate, the therapist's faulty attitudes. Suppose the
therapist fails to focus on the patient in the initial session, e.g., by
discussing in detail the personal circumstances which preclude reduction of his fee, or by talking of the patient as the kind of case he is
currently studying in his research, or by demanding that an ambivalent
patient make his decision on the spot. The therapist should not be
astonished if the patient flees in dismay or has a hard time getting
started. Or let us take the case of a therapist who during the initial
period works hard at keeping a doubtful patient in therapy. If the
patient brings a dream about a persuasive automobile salesman, the
therapist might well ask himself whether he has not slipped into making unrealistic promises and what is at the root of his zeal. By the same
token, the therapist's genuine positive attitudes will also register from
the start. Reminiscing about their first meeting, the patient may describe his first impression of the therapist as of someone sympathetic,
or confident, or one who would not push him around yet would not let
matters get out of control, a person on whom he could rely. Patients
who both wish and fear dependence are put at case by the therapist's
implicit or explicit assurance that he will not let them use him as a
crutch any longer than is necessary. Often the first positive impressions are summed up in the words, "It was easy to tell it to you; I
thought it would be dreadful."
    Even after an auspicious beginning, the relationship develops only
slowly since it is constantly beclouded by the patient's hopes, wishes,
and fears. He may mishear or misunderstand the therapist's remarks,
e.g., take neutral or favorable comments as criticism; such mistakes are
best corrected simply and factually. Little by little the patient relaxes.
He may say that he senses a friendly atmosphere in the sessions but is

afraid to believe it. Later on the patient may, with increasing boldness, test the therapist's sincerity—his attention, memory, sensitivity, his respect for the patient's autonomy, his tolerance of criticism and of other forms of attack, his reaction to flattery and similar bribes, his firmness in not yielding to excessive demands, and his readiness to take a stand when this is necessary to prevent extremes of destructive or self-destructive behavior. However, the patient does not readily accept these tests as conclusive; he has many methods at his disposal to invalidate the encouragement he receives. If, for instance, the therapist continues to treat him with respect in spite of being shown more and more of his faults, the patient may secretly judge him a well-meaning fool who cannot see him as he really is; as we know, the neurotic has great confidence in his ability to deceive others. All these tests have a common core: "Is this person genuine? Can he be trusted? Does he really care?"

In putting the therapist to a severe test, the patient yields to the same compulsions that complicate his relations with people in general. Many a patient, though he craves acceptance, does everything he can to be disliked and rejected. One could therefore use the testing process to demonstrate to the patient his twisted neurotic ways of approaching people, but in doing this one might jeopardize its more vital function. Most important is that the experience with the therapist should turn out differently from the past fiascos. It is best if the therapist can credibly pass the tests to which he is subjected without resorting to interpretations. He may point out the patient's obvious doubts but without too much stress on transference. To discourage the testing is to deprive the patient of a means to build up some trust in another. You can tolerate the discomfort of being put on the spot if you realize the anxiety that accompanies the "acting out." The patient's awakening real self desperately wants the therapist to pass the test and desperately fears that he will not, and his neurotic self is threatened by the therapist's genuineness. It is as important to avoid trying to do more than one can for the patient as it is to keep one's equanimity. If in trying to "pass the test" or to meet the patient's needs for sympathy or anything else the therapist goes beyond what is reasonable and comfortable for him, he is bound to feel resentment and the patient is certain to notice it.

To avoid the anxiety involved in trusting or testing another, the patient may retreat into viewing the therapeutic interaction as purely professional. He can afford to perceive and use the therapist's positive attitudes if he sees them as mere techniques which tell nothing about him as a person. If the therapist is merely an actor playing a role according to the rules of the game, the patient is reduced to the same status. Much as he may resent the role of patient, he welcomes being confirmed in it, e.g., by being given some procedural rules; playing a role is an excuse for not entering the situation fully and personally. He does not want to have any feelings toward the therapist—it is all impersonal anyway, his feelings would not be reciprocated—and he may succeed in suppressing them for a long time, using his customary ways of keeping distance. The emotions are there, nevertheless, and can be brought to the surface at opportune moments.

> One of my patients maintained for a long time that he had no feelings about me and neither liked nor disliked me. The whole process was to him a cold business-like transaction. When I agreed to reduce the number of weekly sessions, I took the opportunity to ask him what he thought my feelings about it might be. He said he was ashamed to tell, but his first thought had been that I might be sorry to lose the fee. I pointed out his assumption that I valued him mainly as a source of income, then asked him what his reaction would be to the following hypothetical situation: "Suppose you had some incontrovertible proof that I like you and am genuinely interested in you, and that much of my thought about our work relates not to my selfish interests but to a desire to see you well and happy." He was visibly stirred and said that the idea filled him with anxiety. Tears came to his eyes as he glimpsed the possibility that his emotional coldness and his assumption of coldness on my part were protective rather than genuine.

The therapist should not try to force himself on the patient's attention, e.g., by being too familiar; without being chummy, he can find ways of expressing personal concern and furthering the relationship. What hinders and what promotes the relationship is plain enough to see. Any ritualization or rigidity of procedure or anything that smacks of artificiality fosters distance and impersonality. When the time comes and the patient himself wants to focus on the real relationship, he will often want to get up from the couch and face the therapist. He will object to the taking of notes when he wants the therapist as "the other," i.e., a participant, not an observer. An important issue is the therapist's response to the patient's direct questions. No competent therapist will handle this issue uniformly in accordance with some general rule. If he is careful of the relationship, he will not leave the patient puzzled for long about the treatment of any of his questions since such a course might kill the possibility of genuine dialogue. If the therapist uses interpretations to the exclusion of other methods, he will seem impersonal and thereby lose therapeutic potency.

If rules and routines mean detachment, occasional departures from them express and foster a freer, more personal tone. This happens, e.g., when the therapist enters into a discussion of some of the patient's practical problems freely and naturally, as a friend might do, dispensing with interpretations, or when he responds spontaneously to a report of a genuinely pleasant or harrowing experience, or lapses into humanity by telling a joke and sharing a good laugh with the patient. I have often been struck by the importance of the brief exchanges preceding and following the session proper. Since they take place outside the professionally defined situation, they imply equality and simple human contact. One patient formulated the difference clearly: "While I am here I don't look on you as a real person, you are to me just a psychiatrist doing a competent job. But in coming in and in leaving, I briefly have a different feeling, as if I have been to see a friend." Reviewing the course of therapy, some of my patients have claimed that the brief interchanges "between the couch and the door" were at times what they relied on most.

If the therapist passes all the tests and, in spite of being a constant critic of the patient's neurosis, steadfastly maintains his attitude of care and respect for him, the patient's trust grows regardless of transference. An important condition for his belief in the therapist's genuineness is consistency of "deeds" and "teachings."

> One patient told me that I had unwittingly passed this test simply by not trying too hard to interpret a complex dream. "It was obviously an important dream, and in your position I would have felt compelled to wrap up the whole session in a single formulation along the lines of the dream. Not being able to do it, I would have become a nervous wreck trying to do it. You did not do it and made no apparent effort to. This was a revelation to me. You were not selling me anything; you really meant what you said about accepting one's limitations, and now I feel it is safe for me, too, to try it."

The invariably positive response to a nondefensive admission of a mistake by the therapist has similar roots. As one patient put it, "When you try to accept yourself, it is helpful that your analyst accepts you with all your faults, but it is so much more convincing if you find that he can accept himself and his own shortcomings."

As the patient comes to rely on the relationship, it begins to dawn on him that the therapist's regard for him means that there is indeed some valuable core in himself, discernible within and behind his neurosis. This realization is a potent stimulus to the patient's attempts to discover his real self and to move, in spite of anxiety, into the difficult stages of the struggle for health. The struggle is easier if the patient feels that the therapist is constantly at his side as an ally of health. As he starts discarding his conceptions of himself as weak and worthless and of his interpersonal world as alien and dangerous, transference—the product of these distorted conceptions—recedes into the background, and the real relationship comes to the fore. Now the relationship can be more real because the patient himself is more nearly his real self, and it offers him a concrete opportunity to replace his fantastic image of people with more realistic perceptions. During the terminal period many sessions take place entirely within this realistically personal framework. There is a feeling of equality, a spontaneity in interchange, and effortless pleasurable teamwork.

When the patient feels firmly rooted in his new attitudes the therapist has fulfilled his role of mediator, of spokesman for the world of health. The patient can now dispense with putting idealized or frightening masks on the therapist and can appreciate him for what he is—a person who has wanted to help and has been helpful but who has his faults as well as his virtues. One patient, in taking leave of me, said that he wanted to ask a personal question. The question was a check on my own neurosis: "Have you ever had feelings like those I used to have? . . . Do you still have them sometimes?" At this point the patient can ask such a question without anxiety and he can also express his affection for the therapist. He no longer needs him to be perfect; he is certain of the reality of their mutual feeling, and he has other friends he can turn to.

The patient may feel genuine grief at the parting, but if therapy has been successful, the separation does not loom large. The separation issue is sometimes blamed for unduly prolonged analyses. It is assumed that the patient "hangs on" because he cannot face separation or free himself from the transference. I do not consider these formulations exact or particularly useful. A mismanagement of the transference can, of course, lead to difficulties in the terminal stage, but the problem of weaning the patient is not the main issue in termination. The main issue is whether the goal of treatment has been achieved and a significant change has taken place. If it has, the patient will be ready to leave or his reluctance will not last.

Continued reluctance means that, in spite of obvious improvement, a decisive shift from neurosis to health has not occurred. The patient's wish for something "bigger and better" results from this lack of a significant change rather than from perfectionism or from unresolved transference, which itself is part and parcel of unresolved neurosis. Something essential must have been omitted from therapy. Large areas may have been left unexplored in the origins or structure of the neurosis, including perhaps some that make termination a difficult problem, e.g., fear of success. Still, it would be rash to assume that the insufficiency is always one of exploration and understanding. In the present state of our practices it is more likely to be found in that part of our work which is needed to make the issue of change vital and pressing for the patient or in our failure to uncover and foster his personal pattern of health. We must begin to prepare for termination from the very start by facilitating experiences that can mediate change. The specific failures vary, but my observation of unduly prolonged analyses leads me to think that the following formulation fits many cases. The therapist lacks knowledge or skill in handling some area crucial for the given patient—e.g., the area of guilt in obsessive-compulsive cases—or he has made major mistakes in handling some aspect of the relationship. Yet the therapist has maintained basically positive attitudes toward the patient, who consequently has come to rely on him and to value his sympathy. In such cases the patient will not want to leave him even if progress has slowed down to nothing; his dissatisfaction and his unfulfilled hopes will result in an unhealthy dependence on continued contact with the therapist.

Interaction of Relationship and Transference

Does the real relationship between the patient and therapist interfere with the development of transference and thus deprive the analyst of one of his most effective tools? This is hardly the case. The notion that the therapist's detachment invariably increases transference seems fallacious to me. The therapist's aloofness may help the patient to stay aloof, and his failure to become emotionally involved prevents both transference and the real relationship from becoming vital and fully effective. A more personal attitude on the part of the therapist encourages the development of feelings in general and may greatly contribute to transference. What is certain is that interpretations of transference are best made against a background of real relationship. I don't mean merely the use of the therapeutic "contract" for calling the patient back to reality, but also the effect of the personal relationship that develops in the situation. The revealing and abandoning of old patterns is facilitated by the support offered by this relationship. Transference fantasies can be more convincingly shown up as distortions when compared with the therapist's plausibly real behavior than when held up against a "blank screen" which because of being nothing could in fact be anything. Even more important, a measure of realistic trust in the therapist provides a steadying background to which the patient can safely return from the transference flights, thus making him more willing to risk them. In favorable cases, prolonged periods of stubborn negative transference, exhausting alike for patient and therapist, need not occur at all. If the patient keeps up an unremitting attack on the analyst, chances are that something has gone wrong with their real relationship.

The fact that the transference and the real relationship coexist and intermingle raises the question of when each of them should be pointed out and used in interpreting. In most of the patient's productions both aspects are present, but one may clearly predominate. One patient, after having started and then stalled on a difficult discussion of a neurotic trend, dreamed that a stranger had criticized her party dress and that she challenged him to a fight; but as they approached each other, he made no effort to strike her and the fight turned into shadowboxing. Here the references to the real events and the therapist's real behavior are unmistakable. The patient learned from the dream how much she was bent on defending the trend in question. However, dreams referring to the real relationship may also have pronounced transference aspects so that interpretation is to some degree a matter of choice. If the therapist appears in the dream in a negative role, it is a sound policy to explore the recent interactions first; his own behavior may have contributed to this image. Such an exploration is a means of detecting and correcting possible misunderstandings and errors. When the therapist admits his mistake, this closes the issue; only if it does not is there anything to interpret. If the patient has distorted or greatly magnified the occasion, the transference interpretation becomes plausible. It is not safe to skip the exploration of reality aspects even if the transference reaction is obvious and striking. The patient will have to admit its presence, but a steady diet of transference interpretations gives him a feeling of not getting a fair deal; it looks as if the responsibility for any misunderstanding were always his, never the therapist's. This is indeed a distortion of reality which increases the patient's confusion. The transference aspect must, of course, be dealt with. The therapist deals with it both by interpretations and by not being the person the patient imagines him to be.

When the dream projects a positive image of the therapist, he must carefully analyze the transference aspect even in the presence of a realistic reference point.

One patient, in a phase when she found all of the therapist's comments stimulating and highly important, dreamed the therapist ejaculated and that the jet went into her ear. This led to a disclosure of fantasies in which the therapist appeared as a cross between a superman and a kangaroo who carried her through the air in its pouch and provided warmth, nourishment, and sexual stimulation. This dream presented an opportunity to clarify the patient's infantile needs and relationships and their expression in her present life, including her expectations of the therapist. When this patient once met the therapist in the street in the company of a woman, she felt her heart sink and became aware of her hopes that he would be her reward for success in analysis and that he would provide for all her needs.

Not to analyze the transference thoroughly in such dreams and daydreams would be crass negligence. They have to be shown up as fantasies and placed in their proper context.

This is not true of all "positive transference" dreams, however; in some cases the patient would lose a great deal if the positive image of the therapist were analyzed away as transference because of its containing an element of idealization.

One of my patients, during a period of my brief absence, engaged in some acting out for which she feared censure from me. She came to the session with the attitude, "I did it, and I don't care what you think," as if trying to make herself numb to the expected blow. It did not come, and she dreamed, the following night, that she had fallen asleep on the couch in a comfortable position which she considered forbidden and on waking up found me not angry but kind. Then she herself faded out of the picture, and she saw me making arrangements for the care of a sick child. As the next patient was announced she walked out of the office. I did not interpret the dream, remarking merely that she had dreamt I was intent on making the child well.

The dream correctly represented her real experience in therapy and therefore did not have to be interpreted or explicitly related to the particular precipitating event. One interprets and puts into words that which one wants to reduce or remove and leaves alone what one wants the patient to keep. The next time the patient came in looking and acting like a new person. "I feel I am all right. I don't need my fantasies any more." Therapy was completed a few weeks later. The experience communicated through the dream remained alive, although —or because—it was never discussed and it proved a crucial step toward recovery. Some things are best not talked about or should merely be hinted at. Repeated verbal formulations can easily kill the living core of experience.

If the therapist does not leave to the patient that part of the positive image of himself which approximately corresponds to reality, he deprives him of something needed to mobilize and focus his motive power for change—a fulcrum outside his neurosis. Such a fulcrum is absolutely necessary. It may be provided by the patient's own healthy positions or by chance external events, but in a planned, systematic way it must be provided by the therapist. His relationship to the patient is one of the two most constructive factors in therapy; the second is the discovery of the healthy roots of neurotic trends.

However, functioning as a representative of health and as an example to the patient may be fraught with conflict for the therapist, who, aware of his weaknesses and his occasional lapses into neurosis, feels that he is a fake in trying to fill this role. To deal with this fear, the therapist should remind himself that only a part of his life is relevant to the patient's welfare; what kind of person he is does matter but only insofar as it is reflected in his psychological state during the therapy hour. Within the protective confines of this situation it is possible, fortunately, to guard against neurotic reactions and in general to function on a higher level than is typical of one's daily life. By cultivating certain attitudes the therapist can almost live up to the positive image the patient has of him and earn the credit he gets. In the therapeutic hour he can, e.g., far exceed his usual level of equanimity; he can be a very fine lovable human being in fulfilling his task in relation to the patient. This makes the patient's positive perceptions correct even if they cannot be generalized to all situations.

A therapist who himself is clearly aware of the difference and lives up to his obligation to keep his own neurosis out of the treatment hour need not feel insincere and need not be defensive if the patient tries to penetrate his "true personality." If the patient complains that he does not know him as a person, the therapist can point out that indeed he does to a degree, and can hold him to the responsibility of forming judgments on the basis of his own perceptions. He can feel free to answer some of the patient's questions about his personal life and keep his privacy about others, depending both on his own feelings and on his estimate of the patient's needs. If on the basis of chance observations or rumors the patient "has the goods" on the therapist, the therapist should not deny what is true or partially true, but he need not try to explain. He can point out that the patient does not know the whole story, taking care, however, not to imply that if the whole truth were known he would be shown to be blameless. He must at all times keep in focus the fact that the patient's need to know him as a real person can be satisfied to his best advantage through their actual direct interaction.

How far can, or should, the therapist go in making this interaction personal, perhaps even extending it beyond the therapeutic hour? If the relationship is beneficial for the patient, one might ask why therapist and patient should not exchange favors and presents, meet for discussions of some shared interests, invite each other to their homes. There can be no general ruling on just what measure of personal interaction is best. Every therapist must determine the limits within which, with a given patient, he can move without strain and without harming the other or himself. These limits depend in part on the therapist's personality. Some rare people can make them quite wide, but no one should go beyond what is genuine and comfortable for him or go far enough to lose sight of what is going on between him and the patient at any time. I feel that on this score serious caution is needed to prevent one from going too far. Outside of the therapeutic hour the therapist is not obligated to keep the interaction in focal awareness and to let it be guided by the therapeutic intent; he may even feel within his rights in seeking from a patient the satisfaction of his own needs. In doing so, however, the therapist may lose sight of the fact that some of these needs, no matter how natural, may feed into the patient's neurosis and prove a powerful stimulus to transference. If this happens, the patient's neurotic wishes and fears will be greatly intensified, as will the subsequent disappointments. The confusion between fantasy and reality created in the patient's mind can grow to tremendous proportions if the therapist permits some of his own neurotic attitudes to become involved in the interaction, and, having lost his vantage point outside his own and the patient's neurosis, he will be helpless to dissipate this confusion.

This state of affairs places insuperable obstacles in the path of therapy. I have said before, and it has been stated by others,* that a genuinely positive experience with the therapist, occurring during the period of strong transference, may have an almost miraculous effect. This happens in particular if the situation created by the patient repeats an early one that led to a trauma, but is then given a different outcome by the therapist's response. Since he stands for the world, as the primal mother once stood for the world, the therapist's response has a powerful effect in resolving the trauma and in changing the patient's attitude to the world at large. By the same token, if, in a similar situation, the therapist is led by his own involvement to respond inadequately, the effect of this response may be tremendously magnified by transference. The patient may literally re-experience the earlier trauma in its full force, and the result may be a perpetuation of the neurosis. No therapist can afford to risk such outcomes by an uncontrolled personal involvement with the patient. Timing is of the essence. The last recon-

* I. deForest, *The Leaven of Love.* Harper, New York, 1954, pp. 45 ff.

structive phase of therapy may be greatly facilitated if the therapist enters into a natural human relationship with the patient to an exent that does not overtax him. However, as long as neurosis and transference prevail, mixing therapy with personal friendship means taking great risks at the patient's expense.

Some Guidelines

Is there anything the therapist can do to improve his way of functioning in the therapeutic relationship, once he has done all he can to overcome and keep in check his own neurotic pattern? Since effectiveness in this area is a matter of attitudes and not of techniques that can be taught, such a discussion might seem useless when our aim is to sharpen our therapeutic tools. I think, however, that it is of some use. Though attitudes cannot be taught, they can be learned and developed. The therapist learns his in very personal ways as he gradually discovers that, apart from methods and techniques, he influences his patients by what he is and as he realizes the responsibility this places on him. One can grow as a therapist simply by reaching this conviction and by being constantly aware of the issues involved. There is no substitute for this experiential learning, but it can be facilitated by a discussion that sharpens awareness of these issues.

It is well for the therapist to realize, e.g., that his confidence in the patient, which is the patient's strongest support, depends partly on his confidence in himself not merely as an expert but also as a person. To acknowledge this is not to disregard the necessity of steadily improving one's understanding of neurosis and one's technical skills; sympathy *alone*, no matter how genuine, will not help the patient but merely develop in him an unhealthy dependence. The therapist's confidence in himself will grow with experience in proportion to his ability to learn from experience.

It should also be kept in mind that we can both overestimate and underestimate our role and responsibility in the success of therapy. When we fail to look squarely at the matter we are apt to develop a notion that it is our task to get the patient well, and we are then weighed down by this tremendous responsibility. It is helpful to remind ourselves from time to time of what we all know in our more lucid moments, namely that it is not up to us to heal and that we cannot heal anyone; the patient and the good Lord take care of that. We merely promote the conditions favorable to self-healing. But it is precisely when we are aware of these limits that we also realize what a tremendous amount of helpful work we can do. Such realizations are a source of confidence.

To handle the personal relationship well, the therapist must start early establishing contact with what is really valuable in the patient. He can confidently expect some mutual liking to develop with continued contact, which will supply motive power not only for the patient's but also for his own efforts and make his therapeutic attitudes more personal and effective. It is doubtful, in fact, whether a therapist should continue working with a patient in whom, after some contact, he finds nothing likable whatsoever; he is not the best person to help him.

Once a relationship is established, it must be kept sound and functioning. The therapist should ask himself every now and then, "Am I satisfied with the human aspect of our interaction? Are things all right between us and if not, why not?" If he is certain that things are going well and that his attitudes toward the patient are sound, he gains greater freedom of expression and action, including the freedom to enjoy his own competent performance. He will feel equally free to point out the patient's neurotic distortions and to enjoy him in his happier moods; he can be outspoken and forceful if the situation demands. Some therapists, particularly the "client-centered" ones, make too much of rules devised to prevent the therapist from impinging on the client's freedom. If he in fact respects the patient's autonomy and has no need to dominate him, he can afford, when appropriate, to express his opinions and feelings, make suggestions, or take a firm stand on an issue. He is a person in his own right, and patients are reassured if he speaks and acts at times with an authority born of confidence: he is the one, after all, who has assumed responsibility for the conduct of treatment.

The last point I wish to stress is that psychotherapy is to a large extent a special problem in communication. There is room in it for careful thought and explicit formulations, but the most important and vital things are not relayed in this way. Words are always suspect. As all experienced therapists know, their attitudes toward the patient cannot be communicated to him through verbal declarations. Explicitness here is in fact deleterious. If these things need to be said, the patient is not ready to hear them, and if he is ready to hear them, they do not need to be said; the therapist can find better means to express them. One does not convince the patient that he is worth caring about by saying to him, "I care." If, however, in your responses to him you show that you appreciate the magnitude of the undertaking, if you respond with action to his unspoken wishes, remember every detail of what he has told you, and make something significant of what he considers unimportant, then he will feel that you really think about him; you do not merely sleep through the session and wake up when he leaves.

The therapist will develop his ability to communicate in other vital ways—by hints, implications, allusions, and also by a realistic dramatization of the issues—if he constantly keeps in mind that the therapeutic encounter is nothing if not dramatic; it must never turn into a lifeless routine. The motives that have brought the patient to the therapist are among the most intense of his life; they must grow in intensity if therapy is to succeed. The manner in which the therapist conducts the sessions should reflect his awareness of this fact.

Andras Angyal: A Bibliography

Der Schlummerzustand (The Hypnagogic State), *Zeitschr. f. Psychol.* 103:65–99, 1927.

Kritikai Attekintes az Eidetika-Kutátasról (A Critical Survey of the Eidetic Research), *Magy. Psychol. Szemle* 2:114–127, 1929.

Due Forme di Orientamento Spaziale (Two Types of Spatial Orientation), *Atti Congr. Ital. Psicol.*, 1929.

Einige Beobachtungen ueber raumhafte Tastphaenomene (Observations on Certain Phenomena of Tactual Space Perception), *Arch. ges. Psychol.* 71:351–356, 1929.

Sullo Stato del Dormiveglia (The State of Slumber), *Arch. Ital. Psicol.* 10:89–94, 1930.

Ueber die Raumlage vorgestellter Oerter (Space Orientation), *Arch. ges. Psychol.* 78:47–94, 1930.

Warum vergisst man die Traeume? (Why Does One Forget Dreams?), *Zeitschr. f. Psychol.* 118:191–199, 1930.

Zur Frage der Traumsymbolik (The Problem of Dream Symbolism), *Zentralbl. Psychotherapie* 4:107–119, 1931.

Esiste nell' Sangue dei Alcoolisti una Diminuzione del Potere Battericido? (Is There any Decrease of the Bactericide Capacity in the Blood of Alcoholics?), with S. Segrè, *Gior. Batterol. Immunol.* 6:61–70, 1931.

Die Lagebeharrung der optisch vorgestellten raeumlichen Umgebung (The Persistence of Orientation Schemata), *Neue Psychol. Stud.* 6:293–309, 1931.

Die Bedeutung der Lage bei raeumlichen Gebilden (The Significance of the Position Factor in Space Perception), *Kwartalnik Psychologiczny* 3:5–42, 1932.

Osservazioni su Alcuni Fenomeni di Moto Apparente (Observations on Some Phenomena of Apparent Motion), *Arch. Ital. Psicol.* 10:25–28, 1932.

Zur Systematik der Gewichts-Empfindungen (A Study of Baragnosis), with M. Ponzo, *Arch. ges. Psychol.* 88:629–634, 1933.

The Perceptual Basis of Somatic Delusions in a Case of Schizophrenia, *Arch. Neurol. and Psychiat.* 34:270–279, 1935.

The Experience of the Body-Self in Schizophrenia, *Arch. Neurol. and Psychiat.* 35:1029–1053, 1936.

321

Phenomena Resembling Lilliputian Hallucinations in Schizophrenia, *Arch. Neurol. and Psychiat.* 36:34–41, 1936.

Disturbances of Activity in a Case of Schizophrenia, *Arch. Neurol. and Psychiat.* 38:1047–1054, 1937.

The Concept of Bionegativity, *Psychiatry* 1:303–307, 1938.

The Structure of Wholes, *Philosophy of Science* 6:25–37, 1939.

Vestibular Reactivity in Schizophrenia, with N. Blackman, *Arch. Neurol. and Psychiat.* 44:611–620, 1940.

Physiologic Aspects of Schizophrenic Withdrawal, with H. Freeman and R. G Hoskins, *Arch. Neurol. and Psychiat.* 44:621–626, 1940.

Foundations for a Science of Personality, New York, The Commonwealth Fund, 1941.

Disgust and Related Aversions, *J. Abnormal and Social Psychol.* 36:393–412, 1941.

Paradoxical Vestibular Reactions in Schizophrenia Under the Influence of Alcohol, of Hyperpnea and CO_2 Inhalation, with N. Blackman, *Amer. J. Psychiatry* 97:894–903, 1941.

Postural Reactions to Vestibular Stimulation in Schizophrenic and Normal Subjects, with M. Sherman, *Amer. J. Psychiatry* 98:857–862, 1942.

Predisposing Factors in Bromide Intoxication, *Arch. Neurol. and Psychiat.* 49:359–382, 1943.

Schizophrenia, pp. 391–394, in *Encyclopedia of Child Guidance;* edited by R. B. Winn, New York, The Philosophical Library, 1943.

Types of Personality, pp. 439–444, in *Encyclopedia of Child Guidance;* edited by R. B. Winn, New York, The Philosophical Library, 1943.

Basic Sources of Human Motivation, *Trans. N.Y. Acad. Sci.* 6:5–13, 1943.

Disturbances of Thinking in Schizophrenia, pp. 115–123, in *Language and Thought in Schizophrenia;* edited by J. S. Kasanin, Berkeley, Univ. of California Press, 1944.

An Experimental Study of Bromism, with E. M. Jellinek, L. H. Cohen, and D. P. Miller, *J. Psychol.* 18:235–258, 1944.

The Holistic Approach in Psychiatry, *Amer. J. Psychiatry* 105:178–182, 1948.

The Psychodynamic Process of Illness and Recovery in a Case of Catatonic Schizophrenia, *Psychiatry* 13:149–165, 1950.

The Convergence of Psychotherapy and Religion, *J. Pastoral Care,* V, 4, 1951.

A Theoretical Model for Personality Studies, *J. Personality* 20:131–142, 1951.

Evasion of Growth, *Amer. J. Psychiatry* 110:358–361, 1953.

Index